Pen drawing by Kerr Eby, after
a drawing by D. Wilkie, 1828

WASHINGTON IRVING

ÆT. 45

Washington Irving

REPRESENTATIVE SELECTIONS, WITH
INTRODUCTION, BIBLIOGRAPHY, AND NOTES

BY

HENRY A. POCHMANN

*Professor of English
Mississippi State College*

Washington Irving

AWS

AMERICAN BOOK COMPANY

New York · Cincinnati · Chicago

Boston · Atlanta

Republished 1971
Scholarly Press, Inc., 22929 Industrial Drive East
St. Clair Shores, Michigan 48080

PREFACE

The editor of these selections has endeavored to represent, as judiciously and as comprehensively as is possible within the limits of a single volume, the entire literary output of Irving from 1802 to 1859. An effort has been made to select representative "units," arranged in a roughly chronological order, to illustrate Irving's work in its several aspects.

The Introduction aims to portray Irving in his relations to society, politics, philosophy, religion, and literature, and thus to trace the history of his development and achievement as a writer.

The bibliography in the *Cambridge History of American Literature* was made as long ago as 1917. Mr. Langfeld made no effort at completeness in the biographical and critical portions of his extended bibliography of Irving (1933). An attempt has been made in this volume to bridge the gap by listing in the Selected Bibliography all materials dealing with Irving as a person and as a writer up to the present time.

All selections follow the "author's revised edition" which Irving himself undertook to arrange and edit in 1848 for the publisher, George P. Putnam, and which was supplemented by the works published subsequently, as well as by the uncollected papers and miscellanies, arranged and edited by Pierre M. Irving after the author's death in 1859.

Irving took many liberties in punctuation, spelling, and sentence structure. The editor has not felt free to make any changes in Irving's text except in a few cases of obvious typographical errors. All footnotes to the text have been transferred to the Notes at the end of the volume, where, unless they are by the present editor, specific indication of authorship is made in each instance.

The editor thankfully acknowledges the permission granted
him by the editors and publishers of Diedrich Knickerbocker's
A History of New York (edited by Stanley T. Williams and
Tremaine McDowell, New York, Harcourt, Brace and Company,
1927) to reproduce several passages from the introduction to
that volume. The editor is indebted, also, to the author and
the publishers for permission to quote short passages from
Henry Seidel Canby's *Classic Americans* (New York, Harcourt,
Brace and Company, 1931).

HENRY A. POCHMANN

CONTENTS

Contents   ix

INTRODUCTION

"First American Man of Letters," "Ambassador of the New World to the Old," "Dean," and "Father of American Literature" are among the decorative titles showered upon Irving by his countrymen. It may fairly be asked what qualities enabled Irving to capture and hold, in both America and Europe, a literary reputation which had escaped all his predecessors— some of them manifestly better educated, more widely experienced, and intellectually greater men. To be sure, he was exceedingly lucky in making his entry upon the British literary horizon in 1819 with *The Sketch Book* at the psychological moment when the quizzical English attitude, which refused to be impressed by the linear dimensions and the show of wealth and power of the young nation across the waters, had just found expression in Sydney Smith's contemptuous query, "In all the four quarters of the globe, who reads an American book?" The answer came more quickly than Sydney Smith expected, for at the moment Washington Irving was seeing through the press the separate numbers of *The Sketch Book*, which literally every Englishman read. Not that, as Mr. Canby remarks, Americans had not previously produced good prose, but because the beauties of earlier compositions, such as the Declaration of Independence, had been largely lost on them. There was an element of good fortune, also, in the fact that Irving should have put forward, as an answer to Sydney Smith's question, precisely his best book instead of some other of his less estimable writings.

Certainly Irving was the first to scotch the old prejudice and distrust—as old at least as Dr. Samuel Johnson, who said what most Englishmen felt, namely, that America produced a degenerate race and civilization. The great Jeffrey, in his

review of the book, expressed surprise that so fine a thing
should have come from an American, and the sage Godwin
admitted: [1]

> Everywhere I find in it the marks of a mind of the utmost
> elegance and refinement, a thing . . . I was not exactly prepared
> to look for in an American. .

Less reserved were the comments of Scott, who wrote:" . . . it
is positively beautiful, and increases my desire to *crimp* you if
it be possible." [2]

[1] Pierre M. Irving, *The Life and Letters of Washington Irving* (3 vols.,
New York, Putnam, 1869), I, 320. This work is hereafter referred to
simply as *Life*.
In England, where "Geoffrey Crayon, Gent." was not immediately
recognized, and where *The Sketch Book* had to stand on its own merits
(not having, as in America, the popularity of Launcelot Langstaff and
Diedrich Knickerbocker to prepare the way), not everyone knew who the
real author was. Many people believed that no one less than the author of
Waverley could be responsible; and even after Jeffrey's favorable article in
the *Edinburgh Review* Irving felt called upon to explain that though he
could not help smiling at the idea of having to vindicate anything he had
written from the honor of Scott's parentage, he was "too good a patriot to
give up even the little ground" he had gained in staggering "the old notion
that it is impossible for an *American to write decent English*." (Irving's
italics; *Life*, I, 363–368.) While he declared this episode to be "one of the
most gratifying circumstances . . . in the whole course of my literary
errantry," he nevertheless remained aware of all the implications raised by
this critical British attitude, and in *Bracebridge Hall* (1822) referred to
the matter, in his best vein, by saying he would willingly attribute the
success of his earlier writings to their intrinsic merit were he not sensible
that their success was owing to a less flattering cause,—novelty. (See
Bracebridge Hall, 9; all references, except where otherwise indicated, are
to the author's revised, or Spuyten Duyvil, edition, 12 vols., New York,
Putnam, 1881.)
While the old spectre was not laid overnight, and Americans continued
to complain (as they still do) of an attitude of superiority on the part of
the Britisher, henceforth the complaints were more frequently couched in
terms of good-natured raillery and banter instead of invective and acri-
mony, so that Irving was truly the Ambassador of Good Will between
America and England. (Cf. Lowell's *Fable for Critics*, ll. 1069–1132,
1436–1455.)
[2] Scott did more. He first urged Constable and later induced Murray,
the "Prince of Booksellers," to undertake the English edition. At Scott's
suggestion, also, Lockhart wrote the appreciative article in *Blackwood's
Edinburgh Magazine*, which did so much to prepare for the popular reception which *The Sketch Book* enjoyed in England. (See the Preface to *The*

In America, this popularity which Irving had gained in England had its salutary effect. But the fact that Americans applauded because Englishmen did, while it may account for some of the early adulation, does not explain Irving's staying power; moreover, literary reputations, while they may be won, are not maintained, in that way. Equally inadequate is the reason advanced that he maintains his place simply because he was the *first*. Neither can his success be attributed to originality or profundity of thought, to insight into the great ideas that swept through the world, to superior ability in character portrayal or plot structure; for precisely in these provinces was he weakest. Reduced to essentials, his forte lay in (1) his temperament, and (2) his style:—a temperament that would vary from pure sentiment and romance to wit and urbanity, and a style that can best be described by the much-maligned word "elegant,"—in the sense that his manner was graciously suave and his expressions in gentlemanly good taste so that no one has yet fallen into the error of failing to recognize behind his words the soul of geniality.

Here, apparently, are qualities which do not loom very large but appear rather trivial by the side of the high seriousness of the Mathers, the intellect of Jonathan Edwards, the fecundity of Thomas Jefferson, or the ponderousness of Timothy Dwight. Nor is it patently clear, until the events and experiences and conditions of his life are scrutinized, how and by what means Irving came by the peculiar literary capabilities which have sustained him through the years while the writings of men built after a larger mould have been suffered to lie neglected for want of readers. For no other major American writer was so literally influenced and determined both by conformity with and by opposition to his "race plus place plus time" as was Irving.

Sketch Book and *Life*, I, 337–343, 350–351. For a convenient list of English criticisms of Irving's writings, see W. B. Cairns, *British Criticisms of American Writings, 1815–1833*, Madison, Wis., 1922.)   .

I. IRVING AS CONDITIONED BY HIS SOCIAL MILIEU

Born in New York City on April 3, 1783, the favorite and last of eleven children of an austere Presbyterian father and a more genial mother, Washington Irving spent his boyhood in what was then a relatively unexciting town just recovering from the ravages of war and conflagration but already a potential commercial and political center. His delicacy of health secured for him more indulgence from his elders than his brothers and sisters enjoyed, and apparently he capitalized upon his favoritism to the extent of making unauthorized tours of discovery into foreign parts of the city and its environs, much to the alarm of his parents and the emolument of the town crier, sometimes even going so far as to slip out in the evenings to enjoy the forbidden theatre in John Street and making his way stealthily back to his room in time for stated evening prayers. Except for a disposition toward physical frailty and a fine sensitiveness, young Irving was a perfectly normal boy, absorbed in childish things, loving play, regarding *Robinson Crusoe* and *Sindbad the Sailor* as the end of literary things, shirking his duties and studies—in short, all that a mother might deplore and an uncle delight in.[3]

After eleven years of elementary schooling, in four different schools, where, besides absorbing a negligible dose of Latin, he received a smattering of the other regular subjects, as well as a little instruction in music and a few lessons in dancing (the latter carefully kept from the knowledge of his father), Irving was ready for life; or rather, he was free to learn after his own fashion, for there is little doubt that Irving learned more of what accounts for his eminence as an author in the school of experience than in the schoolroom. Henceforth his develop-

[3] Along with Burns and Wordsworth, Irving enjoys the dubious distinction of having been eyed, after some boyish escapade, in half-mournful admiration by his mother and reproached with, "O Washington! if you were only good!" (C. D. Warner, *Washington Irving*, 26.)

ment, both intellectual and literary, can be traced in his observations and experiences as a travelling gentleman, the literary stimulation of his varied and somewhat scattered reading (for he was never a regular student or scholar), and the formative influence of his social contacts,—his many friendships and several loves.

Precisely how or why he escaped going to college he could never, in after life, satisfactorily explain; neither is it clear why he was permitted to engage upon the study of the law, for his father had previously interposed his parental authority to prevent Peter's embracing the legal profession—a calling which did not enjoy the Deacon's good opinion. Possibly because nothing else presented itself, he read law after a fashion for some half-dozen years in three different law offices, and grew into a young-man-about-town, eager for society and social gaiety, in the stream of which he swam easily and naturally. Women always attracted him strongly—first his mother, then his Scotch nurse (who is reputed to have taken him to his eponym to have the great Washington bless his namesake), his sisters (notably Anne, who called him "a little rack of bones" and sang songs to him), later the belles of the fashionable society in which he moved, through a long line of "pretty women" whom he met in his lifelong travels and took care to commemorate in his diaries, until finally he basked in the sunshine of Sunnyside, surrounded by the loving and tender ministrations of his nieces, "the most fortunate old bachelor in all the world." [4] He was, in the end as in the beginning, sensitively alive to feminine beauty and influence and consciously sought the company of women throughout his life.

Another equally pleasant and absorbing engagement during the days of his legal apprenticeship was hobnobbing with a knot of likely young men, some of whom later formed the

[4] Theodore Tilton, "Half an Hour at Sunnyside," *Independent*, Nov. 24, 1859; more readily accessible in *Irvingiana*, ed. by E. A. Duyckinck, lii.

famous Knickerbocker group of wits, who visited the theatre, talked of literary aspirations, met for mutual intellectual improvement in the Calliopean Literary Society, and lived life as if it were a pleasant summer's mood.[5] This led to some ephemeral contributions of his to the *Morning Chronicle* under the pseudonym of Jonathan Oldstyle, Gent.

Partly for his health, partly to see something of the world, he undertook several excursions up the Hudson, penetrating as far as Montreal and Quebec, getting his first glimpse of the frontier and encountering his first experience of "roughing it."[6] Presumably because of an alarming consumptive tendency with which he was threatened, he was bundled up and sent, in 1804, on a voyage to southern Europe, the itinerary of which included Bordeaux, Montpellier, Marseilles, Nice, Genoa, Messina, Syracuse, Palermo, Naples, Rome, Paris, and London, acquiring, during the twenty-three months abroad, health for his body, a brush for his manners, several volumes full of experiences for his notebooks, and a vast store of impressions for his mind.[7]

[5] G. S. Hellman, *Washington Irving, Esquire*, 15–19.
[6] *Life*, I, 16–37.
[7] Although he had to be helped up the side of the vessel upon which he sailed, the captain remarking to himself, "There's a chap who will go overboard before we get across," the voyage braced his body and spirits to such an extent that no madcap escapade of that citizen-of-the-world, Dr. Henry, with whom he fell in at Bordeaux, was too much for him. He withstood successfully pirate attacks, quarantine and passport detentions, and long rides over banditti-infested deserts, thrilling at every new adventure, picking up smatterings of French, Spanish, and Italian, reading books of travel, visiting convents and trying rather indiscreetly to flirt with the novices, scaling mountain peaks and descending into subterranean caverns, and after falling in with two young artists, Cabell and Allston, going the merry round of Parisian pleasures.
Together with Cabell, a young Virginian, who, like Irving, had been bred to the law, which he was never to engage in, and who, again like Irving, had come to Europe to combine education with pleasure, he was more bent upon pleasure-seeking than upon intellectual profit. With Allston, who henceforth was to be one of his most intimate friends, he visited picture galleries and played some with the idea of turning painter, but only played with it. For at the moment he was too busy tasting for the

Pierre M. Irving's biography of his uncle rather slurs over the slight irregularities and general light-heartedness which Irving exhibited during his first European trip,—partly, perhaps, because the nephew-biographer drew mainly upon the letters which his uncle wrote home, and relatively little upon his letters to others and upon the diaries in which Irving felt under less restraint in dwelling upon what his parents and brothers would certainly have considered frivolous trivialities. The journals, most of which have only recently been given to the world,[8] indicate that he was less absorbed in cathedrals and picture galleries than with the theatre and the opera, dancing and masquerading, pleasantry and flirtation. From the first, Irving was more vitally interested in people than in institutions. Nelson's fleet in search of the French spoke little to him of the great exciting drama of European politics and diplomacy beyond the spectacle of Nelson's flagship. The classic attractions of Rome drew hardly as much mention in his diaries as the absence of lovely women in the city. He could not see "the grandeur that was Rome" for the present squalor. In France it was not the clash of political opinions and parties so shortly

---

first time those pleasures and living those good things which his father had declared wicked. Even the Italians, he confessed, "stared at us often with surprise and called us the *wild Americans*." (Hellman, *op. cit.*, 26.) After all, however, he was already, perhaps unconsciously, dallying with the idea of turning author. Not that the proposition of making letters, or anything else (least of all, the law) his profession had as yet presented itself to him in so many words. The time to worry over making a livelihood seemed far off. But certainly the copious journals and diaries of the period cannot be explained except on the ground that he was recording impressions and laying by such memorabilia as might be valuable in a "fit of scribbling" if and when it should come. Meanwhile he was pleasantly engaged in seeing and enjoying the world; and so little was he concerned with any but the more noteworthy of the antiquities of the Eternal City and the educational advantages of its classic past that when Cabell suggested hurrying on to "gay Paree," he readily assented, and thus failed to go to either Florence or Venice, a dereliction for which his brother William roundly chided him, adding that he considered Washington's meeting with young Cabell unfortunate.

[8] See bibliography, but especially Williams, "Washington Irving's First Stay in Paris," *American Literature*, II, 15–20 (March, 1930).

after the Revolution, but the personality of "this wonderful" Napoleon[9] and the splendor of individual Frenchmen that attracted him. His first day in Paris was spent in establishing himself comfortably and strolling in the classic garden of the Palais Royal "throngd with the frail nymphs that wander about it."[10] Then follow such entries as these:

Had a levee of Taylors—Shirt makers bootmakers &c to rig me out *a la mode de Paris*. . . .

In the evening went to the Theatre Montansier in the Palais Royal. This is a little theatre much frequented by the frail fair ones. . . .

. . . Mercer joked me about my going to Theatre Montansier before any of the other theatres—it being the most disreputable theatre in the city Told him I had caught paris by the Tail. . . .[11]

How different from the manner of Wordsworth's first entering Paris some years earlier, occupying his time visiting the places made famous by the Revolution and the Terror, and stealthily pocketing a relic from the Bastille! By comparison with the southern countries just traversed, he is frankly delighted with everything he sees in France, and Paris is simply superb. How much more searching and penetrating would have been the comments of Thomas Paine or Thomas Jefferson had they been youths in their early twenties on their first tour of France in 1804–1805!

This reference to the theatre is only one of hundreds to be found in his notebooks both at this time[12] and later, the theatre exerting upon him from the first a profound influence at once

[9] See his comments on Napoleon in T. T. P. Luquer, "Correspondence of Irving and Payne," *Scribner's Magazine*, XLVIII, 467–468 (October, 1910). See also *Life*, I, 107, 248–250.   [10] Williams, *loc. cit.*, 16–18.
[11] *Ibid.*, 16-17. Compare the "discreet" editing of these memoranda by Irving's nephew in *Life*, I, 104.
[12] During the twenty-five days between May 24 and June 19 on which he kept a diary record, he went to the theatre seventeen times and once to "a 15 sous ball in Palais Royal with Vanderlyn—Crowded with filles de joies." (Williams, *loc. cit.*, 20.)

literary and social. Even in his old age he frequently made protracted trips from Sunnyside to New York in order not to forego the pleasures of the theatre season.[13]

After four months in Paris, which, in the few letters he found time to write home during this period, he set down as "of all the places . . . I have seen in Europe . . . the most fascinating,"[14] he proceeded to London via Brussels and Rotterdam. He found his three-months' sojourn in London rather dreary (partly because his boon companions had remained behind in Paris, and partly because expected letters of introduction to notable Londoners had miscarried), and early in 1806 he found himself once more in his native city ready for another bout with his "inveterate enemies, the fathers of the law."[15] By the grace of God and Josiah Ogden Hoffman (his last legal preceptor and chairman of the Board of Examiners), he passed the bar examination,[16] and in February, 1807, set up as a lawyer, at least to the extent of moving into the law office of his brother John, at No. 3 Wall Street, and of invoking somewhat hesitatingly the influence of Mr. Hoffman to put in "a word in

[13] One would be rather hard put to find in his early diaries and letters passages showing greater interest and knowledge than the critiques he wrote of various actors, among them John Kemble, George Frederick Cooke, Mrs. Siddons, and Talma. Modern actors would doubtless be very well content to have more Washington Irvings in their audiences. See *Life*, I, 112–115, 384–387; II, 16–18; and Irving's "Conversations with Talma," arranged, from rough notes in a commonplace book, by Pierre M. Irving, *Biographies and Miscellanies*, 151–160.

[14] *Life*, I, 107.

[15] Cf. *Knickerbocker's History of New York*, ed. by S. T. Williams and T. McDowell (New York, 1927), intro., xiv.

[16] Irving once illustrated his legal attainments at this time by relating the following comments which were passed between the two examiners, Martin Wilkins and Josiah Ogden Hoffman (who served also in Irving's case), when they came to consider a candidate who had acquitted himself rather lamely. Hoffman said, as if in hesitation, though all the while intending to admit the candidate, "Martin, I think he knows a *little* law," to which Wilkins replied, "Make it stronger, Jo, d——d little." (Warner, *op. cit.*, 43.) Many years later, G. P. Putnam, Irving's publisher, noticed the twinkle in Irving's eye when he said in reply to some question about his legal experience, "I was one of the counsel for Burr, and Burr was acquitted." (*Cambridge History of American Literature*, I, 247.)

season" for him with the Committee of Appointments in Albany that, at the expected "liberal dispensation of loaves and fishes . . . a crumb from the table" might fall his way.[17]

Of real importance during the next few years were (1) his travels,[18] and (2) his literary companionship with "the nine worthies," or, as Irving sometimes designated them, "the lads of Kilkenny,"—Peter and Gouverneur Kemble, Henry Brevoort, Henry Ogden, James K. Paulding, and his own brothers, William, Peter, and Ebenezer,[19]—who frequently resorted to an old family mansion of the Kembles on the Passaic, designated as Cockloft Hall in *Salmagundi*, for frolicsome days and nights; sometimes they met for convivial suppers and literary pow-wows at a genteel public house known as Dyde's, and when their purse was low, contented themselves with what they termed "blackguard suppers" at a porterhouse on the corner of John Street and Nassau.[20]

It would have been surprising if the energies of this colorful group had been expended completely in wine, women, and song; and so it is not peculiar that there should have appeared, on January 24, 1807,[21] the first of the *Salmagundi* papers, in which the co-authors, Paulding and William and Washington Irving, proposed, in true *Spectator* fashion, "to instruct the young, reform the old, correct the town, and castigate the age." [22]

[17] *Life*, I, 126.
[18] To Richmond in the summer of 1807 during the trial of Aaron Burr, to Lake Champlain and Montreal in 1808 with the Hoffmans, and to Philadelphia and Washington for adventures in society.
[19] Richard McCall and David Porter were occasional members of this coterie. "Who would have thought," said Irving to Gouverneur Kemble, in alluding to these scenes of jollity, at the age of sixty-six, "that we should ever have lived to be two such respectable old gentlemen!" (*Life*, I, 122)
[20] *Life*, I, 123–124.
[21] The series of twenty numbers was discontinued on Jan. 25, 1808, not "for want of subjects," but because of differences with the publisher. (*Life*, I, 155.) For the authorship of the several papers, see *Life*, I, 129–131.
[22] *Salmagundi*, 14. The reader was assured that the editors wrote for neither fame nor money, and that "so soon as we get tired of reading our

While these papers did not bring a fortune to the authors, they created an impression and stir. There were no coffee-houses in New York, but they were read at every tea-table and found their way to many a proper young belle's toilet-table. The "characters" sketched in them were drawn more or less from life, and included most of the notables of the town, as well as a few from out of town.[23] The "fascinating [Mary] Fairlie" was obviously the original of Sophie Sparkle,[24] and there was no lack of young ladies who envied her the notoriety; neither did the, at that time, shallow disguisings under the names of Ding Dong, Ichabod Fungus, and Dick Paddle provoke affairs of honor. All was good humor; yet asinine theatrical critics, taking a glance at themselves in the mirror of 'Sbidlikens, found it advisable to hold their peace; fashionable upstarts shrank before the portraits of the Giblets; the small beer of politicians soured at the thundering satire of Dabble; and the feathers of carpet soldiers wilted when they were

own works, we shall discontinue them without the least remorse, whatever the public may think of it. While we continue to go on, we will go on merrily: if we moralize, it shall be but seldom; and, on all occasions, we shall be more solicitous to make our readers laugh than cry; for we are laughing philosophers, and clearly of opinion that wisdom, true wisdom, is a plump, jolly dame, who sits in her arm-chair, laughs right merrily at the farce of life—and takes the world as it goes." (*Salmagundi*, 18.)

In conformity with the Addisonian scheme of securing variety, the several subjects were to be dealt with by several gentlemen, each of them gently reminiscent of the several members of the Spectator Club. The department of society was under the direction of Anthony Evergreen, Esq.; the territory of criticism was reserved to William Wizard, Esq.; poetry came from Pindar Cockloft, and so on; and in order the better to motivate their instructions, the authors presented characters and family relationships reminiscent of the Distaffs. And so the editors, posing as "critics, amateurs, dilettanti, and cognoscenti," proceeded merrily through twenty numbers, satirizing the ways of the fashionable world, inserting squibs on the theatre, occasionally mixing a little political satire, waging war against "folly and stupidity," and teaching "parents . . . how to govern their children, girls how to get husbands, and old maids how to do without them." (*Salmagundi*, 14, 23.)

[23] For example, Joseph Dennie, essayist, critic, and editor of the Philadelphia *Port Folio*, was generally understood to be the model of Launcelot Langstaff, Esq. See *Salmagundi*, No. VIII, and *Life*, I, 135.

[24] *Cambridge History of American Literature*, I, 238.

paraded in the regiment of the Fag-Rags. *Salmagundi* was a mild terror of the town.[25]

Thus it is that Irving the lawyer (although he continued for some time longer to share his brother's office) fades into the background, and Irving the writer emerges directly out of the social milieu of early nineteenth-century New York.

His next literary production owes its inception to the same love of fun-making and the same social background, with the difference that the materials are not contemporary Manhattan but the New Amsterdam of former years. Begun as a *jeu d'esprit*, in collaboration with his brother Peter, and intended merely as a take-off on Dr. Samuel Mitchill's *Picture of New York; or, The Traveller's Guide through the Commercial Metropolis of the United States* (New York, 1807), it developed eventually into a comic history of the Dutch settlements in New York, but embodied, at the same time, a great deal of contemporary personal and political satire, now almost as forgotten as that which lies neglected in *Gulliver's Travels*. The book also introduces us to Irving the antiquarian—the result of an impulse that plays henceforth an increasingly prominent role in the development of Irving as a man of letters.

Possibly the greatest single conditioning fact in Irving's early life was the death, in 1809, of his betrothed, Matilda Hoffman—a blow which disrupted for a time his literary labors, and possibly accounts for much of the easily recognizable note of sentiment in his subsequent work—an element almost entirely lacking in his writings before 1809. His falling in love with Matilda Hoffman, shortly after the time when he had been quite struck by the brilliance of Mary Fairlie, as well as a dozen other belles of New York, Philadelphia, and Washington, and, for that matter, with Matilda's older sister, the bright and witty Ann, seems to have been quite sudden—at all events, genuine.[26]

---

[25] *Salmagundi*, "Editor's Preface," xii.
[26] Finding his charge but an indifferent student of the law, Josiah Ogden

Naturally her sudden death of consumption left him profoundly affected—possibly not as permanently as his nephew-biographer suggests with his sentimental stories of Irving's forbidding Matilda's name to be mentioned in his hearing and his carrying about with him through all the years her miniature and her prayer book. Disregarding the vast amount of conjectural surmising, conflicting opinion, and unsupported internal evidence on the subject of Irving's love for Miss Hoffman, or rather, the effect upon him of her untimely death, there is little authentic information upon which to arrive at the truth, the most important direct evidence being Irving's own bald diary-entry for 1809: "Mat. died in April," and a sixteen-page manuscript fragment (written fourteen years later and now preserved in the Yale University Library), in which Irving unburdened his heart to Mrs. Foster and her daughters, particularly Emily, in whose company he was finding pleasure at the time. This much seems certain: that he loved deeply and grieved sincerely at the time, and that the mood of memory and grief was recurrent.

During Irving's lifetime, sentimental Americans, intent upon marrying off America's most charming bachelor, enveloped Irving in a mass of romantic story and gossip. All his youthful attachments were recalled. Once it had been the fascinating daughter of Major Fairlie; then the brilliant young Jewess in Philadelphia, Rebecca Gratz, whom Scott, from Irving's

---

Hoffman nevertheless took a liking to Irving and opened up to him his home. Matilda was then but a girl, provokingly silent at times and given to what seemed fits of petulance. But the passing of the years made a difference, and doubtless Ann was right when she said "that people began by admiring her, but ended by loving Matilda." (S. T. Williams, "Washington Irving and Matilda Hoffman," *American Speech*, I, 468, June, 1926.) Among Irving's own rare references to Matilda is this one: "We saw each other every day, and I became excessively attached to her. . . . Her mind seemed to unfold itself leaf by leaf, and every time to discover new sweetness." (*Notes while Preparing Sketch Book*, 40.) Here, apparently, is no great mystery, but simply the reënactment of what has happened to thousands upon thousands of young people much thrown in each other's company.

description of her to him, is supposed to have used as the proto-type of the Rebecca in *Ivanhoe;* and after the death of Matilda Hoffman, rumor connected the names of Irving and Jean Jeffrey Renwick, to whom Bobbie Burns had sung songs of love.[27] It was impossible that Irving, after *The Sketch Book* had made him one of the most eligible young bachelors of two continents, should have escaped the sharp eyes and ears of rumor and report. In 1826 he was reported engaged to the Empress Maria Louisa,[28] while, if the authority of Charles Felton Pidgin[29] can be trusted, he had already been rejected by Theodosia Burr. Later it was Emily Foster, or Madame de Bergh, or Antoinette Bolviller, or Mary Godwin Shelley, and so the list continued to be aug-mented; but still Irving disappointed the romantic match-makers. By the time of his death, they had given up hope and were drawing what consolation was to be derived from the picture of Irving basking in the affections of his nieces at Sunnyside, feeling, nevertheless, that his celibacy remained the "one defect in this otherwise well-filled life." [30] To supply a plausible story that might account for this persistent bachelor-hood became the sacred duty of Pierre M. Irving, who launched the Matilda legend and embroidered it sufficiently to please all tastes until the advent of the twentieth-century biographer, all compact of inquisitiveness and intent upon pricking the bubbles of the sentimentalist. A few years ago Mr. George S. Hellman[31] made out what seemed a plausible case for his theory that Irving, far from remaining true to his dead love, proposed marriage to Emily Foster in Dresden in 1823 and possibly again later, but recently Professor Williams has advanced evidence and argu-

---

[27] Cf. Hellman, *Washington Irving, Esquire,* 50–53.
[28] E. A. Duyckinck, *Irvingiana,* xii.
[29] *Theodosia [Burr], the First Gentlewoman of Her Time,* 223; see also "Theodosia Burr," *Harper's New Monthly Magazine,* XXIX, 302 (Aug., 1864).
[30] S. T. Williams (ed.), *Notes while Preparing Sketch Book,* 28.
[31] *Washington Irving, Esquire,* 49–58.

ments to show that Mr. Hellman's theory must remain a surmise until more conclusive evidence is produced.[32]

That Irving was very attentive to Emily Foster is plain; that he may have loved her is highly probable; that he sought her in marriage remains to be proved. Until further facts come to light, it seems a warrantable conclusion to say that Irving's love for Matilda was his one great emotional experience; but that in Irving's case, as in many another, time healed the wound, and that he came, in time, to find pleasure, as he always had, in women. That in his moments of melancholy and depression (and Irving was enough the man of sentiment to have many of them) his thoughts should not have reverted to Matilda and his lost happiness would have been unnatural, and that the recurrence of grief tinged some of his more sentimental writings appears not unlikely; but that he should have gone repining through life, remaining a lifelong bachelor because of Matilda Hoffman's death half a century before his own, is hard to believe.[33] For essentially Irving was one of those whom

[32] S. T. Williams, "Washington Irving, Matilda Hoffman, and Emily Foster," *Modern Language Notes*, XLVIII, 182–186 (March, 1933). See also Professor Williams's article, "Washington Irving and Matilda Hoffman," *American Speech*, I, 463–469, and Mr. Hellman's review of the *Journal of Washington Irving (1823–1824)* (ed. by S. T. Williams), in *Modern Language Notes*, XLVII, 326–328 (May, 1932). Important references, in addition to the ones already cited, on the Irving-Matilda-Emily problem include the following: *Life* (4 vols., New York, 1862–1864), I, 185–186, IV, 337, 361; *Notes While Preparing Sketch Book*, 40, 63–65; *Tour in Scotland, 1817*, 24; *Journal of Washington Irving (1823–1824)*, 104–105, 117; *Journals of Washington Irving* (ed. by W. P. Trent and G. S. Hellman); the manuscript fragment in the Yale University Library; *The Sketch Book*, 132, 320; and "St. Mark's Eve," *Bracebridge Hall*, 131.

[33] As early as May 27, 1820, he complained to Paulding that his financial reverses "doomed" him "to remain single." "With all my wandering habits, which are the result of circumstances rather than of disposition, I think I was formed for an honest, domestic, uxorious man. . . . Matrimony . . . I absolutely believe indispensable to the happiness and even comfort of the after part of existence." (*Life*, I, 355.) "God knows," he wrote twenty years later from Madrid, "I have no great idea of bachelor hood and am not one of the fraternity through choice—but providence has some how or other thwarted the warm wishes of my heart and the tendencies of my nature in those earlier seasons of life when tender and happy unions are

Wordsworth designated as the fortunate "glad hearts" of this earth. He often suffered from moments of depression, but possessed too volatile a nature to have harbored and hugged to his bosom an unnatural grief. Although Irving refrained from confession and self-revelation in his diaries, one does not have to read very far to realize that he was a romanticist, given to moods of sentiment and sensibility, and especially between 1809 and 1832, much given to memories and disillusionments as well as doubts and misgivings of the future; yet the one fundamental trait of his character was geniality, which, consciously[34] or unconsciously, became the habit of his mind.

At all events, the hard work necessary to complete *Knickerbocker* and the success of the book, as well as his transfer, in 1811, to the newer and wider scene of Washington in the interest of the Irving brothers' hardware importing business (in which he had become gratuitously a silent and generally inactive but profit-sharing partner) helped transmute grief into the realm of memory. Ostensibly a lobbyist and possibly an angler for some political plum, he set out "determined to be pleased with every thing, or if not pleased, to be amused";[35] and so he arrived in the capital city on the evening of January 9, just in time to get shaved, put on his "pease blossoms & silk stockings," and sally forth to one of Dolly Madison's brilliant levees, where, as he informed his friend Brevoort four days later, he found "a crowded collection of great and little men, of ugly old women, and beautiful young ones—and in ten

---

made; and has protected me in those more advanced periods when matrimonial unions are apt to be unsuited or ungenial; but I have often repined at my single state and have looked forward with doubt and solicitude to the possibility of an old age solitary, uncherished, and unloved." (Dec. 12, 1842; *Letters from Sunnyside and Spain*, 55–56.)

[34] "Let me not," he confides to himself, "indulge in this mawkish feeling and sentiment . . . which has produced a morbid sensibility and fostered all the melancholy tendencies &c." (*Notes while Preparing Sketch Book*, 24, 78.)

[35] *Letters of Irving to Brevoort*, 20.

minutes was hand and glove with half the people in the assemblage." [36] Next he wrote: [37]

To shew you the mode of life I lead, I give you my engagements for this week. On Monday I dined with the mess of Officers at the Barracks—in the evening a Ball at Van Ness's. On Tuesday with my cousin Knickerbocker & several merry Federalists. On Wednesday I dined with General Turreau who had a very pleasant party of Frenchmen & democrats—in the evening at Mrs. Madison's levee, which was brilliant and crowded with interesting men & fine women. On Thursday a dinner at Latrobe's. On Friday a dinner at the Secretary of the Navy's, and in the evening a ball at the Mayor's. Saturday as yet is unengaged—at all these parties you meet with so many intelligent people, that your mind is continually & delightfully exercised.

While it does not appear that he accomplished much, or anything, for his firm (indeed, his letters to his brothers seem to have been regarded by them of so little worth as not to require immediate answers; for we find him writing rather testily to Brevoort, saying, "Tell my brothers that when I receive an answer to any one of the letters I have written, I will begin to write again—but if I do before damme"),[38] he was very profitably employed. "I may compare," he says, "a place like this to a huge library, where a man may turn to any department of knowledge he pleases, and find an author at hand into which he may dip until his curiosity is satisfied." [39]

[36] In the same letter he writes: "Mrs. Madison is a fine, portly, buxom dame—who has a smile & pleasant word for every body . . . but as to Jemmy Madison—ah! poor Jemmy! he is but a withered little apple-John."

"Delightfully moored, 'head and stern'" in the home of John P. Van Ness, which contained several belles, he considers himself "in clover—happy dog! clever Jacob! & all that." (*Ibid.*, 23–25.)

[37] *Ibid.*, 31–32.　　　　[38] *Ibid.*, 35.

[39] *Ibid.*, 32. That he was, even then, on the alert for literary materials appears in the following report to Brevoort: "Congress has been sitting with closed doors, so that I have not seen much of the wisdom of the

Although a Federalist by rearing and temperament, he had not been in Washington a month before he had concluded that he would be no party man.[40] He was quite as happy dining with Democrats as with Federalists so long as they proved gentlemen and good company.[41] Apparently his brothers, especially William, entertained the hope and expressed some concern that Washington might receive some appointment, more particularly the Secretaryship of the Legation to France, with Joel Barlow as Minister; but Washington was too much the dawdler and gentleman of leisure to take the matter seriously, and when it developed that nothing was to be expected from Barlow (who was cool toward Irving in consequence of some critical strictures on the *Columbiad*, for which he believed Irving responsible), he reported the matter so nonchalantly that William must have felt some chagrin at his brother's light-heartedness.[42]

He lived "a constant round of banquetting, revelling, and dancing"[43] until the adjournment of Congress in March, when Washington became deserted, and Irving was glad to leave for

Nation, but I have had enough matter for observation & entertainment to last me a handful of months." (*Irving to Brevoort*, 24–25.)

[40] As a matter of fact, this resolution had been taken as early as May 2, 1807 (see *Life*, I, 138); still he had injected a good deal of political satire into *Salmagundi* (1807–1808) and *Knickerbocker* (1809). But now, apparently, he meant it.

[41] *Irving to Brevoort*, 30–32.

[42] On Feb. 16, Irving wrote: "As to the appointment . . . I do not indulge any sanguine hopes about it, and don't trouble myself on that score. I find that it has been the custom to leave the choice to the minister himself, in which case I have no chance. The Secretary of State was the first person who suggested the idea, and he is very solicitous for it; indeed, I have experienced great civility from him while here. The President, on its being mentioned to him, said some very handsome things of me, and I make no doubt will express a wish in my favor on the subject, more especially as Mrs. Madison is a sworn friend of mine, and indeed all the ladies of the household and myself great cronies. I shall let the thing take its chance. I have made no application, neither shall I make any; and if I go away from Washington with nothing but the great good will that has been expressed and manifested towards me, I shall thank God for all his mercies, and think I have made a very advantageous visit." (*Life*, I, 203–204.)

[43] *Irving to Brevoort*, 24.

Baltimore,[44] where "three days & nights' stout carousal, and a fourth's sickness, sorrow, and repentance" resolved him to resist "the world, the flesh, and the devil at . . . that sensual city" and "push homewards, as expeditiously as was reasonably possible."[45] But Philadelphia lay on the route home; and Philadelphia, his and Brevoort's "old seat of war,"[46] was especially hard to get by, partly because Ann Hoffman was visiting in the city, partly because of the attractive powers of "that little assemblage of smiles and fascinations, Mary Jackson,"[47] and not the least, because the great Cooke was then making his famous Shakespearean appearances there. " 'But this eternal blazon must not be' (Shakespeare), so in two or three days I'll gird up my loins, take staff in hand and return to the land of my fathers."[48]

The distractions of a brilliant social season behind him, Irving resolved, upon his return to New York, to get down to work and stick by it, but oftener than not the day terminated in convivial parties and midnight serenades—anything but work accomplished. Restlessness seized him, and he showed all the symptoms of a young romanticist vacillating between strongly contrasted moods,—hating himself for wasting his time and yet returning to the "transient stimulus of pleasure."

The old grief must have returned occasionally, but there is not the least sign of it in the published record of these years. And so he drifted back, easily and naturally, into the circle of old friendships and pursuits in New York. He now left the home of his mother and shared quarters with Henry Brevoort in Broadway, near Bowling Green, not far from the house of Mrs. Renwick, where both the young gallants were in frequent attendance. The influence of Brevoort upon Irving has not been properly evaluated, even after the publication of the Irving-

[44] *Life*, I, 204.
[46] *Irving to Brevoort*, 37.
[48] *Life*, I, 208; *Irving to Brevoort*, 45.
[45] *Irving to Brevoort*, 40.
[47] *Irving to Brevoort*, 42, 45–47.

Brevoort correspondence focused attention upon the friendship. For one thing, Brevoort directed Irving's attention to the American Indian, a theme which elicited Irving's most impassioned and fearless writing. More significant, however, is the fact that Brevoort was a great reader, and having an ample supply of money, had already gathered a fine collection of books.[49] If we could arrive at accurate and complete information regarding the titles in Brevoort's library about 1811–1812, to which Irving, of course, had ready access, we should doubtless come upon important findings. Unfortunately Brevoort was soon to leave, spending some months of 1812 among the fur hunters and the year 1812–1813 in Europe; but he continued his collecting, and there are references in their correspondence of Brevoort's keeping an eye open for "old odd Books," which Irving requested, and of which Brevoort says, "I have already got a number, and shall get many more in the purlieus of London." [50] Irving, for his part, having mapped out a course of reading and study for himself, had happy recourse to Brevoort's bookshelves, both now and during 1813–1815 (when they again shared bachelor quarters), thus enriching his knowledge of European thought and *belles-lettres*, developing his taste for literature, and making amends for the general neglect of his education as a youth.[51]

And so the years rolled on. He read a good deal; he played with several literary ideas; but, except for a revision of *Knickerbocker*,[52] his pen produced nothing he considered worth publishing. The editorship of the *Analectic Magazine* and the

[49] This library was ultimately to grow into a collection of some 10,000 rare volumes.
[50] *Brevoort to Irving*, 82. Irving had previously commissioned him to "look for scarce and odd books, and make up a collection of quaint and curious works." (*Life*, I, 222.) Not the least of Professor Williams's contributions in his promised definitive life of Irving, it is expected, will be a thoroughgoing examination into Irving's reading.
[51] *Life*, I, 211–212; see also Hellman, *Washington Irving, Esquire*, 77.
[52] In the many editions which followed, but chiefly in this one of 1812

War of 1812 furnished some temporary distraction and excitement, but he remained generally dissatisfied with the world and
with himself. He thought of marrying, but considered himself
too poor. Meanwhile the prospect of further travel intrigued
him most, a taste whetted by Brevoort's enthusiastic letters
regarding literati he was meeting in Europe.[53] "I always keep
it in view as a kind of succedaneum for matrimony, and promise
myself, in case I am not fortunate enough to get happily married to console myself by ranging a little about the world." [54]
When, therefore, in consequence of international complications,
the prospect of a Mediterranean cruise, upon which he had been
invited by his friends among the United States Naval officers,
fell through, he reluctantly unpacked his trunks and looked
forward drearily to sinking back into the workaday world,
which, by contrast with what he had just missed, looked drab.

---

and the one of 1848, Irving made innumerable changes not only in correcting misprints and improving the punctuation but especially in the diction,
omitting or softening numerous expressions which his age considered too
racy, deleting several anti-Catholic passages, and paring down severely
both contemporary and classical allusions. To turn to the critical edition
of the original version, as prepared by S. T. Williams and T. McDowell,
and to make comparisons with Irving's last authorized edition will amply
repay the reader who is familiar only with the latter.

[53] While attending lectures at the University of Edinburgh in 1812–
1813, Brevoort had become a welcome member of that notable Edinburgh
group which included the philosopher, Mackenzie; the savants, Professors
Playfair and Jameson; and the critics, Wilson ("Christopher North") and
Jeffrey. When, in 1813, Jeffrey came to America, Brevoort had appointed
Irving host to the distinguished critic, which opportunity Irving did not
allow to go unimproved. Later, in London and elsewhere, Brevoort had
met Thomas Campbell, Sir James Mackintosh, Madame D'Arblay, Miss
Edgeworth, Madame de Staël, Mrs. Barbauld, and Joanna Baillie, to all of
whom he advertised the excellence of Diedrich Knickerbocker, at the same
time writing Irving animated accounts of his meetings with these illustrious
people. He had also been on familiar terms with Charles Kemble, Mrs.
Siddons, John Howard Payne, and other stage luminaries. But the most
considerable service of Brevoort consisted in his introducing Irving's
writings to Scott, thus laying the foundation for a friendship from which
Irving was to derive so much benefit and stimulation. (*Brevoort to Irving*,
63–100; *Life*, I, 225–227.)

[54] July 8, 1812; *Irving to Brevoort*, 84.

But his brothers again came nobly to the rescue,[55] and on May 25, 1815, he embarked upon his second journey to Europe, little dreaming that seventeen years were to elapse before he would return.

After some pleasant wandering about England and a visit to the home of his sister Sarah in Birmingham (where there was as yet little thought of the hardships in which the Irvings were soon to be involved), he found himself suddenly transferred from a life of ease and indolence to the world of business cares— in charge of the Liverpool branch of the Irving firm, his brother Peter having been incapacitated by illness. By dint of slaving and unceasing attendance upon "the sordid cares of the counting-house," he managed to tide the firm over the first wave of business depression during 1815–1816 (the aftermath of the Napoleonic wars) until Peter returned to assume charge. But by the middle of 1817, the brothers saw the handwriting on the wall, and in January, 1818, they accepted the inevitable—bankruptcy.[56] By March, the formalities were over. Washington was the better for the crisis. Precisely when things looked darkest, he determined no longer to follow the line of least resistance. Thrown now definitely upon his own initiative, he resolved to live by his wits and his pen. Twice temptation assailed him in the form of governmental appointments, but he firmly put them by. It was a brave step to take; his brothers thought—foolhardy. And Irving would not have been Irving if misgivings had not promptly assailed him. He realized

[55] They continued, as long as they had the means, to act upon the sentiment expressed by William in 1804: "It is with delight we share the world with you; and one of our greatest sources of happiness is that fortune is daily putting it in our power thus to add to the comfort and enjoyment of one so very near to us all." (*Life*, I, 38.) When, later, their circumstances were reversed, Irving reciprocated quite as cheerfully.

[56] "So harassed and hag-ridden by the cares and anxieties of business" was he that he had been on the point of chucking it all and returning to New York, only to be met with the news of his mother's death, whereupon he resolved to stick by his invalided brother Peter. (*Irving to Brevoort*, 231, 232; *Life*, I, 254–256, 261–266, 269, 270.)

keenly that his literary promise, born of *Knickerbocker*, remained, after ten years, unfulfilled; and that he puzzled his
family. The muse had been unkind to him,[57] and he had no
assurance for the future; yet he stuck doggedly by his guns,
determined to see if his friend Ogilvie had been right in saying,
"You will look back on this seeming disaster as the most
fortunate incident that has befallen you." [58] And such, indeed,
it proved to be.

Aside from the exigencies of the practical situation of being
forced to make a living, the greatest credit for reclaiming Irving
from his life of indolence and ineffectuality goes to the literary
and social contacts which he made and from which he drew the
necessary stimulus to go on. Among these, the influence of
Scott is, of course, of primary importance. Irving had visited
Edinburgh during August and September of 1817, had moved in
the provocative company of Jeffrey, Blackwood, and Constable,
and had been royally entertained at Abbotsford by Sir Walter
Scott. Now that the nightmare of commercial agony was over,
the decisive step taken, in the summer of 1818, of going to London and setting up as author, and the several literary acquaintances in London renewed and cultivated, the business of putting
words together prospered for the first time since 1809. By February he had the first number of *The Sketch Book* ready and
succeeding numbers partly done. Not that the seven numbers
of this work [59] were dashed off in a twinkling. The moods of
sterility and fits of depression returned,[60] and doubtless it was

[57] He was especially disappointed in having literally nothing to show
for his four years in England—years during which he had hoped he would
hit his stride. (*Life*, I, 256–257, 264, 265, 273, 302.)
[58] *Life*, I, 274.
[59] Published at irregular intervals from May 15, 1819, to Sept. 13, 1820.
[60] To Ebenezer he wrote: "Should my writings not acquire critical
applause, I am content to throw up the pen and take to any commonplace
employment." (*Life*, I, 311.) With hardly more self-confidence, he confided to Brevoort: "I feel great diffidence about this reappearance in literature. I am conscious of my imperfections, . . . I have attempted no lofty
theme, nor sought to look wise and learned, which appears to be very

only the stern taskmaster, necessity, and the bracing influence of Scott in the background that whipped his wayward faculties into line. His progress was somewhat halting, and even the remarkable success of the first numbers, instead of enlivening him, served only to fluster and appall him lest he should not be able to "act up to expectations";[61] but he persevered. Even before _The Sketch Book_ was completely and successfully launched, and when "bread and cheese" were still items of some importance to him, he turned a deaf ear to Scott's urging him to undertake the editorship of an anti-Jacobin periodical in Edinburgh, with "£500 a year certain."[62] The reception of _The Sketch Book_ in America and subsequently in England left no doubt in Irving's mind about the success he had attained. The solid pudding which it returned set him up for the time being, and eventually he realized the "stock of copyright property" and "little capital," which enabled him to become something more than merely the ornamental genius of his family. But in 1820 the battle was far from won. There remained still the disturbing and gnawing thought, "What next?" Referring to the newly-won plaudits, he wrote to Leslie:[63]

Now you suppose I am all on the alert, and full of spirit and excitement. No such thing. I am just as good for nothing as ever I was; and, indeed, have been flurried and put out of my way by these puffings. I feel something as I suppose you did when your picture met with success—anxious to do something better, and at a loss what to do.

---

much the fashion among our American writers, at present. . . . I seek only to blow a flute accompaniment in the national concert, and leave others to play the fiddle and French horn." (_Life_, I, 313, 314.)

[61] _Life_, I, 330–331; cf. _Irving to Brevoort_, 327.

[62] _Life_, I, 338–340. For Irving's reply to Scott's offer, see the Preface to _The Sketch Book_. Later, when Murray offered him a thousand pounds a year to edit a periodical to be published by himself, Irving declined, as well as Murray's offer of a hundred guineas per article which Irving might contribute to the _London Quarterly_. (_Life_, II, 128, 130.)

[63] _Life_, I, 333.

"What to do next" became from now on Irving's haunting worry. For the moment there were too many interruptions and distractions to do much work. Associations formed through Scott and the booksellers, as well as his own well-earned popularity, led to a "round of routs, dinners, operas, balls & blue stocking coteries."[64] Then followed eleven months in Paris (August, 1820, to July, 1821), during which he enjoyed the gay Parisian life enough to find it a serious hindrance to his literary projects.[65] But there were compensations in the companionship of Tom Moore and John Howard Payne. With Payne to introduce him to the great actor, François Joseph Talma,[66] and to lead him more and more into the realm of the drama and theatre, with Lord and Lady Holland offering him frequent hospitality, with "Anacreon Moore" to make him "a gayer fellow than I could have wished,"[67] with Lord Russell, Sydney Smith, Kenney, Luttrel, L'Herbette, and young George Bancroft among his more gifted companions, besides the gracious women of the English and American sets, the year went idly by except for an occasional stroke of the pen on manuscripts which eventually became *Bracebridge Hall*.[68] In July, 1821, drawn by a desire to be of some service in connection with one of the English adaptations of French plays which Payne had prepared for the English stage,[69] and more particularly, to proceed with the writing and arranging for

[64] *Irving to Brevoort*, 386–387.
[65] Meanwhile his desire to set up Peter in a suitable and remunerative occupation had led him to invest $5,000 of borrowed money in a steam-navigation enterprise on the Seine, an arrangement which occasioned much anxiety from the start and led eventually to Irving's losing much more than the original investment. (*Irving to Brevoort*, 349–350, 352, 353, 366–374, 379–381.)
[66] See Irving's "Conversations with Talma," *Biographies and Miscellanies*, arr. and ed. by Pierre M. Irving, 151–160; "Correspondence of Irving and Payne," *Scribner's Magazine*, XLVIII, 465–467; and *Life*, I, 384–386.
[67] *Life*, I, 391; see also 377–383, 388–390, 392, 393.
[68] *Irving to Brevoort*, 356–358, 375, 376; *Life*, I, 374–394.
[69] Hellman, *Washington Irving, Esquire*, 118.

publication of *Bracebridge Hall* (published May, 1822), he left
for London.

If anything had been lacking to raise Irving's popularity to
the heights, this book supplied it. There seemed to be "a kind
of conspiracy to hoist him over the heads of his contemporaries."[70] "Geoffrey Crayon is the most fashionable fellow of
the day," wrote Leslie; and Lord Byron, in a letter to Murray,
underscored his admiration for Irving.[71] It is worth noting
that Irving's flute-like notes were able to captivate public attention at the moment when the virile Scott and the sensational
Byron were the idols of the English-reading world.

Irving now entered upon his great English social triumph.
His letters are full of the chitchat of Murray's drawing-rooms
and the amusing bluestocking coteries of fashion of which Lady
Caroline Lamb was the promoter.[72] There pass in review
Murray, Longmans, Scott, Gifford, Campbell, Hazlitt,[73]
Southey, Mitchell (the translator), Cohen (the antiquary), Sir
James Mackintosh, Foscolo, Milman, Hallam, Belzoni, and the
elder D'Israeli.[74] Mrs. Siddons gives him "the greatest dra-
matic treat" one evening when she reads to him "the part of
Constance at her own house,"[75] and with Charles Kemble he is
"on good terms."[76] In company with Moore, he calls upon
Lady Blessington; at Lady Besborough's house he meets Lord
Wellington; he breakfasts at Holland House; and he accepts
invitations to Wimbledon, one of the country-seats of Lord

---

[70] Warner, *Washington Irving*, 129; see also *Life*, I, 375–376.

[71] Cf. *Life*, I, 370. See also William Godwin's comments, quoted in
Life, I, 320.

[72] Concerning her, he wrote to Brevoort: "She is a strange being, a compound of contradictions, with much to admire, much to stare at, and much
to condemn." (*Irving to Brevoort*, 343.)

[73] "Correspondence of Irving and Payne," *Scribner's Magazine*, XLVIII,
466.

[74] *Irving to Brevoort*, 342–345, 386–392; *Life*, I, 348–354.

[75] *Irving to Brevoort*, 388.

[76] "Correspondence of Irving and Payne," *Scribner's Magazine*, XLVIII,
469 *et. seq.*

and Lady Spencer. He is even asked "occasionally" to Rogers's classic breakfasts, and there he meets the old poet Crabbe "and others of his [Rogers's] literary friends."[77] But to Peter he confides in June, 1822:[78]

I have been leading a sad life lately, burning the candle at both ends . . . have been at the levee and the drawing-room, been at routs, and balls, and dinners, and country-seats; been hand-and-glove with nobility and mobility . . . and am now preparing to make my escape from all this splendid confusion.

The means of escape was a trip to Germany. The resolution to go was taken in consequence of a rheumatic malady in his feet, which made it advisable to try the German baths. But there were several contributing causes that sent him to Germany, not the least of which was the contagion caught from Scott's enthusiasm for German literature and lore. Shortly after his visit to Abbotsford, while the bankruptcy matter was being adjusted, he spent his days and nights studying German. By May 19, he could report progress to his friend Brevoort:[79]

I have been some time past engaged in the study of the German Language, and have got so far on as to be able to read and *splutter* a little. It is a severe task, and has required hard study; but the rich mine of German Literature holds forth abundant reward.

The belief that the rewards were indeed abundant was emphatically confirmed by the particular success of the three stories[80] in *The Sketch Book* which owed most to his readings in German literature. The results of the German tour will be dealt with under the head of Irving's literary development; here it is enough to record the fact that personal and social, as well as

---

[77] *Irving to Brevoort*, 338–339, 391; see also *Life*, I, 418.
[78] *Life*, I, 419.   [79] *Irving to Brevoort*, 286–287.
[80] For the Germanic influences in "Rip Van Winkle," "The Legend of Sleepy Hollow," and "The Spectre Bridegroom," see Henry A. Pochmann, "Irving's German Sources in *The Sketch Book*," *Studies in Philology*, XXVII, 477–507 (July, 1930).

literary, contacts and considerations sent him to Germany, and that, once there, other social factors profoundly affected him.

He entered the Rhineland in search of health and literary materials, and having acquired the former, set out with the avowed intention of preparing for spring publication a German Sketch Book, and went adroitly about making observations and keeping accurate travel notes.[81] The German journals indicate the truly antiquarian spirit in which he proceeded via Frankfurt, Darmstadt, Heidelberg, Karlsruhe, Strassburg, Ulm, Augsburg, and Salzburg, to Vienna, and thence to Dresden, the "little

[81] However, as long as he remained in Germany, the mood to write was lacking, and later in Paris, the "German materials" would not yield readily to such "fits of scribbling" as he was able to muster. While his journals are full of plans, little was accomplished. For example, "In course of the walk tho[ugh]t of preparing a collection of tales of various countries, made up from legends, etc., etc., etc." (*Journals*, I, 101, Nov. 2, 1822.) Again: "Tried to commence work on Germany, but could do nothing. . . . Toward twelve o'clock, an idea of a plan dawned on me—made it out a little, and minuted down heads of it. Felt more encouraged." This, as he told his nephew, was a plan "to mingle up the legendary superstitions of Germany, in the form of tales with local descriptions and a little of the cream of travelling incidents." (*Life*, II, 13.) But as late as Dec. 17, 1823, he had made little progress: "Woke early— felt depressed & desponding—suddenly a tho[ugh]t struck me how to enlarge the MSS on hand so as to make 2 vols. of Sketch Book— that quite enliven'd me." (*Journal of Washington Irving, 1823–1824*, 89.) Under the stimulating impulse he wrote Murray that he would have two volumes ready for the spring. He played with the Sketch-Book idea until March, 1824, and then switched to the plan adopted in *Tales of a Traveller*. (*Life*, II, 23.) At such times as the inspiration was upon him, he wrote frantically and produced an astonishing amount of manuscript in a short period, but he often waited and fretted through barren weeks and months for the movement of his fitful genius. Although he always considered *Tales of a Traveller* the best of his productions, its inception was slow, its composition spasmodic, and its final revision troublesome, so that when it finally appeared, on August 25, 1824, it was a book of pieces, ill-arranged like a crazy-quilt—more so even than *The Sketch Book* and *Bracebridge Hall*, in both of which, but especially in the latter, Irving often succeeds but poorly in his devices of motivation to bring the heterogeneous materials into some sort of unity.

For the influence of German literature on this book, see Henry A. Pochmann, "Irving's German Tour and Its Influence on His Tales," *Publications of the Modern Language Association*, XLV, 1150–1187 (Dec., 1930).

Florence of Germany," where, arriving on November 28, 1822, he little thought he would spend eight months. The time was spent most pleasantly in attendance upon court functions,[82] mingling in the gay and colorful diplomatic circles, enjoying the opera, studying German [83] while Mrs. Foster taught him Italian and Emily superintended his French lessons,[84] making excursions into neighboring regions famous in history and fable, engaging in private theatricals at the home of Mrs. Foster, and paying gallant court to Emily. The varied social distractions were too much for Irving's easily diverted genius; nor was the progress he made in the affairs of the heart (if, indeed, Mr. Hellman's shrewd surmises are correct) any greater than his accomplishments with the pen.[85]

The interval between his German residence and his years in Spain was an unhappy one, representing, as far as the development of his mind's originality and power are concerned, retrogression rather than advance. To be sure, he finally brought *Tales of a Traveller* to press, worked spasmodically on a series of "American Essays" (never completed or published), thought something of writing various biographies, and, more important, was led by Payne into collaborating with him in several plays,

---

[82] This ancient court in Saxony with "its stiff old-fashioned formalities, and buckram ceremonies," where, he admits, "I have been treated uniformly with the most marked attention, by all the members of the royal family, and am in great favor with the old queen," afforded him his first intimate glimpse into the life of royalty. The punctilio exercised in courtly ceremonies and the royal boar hunt, with regular retinue and accoutrements, given Irving's love for the picturesque, seemed like a chapter of history out of the Middle Ages and must have worked strongly upon Irving's imagination. (See Irving's letters reprinted in *Life*, I, 429–436.)

[83] His daily German lessons were punctually attended to, from seven to nine in the morning. On May 16, 1823, he "paid Schott forty dollars for ninety-six hours of German teaching," and the next day he recorded: "Pay off Mr. Keysler for five and one half months, German tuition at eight doll. a month. Forty-four doll[ar]s." (*Journals*, I, 194–195.)

[84] "So that," he wrote to Mrs. Sarah Van Wart, "if I am not acquiring ideas, I am at least acquiring a variety of modes of expressing them when they do come." (*Life*, I, 431.)

[85] See *Journals*, II, 146; *Life*, I, 437–438.

notably *Charles II* and *Richelieu*, besides finishing his translations, begun in Germany, of the operas, *Der Freischütz* (or *The
Wild Huntsman*) and *Abu Hassan*.[86]

The years 1824 and 1825 mark a transition period during
which Irving turned from original composition to compilation.
The hesitancies and doubts expressed in his diaries and the
many different kinds of work attempted, always with little
satisfaction to himself, give evidence of that uncertain state of
mind which did not end until he was fairly launched upon the
routine work of biographical and historical research in Spain.[87]
The caustic reviews elicited by *Tales of a Traveller*, the ugly
attacks upon his patriotism for remaining so long abroad, and
worries over financial investments,[88] all conspired to complete
his discomfiture. But the chief harassment arose from his
inability to find a suitable subject, something that would fix
his mind and make his wayward powers tractable. In no year of
his life was he so indefatigable a reader as during 1825—reading,
as the journals suggest, with a view to stimulating his mind and
pen. The year brought him forcibly (although he had long ago
recognized his mind's very definite limitations) to the realization
that he was not an inventive genius of the first order. In short,
he found himself, at the age of forty-two, pretty well written
out.[89]

[86] Irving's sketch of a play based on the life of Shakespeare belongs also
to this period. See *Journal of Washington Irving (1823–1824)*, ed. by
S. T. Williams, 57–58, and "Correspondence of Irving and Payne,"
Scribner's Magazine, XLVIII, 470–482 (Oct., 1910); 597–601, 604–606,
608–616 (Nov., 1910).

[87] Compare diary entries for the closing days of 1827 and 1828, *Life*, II,
83, 139.

[88] Not only was the navigation scheme, in which he had sunk $5,000,
going badly, but his investment, in 1825, in the Bolivar mines occasioned
much concern from the first. Irving was never a lucky investor, and
speculative enterprises continued to absorb a large part of his earnings.

[89] To be sure, he had shown in *Knickerbocker* a remarkable felicity in
one genre of literature, and ten years later, a similar excellence in another
type, namely, the short story (see F. L. Pattee, *The Development of the
American Short Story*, 20–23, for a statement of the nine services Irving

Thus was born, or confirmed, Irving the biographer and historian; thus, too, came home the melancholy truth of Thoreau's aphorism that routine presents a good wall to which to retreat. The last half of his life was full of high honors for him, rich in notable services to his country, and productive of a dozen respectable books; but the Irving who lives and is vital is the young Irving, the Irving before 1832. One naturally comes, therefore, to ask what formative influences, aside from his social environment, shaped and qualified him so as to make him what he was. One of the most potent influences, all appearances to the contrary, was politics, more specifically, his incipient Federalism.

---

performed for the modern short story); but these works, as well as *Brace-bridge Hall* and *Tales of a Traveller*, had, after all, been largely the product of the literary antiquary. Much of his time since writing *The Sketch Book* had been spent in searching for new materials. Whenever he had run out of literary thunder, he had resorted to change of scene, to travel. To Scott he had confided, in 1819, "I shall occasionally shift my residence and write whatever is suggested by objects before me, or whatever rises in my imagination." (Preface to *The Sketch Book*, 9.) He continued now as he had begun, with the result, particularly after the German period, that his books are less originatively creative than skillful pieces of bookmaking. His remarkable fecundity during the Spanish sojourn (productive in four years of more books than the first forty-two years of his life) was chiefly in the realm of biography and history. *Columbus* (1828), *Granada* (1829), *Companions of Columbus* (1831), *The Conquest of Spain* (not published until 1835), and the other works that owe their inception to his life in Spain were all works that needed little invention,—subjects that were all ready to hand. Even *The Alhambra* (1832) was largely a transcription of legends that he heard or read in Spain,—the result, he says rather pointedly, of "many delightful hours of quiet, undisturbed, literary foraging," and we might add, "dreaming." (See *The Alhambra*, 81.) Certainly none of these books is conceivable without Irving's sojourn in Spain, particularly his residence in the Alhambra.

During one other period of his career, immediately after his return home in 1832, when he was stirred by the dramatic romantic expansiveness of the New West, he was profoundly affected by the scene round about him; and the result is to be seen in *A Tour on the Prairies* (1835), *Astoria* (1836), and *Captain Bonneville* (1837), partly the result of a true inspiration, but still more than half in the nature of potboilers. For the rest of his life he stuck to biography—*Goldsmith* (1849), *Mahomet* (1850), and *Washington* (1855–1859)—works which lean toward compilation rather than original composition.

II. IRVING'S POLITICS AS A DETERMINING FACTOR

Irving, as far as his modest abilities permitted, represented
the Federalistic spirit in American *belles-lettres*. "For Federalism
was essentially an aristocratic ideal struggling to adapt itself
to the conditions of a republic and the equalities of a new country";[90] and Irving belonged by birth and inclination to the
aristocratic circle of New York. It was his heritage,[91] and, in
common with his friends, he instinctively distrusted the leveling
tendencies of democracy and Jeffersonianism. Not that he was
intensely interested in the political aims of either party, or that
he troubled his head much about the abstract principles involved
in the struggle between Federalism and Republicanism. He
came by his "political principles" pretty much as most Americans
come by them today: by inheritance from his father and older
brothers and by association with his Federalist friends; and perhaps more unconsciously than consciously held to their principles of privilege, class interests, capitalism, stability, and
centralization in government. Having a happy disregard (soon
to develop into a distinct dislike) for money-getting and commercial pursuits, this urbane New Yorker was no more personally or vitally interested in the economic ideals of the Federalists than in the abstract principles of man's natural rights
held by the opposing party, which, as his Federalist friends told
him, existed primarily to give mechanics, yokels, and clodhop-
pers their Rights. As a practicing politician he did not cut a
great figure. He was not impressed by drawers, tinkers, and
tradesmen, however vociferous they might be on election day in
proclaiming their stout and solid Federalism; and after one
electioneering experience as a Federalist,[92] he had enough of it,

[90] H. S. Canby, *Classic Americans*, 77.
[91] It is noteworthy that Irving never moved much among those of the
station which would have been his had his family never emigrated to this
side of the Atlantic.
[92] Having just become a duly licensed lawyer, and having just hung

as a letter to Mary Fairlie, dated May 2, 1807, amply illus-
trates: [93]

We have toiled through the purgatory of an election, and
may the day stand for aye accursed on the Kalendar, for never
were poor devils more intolerably beaten and discomfited than
my forlorn brethren, the Federalists. What makes me the more
outrageous is, that I got fairly drawn into the vortex, and before the third day was expired, I was as deep in mud and politics
as ever a moderate gentleman would wish to be; and I drank
beer with the multitude; and I talked handbill-fashion with the
demagogues, and I shook hands with the mob—whom my
heart abhorreth. 'Tis true for the first two days I maintained
my coolness and indifference. The first day I merely hunted
for whim, character, and absurdity, according to my usual custom; the second day being rainy, I sat in the bar-room at the
Seventh Ward, and read a volume of Galatea, which I found on
a shelf; but, before I had got through a hundred pages, I had
three or four good Feds sprawling around me on the floor, and
another with his eyes half shut, leaning on my shoulder in the
most affectionate manner, and spelling a page of the book as if
it had been an electioneering handbill. But the third day—ah!
then came the tug of war. My patriotism all at once blazed
forth, and I determined to save my country! O, my friend, I
have been in such holes and corners; such filthy nooks and
filthy corners, sweep offices and oyster cellars! "I have been
sworn brother to a leash of drawers, and can drink with any
tinker in his own language during my life"—faugh! I shall
not be able to bear the smell of small beer or tobacco for a
month to come! . . .

Truly this saving one's country is a nauseous piece of business, and if patriotism is such a dirty virtue—prythee, no more
of it.

His feeble solicitations at Albany procured him no office,
and his experience in the Seventh Ward disgusted him. Indeed,

out his shingle at No. 3 Wall Street, Irving doubtless felt he should take a
small hand in city politics.   [93] *Life*, I, 137–138.

he could not run with the hungry pack of office-seekers, "who, like a cloud of locusts . . . devour every plant and herb, and every 'green thing' ";[94] so he speedily gave up the idea of saving his country on a government salary.[95] Henceforth, he stuck to his resolution of refraining from active participation in politics. This does not mean, however, that he was not politico-conscious. Certainly *Salmagundi* and *Knickerbocker*, belonging as they do to the period when Hamilton and Jefferson divided all Americans into two classes, are permeated with the doctrine of Federalism; but these books both belong to the history of the young New Yorker—both born of youthful exuberance, effrontery, bravado, with the difference that into the latter entered, in addition, a genuine antiquarianism and a humanizing sorrow. In 1811, just arrived in Washington, he resolved once more "to dismiss from my mind all party prejudice and feeling

[94] His commission in 1812 to Washington, as a member of the Committee of Merchants from New York to obtain the remission of their bonds involved negotiations—half commercial, half political—which led him into quarters and to men whose ways he abhorred.

[95] Not, however, until he had repeatedly offered his services only to find them rejected or to find that he did not want what was offered. For example, soon after his first application for political spoils at Albany went unheeded, he tried, equally unsuccessfully, for a clerkship in one of the courts of New York. (*Life*, I, 126-127, 178-182.) Later in Washington, he half-heartedly angled for the Secretaryship of the Legation to France, but explained privately to his brothers that he should look upon it merely as an opportunity to travel and gather literary stock. (*Life*, I, 202.) Afterwards, during the impending financial collapse of the Irving business, when he had more need than ever for money, and when the hitherto unattainable came to him unsolicited, he had grown philosophical enough to observe that what he had formerly desired he hoped now to get along without: "I have repeatedly applied for some paltry public situation but have been as often disappointed—It has pleased heaven that I should be driven on upon my inner strength—and resort to the citidel [?] within me." (*Tour in Scotland, 1817*, 104.) Only after he found the "citidel within" not as strong a resource as he had hoped, he turned, in 1826, once more to political employment in the form of a diplomatic secretaryship in Spain. Then followed other more substantial and honorable ministerial appointments, which were given and accepted in such a manner as hardly to justify their being classed as political. His appointment by Jackson as Minister to Spain was concurred in unanimously by the Senate and was executed by Irving in as nonpartisan a manner as it is possible to perform the duties of such an office.

as much as possible, and to endeavor to contemplate every subject with a candid and good-natured eye," [96] to divest himself
of all "jaundiced representations" and "party bigotry." [97] Pur-
suant to this resolution, he had to report to his friend Brevoort: [98]

As I do not suffer party feelings to bias my mind I have
associated with both parties—and have found worthy and intelligent men in both—with honest hearts, enlightened minds,
generous feelings and bitter prejudices. . . .

You would be amused . . . to see the odd & heterogeneous
circle of acquaintance I have formed. One day I am dining with
a knot of honest, furious Federalists, who are damning all their
opponents as a set of consummate scoundrels, panders of Bonaparte, &c &c. The next day I dine perhaps with some of the
very men I have heard thus anathematized, and find them
equally honest, warm, & indignant—and if I take their word
for it, I had been dining the day before with some of the
greatest knaves in the nation, men absolutely paid & suborned
by the British government.

Henceforth, also, he stuck resolutely to his determination to
keep out of his writings such political matters as had, perhaps
involuntarily, crept into *Salmagundi* and *Knickerbocker*. In so
far, however, as Federalism was an attitude toward life, an ideal
of living, Irving remained a Federalist, so that he was, in spite
of his indifference to party, really more Federalist than the
Federalists themselves. Without thinking through the theoretical implications, he was keenly aware of a change that was
coming over the country; he was plainly disturbed by the
rebellious and discontented elements among the common
people who, in their determination not to remain common, had
lost all sense of respect for their betters. He was thoroughly
cognizant of this deeper struggle of which "the brawls of
politicians and the ideology of statesmen were only symptoms." [99]

[96] *Life*, I, 202. [97] *Life*, I, 200.
[98] *Irving to Brevoort*, 29–30. [99] Canby, *op. cit.*, 80.

He cast his eyes lovingly toward the "good old days" and viewed with suspicion the present with its tendency to forget the graces of living in its grasping for power and money, for privileges and rights. "He felt, with the sensitiveness of a dreamer, the raucousness of a trading, manufacturing, exploiting society. Sprung from trade himself, and hating it, spending his youth in an illusion of a gay gentleman's world of the arts and conversation in a commercial town, he did not rationalize his desires, yet clearly lived and wrote them."[100] Hence *Salmagundi*, like the *Spectator*, is an onslaught upon the vile manners of a mercantile, middle-class, seaport town; and *Knickerbocker's History*, in its Dutch aspects, is a satire upon their sluggish bourgeoisity, their lack of grace, and the "happy equality" of their earth-creeping minds; in its attacks upon the Yankees, a satire on their ungainly manners and odious practices of pilfering and money-getting. In *The Sketch Book* and *Bracebridge Hall*, the life of a *gentleman*, in the eighteenth-century sense of the word—whether the urbane man-of-parts or the eccentric but worthy country squire—is lovingly idealized; while tradesmen, demagogues, upstarts, innovators, levelers, and dullards are ridiculed.[101]

The point is, of course, quite well taken that, by nature and training, Irving was unfitted to apprehend the ideology which underlies the formative period of the United States, that many of the principles, great and small, passed over his head, that he could hardly have become an acute politician, and that he had little desire to achieve distinction in political pursuits. The fact remains, however, that he was at various times of his life an

---

[100] *Ibid.*, 80.

[101] *Ibid.*, 85. "Half of Irving's heart is in 'Rip Van Winkle,' where the picturesque Rip and his cronies, so full of humor and honest . . . happiness, are set in contrast to the shabby pretentiousness of the village twenty years later. And the other half is in 'Bracebridge Hall' and 'The Alhambra,' for in each is a life tinged with the melancholy of departing, yet rich in loyalty, solidity, and human worth instead of human rights." (*Ibid.*, 81.)

eager follower of political affairs, as, for instance, during his first stay in Washington when he listened with attention to the arguments of both Federalists and Republicans, to both the Anglophile and the pro-French contingents; and that, in 1833, he found the South Carolina nullification hiatus so interesting that he spent some three months in Washington haunting the Congressional halls. His comments upon the situation may sound somewhat like the words of the tyro, but there can be little doubt of his interest. To Peter he wrote:[102]

My sojourn in Washington prolonged itself through the whole session. I became so deeply interested in the debates of Congress, that I almost lived in the capitol. The grand debate in the Senate occupied my mind as intensely for three weeks, as did ever a dramatic representation. I heard almost every speech, good and bad, and did not lose a word of any of the best. I think my close attendance on the legislative halls has given me an acquaintance with the nature and operation of our institutions, and the character and concerns of the various parts of the Union, that I could not have learned from books for years.[103]

During the anti-slavery agitation he remained, it is true, largely a passive spectator, not because he had not pretty clearly defined views on the subject, but because he was never an extremist, because he had old friends on both sides and did not court alienation of friendships by a precipitous entrance into the sphere of politics (which, as a young man, he had forsworn),

[102] *Life*, II, 277–278.
[103] These comments, it must be admitted, bear more the marks of a youth's first visit to his national capital during stirring times than the observations of a fifty-year-old traveller, diplomat, and lawyer; but it must be remembered that he had been out of touch with the American scene and Washington affairs for seventeen years, so that the note of immaturity which we fancy can be detected is probably ascribable to a rediscovered novelty which he found in this land of his birth. After all, his protracted tour as far west as Oklahoma and as far south as New Orleans just prior to his stop in Washington had opened up a new vision to him which could have been matched by few of the august Congressmen then deliberating and debating the nation's problems.

and because he was not the man to cross a bridge before he came to it. He looked upon slavery exactly as Washington looked upon it, and there can be little doubt where he would have stood had he lived until 1861; for already in 1832, while the nullification legislature of South Carolina was in session, he had definitely settled the secession question in his own mind. After dining with Governor Hamilton, "the nullifying Governor" and his "leading nullifiers . . . so madly in the wrong," he replied playfully but suggestively to the Governor's warm invitation to "come again soon" by saying, "O yes! I'll come with *the first troops*."[104]

The ease with which Irving, who in his youth had gone with the dominant Federalism of the time, fitted himself into the scheme of things about 1832 has occasioned some wonderment; but the seeming inconsistencies are not as great as they may appear. The Federalism of his youth had been largely the result of association with his brothers and their friends, all good Federalists; with Josiah Ogden Hoffman, his law preceptor, an ardent "Fed"; with Mrs. Hoffman, the mother of Matilda and daughter of John Fenno, Hamilton's editor. Under such tutelage it was natural for him to poke good-natured fun at President Jefferson's red velvet breeches (in *Salmagundi*) and his "logocratic" government (in *Knickerbocker*). After one unsavory experience in the murky waters of New York politics, "which, not to speak profanely, is a perfect Hell Gate," [105] he had resolved not to allow his good disposition to be ruined by political pettiness. Then had followed seventeen years of detachment from the fierce partisanship of American politics, during which time he had seen something of the workings of several forms of European government.[106] He had also grown

---

[104] *Life*, II, 272.   [105] *Life*, II, 341.
[106] Only once in the interim between his first venture into politics and his return to America in 1832 had he even remotely entered the political arena. As editor of the *Analectic Magazine* during 1813–1814 he had naturally taken greater cognizance of public and national affairs than was

seventeen years older. To be sure, he had his misgivings, expressed in a letter to Alexander H. Everett, dated February 14, 1829: [107]

Your statement of the relative number of votes for General Jackson and Mr. Adams quite surprises me. . . . I was rather sorry when Mr. Adams was first raised to the Presidency, but I am much more so at his being displaced; for he has made a far better President than I expected, and I am loth to see a man superseded who has filled his station worthily. These frequent changes in our administration are prejudicial to the country; we ought to be wary of using our power of changing our Chief Magistrate when the welfare of the country does not require it. . . . As to the old general, with all his *hickory* characteristics, I suspect he has good stuff in him. . . . As I give the old fellow credit for some degree of rough chivalry, I have no idea that he will play a petty, persecuting game with his opponents, when their opposition has been fair and honorable.

One thing here is plain: Washington Irving, still suspicious of change, held with old Samuel Sewall, whom he does not otherwise resemble in many respects, "I am for government, whether in or out." He was inclined to make the best of any government *de facto;* and when he found Old Hickory to have all the disposition in the world to be friendly toward him, he

---

his wont; and although at the outset of the War of 1812 he was less than lukewarm (never having been an enthusiastic supporter of Madison or of Madison's policies), he soon caught the national contagion and joined in the enthusiasm occasioned by the American naval victories. On at least one occasion, when news came of the British capture of Washington, attended by the ruthless burning of the nation's public buildings, the messenger reporting the news in a tone of complacent derision at the national administration, Irving flared up and "let fly at him." He was sufficiently aroused to offer his service to Governor Daniel D. Tompkins, who made him his aide and military secretary, with the rank of colonel, and sent him on several military details; but Irving participated in no bloody encounters, and later he said that his greatest service was rendered in allaying the discomfiture of his chief, the "General and Commander-in-Chief of the Militia, and Admiral of the Navy of the State of New York," when that dignitary fell off his horse. (*Life*, I, 234, 246.)

[107] *Life*, II, 143.

came easily to the position of saying, "The more I see of this old cock of the woods, the more I relish his game qualities."[108] Possibly Paulding had something to do with Irving's ready acceptance of the new order;[109] certainly his intimacy with Martin Van Buren at the London Legation was a contributing factor.[110]

In his talks with business men and politicians in Washington and New York—that is, with those who were prosperous and prominent—he gathered enthusiasm for the new regime, and became impressed by the romantic expansiveness of his country, which he had just re-discovered. Although still distrustful of some of the "elbow-counsellors" of the new democracy, he was less disposed to criticize than eager to discover the romantic charm of the vast changes that had taken place or were about to take place. Still far from being a politician, he moved easily among the Jacksonians, and, for their part, was regarded as one of them. They were eager to make political capital out of his literary reputation and urged upon him various offices, all of which he had the good sense to decline until, in 1842, came the offer of the Ministership to Spain. That he little understood the intricacies of the several economic factors involved, and that he discovered nothing more significant in the great struggle between agrarianism and capitalism for control of the government than the ungenerous suspicions and novel theories which it bred appears pretty plainly. It was enough for him to be on the same side with respectable people like John Jacob Astor, whose motive in financing Astoria he scarcely comprehended for the glamor and romance which the undertaking presented to his romantic mind. He lacked Cooper's intuitive penetration into the mainsprings of human motives, and he was less influenced by the outstanding liberals of the time than by the masters of Wall

[108] *Life*, II, 274.
[109] V. L. Parrington, *The Romantic Revolution in America, 1800–1860*, 207.
[110] *Life*, II, 232–235; Hellman, *op. cit.*, 221–224, 243–256.

Street. From the courageous movement of Locofocoism he drew back in distrust. In his youth he had held with gentlemen that gentlemen, and not the people, should govern the country. He held the same belief still, except that, as the emphasis had shifted from a government by aristocrats to a government by capitalism, he followed the natural trend of those who, seeing their ideal of Federalism little more than a political carcass, shifted their position accordingly. It was easier for a Federalist to side with the stability which a regime of the moneyed interests seemed to portend than to go with the Locofocos or the Democrats. Irving's position is pretty clearly set forth in a letter to Gouverneur Kemble,[111] which, while it shows no great circumspection, does not involve a severe wrench of thought from the position he had formerly taken:

As far as I know my own mind, I am thoroughly a republican, and attached, from complete conviction, to the institutions of my country; but I am a republican without gall, and have no bitterness in my creed. I have no relish for puritans either in religion or politics, who are for pushing principles to an extreme, and for overturning everything that stands in the way of their own zealous career. I have, therefore, felt a strong distaste for some of those loco foco luminaries who of late have been urging strong and sweeping measures, subversive of the interests of great classes of the community. Their doctrines may be excellent in theory, but, if enforced in violent and uncompromising opposition to all our habitudes, may produce the most distressing effects. The best of remedies must be cautiously applied, and suited to the state and constitution of the patient. . . . Ours is a government of compromise. We have several great and distinct interests bound up together, which, if not separately consulted and severally accommodated, may harass and impair each other. . . .
I always distrust the soundness of political councils that are accompanied by acrimonious and disparaging attacks upon any

[111] *Life*, II, 337–340.

great class of our fellow-citizens. Such are those urged to the
disadvantage of the great trading and financial classes of our
country. You yourself know ... how important these classes
are to the prosperous conduct of the complicated affairs of this
immense empire. You yourself know, in spite of all the common-place cant and obloquy that has been cast upon them by
political spouters and scribblers, what general good faith and
fair dealing prevails throughout these classes. Knaves and swind-
lers there are doubtless among them, as there are among all great
classes of men; but I declare that I looked with admiration at the
manner in which the great body of our commercial and financial
men have struggled on through the tremendous trials which have
of late overwhelmed them, and have endeavored, at every
pecuniary sacrifice, to fulfill their engagements. . . .

For my own part, I cannot but think a national bank, properly
restrained and guarded (especially as it respects dealing in
foreign exchange), will, after all, be the measure most likely to
suit the circumstances of the country, and restore the prosperous
action of trade. It would be a salutary check upon all minor
banks, and would curb the power of Mr. Biddle, who is now
getting a complete financial sway.

"This persuasive presentation of the philosophy of compromise, with its implicit defense of capitalism"[112] was a creed
which Irving himself fully realized had certain vulnerable points,
but what else was there for a practical gentleman to embrace?

As to the excessive expansions of commerce, and the extravagant land speculations, which excited such vehement censure, I look upon them as incident to that spirit of enterprise
natural to a young country in a state of rapid and prosperous
development; a spirit which, with all its occasional excesses, has
given our nation an immense impulse in its onward career, and
promises to carry it ahead of all the nations of the globe. There
are moral as well as physical phenomena incident to every state
of things, which may at first appear evils, but which are devised

[112] Parrington, *op. cit.*, 209.

by an all-seeing Providence for some beneficent purpose. . . .
The spirit of speculative enterprise . . . grows out of the very
state of our country and its institutions, and, though sometimes
productive of temporary mischief, yet leaves behind its lasting
benefits.[113] The late land speculations, so much deprecated,
though ruinous to many engaged in them,[114] have forced agri-
culture and civilization into the depths of the wilderness; have
laid open the recesses of primeval forests; made us acquainted
with the most available points of our immense interior; have
cast the germs of future towns and cities and busy marts in
the heart of savage solitudes, and studded our vast rivers and
internal seas with ports that will soon give activity to a vast
internal commerce.[115]

This was more than merely a lyrical outburst, for he himself
was sufficiently affected by the mania for speculation in lands
and railways to make investments and to commercialize his pen
by such money-making ventures as *A Tour on the Prairies*,
Astoria, and *The Adventures of Captain Bonneville*.

Irving is a man who, as a politician, is not brought readily to
a rule of thumb—does not fall neatly into a nice classification.
In 1804 he spoke of himself as "an admirer of General Hamilton,
and a partisan with him in politics."[116] By 1807 he had worked

[113] As Irving himself was soon to realize when commercialism, in the
guise of the railway, with its "unearthly, infernal, and horrific alarum"
disturbed the calm of Sunnyside and made him wish "he had been born
when the world was finished," for "if the Garden of Eden were now on
earth, they would not hesitate to run a railroad through it." (*Life*, III,
142–143, 173.) But he soon found that there were certain compensations,
for "this railroad makes every place accessible on the easiest terms."
(*Life*, III, 179.) "Why," he said on another occasion, "travellers now
walk Broadway with the dust of the prairies on their boots." (*Life*,
III, 343.)
[114] As he had experienced to his own hurt, though his investments later
turned out profitably.
[115] *Life*, II, 339.
[116] *Life*, I, 62. Upon his first visit to Paris (1805), the youth records
this remarkable statement in his diary: "Selective gov ᵗˢ most calculated
to render nation great—France owes her power [to?] years of elective
government in which time the men of abilities rose to the top & managed
affairs—It is the number of those men that still remain in office that gives

up an enthusiasm that sought to save his country by waving the flag of the "Feds." In Washington, early in 1811, he had grown so liberal in his political principles and friendships that the sage Peter Kemble thought it wise to warn him "against the danger of keeping company with French Ambassadors, who . . . are exceedingly apt to corrupt young gentlemen." [117] By 1829, he had come to think indulgently of Andrew Jackson,[118] and in 1833, he was classed as "a Jackson man." In 1850, his position was with Webster and Clay; but in 1856, instead of listening to the considerations urged by timid gentlemen of the old school

---

the french gov^t its present vigor. Crowned heads make a most contemptible appearance at present. Bonaparte is the most brilliant and most intelligent—next to him is the Emperor of Prus[sia] who is assisted by able counsellors." (Williams, "Washington Irving's First Stay in Paris," *American Literature*, II, 17–18,.March, 1930.)

[117] *Brevoort to Irving,* 12.

[118] He was, all his life, if not an active participator, nevertheless in close rapport with those who were within the Washington circle. Although his early solicitations for political spoils for himself had gone unrewarded, he was more successful in asking for his friends, and they, in turn, did nobly by him. Especially during the 'thirties do we find him "asking" various favors for his friends and relatives of Martin Van Buren, with whom he had been intimate in London. The tone of his letters recently made public indicate that Washington Irving, Esquire, understood very well how places were made and dispensed in politics. See the chapter, "The Letters to Martin Van Buren," in Mr. Hellman's biography of Irving.

It must be borne in mind, however, that he was never a truckler; in his intercourse with high officials, regardless of the possible gains or losses to himself, he spoke his mind freely and unconcernedly. Shortly after Van Buren's election, he dared to offer this advice:

"You have now arrived at the most distinguished post in the world, at the head of the *great republic:* it depends upon yourself to make it the most honorable. There is but one true rule for your conduct: act according to the sound dictates of your head and the kind feelings of your heart, without thinking how your temporary popularity is to be affected by it, and *without caring about a re election.*" (New York, Feb. 6, 1837; Hellman, *op. cit.,* 251.)

A half-year later he again offered gratuitously:

"Never think how any measure is to affect your political fortunes, and *dare to be unpopular rather than to do wrong.*" (The italics are Irving's. Hellman, *op. cit.,* 253.)

One wonders how many other private citizens have dared to address the President of the United States in such frank terms and been rewarded with the offer of a seat in his Cabinet.

in favor of Fillmore and the *status quo*, he voted, so he told Mr. Putnam, for Frémont, on the ground that his comparative youth and inexperience in party-politics were points in his favor,—that the country stood in need of a man with nerve and energy, one in his prime, and unfettered by party traditions and bargains for the spoils.[119]

"Though born and brought up in a republic, and more and more confirmed in republican principles by every year's observation and experience," he wrote in *Bracebridge Hall*,[120] "I am not insensible to the excellence that may exist in other forms of government." In the same book he makes some rather pungent observations on the constitution of the several classes of society in England, indicating that he was not as superficial an observer of society and government as he has been made out to be.[121] To be sure, during his earlier years in England, he was only vaguely aware of the miserable living conditions of the English proletariat. He was never thrown with the working classes: he never saw children working in the factories and the coalpits simply because he did not visit the sweatshops and the collieries. During the *Sketch Book* and *Bracebridge* days most of his sympathies were on the side of the English squire who lamented "the national

[119] G. P. Putnam, "Recollections of Irving," in *Studies of Irving*, 153–154. Of interest, also, is the fact that during the last year of his life, while engaged upon an exposition of Washington's party connections to be incorporated in the last volume of his biography, Irving said, "I must deal cautiously with the party questions. I wish to stand in my History, where Washington stood, who was of no party." (*Life*, III, 348.)

[120] P. 240. From Spain he wrote on August 25, 1843: "I consider, under all circumstances, a constitutional monarchy the best form of government for Spain in its present state of knowledge and improvement, and I believe it is the form desired by the great mass of the people; but there are some bigots in politics who would fain restore an absolute monarchy and zealots who would hurry every thing into a wild democracy. One of the latter made a startling speech in a recent political meeting, wherein reforms in the constitution were proposed abridging the power of the crown and taking from it the *Veto*. I shall be satisfied said this Loco Foco if you do away with the *veto*—but I should be much more satisfied if you would do away with the *Queen!*" (*Letters from Sunnyside and Spain*, 64–65.)

[121] *Ibid.*, 238–243.

industry and public improvement" which threatened to destroy
the charm of life, and who held that in proportion as commerce
and manufactures increased, the spirit of "Merry England"
subsided.[122]   To be sure, Irving made one visit to a debtor's
prison, but it was in the spirit of fun and curiosity that he went
with Tom Moore, who wanted to show him the place where,
"with fifty pounds or so in the pocket, one can make one's
self very comfortable." But he did not tarry long. "From
here," said Irving, "I went to Holland House. What a contrast!"[123]   When, however, on another occasion, he stood in
another prison, with Moore again as his companion—the
dungeon in which Marie Antoinette had awaited the hour of
death—his soul was stirred:

> Never have I felt my heart melting with pity more than in be-
> holding this last abode of wretchedness.   What a place for a
> queen, and such a queen! one brought up so delicately, fos-
> tered, admired, adored.[124]

Distressed royalty always evoked his sympathy.[125]   Later, however, during the momentous years from 1829 to 1832, when he

---

[122] *Bracebridge Hall*, 251.   [123] *Life*, III, 208–209.
[124] *Life*, I, 378–379.
[125] He pitied Marie Antoinette; he pitied, also, Bonaparte. Anent the
latter he said in 1815: "I am extremely sorry that his career has terminated
so lamely; it's a thousand pities he had not fallen like a hero at the battle
of Waterloo.

"I must say I think the Cabinet has acted with littleness towards him.
In spite of all his misdeeds, he is a noble fellow, and I am confident will
eclipse, in the eyes of posterity, all the crowned wiseacres that have
crushed him by their overwhelming confederacy.

"If anything could place the Prince Regent in a more ridiculous light,
it is Bonaparte suing for his magnanimous protection. Every compliment
paid to this bloated sensualist, this inflation of sack and sugar, turns to the
keenest sarcasm; and nothing shows more completely the caprices of fortune, and how truly she delights in reversing the relative situations of
persons, and baffling the flights of intellect and enterprise—than that, of
all the monarchs of Europe, *Bonaparte* should be brought to the feet of
the *Prince Regent*.
> " 'An eagle towering in his pride of place
> Was by a mousing owl hawked at and killed.' "
>   (*Life*, I, 250; Irving's italics.)

was secretary of the legation at London, the years during which the Reform Bill was coming to a head, he seems to have been more keenly alive to the tremendous stir all about him and felt most deeply the significance of the current of unrest occasioned by social and political inequalities. On March 31, 1831, he wrote to Brevoort in a vein which leaves little room for doubting that for once he was thoroughly aroused: [126]

We are in the beginning of an eventful week. This evening will determine the fate of the present cabinet, which is in a tottering condition, & we are looking daily for decisive news from Paris. We must have tidings of moment, too, from Poland though I fear we shall have dismal news from that quarter. However, the *great cause of all the world* will go on. What a stirring moment it is to live in. I never took such intense interest in newspapers. It seems to me as if life were breaking out anew with me, or that I were entering upon quite a new and almost unknown career of existence, and I rejoice to find my sensibilities, which were waning as to many objects of past interest, reviving with all their freshness and vivacity at the schemes and prospects opening around me. I trust, my dear Brevoort, we shall both be spared to see a great part of this grand though terrible drama that is about to be acted. There will doubtless be scenes of horror & suffering, but what splendid triumphs must take place over these vile systems of falsehood in every relation of human affairs, that have been woven on the human mind & for so long a time have held it down in despicable thraldom.

This outburst, the first and last utterance of the kind, though couched in rather vague terms and veering on absurdity, is, nevertheless, significant as indicating that, after the turn of the century, Irving shared with Americans in general the enthusiasm for republican principles. It is quite possible that Jackson's concurrence in Irving's diplomatic appointments had something to do with it. It is quite certain that Irving's realization of the

[126] *Irving to Brevoort*, 443–444.

emptiness and hollowness of certain formularies and ceremonies still attaching to court life, particularly as he observed the tottering state of the Spanish throne, made him rather more critical of European monarchical governments at this time than at any other period of his life,[127] while the controversy over the Oregon question aroused all his latent resentment against England.[128]   His was never a truckling attitude, and his position in the end was not unlike that pronounced in the essay "English Writers on America" in *The Sketch Book* and reiterated in 1822:[129]

> With England . . . it remains . . . to promote a mutual spirit of conciliation; she has but to hold the language of friendship and respect, and she is secure of the good-will of every American bosom. . . . We seek no boon at England's hands: we ask nothing as a favor.   Her friendship is not necessary, nor would her hostility be dangerous to our well-being.   We ask nothing from abroad that we cannot reciprocate. . . . We merely ask, do not estrange us from you; . . . we would fain be friends; do not compel us to be enemies.

As diplomat and ambassador Irving served capably.   His letters indicate that he possessed more than ordinary insight into the peculiarly complex situation of international affairs, and that, without being a profound student of such affairs, he exhibited a good deal of acumen in anticipating and grasping the

---

[127] On the occasion of John Randolph's presentation to the King of England, when the Duke of Sussex, amused at the unconventional court costume of Randolph, asked sneeringly, "Who's your friend, Hokey Pokey?" Irving, jealous of the honor of his country, replied rather sharply, "That, sir, is John Randolph, United States Minister at Russia, and one of the most distinguished orators of the United States." (*Life*, II, 202.)

[128] In connection with the Oregon boundary controversy, Irving acquitted himself as a capable diplomat.   To Bulwer, the English Minister at Madrid, he once said: "Bulwer, I should deplore exceedingly a war with England, for depend upon it, if we must come to blows, it will be serious work for both.   You may break our head at first, but by Heaven! we would break your back in the end." (*Life*, III, 112.)

[129] *Bracebridge Hall*, 462–463.

practical interrelations and interdependencies of the nations. The voluminous official correspondence (now preserved in the State Department and estimated at 100,000 words) which Irving sent from Madrid to Washington bears witness to the fact that, while he never approached the wisdom of a Goethe in international affairs, he always succeeded in carrying through to a successful conclusion his many difficult and often delicate ministerial duties as Envoy Extraordinary to Spain. His abilities, however, lay in the realm of the practical;[130] and where his knowledge of the theoretical intricacies of diplomacy was inadequate, he could always rely upon his innate good sense and intuitive gentlemanliness to see the thing to a happy and graceful conclusion. When he begins to theorize, as he does seldom, he grows vague; and his later pronouncements do not show much advancement in depth over his earlier ones. During his Vienna days he wrote into his journal his belief, which, history has indicated, rests upon a false assumption:

Nations are fast losing their nationality. The great and increasing intercourse, the exchange of fashions, the uniformity of opinions by the diffusion of literature are fast destroying those peculiarities that formerly prevailed. We shall in time grow to be very much one people, unless a return of barbarism throws us again into clans.

Two years, however, and a wider glimpse of the world and its ways led him to sense that the realization of this dream was in the dim distance. At least, there is an implied reservation in the following generalization:[131]

[130] One finds also occasionally an observation of Irving's on the economic aspects between the nations, particularly between England and France. See, for example, *Journal of Washington Irving (1823–1824)*, 63, 64. But one feels that he had no greater aptitude for comprehending the intricacies of this finely constituted maze of cause and effect that obtained between the nations than for grasping the comparatively simple problem of the tariff as it could be seen in 1832 as a background behind the American slavery question.

[131] *Journal of Washington Irving (1823–1824)*, 136.

Until nations are *generous* they never will be wise—true policy is generous policy—all littleness—selfishness &c may gain small ends but lose great ones—it may appear chivalrous but it is true—Expedients may answer for the moment—they gain a point but they do not establish a principle—there is a return of the poisoned chalice.

It has frequently been intimated, as an adverse criticism, that Irving was content to remain ignorant of the momentous political and social issues which dominated his age. While, so far as his writings reveal, this contention appears to be founded on fact, the truth is quite the opposite, for he was, if not keenly, nevertheless sympathetically, alive to the burning problems of the nineteenth century. But feeling a thing and using it for literary subject matter are two different things. The singular absence of "living issues" from his published works is attributable to his conscious exclusion of what he apprehended as matters of passing or temporary interest and of jarring or inartistic content. His conception of *belles-lettres* and his oft-avowed philosophy of good will and geniality simply did not include these subjects in his category of "literature." For Irving was, in his own peculiar way, and in spite of his proverbial indolence, ambitious to achieve distinction in literature; and he deliberately excluded those issues and materials from his writings which, according to his belief, did not give promise of remaining vital for all ages.

III. IRVING'S LITERARY DEVELOPMENT

When Irving held in his hands the fifth and last volume of his life of Washington, a work which had taxed his failing energies to the utmost, he said with relief: "Thank Heaven, . . . henceforth I give up all further tasking of the pen."[132] The general reader of Irving seldom realizes how much "tasking of the pen" went into Irving's books. That composition did not come

[132] *Life*, III, 380.

easily is ascribable to two causes chiefly: (1) his mind was not remarkably imaginative in the sense of being creative, and (2) the standard of excellence which he set for himself was difficult to achieve. As early as 1823, he had realized fully that whatever success he would attain would be the result of his manner more than of his matter.

There are such quantities of these legendary and romantic tales now littering from the press both of England and Germany, that one must take care not to fall into the commonplace of the day. Scott's manner must likewise be widely avoided. In short, I must strike out some way of my own, suited to my own way of thinking and writing. I wish, in everything I do, to write in such a manner that my productions may have something more than the mere interest of narrative to recommend them, which is very evanescent; something, if I dare to use the phrase, of classic merit, *i.e.*, depending upon style, etc., which gives a production some chance for duration beyond the mere whim and fashion of the day.[133]

His scrupulous adherence to this simple literary creed caused him to be his own severest judge and to consign numbers of plans and many half-written manuscripts to oblivion. It accounts also for the fact that Irving's "staying" power depends largely upon his style. Mr. Canby, in commenting upon Irving's style, says very aptly:

Irving's reputation is the remarkable achievement of a style that sometimes rests upon little else than its own suavity. It was formed upon the prose of Goldsmith, Sterne, Swift, Steele, and Addison, with romantic coloring from Mrs. Radcliffe, and as early as the Mustapha letters in those good-natured Salmagundi papers of 1807, which proclaimed the civilization of New York by making fun of it, was elegant, harmonious, and incisive. He sharpened its edge in the Knickerbocker "History" of 1810 [*sic*], sweetened it by 1819 in the best of the "Sketch

[133] *Life*, II, 2.

Book" stories, brought it to full ripeness in "The Alhambra"
of 1832, wrote it by second nature in his "Life of Goldsmith"
of 1849, and did not relinquish it until the halting of old age
appears in the very last page of the "Life of Washington" in
1858 [*sic*]. It was a perfect instrument which ... changes very
little from youth to age, varies scarcely at all in works of very
different character, became, as a style should, the very accent
of the man, but was and is a patina upon the metal of his
thought rather than the flexible soul of the thought itself. Style
with Irving was finish, polish, and when he took old chronicles
of Granada, gave them romantic coloring, and translated them
into his personal diction, it is clear that he felt he was about the
chief business of literature. ... Yet many a more pretentious
author of his age has died utterly, while Irving, in spite of his
modern detractors, lives. Stylists do not die if they are fortunate enough to find even a few themes that summon all their
powers.[134]

His style was part of himself. He had learned, as a young
gentleman of fashion, how to turn a pretty phrase; he continued,
for the rest of his life, often even in his daily diary jottings, to
write gracefully and wittily—like a gentleman. It was part of
his rearing and temperament to be a "gentleman,"[135] and the

[134] Canby, *Classic Americans*, 70–71, 92.
[135] Mr. Hellman (*op. cit.*, 65–67) has called attention to the fact that
during the first fifty years of Irving's life none of his works carried his
name on the title page, and that, among the various pseudonyms adopted,
the word "Gentleman" figures most prominently. His first published work
appeared under the *nom de plume* of "Jonathan Oldstyle, Gent." and
in *Salmagundi* he appeared as "Anthony Evergreen, Gent." and "Launcelot
Langstaff, Esq." His first book, a translation, was by "an American Gentleman," while his biographical sketch of Thomas Campbell was by "a
Gentleman of New York." Even Diedrich Knickerbocker, though he was
down and out, was certainly a gentleman; and the books with which he won
international fame—*The Sketch Book, Bracebridge Hall*, and *Tales of a
Traveller*—are all by the pen of "Geoffrey Crayon, Gent." After 1829,
when he used the name "Fray Antonio Agapida" for his *Conquest of
Granada*, he gives, though not always, his own name (perhaps at the
insistence of the publisher), as in the life of Washington. It appears that
the word "gentleman," though he would doubtless have disclaimed the
connotation, was most to his liking.

word he understood precisely in the sense in which the Federalists understood it.

The second influence upon Irving (second only in time) was one that came, quite as much as Federalism, from without, namely, romanticism. Irving, who before *The Sketch Book* had been the scion of the eighteenth-century literary tradition, producing works strongly influenced by Addison, Steele, Goldsmith, Sterne, and others,[136] came by 1819 definitely under the influence of certain romantic impulses. Instead of continuing in the approved manner of the eighteenth-century prose stylists, as he had begun in *Salmagundi* and *Knickerbocker*, he charted a new track for himself and produced in *The Sketch Book* America's first four short stories, three of which were based upon romantic materials drawn from Germany.[137] How and why Irving was led away from classic models and toward romantic materials are important considerations not only in the study of Irving but also in the study of the genesis of the American short story.

Of course, romanticism was in the air, and possibly Irving was destined, sooner or later, to be influenced by it. Classicism and the eighteenth century were dead; romanticism was inevitable. But "how the new forces laid hold upon him and modified his classicism is a problem tremendously important, for it is at this point, where in him the Addisonian Arctic current was cut across by the Gulf Stream of romanticism, that there was born the American short story, a new genre, something distinctively and unquestionably our own in the world of letters."[138]

[136] See Ferdinand Künzig, *Washington Irving und seine Beziehungen zur englischen Literatur des 18. Jahrhunderts.*

[137] For a fuller discussion, see Henry A. Pochmann, "Irving's German sources in *The Sketch Book*," *Studies in Philology*, XXVII, 477–507 (July, 1930); "Irving's German Tour and Its Influence upon His Tales," *Publications of the Modern Language Association*, XLV, 1150–1187 (Dec., 1930). Professor Walter A. Reichert has recently undertaken to trace Irving's steps in Germany, particularly in Dresden, and to treat exhaustively the subject of German influence upon Irving.

[138] Pattee, *The Development of the American Short Story*, 3. The truth of

The transformation of Irving the classicist to Irving the romanticist, in so far as it occurred (for Irving lived, as Professor Pattee very correctly observes, always a little in the past tense), was effected in ten years,—from the publication of *Knickerbocker* in 1809 to *The Sketch Book* in 1819–1820. The eighteenth-century tone and manner were by no means lacking in the books after 1819; indeed, in so far as his style was concerned, there was hardly any change at all; but in his materials the change is too marked to escape notice. The cause of this new note of romanticism is attributable to a number of influences and literary contacts, not the least of which is his acquaintance, during these ten years, with German literature, though the route was, at first, indirect.

Probably the earliest contact which Irving made with things Germanic was the Gothic novel;[139] next came the plays of Schiller and Kotzebue as they were adapted to the New York stage by Dunlap and others about the turn of the century and shortly after;[140] and, about 1812–1814, the necessity, as editor of the *Analectic Magazine,* he felt for keeping abreast of the periodical literature not only of America but of Europe.[141] Through Brevoort, in Europe, he arranged that the important British reviews and "the different periodical Journals of France, as well as those of note published on the Continent, such for instance as

the sweeping implication left by the concluding appositive phrase in Professor Pattee's assertion may be questioned and remains to be established.

[139] Cf. Hellman, *op. cit.,* 28; S. T. Williams and T. McDowell (eds.), *Knickerbocker's History,* intro., xxxvii; and Irving's early diaries.

[140] S. H. Goodnight, *German Literature in American Magazines Prior to 1846* (Madison, 1907), 122–125.

[141] Although undertaken solely to escape the ennui of his single occupation of treading the rounds of fashionable society, "up to my ears in 'an ocean of peacocks' feathers'—or rather like a 'Strawberry smothered in cream,' " and viewed as nothing more than "an amusing occupation, without any mental responsibility of consequence," it soon turned into serious and often irksome business, partly because of the necessity of conducting the critical department, Irving being temperamentally averse to being either "wise or facetious at the expense of others." (*Irving to Brevoort,* 88; *Life,* I, 217, 223–225.)

Kotzebue's &c." should come to his desk.[142] He could not have
scanned these without becoming aware of the stir that was being
made over German literature and thought.[143] Then followed
the years in England and contacts with Campbell, Foscolo,
Hallam, Southey, Milman, Belzoni, D'Israeli, Mrs. Siddons,
Charles Kemble, Mackintosh, Rogers, Gifford, Jeffrey, Blackwood, Constable, and people who frequented Murray's drawing
rooms, and Scott. All this was at a time when Scott was
exciting wonder with his minstrelsy and romance, when the
Waverley authorship was still a mystery, when Shelley brought
forth *Alastor*, Keats his first volume of poems, Tom Moore his
Lalla Rookh, when Lady Caroline Lamb was forming her amusing bluestocking coteries, and when Byron's escapades were still
fresh enough to gossip about.[144] What an atmosphere for the
first American man of letters! Certainly an infectious one.[145]

But to top it all came personal contacts with Scott, whom
Irving visited at Abbotsford in 1817 at a time when that "glorious old minstrel," as Irving designated Scott, was steeped in
German literature. Scott's hearty welcome and hospitality,
coupled with his innumerable border tales, witching songs,
and legendary stories, which crowded Irving's mind with a
"world of ideas, images, and impressions" so as to keep him in
"a kind of dream or delirium," [146] came at the critical moment to
make of Irving a romanticist. It was Scott, also, who directed, or
re-directed,[147] Irving's attention to Germany. Scott had become

[142] *Brevoort to Irving*, 64–65.
[143] See *Studies in Philology*, XXVII, 482–483 (July, 1930).
[144] Irving was soon to have the pleasure of reading Byron's ill-fated
memoirs in manuscript form, then in the possession of Tom Moore.
(*Life*, I, 406–407; see also II, 28.)
[145] The contacts with English romanticists and artists which Irving
formed at this time and later present a fruitful field of research that has
received little attention so far.
[146] See Irving's account of his reception and entertainment by Scott (*Life*,
I, 285) and his extended essay on Abbotsford in *The Crayon Miscellany*.
[147] For Irving could hardly have been the reader of *Blackwood's Edinburgh* and *Foreign Quarterly* magazines that he was without being already
in a manner acquainted with the newly discovered literature of Germany.

interested in German literature as early as 1792, when he had begun the study of the language.[148] He had already made extensive translations from the German, three of which—Goethe's *Goetz von Berlichingen*, Bürger's *Lenore*, and *Der Wilde Jäger*—had found their way into print. At the moment he was engaged on *The Doom of Devorgoil*, based upon an old Scottish tradition and the German legend, "Stumme Liebe," as told by Musaeus.[149]

Whatever the cause, Irving's visit to Scott was followed by a wild effort to take German by storm.[150] The first fruits of the German influence can be seen in the large borrowings for "Rip Van Winkle," "The Legend of Sleepy Hollow," and "The Spectre Bridegroom"—borrowings which are, however, confined largely to subject matter and little to manner. He does not allow his heart to run away with his classic good sense; he does not, in the manner of the German *Romantiker*, lose himself in a romantic haze and atmosphere, as he does more largely later under the influence of Spanish romanticism. Over all, there plays the quiet, gentle humor of Washington Irving, laughing at his characters, at his situations, at himself, and at his reader, so that these first tales, derivative as they are from the German, are not out-and-out romantic or even Gothic in the sense of Monk Lewis's or Mrs. Radcliffe's Gothicism, but rather sportively Gothic.

An examination of Irving's first attempts in this new genre, the American short story, which he said he had "the merit of adopting for himself instead of following others," leads to the

[148] His library at Abbotsford, we know, contained some three hundred volumes of German literature—Goethe, Schiller, Wieland, Bürger, Fouqué, Oehlenschläger, Grimm, Tieck, Hoffmann, Brentano, Arnim, the Schlegels, and others. (F. W. Stokoe, *German Influence in the English Romantic Period, 1788–1818*, 68, 175–177.)

[149] *The Poetical Works of Walter Scott* (12 vols., Edinburgh, 1880), XII, 116, 117, 365; see also W. Macintosh, *Scott and Goethe: German Influence on the Writings of Sir Walter Scott* (Galashiels, n.d.), 1–5, 38–50, especially 44–49.

[150] See above, p. xxxvii.

conclusion that if he did produce a new type, he was far from presenting new materials in that type. ˙Very probably he never ˙ intended to pass off his stories as absolutely original. Certainly he was frank and comprehensive enough in his apology for using the German legend of Peter Klaus for his "Rip Van Winkle," when he wrote: [151]

I had considered popular traditions of the kind as fair foundations for authors of fiction to build upon, and made use of the one in question accordingly.

Irving's method of composition was none other than that of many of his contemporaries whose works were equally derivative, except that they went more frequently to English than to German models. There was this difference, however, that Irving had the merit and ability to re-dress these old materials in an American cloak and to envelop all with his charming style, which, after all, makes them his own.

Two years after *The Sketch Book* was published, Irving went to Germany, and quite naturally he found there what he went in search of—a new matter for a new genre. *Tales of a Traveller* contains "Buckthorne," a rather weak attempt at an English *Wilhelm Meister;* "The Adventure of My Uncle," "The Story of the Young Italian," and "The Bold Dragoon" are all influenced more or less by German literature, while "The Adventure of My Aunt" and "The Adventure of the German Student" are full of Gothic terror; "The Italian Banditti" of the third part is a collection of tales in the Gothic vein; and the sportive Gothic story of "The Devil and Tom Walker" in the fourth part has been called "a comic New England *Faust.*" *Wolfert's Roost*, a volume of fugitive pieces, contains two stories, "Guests from Gibbet Island" and "Don Juan: a Spectral Research," which are both traceable to German sources.

[151] *Works of Washington Irving* (3 vols., New York, P. F. Collier, n.d.), III, 571, footnote.

Of the forty-five short stories with which Irving is credited, no less than a third are derived, wholly or in part, from German sources. Thus the German tale from the very first brought a powerful influence to bear upon the American short story. Irving was unquestionably the most influential native literary force during the early part of the nineteenth century in America, and his influence, consciously or unconsciously, directed the course that the short story was to pursue in its development.[152]

Finally, *The Alhambra*, in which Irving turns away from German influence and follows the full stream of Spanish romance,[153] contains tales founded on local traditions and legends picked up while visiting Granada. The spirit of these stories is that of the *Arabian Nights*, and their frank supernaturalism rests on magic hidden in the bowels of the earth by the Moors, demon steeds, flying carpets, enchanted beauties, engulfed convents, palaces built by necromancy, and phantom armies that emerge from the heart of the mountains. "The book is an arabesque, as redolent of the Orient as the tales of Scheherezade."[154] There is no more travesty, no more romance tempered with rollicking humor as in "The Bold Dragoon," no more Knickerbocker capering as in "The Stout Gentleman" or "The Adventure of the German Student." His surrender is complete. *The Alhambra* shows Irving more definitely and completely under the spell of romanticism than does any other book of his.[155] The chief importance of the volume is that it is

[152] It should be observed, however, that of such later developments as the carrying power which Hawthorne contributed and the definite technique which Poe gave to the short story, Irving was blandly unconscious.

[153] It is possible that Irving's interest in Spanish literature dates back to his Dresden days, for he could easily have caught the contagious enthusiasm of the German *Romantiker* for the Spanish past. His formal lessons in Spanish did not, however, begin until Dec. 10, 1824; but he progressed so well that on Jan. 15, 1825, he could record in his diary that he was reading Spanish "satisfactorily." Nevertheless, the lessons continued for some time longer.

[154] Pattee, *op. cit.*, 17.

[155] "For my part, I gave myself up, during my sojourn in the Alhambra, to all the romantic and fabulous traditions connected with the pile. I lived

one of the few examples of the Oriental Gothic in this country.[156]

Another cogent impulse that accounts for much of Irving as a writer is the true spirit of literary antiquarianism, replete with gleanings from books, at work already in *Salmagundi* and still more pronounced in *Knickerbocker*.[157] The literary antiquarian-

---

in the midst of an Arabian tale, and shut my eyes, as much as possible, to everything that called me back to everyday life." (*Ibid.*, 17; see also *Irving to Brevoort*, 425–426, 433–434.)

[156] Cf. O. S. Coad, "The Gothic Element in American Literature before 1835," *Journal of English and Germanic Philology*, XXIV, 85 (1925).

[157] We are so accustomed to thinking of *Knickerbocker's History* as a *jeu d'esprit* that the authenticity (in the larger sense) of the history is frequently lost sight of. There are, to be sure, trifling errors. "Van Twiller arrived in 1633, not in 1629, as Irving says; Kieft became governor in 1638, not in 1634, although this is a disputed date. Irving speaks of Van Twiller as the first Dutch governor, when actually he was the fifth; yet until recently none of his predecessors was known save Minuet. When Irving began to write, there was available . . . only one general history of New York, that of William Smith, published in 1757." (S. T. Williams and T. McDowell, editors, *Knickerbocker's History*, intro., li.) Aside from a large freedom in dates and names and Irving's obvious nonsense, whether it be satire, burlesque, travesty, humor, or hoax, Diedrich Knickerbocker is a surprisingly dependable historian. He caught fairly accurately the spirit of William the Testy; and although the picture of Peter Stuyvesant is somewhat distorted to fit the comic purpose of the satirist, and Wouter Van Twiller's picture is not photographically accurate, Irving (the rage of their Dutch descendants notwithstanding) is both a merciful and lenient historian; for the Dutch of this early period were certainly bad administrators, unable to enforce their too numerous laws, forever beset by petty squabbles, and anything but business-like, enterprising, and progressive. (*Ibid.*, intro., li.)

Irving's labors, particularly his honest antiquarianism in this and all his other works, have not been generally appreciated. Although his use of historical sources in *Knickerbocker's History* was not always scholarly, and although his plagiarisms sometimes assume amusing proportions, he worked through literally hundreds of volumes of both ancient and modern authors and historians. An exhaustive study of Irving's sources still remains to be made, but the work of Professors Williams and McDowell in their edition of *A History of New York* reveals the wealth of Irving's reading.

"Passages reminiscent of Sterne jostle others from Cotton Mather. Sometimes a character speaks and acts in the idiom of Cervantes, or there is phrasing, perhaps half unconscious, which recalls his severe training in the Bible. Fielding is here, as are Swift and Rabelais, the New England historians, and the Jesuit fathers. It is not ostentatious learning, but a boyish pleasure of playing with words. Allusions tumble after one another throughout the book, occasionally badly assimilated or badly

ism of such works as *The Sketch Book*,[158] *Bracebridge Hall*, *Tales of a Traveller*, and *The Alhambra* is recognizable on every page, while the biographical and historical works of his later career are by their very nature produced by the same or a similar impulse.

With this much prefaced, namely: (1) an inborn, somewhat incalculable feeling for sentiment and, particularly after 1809, sensibility, or rather, sentimentality, (2) an equally naturally acquired feeling for the Federalistic attitude toward living, (3) an inherent love for the method of the literary antiquary, and (4) a feeling for romanticism, imbibed mainly from Scott and German literature, we may proceed now to the more easily determinable factors that account for Irving as a writer. The chief ones, three in number, all relate chiefly to his style, and are (1) an extraordinary sensibility to sense impressions from without, (2) a remarkable faculty for form within the limits of short units, and (3) an equally remarkable deficiency of analytic power.

---

adapted, but all touched with the curiosity of the young writer's eager mind. . . . Interspersed are echoes from Shakespeare . . . the plays of Ben Jonson and John Dryden or the *Hudibras* of Samuel Butler. Irving can allude to Æsop . . . to Homer, Hobbes, Bacon, Sidney, Tom Paine, or Sheridan's Pizarro. . . . He quotes from Hesiod, and he draws parallels from English, Greek, Roman, and Italian legend. . . . He was deep not merely in Cervantes, Rabelais, and Ariosto, but in Arthurian legend and in out-of-the-way tales of knighthood." (S. T. Williams and T. McDowell, *op. cit.*, intro., xxxvii–xliii.)

Among the major literary influences are to be listed Cervantes, Fielding, Sterne, and Swift; while the mock pedantry and elaborate documentation (much of which was dropped after the first edition) are the fruits of ransacking such ponderous books as John Ogilby's *America* (London, 1671), John Josselyn's *Chronological Observations on America* (London, 1674), Cotton Mather's *Magnalia Christi Americana* (London, 1702), Thomas Prince's *Chronological History of New England* (Boston, 1736), Pierre de Charlevoix's *Historie et Description Générale de la Nouvelle France* (Paris, 1744; Irving using the English translation, London, 1761), and *Hazard's Historical Collections* (New York, 1794). (*Op. cit.*, intro., xliv–xlvii.)

[158] See, for example, "The Author's Account of Himself" in *The Sketch Book*, 15. A mere list, taken from this work alone, of the authors and titles of now long forgotten lore is astonishingly revelatory of Irving's wide knowledge of old authors.

His mind was receptive rather than creative. His pictures, therefore, are transcripts rather than conceptions; his characters, such as have lived and moved among men rather than ideals elaborated by a creative imagination out of the plastic elements of life. They have been seen in his travels or assimilated from books and from fragmentary views of old legends, curious chronicles, and picturesque traditions, and built up by the fancy, which patches rather than creates. His remarkable truth of detail grows out of his fine responsiveness to every faint sense impression. But he not only seizes upon every presentation of form or color, but points it as if he enjoys it, for his receptive power is not merely one of apprehension but as much one of feeling: he is not merely the man of fancy, but also the man of sentiment, the vitalization which his perceptions thus undergo being rather by the agency of feeling than of thought. His sensibility seldom attains to the character of insight, simply because he is not analytical. The same root of sensibility gives character to his moral and religious opinions and practices; but it must be pointed out in the same breath that his opinions are hardly principles; for they are less the result of reasoning than the expression of his instincts.[159]

It is rather odd that Irving, so little given to a cultivation of the forms of thought, should have developed such an exquisite sense of form in style; but, again, the perfection which he attained in form is rather the result of a feeling and taste than

[159] Similarly, the element of humor, which, in varying degrees of intensity, pervades all his work, is more the product of feeling than of thought. "It is the genial coloring of his humorous conceptions, not their mechanism, that wins our interest. He hardly ever puns, for the pun is a logical fallacy, and Irving does not play with forms of thought. His humor seldom becomes wit, for wit is the product of analytic insight, and his mind is neither analytical nor specially gifted with insight." (D. J. Hill, *Washington Irving*, 208–209, 211.) Where, in his humor, he grows most intellectual, as sometimes in *Knickerbocker*, it resolves itself usually into that peculiar juxtaposition of sense and nonsense which has been the characteristic of American humor from Franklin through Mark Twain to our own time. (Cf. B. Wendell, *A Literary History of America*, 173.)

a conscious following of models of structure or a rationalization upon them. He had none of the ordinary advantages for forming a style, though he had some that are extraordinary. "His training in the classics was slender: so he lacked the key of etymology, the classic models of antiquity, and the practice of translating from the ancient languages." [160] He probably never made a hexameter in all his life, and a careful examination of his words reveals the fact that he is much less indebted to the Latin element in his language than would naturally be supposed. These deficiencies, however, were compensated for by extensive contact with cultivated people, an acquaintance with several foreign languages, and, above all, a study of the great masters of English prose and verse. Doubtless his falling often into the form of such eighteenth-century writers as Addison and Goldsmith is a result of this study of their sentences, but more as a result of absorption than of imitation.

The excellence of his style is not in the originality of effects or of figures (for most of them, probably all, may be found in previous English writers), nor is it to be found in a new diction. He did not feel, like Emerson, the desire to clothe his sentiments in a "lapidary" style, or, like Carlyle, to invent for himself anything as distinctive as "Carlylese." It was enough for him to incorporate in his writing "something of classic merit" without straining for new effects—to conform to the recognized standard of graceful and tasteful correctness rather than to exploit such eccentricities as he might be able to develop—in short, to "do it beautifully."

To do it beautifully, he found, required effort and, above all, patience. He was meticulous. His scrupulousness in the arrangement of his periods, the details of language, and the correlation of materials proceeded less from rational processes than from intuitive feeling for form. He may not always have seen the way to do it, but he knew instinctively when he had

[160] Hill, *op. cit.*, 215.

succeeded—more particularly, when he had failed. Re-casting constituted a large part of his literary labor. Interpolations and erasures were common in all his writings, even in his diaries. Whole chapters were often rejected and new ones inserted while a book was already in press, and entire manuscripts were sometimes destroyed because they could not be brought to the artistic finish which he could approve. It is hardly likely that Irving himself was aware of what he had done to secure whatever it was that pleased him when a story did please him. Perhaps he would have been surprised had his attention been called to the fact that in the opening paragraph of Book VI of old Diedrich Knickerbocker's history he had composed four sentences which, if printed word for word as written, but arranged in shortened lines, made perfectly good unrimed iambic pentameter, or blank verse, for every syllable of which good authority and parallel might be cited from the epic poets:

> The gallant warrior starts from soft repose,
> From golden visions and voluptuous ease,
> Where in the dulcet 'piping time of peace,'
> He sought sweet solace after all his toils.
> No more in beauty's siren lap reclined,
> He weaves fair garlands for his lady's brows;
> No more entwines with flowers his shining sword,
> Nor through the livelong lazy summer's day
> Chants forth his love-sick soul in madrigals.
> To manhood roused, he spurns the amorous flute,
> Doffs from his brawny back the robe of peace,
> And clothes his pampered limbs in panoply of steel.
> O'er his dark brow, where late the myrtle waved,
> Where wanton roses breathed enervate love,
> He rears the beaming casque and nodding plume,
> Grasps the bright shield, and shakes the ponderous lance,
> Or mounts with eager pride his fiery steed,
> And burns for deeds of glorious chivalry.

This particular passage is, of course, far from typical, for Irving is here obviously under the necessity of burlesquing the warlike propensities of Peter Stuyvesant and parodying the language of heroic writers; but the passage is not without parallel in others of his works.

Irving was never robust; hence his work is rarely intense. Only in one book, his first, born of youthful exuberance, is there much raciness of expression; and when the charge was brought that Diedrich Knickerbocker was nothing more than a coarse caricaturist, Irving took the matter to heart and discreetly deleted many of the expressions that shocked the squeamish taste of his age.

Neither did he strive for grand effects. No one ever came forward with the suggestion that he, like Timothy Dwight, should furnish with every copy of his books a lightning rod for the reader's protection against the many "grand and terrible" thunder storms. In "The Author's Account of Himself," prefaced to *The Sketch Book*, Irving speaks of his "idle humor and vagrant inclination" leading him "aside from the great objects" to sketch "in nooks, and corners, and by-places":

His sketch-book was accordingly crowded with cottages, and landscapes, and obscure ruins; but he had neglected to paint St. Peter's, or the Coliseum; the cascade of Terni, or the bay of Naples; and had not a single glacier or volcano in the whole collection.

Indeed, Irving's principles of composition were few and simple. Like the teacher of freshman composition, he recommended short and direct phrases, with as few long words as possible, avoiding the use of expletives and conjunctions. He would have concurred heartily in Sydney Smith's advice to a young writer to improve his style by striking out every other word. There is in Irving comparatively little of so-called word-pushing for the sheer fun of doing it. His style, while far from incisive, is nevertheless direct—far from wordy. His best works are brief, and he showed a good deal of acumen when he remarked: "If the tales I have furnished should prove to be bad, they will at least be found short."[161] It may be rather useless to conjecture whether or not he could have written a good novel. Certainly he never did,[162] and there is good reason for believing

[161] "To the Reader," *Tales of a Traveller*, xi.

[162] There is some evidence that he thought at one time to make of "Buckthorne and His Friends" something more than the rambling tale it now is, and Mr. Williams thinks and adduces evidence to show that Irving tried at least once to write a novel, going so far as to write a preliminary sketch or outline for a work to be called "Rosalie." See S. T. Williams (ed.), *Tour in Scotland*, 17, 93–102.

See also his words to Brevoort in a letter dated Dec. 11, 1824:

"My last work [*Tales of a Traveller*] has a good run in England, and has been extremely well spoken of by some of the worthies of literature, though it has met with some handling from the press. The fact is I have kept myself so aloof from all clan ship in literature, that I have no allies among the scribblers for the periodical press; and some of them have taken a pique against me for having treated them a little cavalierly in my writings. However, as I do not read criticisms good or bad, I am out of the reach of attack. If my writings are worth any thing they will out live temporary criticism; if not they are not worth caring about. Some parts of my last work were written rather hastily. Yet I am convinced that a great part of it was written in a freer and happier vein than almost any of my former writings. There was more of an artist like touch about it—though this is not a thing to be appreciated by the many. . . . I have preferred adopting a mode of sketches & short tales rather than long works, because I chose to take a line of writing peculiar to myself; rather than fall into the manner of school of any other writer: and there is a constant activity of thought and nicety of execution required in writings of the kind, more than the world appears to imagine. It is comparatively easy to swell a story to any size when you have once the scheme & the characters in your mind; the mere interest of the story too carries the reader on through pages & pages of careless writing and the author may often be dull for half a volume at a time, if he has some striking scene at the end of it, but in these shorter writings every page must have its merit. The author must be continually piquant—woe to him if he makes an awkward sentence or writes a stupid page; the critics are sure to pounce upon it. Yet if he succeed: the very variety & piquancy of his writings; nay their very brevity; makes them frequently recurred to—and when the mere interest of the story is exhausted, he begins to get credit for his touches of pathos or humour; his points of wit or turns of language. I give these as some of the reasons that have induced me to keep on thus far in the way I had opened for myself—because I find by recent letters from E[benezer] I[rving] that you are joining in the oft repeated advice that I should write a novel. I believe the works I have written will be oftener re-read than

that he did not possess the requirements of a good novelist—
sustained concentration, searching analysis of character, strict
construction of plot, and fine adjustment of numberless details
into a continuous fabric of thought. Even *Knickerbocker* is
more an aggregate of short stories or tales by chapters and
books than a continuous story or history; while his biographies,
his longest productions, exhibit no great structural skill.
Washington, in which he exhibits his greatest power of intellect,
shows him more the scholar than any of his other books, but
even in it he is greater in detail than in conception. The work
did not grow from a germ plan; the incidents crystallize round
a man rather than round a principle. For the critical method
of the philosophical historian or biographer he had little aptitude; he appears at his best when he grasps his subject rather
by his sympathies than by his rationalizations from causes to
effects. Hence, in his *Goldsmith*, which is unquestionably his
most successful biography, his success, apart from his felicity
of style, arises from his perfect sympathy with the man. A more
logical mind would have been puzzled by the inconsistencies of
Goldsmith's character and become involved in metaphysical
theories to effect a reconciliation. Irving appears not to have
been disturbed by such illogicalities. If he sought to reconcile
them, he did so by bringing them to the tribunal of his heart,
not of his head.[163]

He had no body of metaphysical theory concerning literature
comparable with those of Coleridge, Wordsworth, Shelley, or
Poe. Doubtless he formulated certain empirical rules, but it is

---

any novel of the size that I could have written. . . ." (*Irving to Brevoort*,
397–400.)
    In the drama, which requires even more precision and structural
finesse, though he worked at several plays, he could have succeeded little
better. His contributions to Payne's plays, while they were considerable,
were in the realm of skillful dialogue and humorous expression but hardly
in conception and plot-construction. Nor did his structural changes in
the two operas which he adapted or translated improve them greatly.
    [163] Cf. Hill, *op. cit.*, 221.

doubtful whether he could have defended them with substantial philosophical criteria. As a literary critic, for which occupation he had a decided distaste, he was, by and large, a sympathetic impressionist before impressionism became popular. Often he appears content with registering his likes and dislikes; for many of his critical utterances, resolved to their final analysis, amount to little more than "I like it because I do" or "I don't because I don't."[164] Yet Irving is not as easily classified as this would indicate. Possibly because he himself never formulated a systematic literary creed, he cannot be disposed of by simply labelling him a classical, pseudo-classical, romantic, or some other kind of critic. For instance, the half-dozen articles in *The Sketch Book* which, if the term is not too strictly defined, may be classed as critical, his literary antiquarianism, as in "A Royal Poet" and in "Stratford-on-Avon," leads him to be little concerned with values but to content himself, like the historical critic, with explaining how or why the writings of

[164] When he says more, it is often little more than a platitude, as in the passage from his diary of 1817:
"There is an endeavour among some of the writers of the day (who fortunately have not any great weight) to introduce into poetry all the common colloquial phrases and vulgar idioms—In their rage for simplicity they would be coarse and commonplace. Now the Language of poetry cannot be too pure and choice. Poems are like classical edifices, for which we seek the noblest materials—what should we think of the work of the architect who would build a Grecian temple of brick when he could get marble. . . . " (*Tour in Scotland*, 111.)
This is not necessarily a direct reference to Wordsworth, but it refers to the type of thing for which Wordsworth got credit. Although Irving outlived Wordsworth by nine years, and long enough to see Tennyson firmly established—long enough to witness the great changes that came over the spirit of English literature—his conceptions of what constitutes good literature did not change. His tastes were conventional, and he preferred among the romanticists, those who were affected most by the eighteenth-century tradition,—Byron, Scott, and Moore before Wordsworth, Shelley, and Keats. He liked the old-world elegance.
"Leigh Hunt's Rimini," he said, "shows a heterogeneous taste—in which a fondness for gorgeous material is mingled up with an occasional proneness[?] to the most grotesque—we fancy him a common stone mason with dirty apron & trowel in hand sometimes building with marble & sometimes with rubbish. . . . " (*Ibid.*, 111.)

James I or of Shakespeare are what they are. Again, while his attitude toward the royal Scotch poet is, in the main, sympathetically romantic, one detects in Irving's glib phrases about "deficiency of poetic artifice," "cultivated periods," "edifying thoughts," "immodest expression," "purity and grace," "moral purpose," "noble thoughts," "delicate images," "graceful turns of language," and "choice language" the pseudo-classical conventionalist, tinged by eighteenth-century sentimentalism, as when he speaks seriously about "refined and exquisite delicacy," "female loveliness," "tender sentiment," and "elegant taste." And then one is rather surprised, in "The Mutability of Literature," to find him bringing Shakespeare to the test of such classical touchstones as "unchanging principles of human nature" and "intrinsic value."

For his own guidance he followed certain practical principles of composition based on extensive experience in reading and writing, but they were concerned more with practice than with theory, as when he spent hours upon hours correcting his own inaccuracies or expression and errors of grammar[165] (found oftener in his earlier than in his later works), and when he remonstrated with his publisher for having inserted so many commas that they interrupted the flow of his language. Usually his direct literary judgments are limited to such vague expressions as when he indicated his depreciation of *Salmagundi* as full of "errors, puerilities, & impertinences," or when he apostrophized Hawthorne's *Scarlet Letter* as "Masterly! ˙ Masterly! Masterly!"[166]

[165] See *Irving to Brevoort*, 315–323.
[166] *Life*, III, 191. His sketches of Campbell and Margaret Davidson, the latter running to the length of 136 pages, do not reveal striking critical abilities. He is precisely what in his "Desultory Thoughts on Criticism" (*Biographies and Miscellanies*, arranged and edited by Pierre M. Irving, 447–452) he argues the American critic should be, namely, the romantically sympathetic interpreter intent upon pointing out "beauties and excellences." "Give me," he says, "the honest bee, that extracts honey from the humblest weed, but save me from the ingenuity of the spider, which traces its venom even in the midst of a flower-garden." (*Ibid.*, 450.)

In his opinions regarding the proper language of poetry, Irving used, in both passages cited,[167] building figures, suggesting that the arts were associated in his mind, as indeed, they were. Among the diary memoranda for 1824 appears this notation:[168]

However, in his reviews of the works of Robert Treat Paine and of the poems of Edwin C. Holland, more particularly in the latter (*Ibid.*, 324–338), although he begins by disavowing all intention of "being either wise or facetious at the expense of others," his criticisms are a bit sharp. It should be observed that these reviews were published in the *Analectic Magazine* during his editorship of that periodical, that he was assiduously · reading the foreign reviews at this time, and that he may have imbibed something of the stringency of his English and Scotch contemporaries. It would appear, if one may judge from his insistence upon neo-classical standards, his merciless dissection of some of Holland's "grand poetical figures and effects," and his gratuitous advice to the young author, that Irving had read to some purpose the critical animadversions of Jeffrey and Gifford of the *Edinburgh* and the *Quarterly* reviews. Like them and their successors, Lockhart and "Christopher North," when aroused in the crusade of "good versus bad literature," he could lay on quite lustily. But his criticism seldom becomes invective; his stings are not barbed; nor does he seem so apparently to relish his own wit and facetiousness as did his Scotch and English compeers when they were about the business of flaying a young Keats or a sensitive Tennyson. While Irving's review of Holland's poems is doubtless his cleverest piece of critical writing, it does not argue great critical abilities.

In dramatic criticism, the one department for which he should have been best qualified (if constant attendance upon the theatre, some experience in adapting and translating operas, and extensive practice in retouching and revising plays facilitate critical ability), he had almost nothing to say beyond such diary jottings as "good," "bad," "medium," "lively," or "dull" opposite the titles of hundreds of plays he noticed in his journals. Concerning actors and actresses, particularly the latter, he is less chary in his comments, his letters and notebooks being full of critiques of acting. These comments, which indicate that Irving recognized good acting when he saw it, do not, however, show that profound technical knowledge expected of a theatrical critic. Essentially, his principles are the same as those of Jonathan Oldstyle, Gent., who, as early as December 11, 1802, had recommended:

"To the actors—less etiquette, less fustian, less buckram. To the orchestra—new music, and more of it. To the pit—patience, clean benches, and umbrellas. To the boxes—less affectation, less noise, less coxcombs. To the gallery—less grog, and better constables;—and, To the whole house, inside and out, a total reformation." ("Letters of Jonathan Oldstyle, No. 5," *Biographies and Miscellanies*, 33.)

[167] See footnote 164, above.

[168] *Journal of Washington Irving (1823–1824)*, 123–124.

Sunday 8th Feby.... Go to Mr Foys—Meet a Mr ——— there converse about sympathy between the arts. Rules applicable alike to painting Writing—Sculpture, Music & architecture—all the imaginative arts—Present state of the arts & of Literature in England—an Era—great rivalship—greater glory in excelling —Some will excel—as in forest some trees will shoot above the others, tho when in the forest we cannot see their superiority we perceive it when at a distance—so posterity will do justice to those who rise above their contemporaries—no school of painting at present in Italy—Eng[lan]d & France the only two schools.

Of his love for certain picturesque architectural types and styles there can be no doubt. Whether viewing the castles of the Rhine, the cathedrals of Italy, the mosque in Spain, the manor house in England, the chateau in France, or his own Sunnyside, "as full of angles and corners as an old cocked hat,"[169] he took more than a passing interest in architectural lines and frequently resorted to his ability at sketching to help his pen commit to paper the impression he wanted to preserve. This attitude of the amateur architect is comparable to his amateur antiquarian interest in old places and historical events. Indeed, Irving was, in almost everything he did best, the amateur; even in his writings he was at his best when he was least the professional. Irving as the gentleman littérateur is better than Irving as the professional historian and biographer, as a comparison of *The Sketch Book* and *The Alhambra*, on the one hand, with his *Conquest of Granada* and *The Life of Washington*, on the other, immediately makes plain. So he was an amateur painter, sketching for pleasure, even toying once with the idea of turning painter.[170] So, also, was he an amateur musician.

[169] *Life*, III, 289.

[170] It has been remarked that Irving gravitated quite as much for companionship toward artists as toward literary people, and that his close friends among artists were more numerous than among writers. (Cf. Hellman, *op. cit.*, 199; see, also, Irving's sketch of Washington Allston in *Biographies and Miscellanies*, 143–150.)

His only musical accomplishment was to perform moderately well on the flute, and there are references to his playing for the delectation of the children or the ladies, as also sometimes for his own entertainment. He learned enough of the technique of music to appreciate the art as "the sweetener of existence," though he was frank to admit that he preferred the opera to the concert.[171]

What has been detailed thus far about Irving as a man of letters but goes to show that he was eminently correct in his appraisal of himself and his decision in 1824 to refuse Brevoort's and Ebenezer's urging him to undertake a novel.

I fancy much of what I value myself upon in writing, escapes the observation of the great mass of my readers: who are intent more upon the story than the way in which it is told. For my part I consider a story merely as a frame on which to stretch my materials. It is the play of thought, and sentiment and language; the weaving in of characters, lightly yet expressively delineated; the familiar and faithful exhibition of scenes in common life; and the half concealed vein of humour that is often playing through the whole—these are among what I aim at, and upon which I felicitate myself in proportion as I think I succeed....I believe the works I have written will be oftener re-read than any novel of the size that I could have written. It is true other writers have crowded into the same branch of literature, and I now begin to find myself elbowed by men who have followed my footsteps; but at any rate I have had the merit of adopting a line for myself instead of following others.[172]

Five years before, in refusing Scott's offer to edit a magazine, he had already realized the path he must pursue:

[171] "I am not over-fond of concerts, and would prefer somewhat inferior talent, when aided by the action and scenic effect of the theatre. I anticipate more pleasure, therefore, from Parodi as *prima donna* of the opera, than from the passionless performances of Jenny Lind as a singer at a concert." When, soon after, he did hear and see Jenny Lind, he was completely captivated by her. (*Life*, III, 180–182.)

[172] *Irving to Brevoort*, 398–401.

My whole course of life has been desultory, and I am unfitted
for any periodically recurring task, or any stipulated labor of
body or mind. I have no command of my talents such as they
are, and have to watch the varyings of my mind as I would a
weather cock. Practice and training may bring me more into
rule; but at present I am as useless for regular service as one of
my own country Indians or a Don Cossack.

I must, therefore, keep on pretty much as I have begun—
writing when I can, not when I would. I shall occasionally
shift my residence and write whatever is suggested by objects
before me, or whatever runs in my imagination; and hope to
write better and more copiously by and by.[173]

He probably never wrote better than he did in 1819. This
much is certain: whenever he wrote "more copiously," he did
not write as well.

One other thing here is pretty clear: he was not bursting with
big ideas and burning messages. He regarded life not from the
philosophic, economic, political, theological, or scientific,[174] but
largely from the literary point of view. He never caught the
restlessness of the century, or the prophetic light that shone on
the faces of Coleridge and Shelley, or the reformer's craze of
his countryman, Cooper. He never embraced the nebulous
ambitions of those who wanted to create in America a great
national literature, nor did he, like Cooper, lose his temper and
harp upon his fellow-citizens' shortcomings and social gauche-
ries and thereby earn their ill-will and hatred. Unlike Cooper,
who aired his criticisms publicly, Irving, when he did become

[173] *Life*, I, 340.
[174] Irving appears to have been less interested in science than in any other
department of human knowledge. Only in botany do his notebooks show
him an occasional dabbler. Among the scattering memoranda of his first
visit to Paris is this reference: "[May] 31 [1805]. Tended lectures on
botany." At the same time he bought a botanical dictionary. His notes
on the botanical lectures are preserved in the New York Public Library.
(Williams, "Washington Irving's First Stay in Paris," *American Literature*, II, 19, March, 1930; and *Life*, I, 108.)

critical, was careful to couch his censures in terms of good-natured raillery and took care to impart them only to people whose sagacity to keep them private could be relied upon. For example, the following remarks to Brevoort, while they evidently proceeded from the same source and impulse as Cooper's animadversions, would hardly have been taken ill even if they had found their way into print:[175]

You seem to be all masking mad in New York. I am afraid our good city is in a bad way as to both morals and manners. What the cities of the old world take moderately and cautiously she gets roaring drunk with. I must say all this rioting and dancing at the theatres with public masquerades every night in the week has a terribly low lived, dissolute, vulgar look. We are too apt to take our ideas of English high life from such vulgar sources as Tom & Jerry and we appear to be Tom and Jerrying it to perfection in New York.

And he did not beard the lion in his den by stirring up trouble with editors and reviewers, though they sometimes tried him severely.[176] He chose to defend himself only when a point of character or honor seemed involved; for the rest, he refused "to sue the praises nor deprecate the censures of reviewers," but left his works "to rise or fall by their own deserts." [177] What he thought of some of the critics he made sufficiently plain in the following words to Brevoort, but it will be observed that even when he is vexed, he does not permit himself to write angrily or nastily:[178]

[175] *Irving to Brevoort*, 430.
[176] *Life*, II, 43–51, 53–60, 73, 294, 316–329; III, 9–17.
[177] *Life*, II, 49–50.
[178] *Irving to Brevoort*, 420–421. In his essay, "Desultory Thoughts on Criticism," he takes the same theme for his text: "Seriously speaking, however, it is questionable whether our national literature is sufficiently advanced to bear this excess of criticism; and whether it would not thrive better if allowed to spring up, for some time longer, in the freshness and vigor of native vegetation." (*Biographies and Miscellanies*, 448.)

We are making rapid advances in literature in America, and have already attained many of the literary vices and diseases of the old countries of Europe. We swarm with reviewers, though we have scarce original works sufficient for them to alight and prey upon, and we closely imitate all the worst tricks of the trade and of the craft of England. Our literature, before long, will be like some of those premature and aspiring whipsters, who become old men before they are young ones, and fancy they prove their manhood by their profligacy and their diseases.

IV. IRVING IN RELATION TO PHILOSOPHY AND RELIGION

By nature and education deficient in analytic power, metaphysics and logic never entered into his professional or amateur pursuits. He lacked that power of continuity of thought, as well as that reflex action of mind, so conspicuous in Hawthorne, that leads to psychological exploration and discovery.[179] His one excursion into the realm of the psychological, in the effort to write a play on the dual nature of man, based cn Goethe's *Faust-motif* and that of Calderon's *Magico Prodigioso*, proved abortive. For such a drama the soul of Washington Irving was not equipped.[180]

The higher problems of existence, intellectual and spiritual, never troubled him much. He even affected to scorn philosophy. He reached his conclusions through the medium of his tastes and the dicta of authorities, rather than by syllogism or formal induction. As a result of this constitution and habit of mind,

[179] Cf. Hill, *op. cit.*, 220.

[180] Cf. Hellman, *op. cit.*, 165–167.

In the realm of the sportive Gothic, Irving was superb, but in his efforts at spiritualism, he was disappointed. His attitude, in the one attempt he made to communicate with the spirit of a departed friend, was quizzical from the start and productive of no results. Recalling this experience later, he said to his nephew: "He did not come, and though I have made similar invocations before and since, they were never answered." He added half playfully, half mournfully: "The ghosts have never been kind to me." (*Life*, II, 136–137; cf. Hellman, *op. cit.*, 178.)

his productions are descriptions and narratives, never disquisitions: he tells us what things are, never why they are.[181] From beginning to end, he was animated by no profound sense of the mystery of existence. The solemn eternities which stir philosophers and theologians engaged his mind but little, except for such obvious thoughts as those on obscurantism in the face of death with which he occupies himself in "St. Mark's Eve."[182] He took his religion in moderate doses; he had had quite too much of it in his father's house, so much that he had been led to believe that all the good things of life belonged to the Devil.[183] His journals do not indicate that he was a regular churchgoer until he reached the age of sixty-five, when he became a regular communicant in the little Episcopal church in Tarrytown. During his youth and through his mature manhood he went his way generally untroubled, frequently expressing surprise at such evidences of religious devotion as he observed on every hand in Europe, particularly among Catholics. He repeatedly referred to "taking the veil" as entering "a living tomb."[184] If we may judge from several diary notes of 1824, when he fell in sometimes, at the house of

---

[181] Cf. Hill, *op. cit.*, 221.

[182] *Bracebridge Hall*, 124–133; see also *Notes while Preparing Sketch Book*, 58–60.

[183] *Life*, I, 8.

[184] See *The Alhambra*, 117–121, and the journals of 1804–1805:

"It is a painful sight," he added in his diary, "to behold young females— endowed with all the graces of person and charm of countenance that can render a woman lovely—with apparent sensibility of mind—sprightliness of manner and susceptibility of heart—shut up forever from the world." Reading the passage carefully and between the lines indicates that Irving is, at this time, little troubled by feelings of religious self-abnegation and devotional exaltation. He had little time to stand reverently before saints' relics or to pause long before religious shrines. Indeed, his early journals reveal him no more reverential but quite as skeptical of much he is told regarding saints and holy vessels as he was later when asked to believe in the authenticity of all the Shakespeare relics at Stratford-on-Avon. See *The Sketch Book*, 319 *et. seq.* He does not scruple to set down his doubts. "Such," he says, "is the origin of Catholic Saints and reminds one forcibly of the manner in which gods and goddesses of the Ancients originated. . . . Priesthood has been the same in all ages and scruples at no falsehood

the Fosters, with an over-zealous curate and other theologically minded persons, Irving preferred his tea without sacred music, a chapter from the Bible, and prayers.[185] He felt ill at ease in this religious atmosphere, and later confessed as much to Emily Foster, who had written to him in 1825 making an "appeal on the subject of religion." He put her off gently but firmly saying "it [religion] is a subject about which I am disposed to *think* rather than *talk*," and hinting that he preferred not to have her urge religion upon him:[186]

I must manage myself with respect to it, and must be left a little to my own management. . . .When I was a child religion was forced upon me before I could understand or appreciate it. *I was made to swallow it whether I would or not, and that too in its most ungracious forms. I was tasked with it; thwarted with it; wearied with it in a thousand harsh and disagreeable ways; until I was disgusted with all its forms and observances.* It was not until I had been my own master for several years that I voluntarily returned to what I had disliked so much in childhood. It required much effort of my reason to divest the outward ceremonies of religion of the dismal associations with which my

or contrivance to support its impositions." (Cf. Hellman, *op. cit.*, 24, 29–30.)

Here, too, may be quoted several opinions he overheard during his first tour of France, opinions in which he evidently concurred and thought enough of to record in his commonplace book:

"M McC[lure] said he had observed that there was as it were a line running from ——— like the line of vine countries and that all to the south were generally catholic & to the north Protestants. Mr Cabell has no opinion of southern climates—thinks the further we go south the more abject & degraded we find the people—a remark that I have found true as far as my experience extends. The greatest improvements in arts & sciences originate in northern countries." (Williams, "Washington Irving's First Stay in Paris," *American Literature*, II, 17–18, March, 1930.)

[185] Cf. *Journal of Washington Irving (1823–1824)*, 221–225.

[186] S. T. Williams, "Washington Irving's Religion" [reprint of a letter from Irving to Emily Foster, Paris, Aug. 23, 1825], *Yale Review*, XV, 414–416 (Jan., 1926). The italics in the quotation from Irving's letter are mine.

young imagination had clothed them, and to behold religion itself in its real amiableness and beauty. I have all my life seen so much hypocrisy, cant and worldliness imposed upon mankind under the external forms of religion, that I remain to this day sensitive on the subject. If at any time it is pressed upon me I involuntarily shrink back. I am like a child that has once been thrust under the water and is afterward shy of approaching the stream even to drink. I must be left to approach of my own accord. But you must not conclude from this that I am heedless and insensible, nor because I am disinclined to discuss religion as a topic that I neither feel nor appreciate it. *I have opinions and principles instilled into me by my early religious education, harsh and ill judged as it was, which still remain with me and influence my conduct. I have high feelings of reverence and veneration, which I believe to be, as far as they go, the religion of the soul, and, although doubtless far short of absolute devotion, are the sparks that in time may kindle up into it;* but I know my own weak and imperfect nature & the treatment it requires. I feel that these sparks must be managed and in some measure left to themselves. A little eagerness to heap on fuel might smother them and in seeking too eagerly to blow them into a flame they might be blown out.

You are not to judge of my feelings in respect to religion for [?] what might have been my deportment when at Buckhill. *I felt out of tune there where you were all wound up to so high a key. I was a little jarred too by the well meant but unskillful and unseasonable handling of some of the professional persons I met there.* If I held myself aloof in any degree, it was not from a want of proper feeling for religion itself, but from an anxiety to avoid any chance of distaste to the form & manner in which it was administered. And now let me withdraw from this subject, on which I have entered [?] with hesitating and unwilling feet, with deep acknowledgement of my sense of the amiable and generous motives which have governed you in leading to it. In the elegance of your style I beheld the conviction of your mind and the elevation of your soul, and I feel the extent of your friendship in the zeal you manifest for my welfare.

This letter makes sufficiently plain the fact that Irving was distinctly repelled by anything in religion bordering upon fanaticism. Not that he denied religion the province of the heart. Not at all. But the enthusiasm of the feelings must be held in check. This is not to say that he held much in common with the still fashionable current of English deism, or that he entered into the mystical pantheism by which some of his contemporaries were inspired, or even that he felt many of the moral emanations of Nature by which the eighteenth-century man had been edified. Somewhere between the two extremes he sought for a sane middle ground. Only once or twice does he write in the following vein: [187]

Those who are in the habit of remarking such matters, must have noticed the passive quiet of an English landscape on Sunday.... The holy repose which reigns over the face of nature, has its moral influence; every restless passion is charmed down, and we feel the natural religion of the soul gently springing up within us. For my part, there are feelings that visit me, in a country church, amid the beautiful serenity of nature, which I experience nowhere else; and if not a more religious, I think I am a better man on Sunday than on any other day of the seven.

This is not Rousseau or Wordsworth or Shelley speaking, nor is it the voice of Peter Bell to whom a primrose was a primrose still. At the age of forty-seven, he wrote his sister, Mrs. Van Wart, what was hardly by intention but certainly by implication a profession of dissatisfaction with his own religious state of mind. Alluding to his brother Ebenezer, he says:[188]

I think him one of the most perfect exemplifications of the Christian character that I have ever known. He has all father's devotion and zeal, without his strictness. Indeed, his piety is

[187] *The Sketch Book*, 130–131. See also *Letters from Sunnyside and Spain*, 10.
[188] *Life*, II, 372–373.

of the most genial and cheerful kind, interfering with no rational pleasure or elegant taste, and obtruding itself upon no one's habits, opinions, or pursuits. I wish to God I could feel like him. I envy him that indwelling source of consolation and enjoyment, which appears to have a happier effect than all the maxims of philosophy or the lessons of worldly wisdom.

Not unnaturally, therefore, we find him, eight years later, after an earnest conversation (which, for his part, terminated in a "moment of overwhelming emotion") with his friend, the Rev. Dr. Taylor, of Christ Church, New York, picking up the lost threads of his youth when he had gone stealthily to Trinity Church to receive the rite of confirmation, if only to escape the rigid Calvinism of his father. He first partook of Communion in Grace Church in the city and then became connected with Christ Church, Tarrytown,[189] where, for the remaining eleven years of his life, he served conscientiously as warden, his chief duty being to present the plate for the silver and copper offerings of the parishioners.[190]

[189] *Life*, III, 150–151. This act of conformity did not, however, satisfy everybody. For example, Daniel Wise, writing in 1883, found two serious shortcomings in (1) Irving's lack of high moral purpose in his writings, and (2) his leanings toward "experimental Christianity." He particularly censured Irving for asserting of the "vain, good-natured, indolent . . . self-indulgent, thoughtless, roystering spendthrift" Oliver Goldsmith that he possessed "the indwelling religion of the soul"; and concluded: "Oh, Washington Irving, if thy writings had been conceived in the spirit of thy soul's Master, they might have ministered not merely to men's amusement and intellectual profit, but also to the promotion of the world's growth of righteousness!" (Daniel Wise, *Washington Irving*, 13–15.)

[190] In the little church, he became an institution; and when he once asked, in a vestry meeting, to be relieved of his duty of taking up the collection, Mr. George D. Morgan immediately sprang to his feet and said: "Mr. Chairman, I protest against any such step on the part of Mr. Irving. It will create great confusion in the congregation; the service will be neglected, and the sermon unheeded. Now, when I bring my friends to church, the first question I am asked is, 'Which is Mr. Irving?' and all I have to say is, 'Mr. Irving is the gentleman who will bye and bye pass the plate in the north aisle.' But if he resigns his duty, I shall have to raise up in my pew and point him out to my friends (here suiting the action to the word), 'There he is, there he is.'" (Edgar M. Bacon, *In Memoriam Washington Irving*, 258.)

His choosing the Episcopal Church was not, of course, the result of a rationalization or a deliberate choice between dogmas and creeds,[191] but, as in most of the important acts of his life, a following of his instincts.[192] What most attracted him in the Episcopal Church appears pretty plainly from the following words of the assistant rector, the Rev. Mr. Spencer: [193]

A firm, though not bigoted Episcopalian, Mr. Irving loved the services of the Church, and often expressed his devoted admiration of her liturgy. . . . He was passionately fond of music. On the occasion of [my] first interview with Mr. Irving, he was expressing his interest in that glorious hymn of the Church, the *Gloria in Excelsis;* and repeating the words, "Glory to God in the highest, on earth peace, and good-will to men," he exclaimed, with his eyes moistened, "That is religion, Mr. Spencer; that is true religion for you." [194]

Here, apparently, is an expression of that same love for music, ceremony, and atmosphere that operated so strongly to elicit feelings of devotion from him in the solemn atmosphere of Westminster Abbey.[195] This close association in Irving's

[191] Although Chapter VIII in *Mahomet*, outlining Mahomet's faith, especially the appended Note, appears to indicate that Irving made elaborate researches into the history and roots of Christianity, in reality he drew his information from such handy secondary sources as he mentions in the preface, particularly from Dr. Gustav Weil's *Muhammed der Prophet, sein Leben und seine Lehre* (Stuttgart, 1843). He was particularly careful to emphasize in the preface that he laid "no claim to novelty of fact, nor profundity of research."

[192] He was not a sectarian, and contributed, even after his membership in the Episcopal Church, to all the different denominations in the neighborhood.

[193] *Irvingiana*, xxv.

[194] Accordingly he spoke to the rector, the Rev. Dr. Creighton, who tells us:
"One Sabbath morning he approached me, and asked, why we could not have the 'Gloria in Excelsis' sung every Sunday. I replied that I had no objection, and that there was nothing whatever to prevent it, and at the same time inquired of him,—'Do you like it?' 'Like it!—like it!' said he; 'above all things. Why, it contains the sum and substance of our faith, and I never hear it without feeling better, and without my heart being lifted up.' " (*Ibid.*, xlii.)

[195] *The Sketch Book*, 219–220.

mind of religion and art is illustrated in the story related by
G. P. Putnam: [196]

Passing a print-window in Broadway one day, his eye
rested on the beautiful engraving of "Christus Consolator."
[Dupont's engraving of Ary Schaeffer's "Christus Consolator."] He stopped and looked at it intently for some minutes,
evidently much affected by the genuine inspiration of the artist
in this remarkable representation of the Saviour as the consoler
of sorrow-stricken humanity. His tears fell freely. "Pray, get
me that print," said he; "I must have it framed for my sitting-
room." When he examined it more closely and found the
artist's name, "It's by my old friend Ary Scheffer [*sic*]!" said he,
remarking further, that he had known Scheffer [*sic*] intimately,
and knew him to be a true artist, but had never expected from
him anything so excellent as this. I afterwards sent him the companion, "Christus Remunerator"; and the pair remained his
daily companions till the day of his death. To me, the picture
of Irving, amid the noise and bustle of noon in Broadway,
shedding tears as he studied that little print, so feelingly picturing human sorrow and the source of its alleviation, has
always remained associated with the artist and his works.

One may take as much of this evidence as one wishes (for
Putnam saw Irving weep rather too often for our credulity),[197]
but the fact remains that Irving's religion consisted less of
theses and texts and sermons than of religious feeling associated
with liturgy and ritual, music, atmosphere, and good will—
truly a religion of the heart.[198]

By way of summary, Irving's own words may be adduced:[199]

[196] "Recollections of Irving," *Studies in Irving*, 154–155.
[197] Putnam also saw Irving weeping over a miniature of Matilda Hoffman.
See G. H. Putnam, *George Palmer Putnam*, 258.
[198] As a youth travelling in Europe, he had observed: "There is certainly
something very solemn and impressive in the ceremonies of the Roman
Church. Unwilling as we may be to acknowledge it we cannot deny that
forms and ceremonies have a great effect on the feelings in matters of
religion." (Cf. Hellman, *op. cit.*, 30.)
[199] "The Author," *Bracebridge Hall*, 14–15.

My only aim is to paint characters and manners. I am no politician. The more I have considered the study of politics, the more I have found it full of perplexity; and I have contented myself, as I have in my religion, with the faith in which I was brought up, regulating my own conduct by its precepts; but leaving to abler heads the task of making converts. . . .

I have always had an opinion that much good might be done by keeping mankind in good humor with one another. I may be wrong in my philosophy, but I shall continue to practise it until convinced of its fallacy.

Here certainly is a sublime, if simple, philosophy. It may be observed that Washington Irving saw no reason to change his views in the matter, possibly because he believed that "a Washington Irving who would take sides in public argument with Calhoun or with Garrison, or, somewhere between the two, with Clay or Webster, was, in Irving's opinion, less serviceable than a Washington Irving who would portray for the American people and for all peoples the illuminating life of George Washington, or the endearing qualities of Oliver Goldsmith";[200] because he believed he could do his countrymen a greater service chronicling Hudson River legends and bringing to them a touch of merry England and romantic Spain than misapplying his slender genius and tiring his readers' patience with theological disquisitions. He calculated correctly that as an intermediary between old-world culture and new-world rawness and as a romancer in the sphere of *belles-lettres* he would speak to better purpose than as politician or preacher.

[200] Hellman, *op. cit.*, 340–341.

SELECTED BIBLIOGRAPHY

(Starred items are of primary importance for the general student.)

I. BIBLIOGRAPHY

Langfeld, William R. "Washington Irving—A Bibliography," published serially in *Bulletin of New York Public Library*, XXXVI, 415–422, 487–494, 561–571, 627–636, 683–689, 755–778, 828–841 (June–Dec., 1932). (A detailed, annotated bibliography, based principally on the Seligman collection of Irvingiana in the New York Public Library.)

*Langfeld, William R. *Washington Irving: A Bibliography.* Compiled by William R. Langfeld with the Bibliographic Assistance of Philip C. Blackburn. New York: New York Public Library, 1933. (A descriptive and annotated bibliographical list of Irving's works, together with additional Irvingiana, reprinted with additions and revisions from the *Bulletin of New York Public Library* of June-Dec., 1932.)

*Long, Shirley V. "Irving Bibliography," *Cambridge History of American Literature*, I, 510–517. (A working bibliography; recently superseded by Langfeld's bibliography except in the biographical and critical items.)

The Seligman Collection of Irvingiana: a Catalogue of Manuscript and Other Material by and about Washington Irving, given to the New York Public Library by Mrs. Isaac N. Seligman and Mr. George S. Hellman. *Bulletin of New York Public Library* for February, 1926.

Vail, R. W. G. (compiler). *The Hellman Collection of Irvingiana:* a Catalogue of Manuscripts and Other Material by or about Washington Irving, given to the New York Public Library by Mr. George S. Hellman. *Bulletin of New York Public Library*, April, 1929. (Indicative of the rich store of Irvingiana in the New York Public Library.)

To keep abreast of current items, the student should consult the annual bibliographies in *American Literature*, *Publi-*

cations of the Modern Language Association, and the bulletins
of the Modern Humanities Research Association.

See, also, below: Adkins, N. F.; Birss, N. J.; Langfeld,
W. R., "The Poems of Washington Irving."

II. WORKS

Irving, Washington. *Abu Hassan* (Hitherto Unpublished).
With an introduction by George S. Hellman. Boston: The
Bibliophile Society, 1924. (A reprint of one of Irving's
operatic adaptations from the German.)

Irving, Washington. *An Unwritten Drama of Lord Byron.*
With an introduction by Thomas Ollive Mabbott. Metuchen,
N. J.: 1925. (A reprint; first published in *The Gift* for 1836.)

Irving, Washington. *Diedrich Knickerbocker's A History of
New York.* Edited with a critical introduction by Stanley
T. Williams and Tremaine McDowell. American Authors
series. New York: 1927. (A verbatim reprint of the first
edition, 1809.)

Irving, Washington. *Knickerbocker's History of New York.*
With a critical introduction by Edwin A. Greenlaw. New
York: 1919. (Selections, with a good introduction.)

Irving, Washington. *The Poems of Washington Irving Brought
Together from Various Sources* by William R. Langfeld.
New York: 1931. (This 20-page pamphlet is reprinted from
the *Bulletin of New York Public Library,* Nov., 1930.)

Irving, Washington. *The Wild Huntsman* (Hitherto Unpublished). With an introduction by George S. Hellman.
Boston: The Bibliophile Society, 1924. (A reprint of
another of Irving's operatic adaptations from the German.)

*Irving, Washington. *The Works of Washington Irving.*
Author's uniform revised edition. 21 vols. New York:
1860–1861. (The standard edition.)

Irving, Washington. *The Works of Washington Irving.*
Spuyten Duyvil edition. 12 vols. New York: 1881. (Same
text as the Author's uniform revised edition and more easily
procurable.)

For other individual works, translations, editorial labors, and numerous contributions to magazines, annuals, newspapers, and other bibliographical addenda, see Langfeld's *Bibliography;* see also Langfeld's "The Poems of Washington Irving," *Bulletin of New York Public Library*, XXXIV, 763–779 (Nov., 1930); and *Cambridge History of American Literature*, I, 510–517.

III. LETTERS, JOURNALS, DIARIES

Brevoort, Henry. *Letters of Henry Brevoort to Washington Irving together with Other Unpublished Brevoort Papers.* Edited with an introduction by George S. Hellman. Library Edition. 2 vols. in 1. New York: 1918. (A valuable supplement to the *Letters of Irving to Brevoort.*)

Irving, Washington. *Journal of Washington Irving (1823–1824).* Edited by Stanley T. Williams. Cambridge: 1931. (A careful reprint; critical introduction.)

Irving, Washington. *Letters from Sunnyside and Spain.* Edited by Stanley T. Williams. New Haven: 1928. (Some of these were published in the *Yale Review;* these and others are here reprinted to make available in book form the most important personal correspondence of Irving between the years 1840 and 1845.)

Irving, Washington. *Letters of Washington Irving to Henry Brevoort.* Edited by George S. Hellman. Library Edition. 2 vols. in 1. New York: 1918. (This correspondence forms an important chapter in the biography of Irving.)

Irving, Washington. *Letters of Washington Irving to Mrs. William Renwick, and her Son, James Renwick. . . . Written between September 10th, 1811 and April 5th, 1816.* Printed for private distribution, no place, no date. (These letters afford an interesting glimpse into Irving's personal and social contacts for the years covered.)

Irving, Washington. *Notes and Journal of Travel in Europe, 1804–1805.* Edited by W. P. Trent. 3 vols. New York: 1921. (Capably edited, with a good introduction.)

Irving, Washington. *Notes while Preparing Sketch Book &c. 1817.* Edited by Stanley T. Williams. New Haven: 1927. (A careful reprint with critical introduction and notes; a valuable addition to Irvingiana.)

Irving, Washington. *Spanish Papers and Other Miscellanies Hitherto Unpublished or Uncollected.* Edited by Pierre M. Irving. New York: 1866. (Includes some personal memorabilia.)

Irving, Washington. *The Journals of Washington Irving.* Edited by William P. Trent and George S. Hellman. 3 vols. Boston: The Bibliophile Society, 1919. (Indispensable, but see Langfeld's bibliography, p. 61, for manuscript diary materials still unpublished.)

Irving, Washington. *Tour in Scotland, 1817, and other Manuscript Notes by Washington Irving.* Edited by Stanley T. Williams. New Haven: 1927. (Including reprints of Irving's *Tour in Scotland, Excursion to Runcorn,* and *Fragments,* together with introduction and notes, this book is a valuable addition to Irvingiana.)

Irving, Washington. *Washington Irving Diary. Spain 1828–29.* Edited by Clara Louisa Penney. New York: 1926. (A reprint of manuscript diary notes in the possession of the Hispanic Society of America.)

Luquer, Thatcher T. Payne (ed.). "Correspondence of Washington Irving and John Howard Payne," *Scribner's Magazine,* XLVIII, 461–482 (Oct., 1910); 597–616 (Nov., 1910). (Interesting data on the several collaborative dramatic efforts of Irving and Payne.)

Williams, Stanley T. "Letters of Washington Irving: Spanish Fêtes and Ceremonies," *Yale Review,* XVII, 99–117 (Oct., 1927). (Letters to his sister and to his niece, Sarah Storrow; reprinted in 1928 in *Letters from Sunnyside and Spain.*)

Williams, Stanley T. *Washington Irving and the Storrows; Letters from England and the Continent, 1821–1828.* Cambridge: 1933.

Williams, Stanley T. "Unpublished Letters of Washington Irving. Sunnyside and New York Chronicles," *Yale Review,*

XVI, 459–484 (April, 1927). (Reprinted in 1928 in *Letters from Sunnyside and Spain.*)

Williams, Stanley T. "Washington Irving's First Stay in Paris," *American Literature*, II, 15–20 (March, 1930). (The first printing of "Travelling Notes" made by Irving during his first visit to Paris; entries from May 24 to June 19, 1805.)

Williams, Stanley T., and Beach, Leonard B. "Washington Irving's Letters to Mary Kennedy," *American Literature*, VI, 44–65 (March, 1934).

For additional letters and diary notes see below: Hellman, G. S., *Washington Irving, Esquire*, especially pp. 243 ff.; Irving, P. M., *Life and Letters of Washington Irving;* Irving, Washington; Mitchell, D. G., *American Lands and Letters* and *Dream Life;* Moore, Thomas; Paulding, W. I.; Poe, E. A., *Tales of the Grotesque and Arabesque; The Romance of Mary Wollstonecraft Shelley, John Howard Payne, and Washington Irving;* Spiller, R. E.; Waldron, W. W.; Williams, Stanley T., "Washington Irving and Fernán Caballero," "Washington Irving and Matilda Hoffman," "Washington Irving's Religion."

IV. BIOGRAPHIES

*Most of the biographies listed below, while based mainly upon *The Life and Letters of Washington Irving*, by his nephew, Pierre M. Irving, add more or less critical material. A definitive life of Irving is promised by Professor Stanley T. Williams.

Adams, Charles. *Memoir of Washington Irving. With Selections from his Works and Criticisms.* New York: 1870. (A 299-page life and book of selections.)

Boynton, Henry Walcott. *Washington Irving.* Riverside Biographical series, No. 11. Boston: 1901. (A 116-page biography typical of the series to which it belongs.)

*Hellman, George Sidney. *Washington Irving, Esquire: Ambassador at Large from the New World to the Old.* New York: 1925. (Hardly a biography in the strict sense of the word, but stimulating; adds some new material, using for the first time Irving's journals published in 3 vols. in 1919.)

Hill, David Jayne. *Washington Irving*. New York: 1879. (One of the earlier works based on Pierre M. Irving's work; adds some good critical estimates.)

*Irving, Pierre M. *The Life and Letters of Washington Irving, by his Nephew.* . . . 4 vols. New York: Putnam, 1862–1864. (At present the most complete and comprehensive biography of Irving; while tempered somewhat by sentiment and the close relationship between biographer and subject, it has long stood as the standard work on Irving.)

Irving, Pierre M. *The Life and Letters of Washington Irving, by his Nephew.* . . . People's Edition, revised and condensed. 3 vols. New York: 1869. (More readily procurable for the general student than the 4-volume life.)

Laun, Adolf. *Washington Irving. Ein Lebens- und Charakterbild.* 3 vols. in 1. Berlin: 1870. (A respectable German biography.)

Underwood, Francis Henry. *Washington Irving*. Philadelphia: 1890. (A concise biography.)

*Warner, Charles Dudley. *Washington Irving*. American Men of Letters series. Boston: 1881.

Wise, Daniel. *Washington Irving*. Home College series, No. 6. New York: 1883. (A biography and critical work from the puritanical point of view.)

Much biographical material, particularly in the form of shorter biographical and memorial sketches, is to be found under the next head: "Biographical and Critical Studies." See, also, above, under the head of "Letters, Journals, Diaries."

V. BIOGRAPHICAL AND CRITICAL STUDIES

A good deal of critical material will be found in the full-length biographies listed above under "Biographies." See also "Letters, Journals, Diaries."

Adkins, Nelson F. "An Uncollected Tale by Washington Irving," *American Literature*, V, 364–367 (Jan., 1934).

(Reprint of "The Haunted Ship," a hitherto unnoticed tale appearing originally in *Friendship's Offering* for 1849.)

Adkins, Nelson F. "Irving's 'Wolfert's Roost': a Bibliographical Note," *Notes and Queries*, CLXIV, 42 (Jan., 1933). (Two additions to Langfeld's bibliography published in the *Bulletin of New York Public Library*, June-Dec., 1932.)

Adkins, Nelson F. *Fitz-Greene Halleck*. New Haven: 1930. (Some reference to Irving.)

Apetz, P. *Washington Irvings Aufenthalt in Dresden, 1822–1823*. Dresden: 1914. (An attempt to reconstruct the record of Irving's residence in Dresden.)

Arens, E. "Washington Irving im Rheinland, 1822," *Eichendorff-Kalendar*, 93–120 (1927–1928).

Axson, Stockton. "Washington Irving and the Knickerbocker Group," *Rice Institute Pamphlet*, XX, 178–195 (April, 1933).

Bacon, Edgar Mayhew. *In Memoriam Washington Irving*. . . . New York: 1909. (Commemorating the fiftieth anniversary of Irving's death.)

Beatty, Elsie Fleming. *Washington Irving and the Sources of his Hudson River Legends*. M. A. thesis in manuscript. Columbia University Library: 1923. (Attempts to find the origins of Irving's Hudson River stories; not always convincing.)

Benson, Adolph B. "Scandinavians in the Works of Washington Irving," *Scandinavian Studies and Notes*, IX, 207–223 (Aug., 1927).

[Benson, E. (?)]. *Brief Remarks on the "Wife" of Washington Irving*. New York: 1819. (A 16-page booklet sometimes attributed to Irving, but not generally accepted as having been written by Irving; possibly by Benson.)

Birss, John Howard. "New Verses by Washington Irving," *American Literature*, IV, 296 (Nov., 1932). (Addenda, consisting of 4 verses, to *The Poems of Washington Irving Brought Together from Various Sources*, by William R. Langfeld.)

Blackburn, Philip C. "Irving's Biography of James Lawrence," *Bulletin of New York Public Library*, XXXVI, 742–743

(Nov., 1932). (A brief collation of the texts and history of the printing of this production, indicating that Irving was not averse to turning out a few pages on a given subject for a given occasion.)

Bowen, E. W. "The Place of Irving in American Literature," *Sewanee Review*, XIV, 171–183 (1906). (A semi-popular estimate.)

Boynton, Henry Walcott. "Irving," in *American Writers on American Literature* (ed. John Macy). New York: 1931, pp. 58–71.

Bruce, Wallace. *Along the Hudson with Washington Irving.* Poughkeepsie, N. Y.: 1913.

Bryant, William Cullen. *A Discourse on the Life, Character and Genius of Washington Irving.* Delivered before the New York Historical Society . . . April 3, 1860. New York: 1860. (A memorial address, somewhat colored by the occasion, but interesting as a contemporary estimate.)

Burton, R. "Irving's Services to American History," *New England Magazine*, N.S. XVI (1897). (A discussion of Irving's contribution to the science of history.)

Cairns, W. B. *British Criticisms on American Writings, 1815–1833.* Madison, Wis.: 1922. (Contains a list of British criticisms upon Irving's works.)

Canby, Henry Seidel. *Classic Americans.* New York: 1931. (A fresh and illuminating chapter, pp. 67–96, included on Irving, with special reference to Irving's Federalism.)

Canby, Henry Seidel. *The Short Story in English.* New York: 1909. (Irving accorded a prominent place in the development of the short story. See also Professor Canby's *A Study of the Short Story.* New York: 1913.)

Clark, L. Gaylord. "Memorial to Irving," *Knickerbocker Magazine*, LV (1860). (A popular memorial sketch occasioned by the death of Irving in 1859.)

Clark, L. Gaylord. "Recollections of Washington Irving," *Lippincott's Magazine*, III (1869). (Personalia.)

Coad, Oral Sumner. "The Gothic Element in American Literature before 1835," *Journal of English and Germanic*

Philology, XXIV, 72–93 (1925). (Some emphasis upon Irving's Gothicism.)

Cody, Sherwin. *Four Famous American Writers: Washington Irving, Edgar Allan Poe, James Russell Lowell, Bayard Taylor*. New York: 1899.

Cook, C. "A Glimpse of Irving at Home," *Century Magazine*, XII (1887). (Personalia.)

Cooke, J. E. "A Morning with Irving," *Southern Magazine*, XII (1887). (Personalia.)

Curtis, George William. "Irving's Knickerbocker," *Critic*, III (1883). (A review.)

Curtis, George William. *Washington Irving. A Sketch.* New York: 1891. (A 115-page Grolier Club publication.)

Dana, Richard Henry. "The Sketch Book," *North American Review*, IX, (1819). (A review.)

Davis, Asahel. *A Visit to Sunnyside in the Life Time of the "Father of American Literature," by a Corresponding Member of the New York Historical Society*. Buffalo: 1860. (Personalia.)

Dennett, J. R. "The Knickerbocker School," *Nation*, Dec. 6, 1867.

Duyckinck, Evert Augustus (ed.). *Irvingiana: a Memorial of Washington Irving*. . . . New York: 1860. (Contemporary estimates and recollections; very valuable.)

Everett, Edward. "Bracebridge Hall," *North American Review*, XV (1822); "A Tour on the Prairies," *North American Review*, XLI (1835); "Astoria," *North American Review*, XLIV (1837); "Remarks before the Massachusetts Historical Society," *Proceedings*, 1858–1860. (Clear-headed reviews and a fair estimate.)

Felton, C. C. "Remarks before the Massachusetts Historical Society," *Proceedings*, 1858–1860. (A contemporary estimate; memorial address.)

Ferguson, John DeLancy. *American Literature in Spain*. New York: 1916. (Irving as intermediary receives some attention, hardly enough.)

Fetterolf, Adam H. *Washington Irving*. Philadelphia: 1897. (A 48-page sketch.)

Foreman, Grant. "An Unpublished Report by Captain Bonneville," *Chronicles of Oklahoma*, X, 326–330 (Sept., 1932). (Additional writings of Bonneville, whose diary Irving edited.)

Gaedertz, K. T. "Zu Washington Irvings Skizzenbuch," *Zur Kenntnis der altenglischen Bühne*. Bremen: 1888.

Gardner, James H. "One Hundred Years Ago in the Region of Tulsa," *Chronicles of Oklahoma*, XI, 765–785 (June, 1933). (A study of the country described in *A Tour on the Prairies*.)

Goggio, E. "Washington Irving in Italy," *Romanic Review*, XXI, 26–33 (Jan.-Mar., 1930). (Suggests that Italy furnished Irving with inspiration for some of his stories in *Tales of a Traveller*.)

Goggio, E. "Washington Irving's Works in Italy," *Romanic Review*, XXII, 301–303 (Oct.-Dec., 1931). (A brief discussion of Irving's popularity in Italy during the second quarter of the nineteenth century.)

Gosse, E. W. "Irving's Sketch Book" *Critic*, III (1883). (A review.)

Greene, G. W. "Life of Washington," *North American Review*, LXXXVI (1858); see also "Irving's Works," in *Biographical Studies*. New York: 1860. (A review.)

Greenlaw, Edwin A. "A Comedy in Politics," *Texas Review*, April, 1916. (With reference to *Knickerbocker's History*, and its satire of Jefferson.)

Grosskunz, R. *Die Natur in den Werken und Briefen des amerikanischen Schriftstellers Washington Irving*. Leipzig: 1902. (A discussion of Irving's treatment of nature; typical dissertation study.)

Guilbert, Edmund. *The House of Washington Irving*. New York: 1867. (Chiefly descriptive.)

Hastings, George E. "John Bull and his American Descendants," *American Literature*, I, 40–68 (1929). (An attempt to discover the extent to which Paulding and Irving were influenced not only by Arbuthnot's *The History of John Bull* but also by one another.)

Haweis, Hugh Reginald. *American Humorists*. Standard

Library, No. 82. New York: [preface 1882]. (Contains a 34-page biographical sketch of Irving.)

Hazlitt, William. "Elia and Geoffrey Crayon," in *Spirit of the Age*. London: 1825; review of Channing's Sermons, *Edinburgh Review*, I (1829). (English comparative estimates.)

Hellman, George Sidney. "Irving's *Washington*; and an Episode in Courtesy," *The Colophon*, Part I, 1930. (The courtesy with which Irving relinquished to Prescott his researches in the history of Mexico was repaid with letters and anecdotes about Washington.)

Hellman, George Sidney. Review of *Journal of Washington Irving (1823–1824)*, edited by Stanley T. Williams, *Modern Language Notes*, XLVII, 326–328 (May, 1932). (Criticizes Professor Williams's position with regard to the Irving-Matilda-Emily problem.)

Hespelt, E. H. "Irving's Version of Byron's *The Tales of Greece*," *Modern Language Notes*, XLII, 111 (Feb., 1927). (Reprinted from an unpublished notebook in the Seligman collection of the New York Public Library.)

Hespelt, E. H., and Williams, Stanley T. "Two Unpublished Anecdotes by Fernán Caballero preserved by Washington Irving," *Modern Language Notes*, XLIX, 25–31 (Jan., 1934). (The first printing of the manuscripts of two anecdotes given by Fernán Caballero to Irving, apparently with the idea that Irving should employ them in his writing.)

Holmes, Oliver Wendell. "Tribute to Irving," Massachusetts Historical Society *Proceedings*, 1858–1860; "Irving's Power of Idealization," *Critic*, III (1883). (Interesting contemporary estimates.)

Howells, William Dean. *My Literary Passions*. New York: 1895, pp. 23–27. (Irving is accorded third place among Howells's "first three loves in literature," and is considered with special reference to his Spanish books.)

Ingraham, C. A. *Washington Irving*. Cambridge, N. Y.: 1922.

[Irving, Washington]. "Excerpts from Two Letters Dated Dec. 16, 1845, and Dec. 20, 1829," *Autograph Album*, I, 71–72 (Dec., 1933).

Jeffrey, Francis. "The Sketch Book," *Edinburgh Review*, XXXIV (1820); "Bracebridge Hall," *Edinburgh Review*, XXXVII (1822); "Irving's Columbus," *Edinburgh Review*, XLVIII (1828). (These reviews did much to prepare the way for Irving's popularity in England.)

Knortz, Karl. *Washington Irving in Tarrytown. Ein Beitrag zur Geschichte der nordamerikanischen Literatur*. Nürnberg: 1909.

Künzig, Ferdinand. *Washington Irving und seine Beziehungen zur englischen Literatur des 18. Jahrhunderts*. Heidelberg: 1911. (An attempt to trace Irving's stylistic roots in eighteenth century English literature; not always convincing.)

Lathrop, G. P. "Poe, Irving, Hawthorne," *Scribner's Monthly*, XI, 799–808 (April, 1876). (Estimates.)

Leslie, Charles Robert. *Autobiographical Recollections*. Boston: 1860. (For Irving-Leslie correspondence, see pp. 204–302.)

Livingston, L. S. "First Books of Irving, Poe, and Whitman," *Bookman* (New York), VIII (1898).

Lockhart, J. G. "On the Writings of Charles Brockden Brown and Washington Irving," *Blackwood's Magazine*, VI (1820). (Contemporary British estimates; see also *Memoirs of the Life of Sir Walter Scott*, chap. xxxix.)

Longfellow, Henry Wadsworth. "Tribute to Irving," Massachusetts Historical Society *Proceedings*, 1858–1860. (A memorial address and testimony of Irving's early influence upon Longfellow.)

Lowell, James Russell. *A Fable for Critics*. Boston: 1848. (Contains a whimsical sketch of Irving.)

Lynch, Virginia. *Washington Irving Footprints*. New York: 1922.

Mabie, Hamilton Wright. *The Writers of Knickerbocker New York*. New York: The Grolier Club, 1912. (A valuable book on the group with which Irving is identified.)

McDowell, Tremaine. "General James Wilkinson in the *Knickerbocker History of New York*," *Modern Language Notes*, XLI, 353–359 (June, 1926). ("Von Poffenburgh is a sketch of James Wilkinson . . . unique among the satirical allusions to contemporary politics in the *History* in its caustic ridicule.")

Memorials of James Fenimore Cooper. New York: 1852. (Contains a letter by Irving regarding Cooper, p. 7.)

Mitchell, Donald Grant. *American Lands and Letters*. New York: 1897. (Contains, on pp. 300–330, a sketch of Irving, including a letter printed for the first time.)

Mitchell, Donald Grant. *Dream Life*. New York: 1863. (Preface reproduces in full a letter by Irving only part of which is quoted in P. M. Irving's *Life*; also some reminiscences.)

Mitchell, Donald Grant. "Washington Irving," *Atlantic Monthly*, XIII (1864); "Memorial Address," in *Bound Together: a Sheaf of Papers*. New York: 1884.

Moore, Thomas. *Memoirs, Journal and Correspondence of Thomas Moore*. Edited by Lord John Russell. 8 vols. London: 1853–1856. (Contain diary references concerning his companionship with Irving.)

Morris, G. D. *Washington Irving's Fiction in the Light of French Criticism*. Indiana University Studies, No. 30. May, 1916. (A suggestive interpretation.)

[Neal, John.] "American Writers, No. IV," *Blackwood's Edinburgh Magazine*, XVII, 58–67 (Jan., 1825).

Parrington, Vernon Louis. *The Romantic Revolution in America, 1800–1860*. New York: 1927, pp. 203–212. (Irving interpreted in the stream of American liberal thought.)

Pattee, Fred Lewis. *The Development of the American Short Story*. New York: 1923. (Chapter I devoted to Washington Irving and his contributions to the short story.)

Paulding, William Irving. *Literary Life of James K. Paulding*. New York: 1867. (Contains, on p. 120, one of Irving's letters, only portions of which are included in P. M. Irving's *Life and Letters*.)

Payne, William Morton. *Leading American Essayists*. New York: 1910. (Includes a chapter on Irving.)

Plath, Otto. "Washington Irvings Einfluss auf Wilhelm Hauff," *Euphorion, Zeitschrift für Literaturgeschichte*. Leipzig: 1913. (An attempt to evaluate Irving's influence upon Hauff.)

Pochmann, Henry A. "Irving's German Sources in *The Sketch Book*," *Studies in Philology*, XXVII, 477–507 (July, 1930). (Contact with German literature partly accountable for Irving's turning from classicism toward romanticism; examination into the German sources for "Rip Van Winkle," "Sleepy Hollow," and "The Spectre Bridegroom.")

Pochmann, Henry A. "Irving's German Tour and Its Influence on His Tales," *Publications of the Modern Language Association*, XLV, 1150–1187 (Dec., 1930). (A study of the influence of German literature upon *Tales of a Traveller*, *The Alhambra*, and *Wolfert's Roost*.)

Pochmann, Henry A. *The Influence of the German Tale on the Short Stories of Irving, Hawthorne, and Poe*. Dissertation in manuscript in the University of North Carolina Library: 1928; abstract in the *University of North Carolina Record: Research in Progress 1927–1928*. Graduate School series No. 19, pp. 45–46. (Points out certain significant affinities in subject matter, style, and technique between the German tale and the early American short story.)

Poe, Edgar Allan. "Irving's Astoria," *Southern Literary Messenger*, III (1837). (A review.)

Poe, Edgar Allan. *Tales of the Grotesque and Arabesque*. Philadelphia: 1840 [actually published 1839]. (Contains several quoted opinions of Poe's work, two of them being from letters of Irving to Poe. See also *The Literati* [First edition. New York: J. S. Redfield, 1850], particularly the introductory memoir by Rufus Griswold, in which short portions of these letters are quoted. The second of these letters is reprinted in full in George E. Woodberry's *Life of Poe*. New York: 1909, II, 216–217.)

Prescott, W. H. "The Conquest of Granada," *North American Review*, XXIX (1828). (A review.)

Putnam, George Haven. "Irving," in *Cambridge History of American Literature*. 4 vols. New York: 1917–1921, I, 245–259; bibliography, 510–517. (A typical CHAL chapter, but telling the story of Irving's relations to his publisher somewhat differently from P. M. Irving's version.)

Putnam, George Haven. *George Palmer Putnam*. New York: 1912. (Includes a discussion of Irving's relations with his publisher, G. P. Putnam.)

Putnam, George Haven. "Washington Irving," *Forum*, LXXV, 397–409 (March, 1926).

Putnam, George Haven. *Washington Irving; His Life and Work*. New York: 1903. (A 56-page biographical and critical sketch, including a brief bibliography of Irving's chief works.)

Putnam, George Palmer. "Recollections of Irving," *Atlantic Monthly*, VI (1860). (Personalia and reminiscences.)

Richards, T. A. "Irving at Sunnyside," *Harper's Magazine*, XIV (1856). (A contemporary view.)

Ripley, George. "Washington Irving," *Harper's Magazine*, II (1851). (Another contemporary estimate.)

The Romance of Mary Wollstonecraft Shelley, John Howard Payne, and Washington Irving. Boston: The Bibliophile Society, 1907. (Suggesting a triangular love relationship.)

Russell, John Adams. "Irving: Recorder of Indian Life," *Journal of American History*, XXV, 185–195 (1931). (Irving's attitude toward the Indian and his services as an historian of the Indian.)

Sanford, O. M. "An Irving Centennial Fifty Years Ago," *Americana*, XXVI, 456–461 (Oct., 1933). (Reminiscences of a centennial address given by Irving's pastor, J. S. Spencer.)

Saunders, Frederick. *Character Studies, with Some Personal Recollections*. New York: 1894. (A short sketch of Irving included.)

Sedgwick, A. G. "Irving," *Nation*, XXXVI (1883).

Small, Miriam R. "A Possible Ancestor of Diedrich Knickerbocker," *American Literature*, II, 21–24 (March, 1930). (Richard Graves' *The Spiritual Quixote* contains a possible source for certain aspects of Irving's characterization of D. Knickerbocker.)

Spiller, Robert E. *The American in England*. New York: 1926.

(Contains, on p. 281, portions of a letter no part of which had been previously published.)

Sprenger, R. *Über die Quelle von Washington Irvings Rip Van Winkle.* Northeim: 1901. (Suggests Germanic influence.)

Stoddard, R. H. *The Life of Washington Irving.* The Elzevir Library, vol. I, no. iv. New York: 1883. (A 70-page biographical sketch.)

Streeter, F. B. "Knickerbocker and the Prairie," Fort Hays Kansas State College *Aerend*, III, 229–230 (Fall, 1932). (A humorous incident in Irving's journey in the western territory—his purchase of a balky horse.)

Taylor, J. F. "Washington Irving's Mexico, a Lost Fragment," *Bookman* (New York), XLI, 665–669 (Aug., 1915).

Thackeray, W. M. "Nil Nisi Bonum," *Cornhill Magazine*, I (1860); *Harper's Magazine*, XX (1860). (Included in *Roundabout Papers.*)

Thompson, J. B. "The Genesis of the Rip Van Winkle Legend," *Harper's Magazine*, LXVII (1883). (Traces the supernatural-sleep *motif* in literature.)

Thorburn, Joseph B. "Centennial of the Tour on the Prairies by Washington Irving (1832–1932)," *Chronicles of Oklahoma*, X, 426–437 (Sept., 1932). (The coöperation of the Oklahoma Historical Society and the State Department of Education with various communities in centennial celebrations.)

Tilton, Theodore. "Half an Hour at Sunnyside: A Visit to Washington Irving," *Independent*, Nov. 24, 1859; reprinted in *Littell's Living Age*, LXIII (Oct.-Dec., 1859); reprinted in Duyckinck, *Irvingiana*, l-lii. (Personalia.)

Tuckermann, Henry Theodore, *Irving.* New York: 1896; also in *Little Journeys to the Homes of American Authors* [Elbert Hubbard, ed.]. New York: 1896, pp. 267–296. (Anecdotal, personal, and descriptive sketches.)

Vincent, Leon Henry. *American Literary Masters.* Boston: 1906. (Chapter devoted to Irving.)

Waldron, William Watson. *Washington Irving and Contemporaries in Thirty Life Sketches.* New York: n.d. [1867].

(Pages 17–54 contain a short life of Irving, together with several letters, including nine to Waldron, not elsewhere published.)

Wallace, H. B. *Literary Criticism.* Philadelphia: 1856. (Contemporary estimate of Irving included.)

Warner, Charles Dudley; Bryant, William Cullen; and Putnam, George Palmer. *Studies of Irving* (Warner, C. D., "Washington Irving," an essay prepared in Jan., 1880, as an introduction to the Geoffrey Crayon edition of Irving's works, pp. 7–73; Bryant, W. C., "Washington Irving: His Life, Character, and Genius, a Discourse Delivered before the New York Historical Society, April 3, 1860," pp. 77–128; and Putnam, G. P., "Washington Irving: Personal Reminiscences, by his Publisher," written for the *Atlantic Monthly,* Nov., 1860, pp. 131–159). New York: 1880. (Three essays in the nature of memorials.)

Webster, Clarence. "Irving's Expurgations of the 1809 *History of New York,*" *American Literature,* III, 293–295 (Nov., 1932). (Although Irving toned down in later editions many of his English expressions, the Dutch passages, even the coarser ones, remained intact.)

Wendell, Barrett. *A Literary History of America.* New York: 1900. (Includes a short treatment of Irving.)

Whitaker, Daniel Kimball. *An Eulogy on the Late Washington Irving.* Delivered by Appointment before the Washington Raven Club, Dec. 22, 1859. Washington: 1860. (A memorial address.)

Williams, Stanley T. "The First Version of the Writings of Washington Irving in Spanish," *Modern Philology,* XXVIII, 185–201 (Nov., 1930). (The first appearance of Irving's writings in Spanish in *Tareas de un solitario,* 1829; a list of 42 Spanish translations of Irving's writings; and a discussion of George Washington Montgomery's skillful work as translator of Irving.)

Williams, Stanley T. "Washington Irving and Fernán Caballero," *Journal of English and Germanic Philology,* XXIX, 352–366 (July, 1930). (Suggests that Irving's popularity in Spain was due, in part, to his sympathy with the Spanish literary form of the "articulo des costumbres.")

Williams, Stanley T. "Washington Irving and Matilda Hoffman," *American Speech*, I, 463–469 (June, 1926). (An effort to arrive at a justifiable evaluation of Matilda Hoffman's influence upon Irving.)

Williams, Stanley T. "Washington Irving, Matilda Hoffman, and Emily Foster," *Modern Language Notes*, XLVIII, 182–186 (March, 1933). (A protest against Mr. Hellman's assumptions and surmises regarding Irving's love for Emily Foster; suggests that Mr. Hellman misread a passage in Irving's journals, which forms the crux of Hellman's argument.)

Williams, Stanley T. "Washington Irving's Religion [Letter from Irving to Emily Foster, Paris, Aug. 23, 1825]," *Yale Review*, XV, 414–416 (Jan., 1926). (Contains Irving's putting by Emily's concern over his lack of religiosity.)

Willis, N. P. "Ollapodiana," *Knickerbocker Magazine*, Oct., 1836; "Willis at Sunnyside," *Living Age*, LIV–LV (1857). (Personalia and estimates.)

Wilson, James Grant. *Bryant and His Friends*. New York: 1886. (Contains some mention of Irving.)

Wilson, James Grant. *Life and Letters of Fitz-Greene Halleck*. New York: 1869. (Contains, pp. 397–398, a quotation from one of Irving's speeches; also several anecdotes not found in P. M. Irving's *Life*.)

Yarborough, Minnie C. "Rambles with Washington Irving: Quotations from an Unpublished Autobiography of William C. Preston," *South Atlantic Quarterly*, XXIX, 423–439 (Oct., 1930). (Preston was Irving's travelling companion on the Scotch tour of 1817.)

Zeydel, E. H. "Washington Irving and Ludwig Tieck," *Publications of the Modern Language Association*, XLVI, 946–947 (Sept., 1931). (Points out the fact that Irving personally knew Tieck and corrects a misreading of Tieck for Treck in the Trent-Hellman *Journals*.)

CHRONOLOGICAL TABLE

1783. April 3, born in New York City.

1787. Sent to Mrs. Ann Kilmaster's school.

1789. Sent to school kept by Benjamin Romaine.

1799. Enters law office of Henry Masterton.

1800. First extended voyage up the Hudson.

1801. Enters law office of Brockholst Livingston.

1802. Becomes clerk in office of Josiah Ogden Hoffman. Contributes juvenile essays under signature of "Jonathan Old-style, Gent." to his brother Peter's paper, the *Morning Chronicle*, Nov. 15, 1802—Apr. 23, 1803.

1803. Makes extended trip, in company with Hoffman, to Montreal and Quebec.

1804–6. Visit to Europe in search of health, education, and pleasure—Bordeaux, Marseilles, Nice, Genoa, Messina, Syracuse, Palermo, Naples, Rome, Milan, Zurich, Paris, Brussels, Rotterdam, London, Oxford, Bath, Bristol. Contacts with Cabell, Allston, Madame de Staël.

1806. Nov. 21, passed bar examination.

1807–8. *Salmagundi*, 20 numbers from Jan. 24, 1807, to Jan. 25, 1808. Father died October 25, 1807.

1809. April 26, Matilda Hoffman died. Dec. 6, *Knickerbocker's History* published.

1810. Goes into partnership with his brothers, William and Peter, in the hardware business, carried on in New York and Liverpool.

1811. Goes as agent of his firm to Washington during Congressional session.

1811. Leaves mother's home to share bachelor quarters with Henry Brevoort at No. 16 Broadway, near Bowling Green.

1812. General business depression. Goes to Washington as member of Committee of Merchants from New York to seek measures of relief. Becomes editor of the *Analectic Magazine*.

1813. Entertains Francis Jeffrey of the *Edinburgh Review*.

1814. Becomes aide-de-camp to Governor Tompkins, with rank of Colonel.

1815. Makes preparations to set off on Mediterranean cruise, and upon collapse of plans, sets out, on May 25, for England, ostensibly to aid in the conduct of the Liverpool business. Remains abroad 17 years. Peter in poor health; business devolves upon Washington. Slaves manfully to avert failure. Occasional visits to Birmingham and London.

1817. Peter's health improved; Washington relieved of business responsibilities. Death of mother. Scotch tour; meetings with Scott and Edinburgh literati; also Murray coterie in London.

1818. Irving firm forced into bankruptcy. Refuses various editorial and governmental positions, throwing himself resolutely upon his ability with the pen.

1819–20. *The Sketch Book* published serially, in America and England.

1820. Extended literary associations in London.

1821. Meets Moore, Payne, and Talma in Paris.

1822. *Bracebridge Hall* pub. Social triumphs in London. Visit to Germany; settles in Dresden.

1823. Intimacy with Foster family during eight months' residence in Dresden. Return to Paris. Collaboration with Payne in plays and theatrical adaptations.

1824. Return to London. *Tales of a Traveller* pub.

1825. Paris.

1826. Goes to Madrid as member of American Legation. Begins work on *Life of Columbus*.

1827. Meets Longfellow. Historical and biographical labors.

1828. *Life and Voyages of Columbus* pub. Tour of Spain; visit to the Alhambra; research in Spanish manuscripts; residence at Seville.

1829. Domiciled in the Alhambra. *Conquest of Granada* published. Goes to London as Secretary of the Legation to the Court of St. James.

1830. Presented with medal by the Royal Society of Literature.

1831. Degree of D.C.L. conferred upon him by University of Oxford. *Voyages of the Companions of Columbus* pub.

1832. Returns to New York; enthusiastically received. *Alhambra* pub. Tour of West and South in company with government commissioners.

1833. Attends Congressional sessions in Washington. Declines nomination to Congress.

1834. John Jacob Astor suggests *Astoria*, joint production of Irving and his nephew, Pierre M. Irving.

1835. *The Crayon Miscellany* (including *A Tour on the Prairies*, *Abbotsford and Newstead Abbey*, and *Legends of the Conquest of Spain*) pub.

1836. Occupies Sunnyside at Tarrytown on the Hudson. *Astoria* pub.

1837. *Adventures of Captain Bonneville* pub.

1838. Declines nomination of Tammany Hall for Mayor of New York; also secretaryship of Navy offered by Van Buren. Abandons writing *Conquest of Mexico* in favor of W. H. Prescott. Begins work on *Life of Washington*.

1840. *Life of Oliver Goldsmith* pub.

1841. *Biography of Margaret Davidson* pub. Appointed Minister to Spain.

1842. Visits England; assumes ministership at Madrid.

1843. Spanish insurrection.

1845. Resigns position as Minister to Spain. Goes to England in interest of Oregon controversy.

1846. Returns to New York.

1847. Sunnyside remodelled and expanded. Begins preparation of complete revised edition of his works.

1848. Arranges with George P. Putnam for publication of revised edition.

1849. *Life of Goldsmith* (new and extended edition) pub.; also *A Book of the Hudson*.

1850. *Mahomet and His Successors* pub.

1853. Research in archives in Washington, D. C.

1855. *Wolfert's Roost* pub.; also vol. I of *Life of Washington*.
1856. Vols. II and III of *Life of Washington* pub.
1857. Vol. IV of *Life of Washington* pub.
1858. At work on last vol. of *Washington;* ill health.
1859. Vol. V of *Life of Washington* pub. Died Nov. 28.

*

Selections from
WASHINGTON IRVING

*

From LETTERS OF JONATHAN OLDSTYLE, GENT.

LETTER III[1]

Sir,—There is no place of public amusement of which I am so fond as the Theatre.[2] To enjoy this with the greater relish, I go but seldom; and I find there is no play, however poor or ridiculous, from which I cannot derive some entertainment.

I was very much taken with a play-bill of last week, announcing, in large capitals, "The Battle of Hexham, or, Days of Old." Here, said I to myself, will be something grand—Days of Old, —my fancy fired at the words. I pictured to myself all the gallantry of chivalry. Here, thought I, will be a display of court manners and true politeness; the play will, no doubt, be garnished with tilts and tournaments; and as to those banditti, whose names make such a formidable appearance on the bills, they will be hung up, every mother's son, for the edification of the gallery.

With such impressions, I took my seat in the pit, and was so impatient that I could hardly attend to the music, though I found it very good.

The curtain rose,—out walked the Queen,[3] with great majesty; she answered my ideas: she was dressed well, she looked well, and she acted well. The Queen was followed by a pretty gentleman, who, from his winking and grinning, I took to be the court-fool; I soon found out my mistake. He was a courtier "high in trust," and either general, colonel, or something of martial dignity. They talked for some time, though I could not understand the drift of their discourse, so I amused myself with eating peanuts.

In one of the scenes I was diverted with the stupidity of a corporal, and his men, who sung a dull song, and talked a great deal about nothing; though I found, by their laughing, there

---

[1] Superior figures throughout the text refer to correspondingly numbered notes at the end of the volume, pp. 375 ff.

was a great deal of fun in the corporal's remarks. What this scene had to do with the rest of the piece, I could not comprehend; I suspect it was a part of some other play, thrust in here by accident.

I was then introduced to a cavern, where there were several hard-looking fellows sitting around a table carousing. They told the audience they were banditti. They then sung a gallery song, of which I could understand nothing but two lines:—

> "The Welshman lik'd to have been chok'd by a mouse,
> But he pull'd him out by the tail."

Just as they had ended this elegant song, their banquet was disturbed by the melodious sound of a horn, and in marched a portly gentleman,[4] who, I found, was their captain. After this worthy gentleman had fumed his hour out, after he had slapped his breast and drawn his sword half a dozen times, the act ended.

In the course of the play, I learnt that there had been, or was, or would be, a battle; but how, or when, or where, I could not understand. The banditti once more made their appearance, and frightened the wife of the portly gentleman, who was dressed in man's clothes, and was seeking her husband. I could not enough admire the dignity of her deportment, the sweetness of her countenance, and the unaffected gracefulness of her action;[5] but who the captain really was, or why he ran away from his spouse, I could not understand. However, they seemed very glad to find one another again; and so at last the play ended, by the falling of the curtain.

I wish the manager would use a drop-scene at the close of the acts; we might then always ascertain the termination of the piece by the green curtain. On this occasion, I was indebted to the polite bows of the actors for this pleasing information. I cannot say that I was entirely satisfied with the play, but I promised myself ample entertainment in the afterpiece, which was called the "Tripolitan Prize." Now, thought I, we shall have some sport for our money; we will, no doubt, see a few of those Tripolitan scoundrels spitted like turkeys for our amusement. Well, sir, the curtain rose—the trees waved in front of the stage, and the sea rolled in the rear; all things looked very pleasant and smiling. Presently I heard a bustling behind the scenes,—here, thought I, comes a band of fierce Tripolitans, with whiskers as long as my arm. No such thing; they were only a party of village masters and misses taking a walk for exercise,—and very pretty behaved young gentry they were, I assure you; but it was cruel in the manager to dress them in buckram, as it deprived them entirely of the use of their limbs. They arranged themselves very orderly on each side of the stage, and sung something, doubtless very affecting, for they all looked pitiful enough. By and by came up a most tremendous storm: the lightning flashed, the thunder roared, and the rain fell in torrents; however, our pretty rustics stood gaping quietly at one another, until they must have been wet to the skin. I was surprised at their torpidity, till I found they were each one afraid to move first, for fear of being laughed at for their awkwardness. How they got off I do not recollect; but I advise the manager, in a similar case, to furnish every one with a trap-door, through which to make his exit. Yet this would deprive the audience of much amusement; for nothing can be more laughable than to see a body of guards with their spears, or courtiers with their long robes, get across the stage at our theatre.

Scene passed after scene. In vain I strained my eyes to catch a glimpse of a Mahometan phiz. I once heard a great bellowing behind the scenes, and expected to see a strapping Mussulman come bouncing in; but was miserably disappointed, on distinguishing his voice, to find out by his swearing that he was only a Christian. In he came,—an American navy officer,—worsted stockings, olive velvet small-clothes, scarlet vest, pea-jacket, and gold-laced hat—dressed quite in character. I soon found out, by his talk, that he was an American prize-master; that, returning through the Mediterranean with his Tripolitan prize, he was driven by a storm on the coast of England. The honest gentleman seemed, from his actions, to be rather intoxicated; which I could account for in no other way than his having drank a great deal of salt-water, as he swam ashore.

Several following scenes were taken up with hallooing and huzzaing, between the captain, his crew, and the gallery, with several amusing tricks of the captain and his son,—a very funny, mischievous little fellow. Then came the cream of the joke: the captain wanted to put to sea, and the young fellow, who had fallen desperately in love, to stay ashore. Here was a contest between love and honor; such piping of eyes, such blowing of noses, such slapping of pocket-holes! But Old Junk was in-flexible,—What! an American tar desert his duty! (three cheers from the gallery,) impossible! American tars forever!! True blue will never stain!! &c. &c. (a continual thundering among the gods.) Here was a scene of distress; here was bathos. The author seemed as much puzzled to know how to dispose of the young tar as Old Junk was. It would not do to leave an Ameri-can seaman on foreign ground, nor would it do to separate him from his mistress.

Scene the last opened. It seems that another Tripolitan cruiser had bore down on the prize, as she lay about a mile off shore. How a Barbary corsair had got in this part of the world, —whether she had been driven there by the same storm, or whether she was cruising to pick up a few English first-rates, I could not learn. However, here she was. Again were we con-ducted to the sea-shore, where we found all the village gentry, in their buckram suits, ready assembled to be entertained with the rare show of an American and Tripolitan engaged yard-arm and yard-arm. The battle was conducted with proper decency and decorum, and the Tripolitan very politely gave in,—as it would be indecent to conquer in the face of an American audience.

After the engagement the crew came ashore, joined with the captain and gallery in a few more huzzas, and the curtain fell. How Old Junk, his son, and his son's sweetheart, settled it, I could not discover.

I was somewhat puzzled to understand the meaning and ne-cessity of this engagement between the ships, till an honest old countryman at my elbow said, he supposed this was the Battle of Hexham, as he recollected no fighting in the first piece. With this explanation I was perfectly satisfied.

My remarks upon the audience, I shall postpone to another opportunity.

JONATHAN OLDSTYLE.

December 1, 1802.

From SALMAGUNDI [6]

As everybody knows, or ought to know, what a SALMAGUND [7] is, we shall spare ourselves the trouble of an explanation; besides, we despise trouble as we do everything low and mean, and hold the man who would incur it unnecessarily as an object worthy our highest pity and contempt. Neither will we puzzle our heads to give an account of ourselves,[8] for two reasons; first, because it is nobody's business; secondly, because if it were, we do not hold ourselves bound to attend to anybody's business but our own; and even *that* we take the liberty of neglecting when it suits our inclination. To these we might·add a third, that very few men *can* give a tolerable account of themselves, let them try ever so hard; but this reason, we candidly avow, would not hold good with ourselves.

There are, however, two or three pieces of information which we bestow gratis on the public, chiefly because it suits our own pleasure and convenience that they should be known, and partly because we do not wish that there should be any ill will between us at the commencement of our acquaintance.

Our intention is simply to instruct the young, reform the old, correct the town, and castigate the age;[9] this is an arduous task, and therefore we undertake it with confidence. We intend for this purpose to present a striking picture of the town; and as everybody is anxious to see his own phiz on canvas, however stupid or ugly it may be, we have no doubt but the whole town will flock to our exhibition. Our picture will necessarily include a vast variety of figures; and should any gentleman or lady be displeased with the inveterate truth of their likenesses, they may ease their spleen by laughing at those of their neighbors—this being what *we* understand by *poetical justice*.

Like all true and able editors, we consider ourselves infallible; and therefore, with the customary diffidence of our brethren of the quill, we shall take the liberty of interfering in all matters either of a public or private nature. We are critics, amateurs, dilettanti and cognoscenti; and as we know "by the pricking of our thumbs," that every opinion which we may advance in either of those characters will be correct, we are determined, though it may be questioned, contradicted, or even controverted, yet it shall never be revoked.

We beg the public particularly to understand that we solicit no patronage. We are determined, on the contrary, that the patronage shall be entirely on our side. We have nothing to do with the pecuniary concerns of the paper; its success will yield us neither pride nor profit—nor will its failure occasion to us either loss or mortification. We advise the public, therefore, to purchase our numbers merely for their own sakes; if they do not, let them settle the affair with their consciences and posterity.

To conclude, we invite all editors of newspapers and literary journals to praise us heartily in advance, as we assure them that we intend to deserve their praises. To our next-door neighbor, "Town,"[10] we hold out a hand of amity, declaring to him that, after ours, his paper will stand the best chance for immortality. We proffer an exchange of civilities: he shall furnish us with notices of epic poems and tobacco; and we, in return, will enrich him with original speculations on all manner of subjects, together with "the rummaging of my grandfather's mahogany chest of drawers," "the life and amours of mine Uncle John," "anecdotes of the Cockloft family," and learned quotations from that unheard of writer of folios, *Linkum Fidelius*.

From NO. XIII.——FRIDAY, AUGUST 14, 1807

From My Elbow-Chair

A RETROSPECT; OR, "WHAT YOU WILL"

Lolling in my elbow-chair this fine summer noon, I feel myself insensibly yielding to that genial feeling of indolence the season is so well fitted to inspire. Every one who is blessed with a little of the delicious languor of disposition that delights in repose, must often have sported among the fairy scenes, the golden visions, the voluptuous reveries, that swim before the imagination at such moments, and which so much resemble those blissful sensations a Mussulman enjoys after his favorite indulgence of opium, which Will Wizard declares can be compared to nothing but "swimming in an ocean of peacocks' feathers." In such a mood everybody must be sensible it would be idle and unprofitable for a man to send his wits a gadding on a voyage of discovery into futurity, or even to trouble himself with a laborious investigation of what is actually passing under his eye. We are, at such times, more disposed to resort to the pleasures of memory than to those of the imagination; and like the wayfaring traveller, reclining for a moment on his staff, had rather contemplate the ground we have travelled, than the region which is yet before us.

I could here amuse myself, and stultify my readers, with a most elaborate and ingenious parallel between authors and travellers; but in this balmy season, which makes men stupid and dogs mad, and when, doubtless, many of our most strenuous admirers have great difficulty in keeping awake through the day, it would be cruel to saddle them with the formidable difficulty of putting two ideas together and drawing a conclusion, or, in the learned phrase, forging *syllogisms in Baroco*—a terrible undertaking for the dogdays! To say the truth, my observations were only intended to prove that this, of all others, is the most auspicious moment, and my present, the most favorable mood for indulging in a retrospect. Whether, like certain great personages of the day, in attempting to prove one thing, I have exposed another; or whether, like certain other great personages, in attempting to prove a great deal, I have proved nothing at all, I leave to my readers to decide, provided they have the power and inclination so to do; but a RETROSPECT will I take, notwithstanding.

I am perfectly aware that in doing this I shall lay myself open to the charge of imitation, than which a man might be better accused of downright housebreaking; for it has been a standing rule with many of my illustrious predecessors, occasionally, and particularly at the conclusion of a volume,[11] to look over their shoulder and chuckle at the miracles they had achieved. But, as I before professed, I am determined to hold myself entirely independent of all manner of opinions and criticisms, as the only method of getting on in this world in anything like a straight line. True it is, I may sometimes seem to angle a little for the good opinion of mankind, by giving them some excellent reasons for doing unreasonable things; but this is merely to show them, that although I may occasionally go wrong, it is not for want of knowing how to go right; and here I will lay down a maxim, which will forever entitle me to the gratitude of my inexperienced readers, namely, that a man always gets more credit in the eyes of this naughty world for sinning willfully than for sinning through sheer ignorance.

It will doubtless be insisted by many ingenious cavillers, who will be meddling with what does not at all concern them, that this retrospect should have been taken at the commencement of our second volume; it is usual, I know: moreover it is natural. So soon as a writer has once accomplished a volume, he forthwith becomes wonderfully increased in altitude! he steps upon his book as upon a pedestal, and is elevated in proportion to its magnitude. A duodecimo makes him one inch taller—an octavo, three inches—a quarto, six; but he who has made out to swell a folio looks down upon his fellow creatures from such a fearful height that, ten to one, the poor man's head is turned forever afterward. From such a lofty situation, therefore, it is natural an author should cast his eyes behind, and having reached the first landing-place on the stairs of immortality, may reasonably be allowed to plead his privilege to look back over the height he has ascended. I have deviated a little from this venerable custom, merely that our retrospect might fall in the dog days—of all days in the year most congenial to the indulgence of a little self-sufficiency, inasmuch as people have then little to do but to retire within the sphere of self, and make the most of what they find there.

Let it not be supposed, however, that we think ourselves a

whit the wiser or better since we have finished our volume than we were before; on the contrary, we seriously assure our readers that we were fully possessed of all the wisdom and morality it contains at the moment we commenced writing. It is the world which has grown wiser,—not us; we have thrown our mite into the common stock of knowledge, we have shared our morsel with the ignorant multitude; and so far from elevating ourselves above the world, our sole endeavor has been to raise the world to our own level, and make it as wise as we, its disinterested benefactors.

To a moral writer like myself, who, next to his own comfort and entertainment, has the good of his fellow citizens at heart, a retrospect is but a sorry amusement. Like the industrious husbandman, he often contemplates in silent disappointment his labors wasted on a barren soil, or the seeds he has carefully sown, choked by a redundancy of worthless weeds. I expected long ere this to have seen a complete reformation in manners and morals, achieved by our united efforts. My fancy echoed to the applauding voices of a retrieved generation; I anticipated, with proud satisfaction, the period, not far distant, when our work would be introduced into the academies with which every lane and alley of our cities abounds; when our precepts would be gently inducted into every unlucky urchin by force of birch, and my iron-bound physiognomy, as taken by Will Wizard, be as notorious as that of Noah Webster, junr. Esq. or his no less renowned predecessor, the illustrious Dilworth of spelling-book immortality.[12] But, well-a-day! to let my readers into a profound secret—the expectations of man are like the varied hues that tinge the distant prospect; never to be realized, never to be enjoyed but in perspective. Luckless Launcelot, that the humblest of the many air castles thou hast erected should prove a "baseless fabric!" Much does it grieve me to confess, that after all our lectures, precepts, and excellent admonitions, the people of NEW YORK are nearly as much given to backsliding and ill-nature as ever; they are just as much abandoned to dancing,[13] and tea-drinking; and as to scandal, Will Wizard informs me that, by a rough computation, since the last cargo of gunpowder-tea from Canton, no less than eighteen characters have been blown up, besides a number of others that have been woefully shattered.[14]

The ladies still labor under the same scarcity of muslins,[15] and delight in flesh-colored silk stockings; it is evident, however, that our advice has had very considerable effect on them, as they endeavor to act as opposite to it as possible; this being what Evergreen calls female independence. As to Straddles,[16] they abound as much as ever in Broadway, particularly on Sundays; and Wizard roundly asserts that he supped in company with a knot of them a few evenings since, when they liquidated a whole Birmingham consignment, in a batch of imperial champagne. I have, furthermore, in the course of a month past, detected no less than three Giblet[17] families making their first onset toward style and gentility in the very manner we have heretofore reprobated. Nor have our utmost efforts been able to check the progress of that alarming epidemic, the rage for punning,[18] which, though doubtless originally intended merely to ornament and enliven conversation by little sports of fancy, threatens to overrun and poison the whole, like the baneful ivy which destroys the useful plant it first embellished. Now I look upon a habitual punster as a depredator upon conversation; and I have remarked sometimes one of these offenders, sitting silent on the watch for an hour together, until some luckless wight, unfortunately for the ease and quiet of the company, dropped a phrase susceptible of a double meaning:—when—pop, our punster would dart out like a veteran mouser from her covert, seize the unlucky word, and after worrying and mumbling at it until it was capable of no further marring, relapse again into silent watchfulness, and lie in wait for another opportunity. Even this might be borne with, by the aid of a little philosophy; but the worst of it is, they are not content to manufacture puns and laugh heartily at them themselves; but they expect we should laugh with them, which I consider as an intolerable hardship, and a flagrant imposition on good nature. Let those gentlemen fritter away conversation with impunity, and deal out their wits in sixpenny bits if they please; but I beg

I may have the choice of refusing currency to their small change. I am seriously afraid, however, that our junto is not quite free from the infection—nay, that it has even approached so near as to menace the tranquillity of my elbow-chair; for, Will Wizard, as we were in caucus the other night, absolutely electrified Pindar and myself with a most palpable and perplexing pun; had it been a torpedo, it could not have more discomposed the fraternity. Sentence of banishment was unanimously decreed; but on his confessing that, like many celebrated wits, he was merely retailing other men's wares on commission, he was for that once forgiven on condition of refraining from such diabolical practices in future. Pindar is particularly outrageous against punsters; and quite astonished and put me to a nonplus a day or two since, by asking abruptly "whether I thought a punster could be a good Christian?" He followed up his question triumphantly by offering to prove, by sound logic and historical fact, that the Roman Empire owed its decline and fall to a pun; and that nothing tended so much to demoralize the French nation, as their abominable rage for *jeux de mots*.

But what, above everything else, has caused me much vexation of spirit, and displeased me most with this stiff-necked nation is, that in spite of all the serious and profound censures of the sage Mustapha,[19] in his various letters—they *will talk!*— they will still wag their tongues, and chatter like very slang-whangers! This is a degree of obstinacy incomprehensible in the extreme; and is another proof how alarming is the force of habit, and how difficult it is to reduce beings, accustomed to talk, to that state of silence which is the very acme of human wisdom.

We can only account for these disappointments in our moderate and reasonable expectations, by supposing the world so deeply sunk in the mire of delinquency, that not even Hercules, were he to put his shoulder to the axletree, would be able to extricate it. We comfort ourselves, however, by the reflection that there are at least three good men left in this degenerate age to benefit the world by example, should precept ultimately fail. And borrowing, for once, an example from certain sleepy writers who, after the first emotions of surprise at finding their invaluable effusions neglected or despised, console themselves with the idea that 'tis a stupid age, and look forward to posterity for redress—we bequeath our volume to future generations—and much good may it do them. Heaven grant they may be able to read it! for, if our fashionable mode of education continues to improve, as of late, I am under serious apprehensions that the period is not far distant when the discipline of the dancing-master will supersede that of the grammarian: crotchets and quavers supplant the alphabet: and the heels, by an antipodean manœuvre, obtain entire preëminence over the head. How does my heart yearn for poor, dear posterity when this work shall become unintelligible to our grandchildren as it seems to be to their grandfathers and grandmothers.

In fact—for I love to be candid—we begin to suspect that many people read our numbers merely for their amusement, without paying any attention to the serious truths conveyed in every page. Unpardonable want of penetration! not that we wish to restrict our readers in the article of laughing, which we consider as one of the dearest prerogatives of man, and the distinguishing characteristic which raises him above all other animals: let them laugh, therefore, if they will, provided they profit at the same time, and do not mistake our object. It is one of our indisputable facts that it is easier to laugh ten follies out of countenance than to coax, reason, or flog a man out of one. In this odd, singular, and indescribable age—which is neither the age of gold, silver, iron, brass, chivalry, or *pills*, as Sir John Carr[20] asserts—a grave writer who attempts to attack folly with the heavy artillery of moral reasoning, will fare like Smollett's honest pedant, who clearly demonstrated by angles, etc., after the manner of Euclid, that it was wrong to do evil—and was laughed at for his pains. Take my word for it, a little well-applied ridicule, like Hannibal's application of vinegar to rocks, will do more with certain hard heads and obdurate hearts, than all the logic or demonstrations in Longinus or Euclid. But the people of Gotham, wise souls! are so much accustomed to see morality approach them clothed in formidable wigs and sable garbs, "with leaden eye that loves the ground," that they can never recognize her when, drest in gay attire, she comes tripping toward them with smiles and sunshine in her countenance.——— Well, let the rogues remain in happy ignorance, for "ignorance is bliss," as the poet says—and I put as implicit faith in poetry as I do in the almanac or the newspaper. We will improve them, without their being the wiser for it, and they shall become better in spite of their teeth, and without their having the least suspicion of the reformation working within them.

Among all our manifold grievances, however, still some small but vivid rays of sunshine occasionally brighten along our path; cheering our steps, and inviting us to persevere.

The public have paid some little regard to a few articles of our advice; they have purchased our numbers freely—so much the better for our publisher; they have read them attentively— so much the better for themselves. The melancholy fate of my dear aunt Charity[21] has had a wonderful effect; and I have now before me a letter from a gentleman who lives opposite to a couple of old ladies, remarkable for the interest they took in his affairs; his apartments were absolutely in a state of blockade, and he was on the point of changing his lodgings, or capitulat- ing, until the appearance of our ninth number, which he imme- diately sent over with his compliments. The good ladies took the hint, and have scarcely appeared at their window since. As to the wooden gentlemen,[22] our friend, Miss Sparkle, assures me, they are wonderfully improved by our criticisms, and some- times venture to make a remark, or attempt a pun in company, to the great edification of all who happen to understand them. As to the red shawls, they are entirely discarded from the fair shoulders of our ladies—ever since the last importation of finery—nor has any lady, since the cold weather, ventured to expose her elbows to the admiring gaze of scrutinizing passen- gers. But there is one victory we have achieved which has given us more pleasure than to have written down the whole administration: I am assured, from unquestionable authority, that our young ladies—doubtless in consequence of our weighty admonitions—have not once indulged in that intoxicating,

inflammatory, and whirligig dance, the waltz—ever since hot
weather commenced. True it is, I understand, an attempt was
made to exhibit it by some of the sable fair ones at the last
African ball, but it was highly disapproved of by all the respectable elderly ladies present.

These are sweet sources of comfort to atone for the many
wrongs and misrepresentations heaped upon us by the world—
for even we have experienced its ill-nature. How often have we
heard ourselves reproached for the insidious applications of the
uncharitable!—how often have we been accused of emotions
which never found an entrance into our bosoms!—how often
have our sportive effusions been wrested to serve the purposes
of particular enmity and bitterness!——Meddlesome spirits!
little do they know our disposition; we "lack gall" to wound
the feelings of a single innocent individual; we can even forgive
them from the very bottom of our souls; may they meet as
ready a forgiveness from their own consciences! Like true and
independent bachelors, having no domestic cares to interfere
with our general benevolence, we consider it incumbent upon
us to watch over the welfare of society; and although we are
indebted to the world for little else than left-handed favors, yet
we feel a proud satisfaction in requiting evil with good, and the
sneer of illiberality with the unfeigned smile of good humor.
With these mingled motives of selfishness and philanthropy we
commenced our work, and if we cannot solace ourselves with
the consciousness of having done much good, yet there is still
one pleasing consolation left, which the world can neither give
nor take away. There are moments—lingering moments of listless indifference and heavy-hearted despondency—when our
best hopes and affections slipping, as they sometimes will, from
their hold on those objects to which they usually cling for support, seem abandoned on the wide waste of cheerless existence,
without a place to cast anchor; without a shore in view to excite
a single wish, or to give a momentary interest to contemplation.
We look back with delight upon many of these moments of
mental gloom, whiled away by the cheerful exercise of our pen,
and consider every such triumph over the spleen as retarding

the furrowing hand of time in its insidious encroachments on our brows. If, in addition to our own amusements, we have, as we jogged carelessly laughing along, brushed away one tear of dejection and called forth a smile in its place—if we have brightened the pale countenance of a child of sorrow—we shall feel almost as much joy and rejoicing as a slang-whanger does when he bathes his pen in the heart's blood of a patron and benefactor, or sacrifices one more illustrious victim on the altar of party animosity.

From BOOK III: IN WHICH IS RECORDED THE GOLDEN REIGN OF WOUTER VAN TWILLER

CHAPTER I

OF THE RENOWNED WOUTER VAN TWILLER, HIS UNPARALLELED VIRTUES—AS LIKEWISE HIS UNUTTERABLE WISDOM IN THE LAW CASE OF WANDLE SCHOONHOVEN AND BARENT BLEECKER—AND THE GREAT ADMIRATION OF THE PUBLIC THEREAT

Grievous and very much to be commiserated is the task of the feeling historian, who writes the history of his native land. If it fall to his lot to be the recorder of calamity or crime, the mournful page is watered with his tears—nor can he recall the most prosperous and blissful era, without a melancholy sigh at the reflection, that it has passed away for ever! I know not whether it be owing to an immoderate love for the simplicity of former times, or to that certain tenderness of heart incident to all sentimental historians; but I candidly confess that I cannot look back on the happier days of our city, which I now describe, without great dejection of spirit. With faltering hand do I withdraw the curtain of oblivion, that veils the modest merit of our venerable ancestors, and as their figures rise to my mental vision, humble myself before their mighty shades.

Such are my feelings when I revisit the family mansion of the Knickerbockers, and spend a lonely hour in the chamber where hang the portraits of my forefathers, shrouded in dust, like the forms they represent. With pious reverence do I gaze on the countenances of those renowned burghers, who have preceded me in the steady march of existence—whose sober and temperate blood now meanders through my veins, flowing slower and slower in its feeble conduits, until its current shall soon be stopped for ever!

These, I say to myself, are but frail memorials of the mighty
men who flourished in the days of the patriarchs; but who, alas,
have long since mouldered in that tomb, towards which my
steps are insensibly and irresistibly hastening! As I pace the
darkened chamber and lose myself in melancholy musings, the
shadowy images around me almost seem to steal once more into
existence—their countenances to assume the animation of life—
their eyes to pursue me in every movement! Carried away by
the delusions of fancy, I almost imagine myself surrounded by
the shades of the departed, and holding sweet converse with the
worthies of antiquity! Ah, hapless Diedrich! born in a degenerate age, abandoned to the buffetings of fortune—a stranger
and a weary pilgrim in thy native land—blest with no weeping
wife, nor family of helpless children; but doomed to wander
neglected through those crowded streets, and elbowed by foreign upstarts from those fair abodes where once thine ancestors
held sovereign empire!

Let me not, however, lose the historian in the man, nor suffer
the doting recollections of age to overcome me, while dwelling
with fond garrulity on the virtuous days of the patriarchs—on
those sweet days of simplicity and ease, which never more will
dawn on the lovely island of Manna-hata.

These melancholy reflections have been forced from me by
the growing wealth and importance of New Amsterdam, which,
I plainly perceive, are to involve it in all kinds of perils and disasters. Already, as I observed at the close of my last book, they
had awakened the attentions of the mother country. The usual
mark of protection shown by mother countries to wealthy
colonies was forthwith manifested; a governor being sent out
to rule over the province and squeeze out of it as much revenue
as possible. The arrival of a governor of course put an end to
the protectorate of Oloffe the Dreamer. He appears, however,
to have dreamt to some purpose during his sway, as we find
him afterwards living as a patroon on a great landed estate on
the banks of the Hudson; having virtually forfeited all right to
his ancient appellation of Kortlandt or Lackland.

It was in the year of our Lord 1629 [24] that Mynheer Wouter

Van Twiller was appointed governor of the province of Nieuw Nederlandts, under the commission and control of their High Mightinesses the Lords States General of the United Netherlands, and the privileged West India Company.

This renowned old gentleman arrived at New Amsterdam in the merry month of June, the sweetest month in all the year; when dan Apollo seems to dance up the transparent firmament —when the robin, the thrush, and a thousand other wanton songsters make the woods to resound with amorous ditties, and the luxurious little boblincon revels among the clover blossoms of the meadows—all which happy coincidence persuaded the old dames of New Amsterdam, who were skilled in the art of foretelling events, that this was to be a happy and prosperous administration.

The renowned Wouter (or Walter) Van Twiller, was descended from a long line of Dutch burgomasters, who had successively dozed away their lives, and grown fat upon the bench of magistracy in Rotterdam; and who had comported themselves with such singular wisdom and propriety, that they were never either heard or talked of—which, next to being universally applauded, should be the object of ambition of all magistrates and rulers. There are two opposite ways by which some men make a figure in the world; one by talking faster than they think; and the other by holding their tongues and not thinking at all. By the first, many a smatterer acquires the reputation of a man of quick parts; by the other, many a dunderpate, like the owl, the stupidest of birds, comes to be considered the very type of wisdom. This, by the way, is a casual remark, which I would not, for the universe, have it thought I apply to Governor Van Twiller. It is true he was a man shut up within himself, like an oyster, and rarely spoke except in monosyllables; but then it was allowed he seldom said a foolish thing. So invincible was his gravity that he was never known to laugh or even to smile through the whole course of a long and prosperous life. Nay if a joke were uttered in his presence, that set light minded hearers in a roar, it was observed to throw him into a state of perplexity. Sometimes he would deign to inquire into the matter, and when, after much explanation, the joke was made as plain as a pike-staff, he would continue to smoke his pipe in silence, and at length, knocking out the ashes would exclaim, "Well! I see nothing in all that to laugh about."

With all his reflective habits, he never made up his mind on a subject. His adherents accounted for this by the astonishing magnitude of his ideas. He conceived every subject on so grand a scale that he had not room in his head to turn it over and examine both sides of it. Certain it is that if any matter were propounded to him on which ordinary mortals would rashly determine at first glance, he would put on a vague, mysterious look; shake his capacious head; smoke some time in profound silence, and at length observe that "he had his doubts about the matter;" which gained him the reputation of a man slow of belief and not easily imposed upon. What is more, it gained him a lasting name: for to this habit of the mind has been attributed his surname of Twiller; which is said to be a corruption of the original Twijfler, or, in plain English, *Doubter.*

The person of this illustrious old gentleman was formed and proportioned, as though it had been moulded by the hands of some cunning Dutch statuary, as a model of majesty and lordly grandeur. He was exactly five feet six inches in height, and six feet five inches in circumference. His head was a perfect sphere, and of such stupendous dimensions, that dame Nature, with all her sex's ingenuity, would have been puzzled to construct a neck capable of supporting it; wherefore she wisely declined the attempt, and settled it firmly on the top of his back bone, just between the shoulders. His body was oblong and particularly capacious at bottom; which was wisely ordered by Providence, seeing that he was a man of sedentary habits, and very averse to the idle labor of walking. His legs were short, but sturdy in proportion to the weight they had to sustain; so that when erect he had not a little the appearance of a beer barrel on skids. His face, that infallible index of the mind, presented a vast expanse, unfurrowed by any of those lines and angles which disfigure the human countenance with what is termed expression. Two small grey eyes twinkled feebly in the midst, like two stars of lesser magnitude in a hazy firmament; and his full-fed cheeks, which seemed to have taken toll of every thing that went into his mouth, were curiously mottled and streaked with dusky red, like a spitzenberg apple.

His habits were as regular as his person. He daily took his four stated meals, appropriating exactly an hour to each; he smoked and doubted eight hours, and he slept the remaining twelve of the four and twenty. Such was the renowned Wouter Van Twiller—a true philosopher, for his mind was either elevated above, or tranquilly settled below, the cares and perplexities of this world. He had lived in it for years, without feeling the least curiosity to know whether the sun revolved round it, or it round the sun; and he had watched, for at least half a century, the smoke curling from his pipe to the ceiling, without once troubling his head with any of those numerous theories, by which a philosopher would have perplexed his brain, in accounting for its rising above the surrounding atmosphere.

In his council he presided with great state and solemnity. He sat in a huge chair of solid oak, hewn in the celebrated forest of the Hague, fabricated by an experienced timmerman of Amsterdam, and curiously carved about the arms and feet, into exact imitations of gigantic eagle's claws. Instead of a sceptre he swayed a long Turkish pipe, wrought with jasmin and amber, which had been presented to a stadtholder of Holland, at the conclusion of a treaty with one of the petty Barbary powers. In this stately chair would he sit, and this magnificent pipe would he smoke, shaking his right knee with a constant motion, and fixing his eye for hours together upon a little print of Amsterdam, which hung in a black frame against the opposite wall of the council chamber. Nay, it has even been said, that when any deliberation of extraordinary length and intricacy was on the carpet, the renowned Wouter would shut his eyes for full two hours at a time, that he might not be disturbed by external objects—and at such times the internal commotion of his mind was evinced by certain regular guttural sounds, which his admirers declared were merely the noise of conflict, made by his contending doubts and opinions.

It is with infinite difficulty I have been enabled to collect these biographical anecdotes of the great man under consideration. The facts respecting him were so scattered and vague, and divers of them so questionable in point of authenticity, that I have had to give up the search after many, and decline the admission of still more, which would have tended to heighten the coloring of his portrait.

I have been the more anxious to delineate fully the person and habits of Wouter Van Twiller, from the consideration that he was not only the first, but also the best governor that ever presided over this ancient and respectable province; and so tranquil and benevolent was his reign, that I do not find throughout the whole of it, a single instance of any offender being brought to punishment—a most indubitable sign of a merciful governor, and a case unparalleled, excepting in the reign of the illustrious King Log, from whom, it is hinted, the renowned Van Twiller was a lineal descendant.

The very outset of the career of this excellent magistrate was distinguished by an example of legal acumen, that gave flattering presage of a wise and equitable administration. The morning after he had been installed in office, and at the moment that he was making his breakfast from a prodigious earthen dish, filled with milk and Indian pudding, he was interrupted by the appearance of Wandle Schoonhoven, a very important old burgher of New Amsterdam, who complained bitterly of one Barent Bleecker, inasmuch as he refused to come to a settlement of accounts, seeing that there was a heavy balance in favor of the said Wandle. Governor Van Twiller, as I have already observed, was a man of few words; he was likewise a mortal enemy to multiplying writings—or being disturbed at his breakfast. Having listened attentively to the statement of Wandle Schoonhoven, giving an occasional grunt, as he shovelled a spoonful of Indian pudding into his mouth—either as a sign that he relished the dish, or comprehended the story—he called unto him his constable, and pulling out of his breeches pocket a huge jack-knife, dispatched it after the defendant as a summons, accompanied by his tobacco-box as a warrant.

This summary process was as effectual in those simple days as was the seal ring of the great Haroun Alraschid among the true believers. The two parties being confronted before him, each produced a book of accounts, written in a language and character that would have puzzled any but a High Dutch commentator, or a learned decipherer of Egyptian obelisks. The sage Wouter took them one after the other, and having poised them in his hands, and attentively counted over the number of leaves, fell straightway into a very great doubt, and smoked for half an hour without saying a word; at length, laying his finger beside his nose, and shutting his eyes for a moment, with the air of a man who has just caught a subtle idea by the tail, he slowly took his pipe from his mouth, puffed forth a column of tobacco smoke, and with marvellous gravity and solemnity pronounced—that having carefully counted over the leaves and weighed the books, it was found, that one was just as thick and as heavy as the other—therefore it was the final opinion of the court that the accounts were equally balanced—therefore Wandle should give Barent a receipt, and Barent should give Wandle a receipt—and the constable should pay the costs.

This decision being straightway made known, diffused general joy throughout New Amsterdam, for the people immediately perceived, that they had a very wise and equitable magistrate to rule over them. But its happiest effect was, that not another lawsuit took place throughout the whole of his administration—and the office of constable fell into such decay, that there was not one of those losel scouts known in the province for many years. I am the more particular in dwelling on this transaction, not only because I deem it one of the most sage and righteous judgments on record, and well worthy the attention of modern magistrates; but because it was a miraculous event in the history of the renowned Wouter—being the only time he was ever known to come to a decision in the whole course of his life.

CHAPTER IV

CONTAINING FURTHER PARTICULARS OF THE GOLDEN AGE, AND
    WHAT CONSTITUTED A FINE LADY AND GENTLEMAN IN THE
    DAYS OF WALTER THE DOUBTER

In this dulcet period of my history, when the beauteous island
of Manna-hata presented a scene, the very counterpart of those
glowing pictures drawn of the golden reign of Saturn, there
was, as I have before observed, a happy ignorance, an honest
simplicity prevalent among its inhabitants, which, were I even
able to depict, would be but little understood by the degenerate
age for which I am doomed to write. Even the female sex,
those arch innovators upon the tranquillity, the honesty, and
gray-beard customs of society, seemed for a while to conduct
themselves with incredible sobriety and comeliness.

Their hair, untortured by the abominations of art, was
scrupulously pomatumed back from their foreheads with a candle, and covered with a little cap of quilted calico, which fitted
exactly to their heads. Their petticoats of linsey-woolsey were
striped with a variety of gorgeous dyes—though I must confess these gallant garments were rather short, scarce reaching
below the knee; but then they made up in the number, which
generally equalled that of the gentleman's small clothes; and
what is still more praiseworthy, they were all of their own
manufacture—of which circumstance, as may well be supposed,
they were not a little vain.

These were the honest days in which every woman staid at
home, read the Bible, and wore pockets—ay, and that too of a
goodly size, fashioned with patchwork into many curious
devices, and ostentatiously worn on the outside. These, in fact,
were convenient receptacles, where all good housewives carefully stored away such things as they wished to have at hand;
by which means they often came to be incredibly crammed—
and I remember there was a story current when I was a boy that
the lady of Wouter Van Twiller once had occasion to empty
her right pocket in search of a wooden ladle, when the

contents filled a couple of corn baskets, and the utensil was discovered lying among some rubbish in one corner—but we must not give too much faith to all these stories; the anecdotes of those remote periods being very subject to exaggeration.

Besides these notable pockets, they likewise wore scissors and pincushions suspended from their girdles by red ribands, or among the more opulent and showy classes, by brass, and even silver chains—indubitable tokens of thrifty housewives and industrious spinsters. I cannot say much in vindication of the shortness of the petticoats; it doubtless was introduced for the purpose of giving the stockings a chance to be seen, which were generally of blue worsted with magnificent red clocks—or perhaps to display a well-turned ankle, and a neat, though serviceable foot, set off by a high-heeled leathern shoe, with a large and splendid silver buckle. Thus we find that the gentle sex in all ages have shown the same disposition to infringe a little upon the laws of decorum, in order to betray a lurking beauty, or gratify an innocent love of finery.

From the sketch here given, it will be seen that our good grandmothers differed considerably in their ideas of a fine figure from their scantily dressed descendants of the present day. A fine lady, in those times, waddled under more clothes, even on a fair summer's day, than would have clad the whole bevy of a modern ball-room. Nor were they the less admired by the gentlemen in consequence thereof. On the contrary, the greatness of a lover's passion seemed to increase in proportion to the magnitude of its object—and a voluminous damsel arrayed in a dozen of petticoats, was declared by a Low Dutch sonneteer of the province to be radiant as a sunflower, and luxuriant as a full-blown cabbage. Certain it is, that in those days the heart of a lover could not contain more than one lady at a time; whereas the heart of a modern gallant has often room enough to accommodate half a dozen. The reason of which I conclude to be, that either the hearts of the gentlemen have grown larger, or the persons of the ladies smaller—this, however, is a question for physiologists to determine.

But there was a secret charm in these petticoats, which, no

doubt, entered into the consideration of the prudent gallants.
The wardrobe of a lady was in those days her only fortune; and
she who had a good stock of petticoats and stockings, was as
absolutely an heiress as is a Kamschatka damsel with a store of
bearskins, or a Lapland belle with a plenty of reindeer. The
ladies, therefore, were very anxious to display these powerful
attractions to the greatest advantage; and the best rooms in the
house, instead of being adorned with caricatures of dame Nature, in water colors and needle work, were always hung round
with abundance of homespun garments, the manufacture and
the property of the females—a piece of laudable ostentation
that still prevails among the heiresses of our Dutch villages.

The gentlemen, in fact, who figured in the circles of the gay
world in these ancient times, corresponded, in most particulars, with the beauteous damsels whose smiles they were ambitious to deserve. True it is, their merits would make but a very
inconsiderable impression upon the heart of a modern fair;
they neither drove their curricles, nor sported their tandems,
for as yet those gaudy vehicles were not even dreamt of—
neither did they distinguish themselves by their brilliancy at
the table, and their consequent rencontres with watchmen, for
our forefathers were of too pacific a disposition to need those
guardians of the night, every soul throughout the town being
sound asleep before nine o'clock. Neither did they establish
their claims to gentility at the expense of their tailors—for as
yet those offenders against the pockets of society, and the tranquillity of all aspiring young gentlemen, were unknown in New
Amsterdam; every good housewife made the clothes of her
husband and family, and even the goede vrouw of Van Twiller
himself thought it no disparagement to cut out her husband's
linsey-woolsey galligaskins.

Not but what there were some two or three youngsters who
manifested the first dawning of what is called fire and spirit;
who held all labor in contempt; skulked about docks and market-places; loitered in the sunshine; squandered what little
money they could procure at hustle-cap and chuck-farthing;
swore, boxed, fought cocks, and raced their neighbor's horses

—in short, who promised to be the wonder, the talk, and abomination of the town, had not their stylish career been unfortunately cut short by an affair of honor with a whipping-post.

Far other, however, was the truly fashionable gentleman of those days—his dress, which served for both morning and evening, street and drawing-room, was a linsey-woolsey coat, made, perhaps, by the fair hands of the mistress of his affections, and gallantly bedecked with abundance of large brass buttons —half a score of breeches heightened the proportions of his figure—his shoes were decorated by enormous copper buckles —a low-crowned broad-rimmed hat overshadowed his burly visage, and his hair dangled down his back in a prodigious queue of eelskin.

Thus equipped, he would manfully sally forth with pipe in mouth to besiege some fair damsel's obdurate heart—not such a pipe, good reader, as that which Acis did sweetly tune in praise of his Galatea, but one of true Delft manufacture, and furnished with a charge of fragrant tobacco. With this would he resolutely set himself down before the fortress, and rarely failed, in the process of time, to smoke the fair enemy into a surrender, upon honorable terms.

Such was the happy reign of Wouter Van Twiller, celebrated in many a long forgotten song as the real golden age, the rest being nothing but counterfeit copper-washed coin. In that delightful period, a sweet and holy calm reigned over the whole province. The burgomaster smoked his pipe in peace— the substantial solace of his domestic cares, after her daily toils were done, sat soberly at the door, with her arms crossed over her apron of snowy white, without being insulted with ribald street walkers or vagabond boys—those unlucky urchins who do so infest our streets, displaying, under the roses of youth, the thorns and briers of iniquity. Then it was that the lover with ten breeches, and the damsel with petticoats of half a score, indulged in all the innocent endearments of virtuous love without fear and without reproach; for what had that virtue to fear, which was defended by a shield of good linsey-woolseys, equal at least to the seven bull hides of the invincible Ajax?

Ah blissful, and never to be forgotten age! when every thing was better than it has ever been since, or ever will be again—when Buttermilk Channel was quite dry at low water—when the shad in the Hudson were all salmon, and when the moon shone with a pure and resplendent whiteness, instead of that melancholy yellow light which is the consequence of her sickening at the abominations she every night witnesses in this degenerate city!

Happy would it have been for New Amsterdam could it always have existed in this state of blissful ignorance and lowly simplicity, but alas! the days of childhood are too sweet to last! Cities, like men, grow out of them in time, and are doomed alike to grow into the bustle, the cares, and miseries of the world. Let no man congratulate himself, when he beholds the child of his bosom or the city of his birth increasing in magnitude and importance—let the history of his own life teach him the dangers of the one, and this excellent little history of Mannahata convince him of the calamities of the other.

CHAPTER IX

HOW THE FORT GOED HOOP WAS FEARFULLY BELEAGUERED—
HOW THE RENOWNED WOUTER FELL INTO A PROFOUND
DOUBT, AND HOW HE FINALLY EVAPORATED

By this time my readers must fully perceive what an arduous task I have undertaken—exploring a little kind of Herculaneum of history, which had lain nearly for ages buried under the rubbish of years, and almost totally forgotten—raking up the limbs and fragments of disjointed facts, and endeavoring to put them scrupulously together, so as to restore them to their original form and connection—now lugging forth the character of an almost forgotten hero, like a mutilated statue—now deciphering a half-defaced inscription, and now lighting upon a mouldering manuscript, which, after painful study, scarce repays the trouble of perusal.

In such case how much has the reader to depend upon the honor and probity of his author, lest, like a cunning antiquarian, he either impose upon him some spurious fabrication of his own, for a precious relic of antiquity—or else dress up the dismembered fragment with such false trappings, that it is scarcely possible to distinguish the truth from the fiction with which it is enveloped. This is a grievance which I have more than once had to lament, in the course of my wearisome researches among the works of my fellow historians, who have strangely disguised and distorted the facts respecting this country; and particularly respecting the great province of New Netherlands; as will be perceived by any who will take the trouble to compare their romantic effusions, tricked out in the meretricious gauds of fable, with this authentic history.

I have had more vexations of the kind to encounter, in those parts of my history which treat of the transactions on the eastern border, than in any other, in consequence of the troops of historians who have infested these quarters, and have shown the honest people of Nieuw Nederlandts no mercy in their works. Among the rest, Mr. Benjamin Trumbull arrogantly declares, that "the Dutch were always mere intruders." Now to this I shall make no other reply, than to proceed in the steady narration of my history, which will contain not only proofs that the Dutch had clear title and possession in the fair valleys of the Connecticut, and that they were wrongfully dispossessed thereof—but likewise, that they have been scandalously maltreated ever since, by the misrepresentations of the crafty historians of New England. And in this I shall be guided by a spirit of truth and impartiality, and a regard to immortal fame —for I would not wittingly dishonor my work by a single falsehood, misrepresentation, or prejudice, though it should gain our forefathers the whole country of New England.

I have already noticed in a former chapter of my history, that the territories of the Nieuw Nederlandts extended on the east, quite to the Varsche or fresh, or Connecticut river. Here, at an early period, had been established a frontier post on the bank of the river, and called Fort Goed Hoop, not far from the site of the present fair city of Hartford. It was placed under the command of Jacobus Van Curlet, or Curlis, as some historians will have it; a doughty soldier, of that stomachful class famous for eating all they kill. He was long in the body and short in the limb, as though a tall man's body had been mounted on a little man's legs. He made up for this turnspit construction by striding to such an extent, that you would have sworn he had on the seven-leagued boots of Jack the Giant-killer; and so high did he tread on parade that his soldiers were sometimes alarmed lest he should trample himself under foot.

But notwithstanding the erection of this fort and the appointment of this ugly little man of war as commander, the Yankees continued the interlopings hinted at in my last chapter, and at length had the audacity to *squat* themselves down within the jurisdiction of Fort Goed Hoop.

The long-bodied Van Curlet protested with great spirit against these unwarrantable encroachments, couching his protest in Low Dutch, by way of inspiring more terror, and forthwith dispatched a copy of the protest to the governor at New Amsterdam, together with a long and bitter account of the aggressions of the enemy. This done, he ordered his men, one and all, to be of good cheer—shut the gate of the fort, smoked three pipes, went to bed, and awaited the result with a resolute and intrepid tranquillity, that greatly animated his adherents, and no doubt struck sore dismay and affright into the hearts of the enemy.

Now it came to pass, that about this time, the renowned Wouter Van Twiller, full of years and honors, and council dinners, had reached that period of life and faculty which, according to the great Gulliver, entitles a man to admission into the ancient order of Struldbruggs. He employed his time in smoking his Turkish pipe, amid an assemblage of sages, equally enlightened and nearly as venerable as himself, and who, for their silence, their gravity, their wisdom, and their cautious averseness to coming to any conclusion in business, are only to be equalled by certain profound corporations which I have known in my time. Upon reading the protest of the gallant Jacobus Van Curlet, therefore, his excellency fell straightway into one of the deepest doubts that ever he was known to encounter;

his capacious head gradually drooped on his chest, he closed his eyes, and inclined his ear to one side, as if listening with great attention to the discussion that was going on in his belly; and which all who knew him declared to be the huge court-house or council-chamber of his thoughts; forming to his head what the house of representatives does to the Senate. An inarticulate sound, very much resembling a snore, occasionally escaped him—but the nature of this internal cogitation was never known, as he never opened his lips on the subject to man, woman, or child. In the mean time, the protest of Van Curlet lay quietly on the table, where it served to light the pipes of the venerable sages assembled in council; and in the great smoke which they raised, the gallant Jacobus, his protest, and his mighty Fort Goed Hoop, were soon as completely beclouded and forgotten, as is a question of emergency swallowed up in the speeches and resolutions of a modern session of Congress.

There are certain emergencies when your profound legislators and sage deliberative councils are mightily in the way of a nation; and when an ounce of hare-brained decision is worth a pound of sage doubt and cautious discussion. Such, at least, was the case at present; for while the renowned Wouter Van Twiller was daily battling with his doubts, and his resolution growing weaker and weaker in the contest, the enemy pushed farther and farther into his territories, and assumed a most formidable appearance in the neighborhood of Fort Goed Hoop. Here they founded the mighty town of *Pyquag*, or, as it has since been called, *Weathersfield*, a place which, if we may credit the assertions of that worthy historian, John Josselyn, Gent., "hath been infamous by reason of the witches therein." And so daring did these men of Pyquag become, that they extended those plantations of onions, for which their town is illustrious, under the very noses of the garrison of Fort Goed Hoop—insomuch that the honest Dutchmen could not look toward that quarter without tears in their eyes.

This crying injustice was regarded with proper indignation by the gallant Jacobus Van Curlet. He absolutely trembled with the violence of his choler and the exacerbations of his valor; which were the more turbulent in their workings, from the length of the body in which they were agitated. He forthwith proceeded to strengthen his redoubts, heighten his breastworks, deepen his fosse, and fortify his position with a double row of abbatis; after which he dispatched a fresh courier with accounts of his perilous situation.

The courier chosen to bear the dispatches was a fat, oily little man, as being less liable to be worn out, or to lose leather on the journey; and to insure his speed, he was mounted on the fleetest wagon-horse in the garrison, remarkable for length of limb, largeness of bone, and hardness of trot; and so tall, that the little messenger was obliged to climb on his back by means of his tail and crupper. Such extraordinary speed did he make, that he arrived at Fort Amsterdam in a little less than a month, though the distance was full two hundred pipes, or about one hundred and twenty miles.

With an appearance of great hurry and business, and smoking a short travelling-pipe, he proceeded on a long swing trot through the muddy lanes of the metropolis, demolishing whole batches of dirt pies, which the little Dutch children were making in the road; and for which kind of pastry the children of this city have ever been famous. On arriving at the governor's house, he climbed down from his steed; roused the grayheaded doorkeeper, old Skaats, who, like his lineal descendant and faithful representative, the venerable crier of our court, was nodding at his post—rattled at the door of the council chamber, and startled the members as they were dozing over a plan for establishing a public market.

At that very moment a gentle grunt, or rather a deep-drawn snore, was heard from the chair of the governor; a whiff of smoke was at the same instant observed to escape from his lips, and a light cloud to ascend from the bowl of his pipe. The council, of course, supposed him engaged in deep sleep for the good of the community, and, according to custom in all such cases established, every man bawled out silence, when, of a sudden, the door flew open, and the little courier straddled into the apartment, cased to the middle in a pair of Hessian boots, which he had got into for the sake of expedition. In his right hand he held forth the ominous dispatches, and with his left he grasped firmly the waistband of his galligaskins, which had unfortunately given way, in the exertion of descending from his horse. He stumped resolutely up to the governor, and with more hurry than perspicuity delivered his message. But fortunately his ill tidings came too late to ruffle the tranquillity of this most tranquil of rulers. His venerable excellency had just breathed and smoked his last—his lungs and his pipe having been exhausted together, and his peaceful soul having escaped in the last whiff that curled from his tobacco-pipe. In a word, the renowned Walter the Doubter, who had so often slumbered with his contemporaries, now slept with his fathers, and Wilhelmus Kieft governed in his stead.

From BOOK IV: CONTAINING THE CHRONICLES OF THE REIGN OF WILLIAM THE TESTY[25]

CHAPTER I

SHOWING THE NATURE OF HISTORY IN GENERAL; CONTAINING FARTHERMORE THE UNIVERSAL ACQUIREMENTS OF WILLIAM THE TESTY, AND HOW A MAN MAY LEARN SO MUCH AS TO RENDER HIMSELF GOOD FOR NOTHING

When the lofty Thucydides is about to enter upon his description of the plague that desolated Athens, one of his modern commentators assures the reader, that the history is now going to be exceeding solemn, serious, and pathetic; and hints, with that air of chuckling gratulation with which a good dame draws forth a choice morsel from a cupboard to regale a favorite, that this plague will give his history a most agreeable variety.

In like manner did my heart leap within me, when I came to the dolorous dilemma of Fort Goed Hoop, which I at once perceived to be the forerunner of a series of great events and entertaining disasters. Such are the true subjects for the historic pen.

For what is history, in fact, but a kind of Newgate calendar, a register of the crimes and miseries that man has inflicted on his fellow-man? It is a huge libel on human nature, to which we industriously add page after page, volume after volume, as if we were building up a monument to the honor, rather than the infamy of our species. If we turn over the pages of these chronicles that man has written of himself, what are the characters dignified by the appellation of great, and held up to the admiration of posterity? Tyrants, robbers, conquerors, renowned only for the magnitude of their misdeeds, and the stupendous wrongs and miseries they have inflicted on mankind—warriors, who have hired themselves to the trade of blood, not from motives of virtuous patriotism, or to protect the injured and defenceless, but merely to gain the vaunted glory of being adroit and successful in massacring their fellow-beings! What are the great events that constitute a glorious era?—The fall of empires—the desolation of happy countries —splendid cities smoking in their ruins—the proudest works of art tumbled in the dust—the shrieks and groans of whole nations ascending unto heaven!

It is thus the historian may be said to thrive on the miseries of mankind, like birds of prey which hover over the field of battle, to fatten on the mighty dead. It was observed by a great projector of inland lock navigation, that rivers, lakes, and oceans, were only formed to feed canals.—In like manner I am tempted to believe, that plots, conspiracies, wars, victories, and massacres, are ordained by Providence only as food for the historian.

It is a source of great delight to the philosopher, in studying the wonderful economy of nature, to trace the mutual dependencies of things, how they are created reciprocally for each other, and how the most noxious and apparently unnecessary animal has its uses. Thus those swarms of flies, which are so often execrated as useless vermin, are created for the sustenance of spiders—and spiders, on the other hand, are evidently made to devour flies. So those heroes who have been such scourges to the world, were bounteously provided as themes for the poet and historian, while the poet and the historian were destined to record the achievements of heroes!

These, and many similar reflections, naturally arose in my mind, as I took up my pen to commence the reign of William Kieft: for now the stream of our history, which hitherto has rolled in a tranquil current, is about to depart forever from its peaceful haunts, and brawl through many a turbulent and rugged scene.

As some sleek ox, sunk in the rich repose of a clover-field, dozing and chewing the cud, will bear repeated blows before it raises itself; so the province of Nieuw Nederlandts, having waxed fat under the drowsy reign of the Doubter, needed cuffs and kicks to rouse it into action. The reader will now witness the manner in which a peaceful community advances towards a state of war; which is apt to be like the approach of a horse to a drum, with much prancing and little progress, and too often with the wrong end foremost.

Wilhelmus Kieft, who, in 1634,[26] ascended the gubernatorial chair (to borrow a favorite though clumsy appellation of modern phraseologists), was of a lofty descent, his father being inspector of wind-mills in the ancient town of Saardam; and our hero, we are told, when a boy, made very curious investigations into the nature and operation of these machines, which was one reason why he afterwards came to be so ingenious a governor. His name, according to the most authentic etymologists, was a corruption of Kyver; that is to say, a *wrangler* or *scolder*; and expressed the characteristic of his family, which, for nearly two centuries, had kept the windy town of Saardam in hot water, and produced more tartars and brimstones than any ten families in the place; and so truly did he inherit this family peculiarity, that he had not been a year in the government of the province, before he was universally denominated William the Testy. His appearance answered to his name. He was a brisk, wiry, waspish little old gentleman; such a one as may now and then be seen stumping about our city in a broad-skirted coat with huge buttons, a cocked hat stuck on the back of his head, and a cane as high as his chin. His face was broad, but his features were sharp; his cheeks were scorched into a dusky red, by two fiery little gray eyes; his nose turned up, and the corners of his mouth turned down, pretty much like the muzzle of an irritable pug-dog.

I have heard it observed by a profound adept in human physiology, that if a woman waxes fat with the progress of years, her tenure of life is somewhat precarious, but if haply she withers as she grows old, she lives forever. Such promised to be the case with William the Testy, who grew tough in proportion as he dried. He had withered, in fact, not through the process of years, but through the tropical fervor of his soul, which burnt like a vehement rush-light in his bosom; inciting him to incessant broils and bickerings. Ancient traditions speak much of his learning, and of the gallant inroads he had made into the dead languages, in which he had made captive a host of Greek nouns and Latin verbs; and brought off rich booty in ancient saws and apothegms; which he was wont to parade in his public harangues, as a triumphant general of yore, his *spolia opima*. Of metaphysics he knew enough to confound all hearers and himself into the bargain. In logic, he knew the whole family of syllogisms and dilemmas, and was so proud of his skill that he never suffered even a self-evident fact to pass unargued. It was observed, however, that he seldom got into an argument without getting into a perplexity, and then into a passion with his adversary for not being convinced gratis.

He had, moreover, skirmished smartly on the frontiers of several of the sciences, was fond of experimental philosophy, and prided himself upon inventions of all kinds. His abode, which he had fixed at a Bowerie or country-seat at a short distance from the city, just at what is now called Dutch-street, soon abounded with proofs of his ingenuity: patent smokejacks that required a horse to work them; Dutch ovens that roasted meat without fire; carts that went before the horses; weathercocks that turned against the wind; and other wrong-headed contrivances that astonished and confounded all beholders. The house, too, was beset with paralytic cats and dogs, the subjects of his experimental philosophy; and the yelling and yelping of the latter unhappy victims of science, while aiding in the pursuit of knowledge, soon gained for the place the name of "Dog's Misery," by which it continues to be known even at the present day.

It is in knowledge as in swimming; he who flounders and splashes on the surface, makes more noise, and attracts more attention, than the pearl-diver who quietly dives in quest of treasures to the bottom. The vast acquirements of the new governor were the theme of marvel among the simple burghers of New Amsterdam; he figured about the place as learned a man as a Bonze at Pekin, who has mastered one half of the Chinese alphabet: and was unanimously pronounced a "universal genius!"

I have known in my time many a genius of this stamp; but, to speak my mind freely, I never knew one who, for the ordinary purposes of life, was worth his weight in straw. In this respect, a little sound judgment and plain common sense is worth all the sparkling genius that ever wrote poetry or invented theories. Let us see how the universal acquirements of William the Testy aided him in the affairs of government.

CHAPTER II

HOW WILLIAM THE TESTY UNDERTOOK TO CONQUER BY PROC-
LAMATION—HOW HE WAS A GREAT MAN ABROAD, BUT A
LITTLE MAN IN HIS OWN HOUSE

No sooner had this bustling little potentate been blown by a whiff of fortune into the seat of government than he called his council together to make them a speech on the state of affairs.

Caius Gracchus, it is said, when he harangued the Roman populace, modulated his tone by an oratorical flute or pitchpipe; Wilhelmus Kieft, not having such an instrument at hand, availed himself of that musical organ or trump which nature has implanted in the midst of a man's face; in other words, he preluded his address by a sonorous blast of the nose; a preliminary flourish much in vogue among public orators.

He then commenced by expressing his humble sense of his utter unworthiness of the high post to which he had been appointed; which made some of the simple burghers wonder why he undertook it, not knowing that it is a point of etiquette with a public orator never to enter upon office without declaring himself unworthy to cross the threshold. He then proceeded in a manner highly classic and erudite to speak of government generally, and of the governments of ancient Greece in particular; together with the wars of Rome and Carthage; and the rise and fall of sundry outlandish empires which the worthy burghers had never read nor heard of. Having thus, after the manner of your learned orator, treated of things in general, he came by a natural, roundabout transition, to the matter in hand, namely, the daring aggressions of the Yankees.

As my readers are well aware of the advantage a potentate has of handling his enemies as he pleases in his speeches and bulletins, where he has the talk all on his own side, they may rest assured that William the Testy did not let such an opportunity escape of giving the Yankees what is called "a taste of his quality." In speaking of their inroads into the territories of their High Mightinesses, he compared them to the Gauls who desolated Rome; the Goths and Vandals who overran the fairest plains of Europe; but when he came to speak of the unparalleled audacity with which they of Weathersfield had advanced their patches up to the very walls of Fort Goed Hoop, and threatened to smother the garrison in onions, tears of rage started into his eyes, as though he nosed the very offence in question.

Having thus wrought up his tale to a climax, he assumed a most belligerent look, and assured the council that he had devised an instrument, potent in its effects, and which he trusted would soon drive the Yankees from the land. So saying, he thrust his hand into one of the deep pockets of his broad-skirted coat and drew forth, not an infernal machine, but an instrument in writing, which he laid with great emphasis upon the table.

The burghers gazed at it for a time in silent awe, as a wary housewife does at a gun, fearful it may go off half-cocked. The document in question had a sinister look, it is true; it was

crabbed in text, and from a broad red ribbon dangled the great
seal of the province, about the size of a buckwheat pancake.
Still, after all, it was but an instrument in writing. Herein,
however, existed the wonder of the invention. The document
in question was a PROCLAMATION, ordering the Yankees to
depart instantly from the territories of their High Mightinesses
under pain of suffering all the forfeitures and punishments in
such case made and provided. It was on the moral effect of this
formidable instrument that Wilhelmus Kieft calculated; pledg-
ing his valor as a governor that, once fulminated against the
Yankees, it would, in less than two months, drive every mother's
son of them across the borders.

The council broke up in perfect wonder, and nothing was
talked of for some time among the old men and women of New
Amsterdam but the vast genius of the governor, and his new
and cheap mode of fighting by proclamation.

As to Wilhelmus Kieft, having dispatched his proclamation
to the frontiers, he put on his cocked hat and corduroy small-
clothes, and mounting a tall raw-boned charger, trotted out to
his rural retreat of Dog's Misery. Here, like the good Numa, he
reposed from the toils of state, taking lessons in government,
not from the nymph Egeria, but from the honored wife of his
bosom; who was one of that class of females sent upon the
earth a little after the flood, as a punishment for the sins of
mankind, and commonly known by the appellation of *knowing
women*. In fact, my duty as an historian obliges me to make
known a circumstance which was a great secret at the time, and
consequently was not a subject of scandal at more than half the
tea-tables in New Amsterdam, but which, like many other
great secrets, has leaked out in the lapse of years—and this was,
that Wilhelmus the Testy, though one of the most potent little
men that ever breathed, yet submitted at home to a species of
government, neither laid down in Aristotle nor Plato; in short,
it partook of the nature of a pure, unmixed tyranny, and is
familiarly denominated *petticoat government*.—An absolute
sway, which, although exceedingly common in these modern
days, was very rare among the ancients, if we may judge from

the rout made about the domestic economy of honest Socrates; which is the only ancient case on record.

The great Kieft, however, warded off all the sneers and sarcasms of his particular friends, who are ever ready to joke with a man on sore points of the kind, by alleging that it was a government of his own election, to which he submitted through choice; adding at the same time a profound maxim which he had found in an ancient author, that "he who would aspire to *govern*, should first learn to *obey*."

CHAPTER III

IN WHICH ARE RECORDED THE SAGE PROJECTS OF A RULER OF UNIVERSAL GENIUS—THE ART OF FIGHTING BY PROCLAMATION—AND HOW THAT THE VALIANT JACOBUS VAN CURLET CAME TO BE FOULLY DISHONORED AT FORT GOED HOOP

Never was a more comprehensive, a more expeditious, or, what is still better, a more economical measure devised, than this of defeating the Yankees by proclamation—an expedient, likewise, so gentle and humane, there were ten chances to one in favor of its succeeding,—but then there was one chance to ten that it would not succeed—as the ill-natured fates would have it, that single chance carried the day! The proclamation was perfect in all its parts, well constructed, well written, well sealed, and well published—all that was wanting to insure its effect was, that the Yankees should stand in awe of it; but, provoking to relate, they treated it with the most absolute contempt, applied it to an unseemly purpose, and thus did the first warlike proclamation come to a shameful end—a fate which I am credibly informed has befallen but too many of its successors.

So far from abandoning the country, those varlets continued their encroachments, squatting along the green banks of the Varsche river, and founding Hartford, Stamford, New Haven, and other border towns. I have already shown how the onion patches of Pyquag were an eyesore to Jacobus Van Curlet and his garrison; but now these moss-troopers increased in their atrocities, kidnapping hogs, impounding horses, and sometimes grievously rib-roasting their owners. Our worthy forefathers could scarcely stir abroad without danger of being outjockeyed in horseflesh, or taken in in bargaining; while, in their absence, some daring Yankee peddler would penetrate to their household, and nearly ruin the good housewives with tin-ware and wooden bowls.[27]

I am well aware of the perils which environ me in this part of my history. While raking, with curious hand but pious heart, among the mouldering remains of former days, anxious to draw therefrom the honey of wisdom, I may fare somewhat like that valiant worthy, Samson, who, in meddling with the carcass of a dead lion, drew a swarm of bees about his ears. Thus, while narrating the many misdeeds of the Yanokie or Yankee race, it is ten chances to one but I offend the morbid sensibilities of certain of their unreasonable descendants, who may fly out and raise such a buzzing about this unlucky head of mine, that I shall need the tough hide of an Achilles, or an Orlando Furioso, to protect me from their stings.

Should such be the case, I should deeply and sincerely lament —not my misfortune in giving offence—but the wrong-headed perverseness of an ill-natured generation, in taking offence at any thing I say. That their ancestors did use my ancestors ill is true, and I am very sorry for it. I would, with all my heart, the fact were otherwise; but as I am recording the sacred events of history, I'd not bate one nail's breadth of the honest truth, though I were sure the whole edition of my work would be bought up and burnt by the common hangman of Connecticut. And in sooth, now that these testy gentlemen have drawn me out, I will make bold to go farther, and observe that this is one of the grand purposes for which we impartial historians are sent into the world—to redress wrongs and render justice on the heads of the guilty. So that, though a powerful nation may wrong its neighbors with temporary impunity, yet sooner or later an historian springs up, who wreaks ample chastisement on it in return.

Thus these moss-troopers of the east little thought, I'll warrant it, while they were harassing the inoffensive province of

Nieuw Nederlands, and driving its unhappy governor to his
wit's end, that an historian would ever arise, and give them
their own, with interest. Since, then, I am but performing my
bounden duty as an historian, in avenging the wrongs of our
revered ancestors, I shall make no further apology, and, indeed,
when it is considered that I have all these ancient borderers of
the east in my power, and at the mercy of my pen, I trust that
it will be admitted I conduct myself with great humanity and
moderation.

It was long before William the Testy could be persuaded
that his much vaunted war measure was ineffectual; on the contrary, he flew in a passion whenever it was doubted, swearing
that though slow in operating, yet when it once began to work,
it would soon purge the land of these invaders. When convinced, at length, of the truth, like a shrewd physician, he
attributed the failure to the quantity, not the quality of the
medicine, and resolved to double the dose. He fulminated,
therefore, a second proclamation more vehement than the first,
forbidding all intercourse with these Yankee intruders; ordering the Dutch burghers on the frontiers to buy none of their
pacing horses, measly pork, apple sweetmeats, Weathersfield
onions, or wooden bowls, and to furnish them with no supplies
of gin, gingerbread, or sourkrout.

Another interval elapsed, during which the last proclamation
was as little regarded as the first, and the non-intercourse was
especially set at naught by the young folks of both sexes, if we
may judge by the active bundling which took place along the
borders.

At length one day the inhabitants of New Amsterdam were
aroused by a furious barking of dogs, great and small, and beheld, to their surprise, the whole garrison of Fort Goed Hoop
straggling into town all tattered and wayworn, with Jacobus
Van Curlet at their head, bringing the melancholy intelligence
of the capture of Fort Goed Hoop by the Yankees.

The fate of this important fortress is an impressive warning
to all military commanders. It was neither carried by storm
nor famine; nor was it undermined; nor bombarded; nor set on

fire by red-hot shot; but was taken by a stratagem no less singular than effectual, and which can never fail of success, whenever an opportunity occurs of putting it in practice.

It seems that the Yankees had received intelligence that the garrison of Jacobus Van Curlet had been reduced nearly one-eighth by the death of two of his most corpulent soldiers, who had overeaten themselves on fat salmon caught in the Varsche river. A secret expedition was immediately set on foot to surprise the fortress. The crafty enemy knowing the habits of the garrison to sleep soundly after they had eaten their dinners and smoked their pipes, stole upon them at the noontide of a sultry summer's day, and surprised them in the midst of their slumbers.

In an instant the flag of their High Mightinesses was lowered, and the Yankee standard elevated in its stead, being a dried codfish, by way of a spread eagle. A strong garrison was appointed, of long-sided, hard-fisted Yankees, with Weathersfield onions for cockades and feathers. As to Jacobus Van Curlet and his men, they were seized by the nape of the neck, conducted to the gate, and one by one dismissed with a kick in the crupper, as Charles XII. dismissed the heavy-bottomed Russians at the battle of Narva; Jacobus Van Curlet receiving two kicks in consideration of his official dignity.

CHAPTER IV

CONTAINING THE FEARFUL WRATH OF WILLIAM THE TESTY, AND THE ALARM OF NEW AMSTERDAM—HOW THE GOVERNOR DID STRONGLY FORTIFY THE CITY—OF THE RISE OF ANTONY THE TRUMPETER, AND THE WINDY ADDITION TO THE ARMORIAL BEARINGS OF NEW AMSTERDAM

Language cannot express the awful ire of William the Testy on hearing of the catastrophe at Fort Goed Hoop. For three good hours his rage was too great for words, or rather the words were too great for him, (being a very small man,) and he was nearly choked by the misshapen, nine-cornered Dutch oaths and epithets which crowded at once into his gullet. At

length his words found vent, and for three days he kept up a
constant discharge, anathematizing the Yankees, man, woman,
and child, for a set of dieven, schobbejacken, deugenieten,
twistzoekeren, blaes-kaken, loosen-schalken, kakken-bedden,
and a thousand other names, of which, unfortunately for posterity, history does not make mention. Finally, he swore that
he would have nothing more to do with such a squatting, bundling, guessing, questioning, swapping, pumpkin-eating, mo-
lasses-daubing, shingle-splitting, cider-watering, horse-jockey-
ing, notion-peddling crew—that they might stay at Fort Goed
Hoop and rot, before he would dirty his hands by attempting to
drive them away; in proof of which he ordered the new-raised
troops to be marched forthwith into winter quarters, although
it was not as yet quite midsummer. Great despondency now
fell upon the city of New Amsterdam. It was feared that the
conquerors of Fort Goed Hoop, flushed with victory and apple-
brandy, might march on to the capital, take it by storm, and
annex the whole province to Connecticut. The name of Yankee
became as terrible among the Nieuw Nederlanders as was that
of Gaul among the ancient Romans; insomuch that the good
wives of the Manhattoes used it as a bugbear wherewith to
frighten their unruly children.

Everybody clamored around the governor, imploring him
to put the city in a complete posture of defence, and he listened
to their clamors. Nobody could accuse William the Testy of
being idle in time of danger, or at any other time. He was never
idle, but then he was often busy to very little purpose. When a
youngling he had been impressed with the words of Solomon,
"Go to the ant, thou sluggard, observe her ways and be wise,"
in conformity to which he had ever been of a restless, ant-like
turn; hurrying hither and thither, nobody knew why or wherefore, busying himself about small matters with an air of great
importance and anxiety, and toiling at a grain of mustard-seed
in the full conviction that he was moving a mountain. In the
present instance, he called in all his inventive powers to his aid,
and was continually pondering over plans, making diagrams,
and worrying about with a troop of workmen and projectors at

his heels. At length, after a world of consultation and contrivance, his plans of defence ended in rearing a great flag-staff in the centre of the fort, and perching a wind-mill on each bastion.

These warlike preparations in some measure allayed the public alarm, especially after an additional means of securing the safety of the city had been suggested by the governor's lady. It has already been hinted in this most authentic history, that in the domestic establishment of William the Testy "the gray mare was the better horse;" in other words, that his wife, "ruled the roast," and, in governing the governor, governed the province, which might thus be said to be under petticoat government.

Now it came to pass, that about this time there lived in the Manhattoes a jolly, robustious trumpeter, named Antony Van Corlear, famous for his long wind; and who, as the story goes, could twang so potently upon his instrument, that the effect upon all within hearing was like that ascribed to the Scotch bagpipe when it sings right lustily i' the nose.

This sounder of brass was moreover a lusty bachelor, with a pleasant, burly visage, a long nose, and huge whiskers. He had his little *bowerie*, or retreat in the country, where he led a roystering life, giving dances to the wives and daughters of the burghers of the Manhattoes, insomuch that he became a prodigious favorite with all the women, young and old. He is said to have been the first to collect that famous toll levied on the fair sex at Kissing Bridge, on the highway to Hellgate.[28]

To this sturdy bachelor the eyes of all the women were turned in this time of darkness and peril, as the very man to second and carry out the plans of defence of the governor. A kind of petticoat council was forthwith held at the government house, at which the governor's lady presided; and this lady, as has been hinted, being all potent with the governor, the result of these councils was the elevation of Antony the Trumpeter to the post of commandant of wind-mills and champion of New Amsterdam.

The city being thus fortified and garrisoned, it would have

done one's heart good to see the governor snapping his fingers and fidgeting with delight, as the trumpeter strutted up and down the ramparts twanging defiance to the whole Yankee race, as does a modern editor to all the principalities and powers on the other side of the Atlantic. In the hands of Antony Van Corlear this windy instrument appeared to him as potent as the horn of the paladin Astolpho, or even the more classic horn of Alecto; nay, he had almost the temerity to compare it with the rams' horns celebrated in holy writ, at the very sound of which the walls of Jericho fell down.

Be all this as it may, the apprehensions of hostilities from the east gradually died away. The Yankees made no further invasion; nay, they declared they had only taken possession of Fort Goed Hoop as being erected within their territories. So far from manifesting hostility, they continued to throng to New Amsterdam with the most innocent countenances imaginable, filling the market with their notions, being as ready to trade with the Nederlanders as ever—and not a whit more prone to get to the windward of them in a bargain.

The old wives of the Manhattoes who took tea with the governor's lady attributed all this affected moderation to the awe inspired by the military preparations of the governor, and the windy prowess of Antony the Trumpeter.

There were not wanting illiberal minds, however, who sneered at the governor for thinking to defend his city as he governed it, by mere wind; but William Kieft was not to be jeered out of his wind-mills—he had seen them perched upon the ramparts of his native city of Saardam, and was persuaded they were connected with the great science of defence; nay, so much piqued was he by having them made a matter of ridicule, that he introduced them into the arms of the city, where they remain to this day, quartered with the ancient beaver of the Manhattoes, an emblem and memento of his policy.

I must not omit to mention that certain wise old burghers of the Manhattoes, skilful in expounding signs and mysteries, after events have come to pass, consider this early intrusion of the wind-mill into the escutcheon of our city, which before had been wholly occupied by the beaver, as portentous of its after fortune, when the quiet Dutchman would be elbowed aside by the enterprising Yankee, and patient industry overtopped by windy speculation.

CHAPTER VII

GROWING DISCONTENTS OF NEW AMSTERDAM UNDER THE GOVERNMENT OF WILLIAM THE TESTY

It has been remarked by the observant writer of the Stuyvesant manuscript, that under the administration of William Kieft the disposition of the inhabitants of New Amsterdam experienced an essential change, so that they became very meddlesome and factious. The unfortunate propensity of the little governor to experiment and innovation, and the frequent exacerbations of his temper, kept his council in a continual worry; and the council being to the people at large what yeast or leaven is to a batch, they threw the whole community in a ferment; and the people at large being to the city what the mind is to the body, the unhappy commotions they underwent operated most disastrously upon New Amsterdam—insomuch that, in certain of their paroxysms of consternation and perplexity, they begat several of the most crooked, distorted, and abominable streets, lanes, and alleys, with which this metropolis is disfigured.

The fact was, that about this time, the community, like Balaam's ass, began to grow more enlightened than its rider, and to show a disposition for what is called "self government." This restive propensity was first evinced in certain popular meetings, in which the burghers of New Amsterdam met to talk and smoke over the complicated affairs of the province, gradually obfuscating themselves with politics and tobacco-smoke. Hither resorted those idlers and squires of low degree who hang loose on society and are blown about by every wind of doctrine. Cobblers abandoned their stalls to give lessons on political economy; blacksmiths suffered their fires to go out while they stirred up the fires of faction; and even tailors, though said to be the ninth parts of humanity, neglected their own measures to criticize the measures of government.[29]

Strange! that the science of government, which seems to be so generally understood, should invariably be denied to the only one called upon to exercise it. Not one of the politicians in question, but, take his word for it, could have administered affairs ten times better than William the Testy.

Under the instructions of these political oracles the good people of New Amsterdam soon became exceedingly enlightened; and, as a matter of course, exceedingly discontented. They gradually found out the fearful error in which they had indulged, of thinking themselves the happiest people in creation; and were convinced that, all circumstances to the contrary notwithstanding, they were a very unhappy, deluded, and consequently ruined people!

We are naturally prone to discontent, and avaricious after imaginary causes of lamentation. Like lubberly monks we belabor our own shoulders, and take a vast satisfaction in the music of our own groans. Nor is this said by way of paradox; daily experience shows the truth of these observations. It is almost impossible to elevate the spirits of a man groaning under ideal calamities; but nothing is easier than to render him wretched, though on the pinnacle of felicity; as it would be an Herculean task to hoist a man to the top of a steeple, though the merest child could topple him off thence.

I must not omit to mention that these popular meetings were generally held at some noted tavern; these public edifices possessing what in modern times are thought the true fountains of political inspiration. The ancient Greeks deliberated upon a matter when drunk, and reconsidered it when sober. Mob politicians in modern times dislike to have two minds upon a subject; so they both deliberate and act when drunk; by this means a world of delay is spared; and as it is universally allowed that a man when drunk sees double, it follows conclusively that he sees twice as well as his sober neighbors.

CHAPTER VIII

OF THE EDICT OF WILLIAM THE TESTY AGAINST TOBACCO—OF THE
PIPE PLOT, AND THE RISE OF FEUDS AND PARTIES

Wilhelmus Kieft, as has already been observed, was a great legislator on a small scale, and had a microscopic eye in public affairs. He had been greatly annoyed by the factious meeting of the good people of New Amsterdam, but, observing that on these occasions the pipe was ever in their mouth, he began to think that the pipe was at the bottom of the affair, and that there was some mysterious affinity between politics and tobacco smoke. Determined to strike at the root of the evil, he began, forthwith, to rail at tobacco, as a noxious, nauseous weed; filthy in all its uses; and as to smoking he denounced it as a heavy tax upon the public pocket; a vast consumer of time, a great encourager of idleness, and a deadly bane to the prosperity and morals of the people. Finally he issued an edict, prohibiting the smoking of tobacco throughout the New Netherlands. Ill-fated Kieft! Had he lived in the present age and attempted to check the unbounded license of the press, he could not have struck more sorely upon the sensibilities of the million. The pipe, in fact, was the great organ of reflection and deliberation of the New Netherlander. It was his constant companion and solace— was he gay, he smoked; was he sad, he smoked; his pipe was never out of his mouth; it was a part of his physiognomy; without it his best friends would not know him. Take away his pipe? You might as well take away his nose!

The immediate effect of the edict of William the Testy was a popular commotion. A vast multitude armed with pipes and tobacco-boxes, and an immense supply of ammunition, sat themselves down before the governor's house, and fell to smoking with tremendous violence. The testy William issued forth like a wrathful spider, demanding the reason of this lawless fumigation. The sturdy rioters replied by lolling back in their seats, and puffing away with redoubled fury; raising such a murky cloud that the governor was fain to take refuge in the interior of his castle.

A long negotiation ensued through the medium of Antony the Trumpeter. The governor was at first wrathful and un-yielding, but was gradually smoked into terms. He concluded by permitting the smoking of tobacco, but he abolished the fair long pipes used in the days of Wouter Van Twiller, denoting ease, tranquillity, and sobriety of deportment; these he con-demned as incompatible with the despatch of business, in place whereof he substituted little captious short pipes, two inches in length, which, he observed, could be stuck in one corner of the mouth, or twisted in the hat-band; and would never be in the way. Thus ended this alarming insurrection, which was long known by the name of The Pipe Plot, and which, it has been somewhat quaintly observed, did end, like most plots and sedi-tions, in mere smoke.

But mark, oh, reader! the deplorable evils which did after-wards result. The smoke of these villanous little pipes, con-tinually ascending in a cloud about the nose, penetrated into and befogged the cerebellum; dried up all the kindly moisture of the brain, and rendered the people who used them as vaporish and testy as the governor himself. Nay, what is worse, from being goodly, burly, sleek-conditioned men, they became, like our Dutch yeomanry who smoke short pipes, a lantern-jawed, smoke-dried, leathern-hided race.

Nor was this all. From this fatal schism in tobacco pipes we may date the rise of parties in the Nieuw Nederlands. The rich and self-important burghers who had made their fortunes, and could afford to be lazy, adhered to the ancient fashion, and formed a kind of aristocracy known as the *Long Pipes;* while the lower order, adopting the reform of William Kieft as more convenient in their handicraft employments, were branded with the plebeian name of *Short Pipes*.

A third party sprang up, headed by the descendants of Robert Chewit, the companion of the great Hudson. These discarded pipes altogether and took to chewing tobacco; hence they were called *Quids;* an appellation since given to those political mongrels, which sometimes spring up between two great parties, as a mule is produced between a horse and an ass.[30]

And here I would note the great benefit of party distinctions in saving the people at large the trouble of thinking. Hesiod divides mankind into three classes, those who think for themselves, those who think as others think, and those who do not think at all. The second class comprises the great mass of society; for most people require a set creed and a file-leader. Hence the origin of party: which means a large body of people, some few of whom think, and all the rest talk. The former take the lead and discipline the latter; prescribing what they must say; what they must approve; what they must hoot at; whom they must support; but, above all, whom they must hate; for no one can be a right good partisan, who is not a thorough-going hater.

The enlightened inhabitants of the Manhattoes, therefore, being divided into parties, were enabled to hate each other with great accuracy. And now the great business of politics went bravely on, the long pipes and short pipes assembling in separate beer-houses, and smoking at each other with implacable vehemence, to the great support of the state and profit of the tavern-keepers. Some, indeed, went so far as to bespatter their adversaries with those odoriferous little words which smell so strong in the Dutch language; believing, like true politicians, that they served their party, and glorified themselves in proportion as they bewrayed their neighbors. But, however they might differ among themselves, all parties agreed in abusing the governor; seeing that he was not a governor of their choice, but appointed by others to rule over them.

Unhappy William Kieft! exclaims the sage writer of the Stuyvesant manuscript, doomed to contend with enemies too knowing to be entrapped, and to reign over a people too wise to be governed. All his foreign expeditions were baffled and set at naught by the all-pervading Yankees; all his home measures were canvassed and condemned by "numerous and respectable meetings" of pot-house politicians.

In the multitude of counsellors, we are told, there is safety; but the multitude of counsellors was a continual source of perplexity to William Kieft. With a temperament as hot as an old radish, and a mind subject to perpetual whirlwinds and tornadoes, he never failed to get into a passion with every one who undertook to advise him. I have observed, however, that your passionate little men, like small boats with large sails, are easily upset or blown out of their course; so was it with William the Testy, who was prone to be carried away by the last piece of advice blown into his ear. The consequence was, that, though a projector of the first class, yet, by continually changing his projects, he gave none a fair trial; and by endeavoring to do every thing, he in sober truth did nothing.

In the mean time, the sovereign people got into the saddle, showed themselves, as usual, unmerciful riders; spurring on the little governor with harangues and petitions, and thwarting him with memorials and reproaches, in much the same way as holyday apprentices manage an unlucky devil of a hack-horse—so that Wilhelmus Kieft was kept at a worry or a gallop throughout the whole of his administration.

CHAPTER XII

CONTAINING THE RISE OF THE GREAT AMPHICTYONIC COUNCIL OF
THE PILGRIMS, WITH THE DECLINE AND FINAL EXTINCTION
OF WILLIAM THE TESTY

It was asserted by the wise men of ancient times, who had a nearer opportunity of ascertaining the fact, that at the gate of Jupiter's palace lay two huge tuns, one filled with blessings, the other with misfortunes; and it would verily seem as if the latter had been completely overturned and left to deluge the unlucky province of Nieuw Nederlands: for about this time, while harassed and annoyed from the south and the north, incessant forays were made by the border chivalry of Connecticut upon the pig-stys and hen-roosts of the Nederlanders. Every day or two some broad-bottomed express-rider, covered with mud and mire, would come floundering into the gate of New Amsterdam, freighted with some new tale of aggression from the frontier; whereupon Antony Van Corlear, seizing his trumpet, the only substitute for a newspaper in those primitive days, would sound the tidings from the ramparts with such doleful notes and disastrous cadence as to throw half the old women in the city into hysterics; all which tended greatly to increase his popularity; there being nothing for which the public are more grateful than being frequently treated to a panic; a secret well known to modern editors.

But, oh ye powers! into what a paroxysm of passion did each new outrage of the Yankees throw the choleric little governor! Letter after letter, protest after protest, bad Latin, worse English, and hideous Low Dutch, were incessantly fulminated upon them, and the four-and-twenty letters of the alphabet, which formed his standing army, were worn out by constant campaigning. All, however, was ineffectual; even the recent victory at Oyster Bay, which had shed such a gleam of sunshine between the clouds of his foul-weather reign, was soon followed by a more fearful gathering up of those clouds, and indications of more portentous tempest; for the Yankee tribe on the banks of the Connecticut, finding on this memorable occasion their incompetency to cope, in fair fight, with the sturdy chivalry of the Manhattoes, had called to their aid all the ten tribes of their brethren who inhabit the east country, which from them has derived the name of Yankee land. This call was promptly responded to. The consequence was a great confederacy of the tribes of Massachusetts, Connecticut, New Plymouth and New Haven, under the title of the "United Colonies of New England;" the pretended object of which was mutual defence against the savages; but the real object the subjugation of the Nieuw Nederlands.

For, to let the reader into one of the great secrets of history, the Nieuw Nederlands had long been regarded by the whole Yankee race as the modern land of promise, and themselves as the chosen and peculiar people destined, one day or other, by hook or by crook, to get possession of it. In truth they are a wonderful and all-prevalent people; of that class who only require an inch to gain an ell, or a halter to gain a horse. From the time they first gained a foothold on Plymouth Rock, they began to migrate, progressing and progressing from place to place, and land to land, making a little here and a little there, and controverting the old proverb, that a rolling stone gathers no moss. Hence they have facetiously received the nickname of THE PILGRIMS: that is to say, a people who are always seeking a better country than their own.

The tidings of this great Yankee league struck William Kieft with dismay, and for once in his life he forgot to bounce on receiving a disagreeable piece of intelligence. In fact, on turning over in his mind all that he had read at The Hague about leagues and combinations, he found that this was a counterpart of the Amphictyonic league, by which the states of Greece attained such power and supremacy; and the very idea made his heart quake for the safety of his empire at the Manhattoes.

The affairs of the confederacy were managed by an annual council of delegates held at Boston, which Kieft denominated the Delphos of this truly classic league. The very first meeting gave evidence of hostility to the Nieuw Nederlanders, who were charged, in their dealings with the Indians, with carrying on a traffic in "guns, powther and shott—a trade damnable and injurious to the colonists." It is true the Connecticut traders were fain to dabble a little in this damnable traffic; but then they always dealt in what were termed Yankee guns; ingeniously calculated to burst in the pagan hands which used them.

The rise of this potent confederacy was a death-blow to the glory of William the Testy, for from that day forward he never held up his head, but appeared quite crest-fallen. It is true, as the grand council augmented in power, and the league, rolling onward, gathered about the red hills of New Haven, threatening to overwhelm the Nieuw Nederlands, he continued occasionally to fulminate proclamations and protests, as a shrewd sea-captain fires his guns into a water-spout; but alas! they had no more effect than so many blank cartridges.

Thus end the authenticated chronicles of the reign of William the Testy; for henceforth, in the troubles, perplexities, and confusion of the times, he seems to have been totally overlooked; and to have slipped for ever through the fingers of scrupulous history. It is a matter of deep concern that such obscurity should hang over his latter days; for he was in truth a mighty and great little man, and worthy of being utterly renowned, seeing that he was the first potentate that introduced into this land the art of fighting by proclamation, and defending a country by trumpeters and wind-mills.

It is true, that certain of the early provincial poets, of whom there were great numbers in the Nieuw Nederlands, taking advantage of his mysterious exit, have fabled, that, like Romulus, he was translated to the skies, and forms a very fiery little star, somewhere on the left claw of the crab; while others, equally fanciful, declare that he had experienced a fate similar to that of the good king Arthur; who, we are assured by ancient bards, was carried away to the delicious abodes of fairy land, where he still exists, in pristine worth and vigor, and will one day or another return to restore the gallantry, the honor, and the immaculate probity, which prevailed in the glorious days of the Round Table.[31]

All these, however, are but pleasing fantasies, the cobweb visions of those dreaming varlets, the poets, to which I would not have my judicious readers attach any credibility. Neither am I disposed to credit an ancient and rather apocryphal historian, who asserts that the ingenious Wilhelmus was annihilated by the blowing down of one of his wind-mills; nor a writer of later times, who affirms that he fell a victim to an experiment in natural history, having the misfortune to break his neck from a garret window of the stadthouse in attempting to catch swallows by sprinkling salt upon their tails. Still less do I put my faith in the tradition that he perished at sea in conveying home to Holland a treasure of golden ore, discovered somewhere among the haunted regions of the Catskill mountains.[32]

The most probable account declares, that what with the constant troubles on his frontiers, the incessant schemings and projects going on in his own pericranium, the memorials, petitions, remonstrances, and sage pieces of advice of respectable meetings of the sovereign people, and the refractory disposition of his councillors, who were sure to differ from him on every

point, and uniformly to be in the wrong—his mind was kept
in a furnace heat, until he became as completely burnt out as a
Dutch family pipe which has passed through three generations
of hard smokers. In this manner did he undergo a kind of animal
combustion, consuming away like a farthing rush-light: so that
when grim death finally snuffed him out, there was scarce left
enough of him to bury!

From BOOK V: CONTAINING THE FIRST PART OF
THE REIGN OF PETER STUYVESANT, AND HIS
TROUBLES WITH THE AMPHICTYONIC COUN-
CIL.

CHAPTER I

IN WHICH THE DEATH OF A GREAT MAN IS SHOWN TO BE NO VERY
INCONSOLABLE MATTER OF SORROW—AND HOW PETER
STUYVESANT ACQUIRED A GREAT NAME FROM THE UNCOM-
MON STRENGTH OF HIS HEAD

To a profound philosopher like myself, who am apt to see
clear through a subject, where the penetration of ordinary
people extends but half way, there is no fact more simple and
manifest than that the death of a great man is a matter of very
little importance. Much as we may think of ourselves, and much
as we may excite the empty plaudits of the million, it is certain
that the greatest among us do actually fill but an exceeding
small space in the world; and it is equally certain, that even that
small space is quickly supplied when we leave it vacant. "Of
what consequence is it," said Pliny, "that individuals appear, or
make their exit? the world is a theatre whose scenes and actors
are continually changing." Never did philosopher speak more
correctly, and I only wonder that so wise a remark could have
existed so many ages, and mankind not have laid it more to
heart. Sage follows on in the footsteps of sage; one hero just
steps out of his triumphal car, to make way for the hero who
comes after him; and of the proudest monarch, it is merely said

that "he slept with his fathers, and his successor reigned in his stead."

The world, to tell the private truth, cares but little for their loss, and if left to itself would soon forget to grieve; and though a nation has often been figuratively drowned in tears on the death of a great man, yet it is ten to one if an individual tear has been shed on the occasion, excepting from the forlorn pen of some hungry author. It is the historian, the biographer, and the poet, who have the whole burden of grief to sustain; who—kind souls!—like undertakers in England, act the part of chief mourners—who inflate a nation with sighs it never heaved, and deluge it with tears it never dreamt of shedding. Thus, while the patriotic author is weeping and howling, in prose, in blank verse, and in rhyme, and collecting the drops of public sorrow into his volume, as into a lachrymal vase, it is more than probable his fellow citizens are eating and drinking, fiddling and dancing, as utterly ignorant of the bitter lamentations made in their name, as are those men of straw, John Doe and Richard Roe, of the plaintiffs for whom they are generously pleased to become sureties.

The most glorious hero that ever desolated nations might have mouldered into oblivion among the rubbish of his own monument, did not some historian take him into favor, and benevolently transmit his name to posterity—and much as the valiant William Kieft worried, and bustled, and turmoiled, while he had the destinies of a whole colony in his hand, I question seriously whether he will not be obliged to this authentic history for all his future celebrity.

His exit occasioned no convulsion in the city of New Amsterdam nor its vicinity: the earth trembled not, neither did any stars shoot from their spheres—the heavens were not shrouded in black, as poets would fain persuade us they have been, on the death of a hero—the rocks (hard-hearted varlets!) melted not into tears, nor did the trees hang their heads in silent sorrow; and as to the sun, he lay a-bed the next night just as long, and showed as jolly a face when he rose, as he ever did on the same day of the month in any year, either before or since. The good people of New Amsterdam, one and all, declared that he had been a very busy, active, bustling little governor; that he was "the father of his country"—that he was "the noblest work of God"—that "he was a man, take him for all in all, they ne'er should look upon his like again"—together with sundry other civil and affectionate speeches regularly said on the death of all great men; after which they smoked their pipes, thought no more about him, and Peter Stuyvesant succeeded to his station.

Peter Stuyvesant was the last, and, like the renowned Wouter Van Twiller, the best of our ancient Dutch governors. Wouter having surpassed all who preceded him, and Peter or Piet, as he was sociably called by the old Dutch burghers, who were ever prone to familiarize names, having never been equalled by any successor. He was in fact the very man fitted by nature to retrieve the desperate fortunes of her beloved province, had not the fates, those most potent and unrelenting of all ancient spinsters, destined them to inextricable confusion.

To say merely that he was a hero would be doing him great injustice—he was in truth a combination of heroes—for he was of a sturdy, raw-boned make like Ajax Telamon, with a pair of round shoulders that Hercules would have given his hide for (meaning his lion's hide,) when he undertook to ease old Atlas of his load. He was, moreover, as Plutarch describes Coriolanus, not only terrible for the force of his arm, but likewise of his voice, which sounded as though it came out of a barrel; and, like the self-same warrior, he possessed a sovereign contempt for the sovereign people, and an iron aspect, which was enough of itself to make the very bowels of his adversaries quake with terror and dismay. All this martial excellency of appearance was inexpressibly heightened by an accidental advantage, with which I am surprised that neither Homer nor Virgil have graced any of their heroes. This was nothing less than a wooden leg, which was the only prize he had gained in bravely fighting the battles of his country, but of which he was so proud, that he was often heard to declare he valued it more than all his other limbs put together; indeed so highly did he esteem it, that he had it gallantly enchased and relieved with silver devices, which caused it to be related in divers histories and legends that he wore a silver leg.[33]

Like that choleric warrior Achilles, he was somewhat subject to extempore bursts of passion, which were rather unpleasant to his favorites and attendants, whose perceptions he was apt to quicken, after the manner of his illustrious imitator, Peter the Great, by anointing their shoulders with his walking-staff.

Though I cannot find that he had read Plato, or Aristotle, or Hobbes, or Bacon, or Algernon Sydney, or Tom Paine, yet did he sometimes manifest a shrewdness and sagacity in his measures, that one would hardly expect from a man who did not know Greek, and had never studied the ancients. True it is, and I confess it with sorrow, that he had an unreasonable aversion to experiments, and was fond of governing his province after the simplest manner: but then he contrived to keep it in better order than did the erudite Kieft, though he had all the philosophers, ancient and modern, to assist and perplex him. I must likewise own that he made but very few laws; but then again he took care that those few were rigidly and impartially enforced: and I do not know but justice on the whole was as well administered as if there had been volumes of sage acts and statutes yearly made, and daily neglected and forgotten.

He was, in fact, the very reverse of his predecessors, being neither tranquil and inert, like Walter the Doubter, nor restless and fidgeting, like William the Testy; but a man, or rather a governor of such uncommon activity and decision of mind, that he never sought nor accepted the advice of others; depending bravely upon his single head as would a hero of yore upon his single arm, to carry him through all difficulties and dangers. To tell the simple truth, he wanted nothing more to complete him as a statesman than to think always right; for no one can say but that he always acted as he thought. He was never a man to flinch when he found himself in a scrape; but to dash forward through thick and thin, trusting, by hook or by crook, to make all things straight in the end. In a word, he possessed, in an eminent degree, that great quality in a statesman, called perseverance by the polite, but nicknamed obstinacy by the vulgar. A wonderful salve for official blunders; since he who perseveres in error without flinching, gets the credit of bold-ness and consistency, while he who wavers in seeking to do what is right gets stigmatized as a trimmer. This much is cer-tain; and it is a maxim well worthy the attention of all legislators, great and small, who stand shaking in the wind, irresolute which way to steer, that a ruler who follows his own will pleases him-self; while he who seeks to satisfy the wishes and whims of others runs great risk of pleasing nobody. There is nothing too like putting down one's foot resolutely, when in doubt, and letting things take their course. The clock that stands still points right twice in the four-and-twenty hours: while others may keep going continually and be continually going wrong.

Nor did this magnanimous quality escape the discernment of the good people of Nieuw Nederlands; on the contrary, so much were they struck with the independent will and vigorous resolution displayed on all occasions by their new governor, that they universally called him Hard-Koppig Piet; or Peter the Headstrong—a great compliment to the strength of his under-standing.

If, from all that I have said, thou dost not gather, worthy reader, that Peter Stuyvesant was a tough, sturdy, valiant, weather-beaten, mettlesome, obstinate, leathern-sided, lion-hearted, generous-spirited old governor, either I have written to but little purpose, or thou art very dull at drawing con-clusions.

This most excellent governor commenced his administration on the 29th of May, 1647; a remarkably stormy day, distin-guished in all the almanacks of the time which have come down to us by the name of *Windy Friday*. As he was very jealous of his personal and official dignity, he was inaugurated into office with great ceremony; the goodly oaken chair of the renowned Wouter Van Twiller being carefully preserved for such occa-sions, in like manner as the chair and stone were reverentially preserved at Schone, in Scotland, for the coronation of the Caledonian monarchs.

I must not omit to mention that the tempestuous state of the elements, together with its being that unlucky day of the week termed "hanging day," did not fail to excite much grave speculation and divers very reasonable apprehensions among the more ancient and enlightened inhabitants; and several of the sager sex, who were reputed to be not a little skilled in the mystery of astrology and fortune-telling, did declare outright that they were omens of a disastrous administration—an event that came to be lamentably verified, and which proves, beyond dispute, the wisdom of attending to those preternatural intimations furnished by dreams and visions, the flying of birds, falling of stones, and cackling of geese, on which the sages and rulers of ancient times placed such reliance—or to those shooting of stars, eclipses of the moon, howlings of dogs, and flarings of candles, carefully noted and interpreted by the oracular sibyls of our day; who, in my humble opinion, are the legitimate inheritors and preservers of the ancient science of divination. This much is certain, that Governor Stuyvesant succeeded to the chair of state at a turbulent period; when foes thronged and threatened from without; when anarchy and stiff-necked opposition reigned rampant within; when the authority of their High Mightinesses the Lords States General, though supported by economy and defended by speeches, protests and proclamations, yet tottered to its very centre; and when the great city of New Amsterdam, though fortified by flag-staffs, trumpeters, and wind-mills, seemed, like some fair lady of easy virtue, to lie open to attack, and ready to yield to the first invader.

From BOOK VII: CONTAINING THE THIRD PART
     OF THE REIGN OF PETER THE HEADSTRONG
     —HIS TROUBLES WITH THE BRITISH NATION,
     AND THE DECLINE AND FALL OF THE DUTCH
     DYNASTY

CHAPTER XI

HOW PETER STUYVESANT DEFENDED THE CITY OF NEW AMSTERDAM
     FOR SEVERAL DAYS, BY DINT OF THE STRENGTH OF HIS
     HEAD

There is something exceedingly sublime and melancholy in
the spectacle which the present crisis of our history presents. An
illustrious and venerable little city—the metropolis of a vast
extent of uninhabited country—garrisoned by a doughty host
of orators, chairmen, committeemen, burgomasters, schepens,
and old women—governed by a determined and strong-headed
warrior, and fortified by mud batteries, palisadoes, and resolutions—blockaded by sea, beleaguered by land, and threatened
with direful desolation from without; while its very vitals are
torn with internal faction and commotion! Never did historic
pen record a page of more complicated distress, unless it be the
strife that distracted the Israelites, during the siege of Jerusalem
—where discordant parties were cutting each other's throats,
at the moment when the victorious legions of Titus had toppled
down their bulwarks, and were carrying fire and sword into the
very sanctum sanctorum of the temple.

Governor Stuyvesant having triumphantly put his grand
council to the rout, and delivered himself from a multitude of
impertinent advisers, despatched a categorical reply to the
commanders of the invading squadron; wherein he asserted the
right and title of their High Mightinesses the Lords States General to the province of New Netherlands, and trusting in the
righteousness of his cause, set the whole British nation at
defiance!

My anxiety to extricate my readers and myself from these

disastrous scenes prevents me from giving the whole of this gallant letter, which concluded in these manly and affectionate terms:

"As touching the threats in your conclusion, we have nothing to answer, only that we fear nothing but what God (who is as just as merciful) shall lay upon us; all things being in his gracious disposal, and we may as well be preserved by him with small forces as by a great army; which makes us to wish you all happiness and prosperity, and recommend you to his protection. My lords, your thrice humble and affectionate servant and friend,

"P. STUYVESANT."

Thus having thrown his gauntlet, the brave Peter stuck a pair of horse pistols in his belt, girded an immense powder-horn on his side—thrust his sound leg into a Hessian boot, and clapping his fierce little war-hat on the top of his head—paraded up and down in front of his house, determined to defend his beloved city to the last.

While all these struggles and dissensions were prevailing in the unhappy city of New Amsterdam, and while its worthy but ill-starred governor was framing the above-quoted letter, the English commanders did not remain idle. They had agents secretly employed to foment the fears and clamors of the populace; and moreover circulated far and wide, through the adjacent country, a proclamation, repeating the terms they had already held out in their summons to surrender, at the same time beguiling the simple Nederlanders with the most crafty and conciliating professions. They promised that every man who voluntarily submitted to the authority of his British Majesty should retain peaceful possession of his house, his vrouw, and his cabbage-garden. That he should be suffered to smoke his pipe, speak Dutch, wear as many breeches as he pleased, and import bricks, tiles, and stone jugs from Holland, instead of manufacturing them on the spot. That he should on no account be compelled to learn the English language, nor eat codfish on Saturdays, nor keep accounts in any other way than by casting them up on his fingers, and chalking them down upon the crown of his hat; as is observed among the Dutch yeomanry at the present day. That every man should be allowed quietly to inherit his father's hat, coat, shoe-buckles, pipe, and every other personal appendage; and that no man should be obliged to conform to any improvements, inventions, or any other modern innovations; but, on the contrary, should be permitted to build his house, follow his trade, manage his farm, rear his hogs, and educate his children, precisely as his ancestors had done before him from time immemorial. Finally, that he should have all the benefits of free trade, and should not be required to acknowledge any other saint in the calendar than St. Nicholas, who should thenceforward, as before, be considered the tutelar saint of the city.

These terms, as may be supposed, appeared very satisfactory to the people, who had a great disposition to enjoy their property unmolested, and a most singular aversion to engage in a contest, where they could gain little more than honor and broken heads—the first of which they held in philosophic indifference, the latter in utter detestation. By these insidious means, therefore, did the English succeed in alienating the confidence and affections of the populace from their gallant old governor, whom they considered as obstinately bent upon running them into hideous misadventures; and did not hesitate to speak their minds freely, and abuse him most heartily—behind his back.

Like as a mighty grampus when assailed and buffeted by roaring waves and brawling surges, still keeps on an undeviating course, rising above the boisterous billows, spouting and blowing as he emerges—so did the inflexible Peter pursue, unwavering, his determined career, and rise, contemptuous, above the clamors of the rabble.

But when the British warriors found that he set their power at defiance, they despatched recruiting officers to Jamaica and Jericho, and Nineveh, and Quag, and Patchog, and all those towns on Long Island which had been subdued of yore by

Stoffel Brinkerhoff; stirring up the progeny of Preserved Fish, and Determined Cock, and those other New England squatters, to assail the city of New Amsterdam by land; while the hostile ships prepared for an assault by water.

The streets of New Amsterdam now presented a scene of wild dismay and consternation. In vain did Peter Stuyvesant order the citizens to arm and assemble on the Battery. Blank terror reigned over the community. The whole party of Short Pipes in the course of a single night had changed into arrant old women—a metamorphosis only to be paralleled by the prodigies recorded by Livy as having happened at Rome at the approach of Hannibal, when statues sweated in pure affright, goats were converted into sheep, and cocks, turning into hens, ran cackling about the street.

Thus baffled in all attempts to put the city in a state of defence; blockaded from without; tormented from within; and menaced with a Yankee invasion, even the stiff-necked will of Peter Stuyvesant for once gave way, and in spite of his mighty heart, which swelled in his throat until it nearly choked him, he consented to a treaty of surrender.

Words cannot express the transports of the populace, on receiving this intelligence; had they obtained a conquest over their enemies, they could not have indulged greater delight. The streets resounded with their congratulations—they extolled their governor as the father and deliverer of his country—they crowded to his house to testify their gratitude, and were ten times more noisy in their plaudits than when he returned, with victory perched upon his beaver, from the glorious capture of Fort Christina. But the indignant Peter shut his doors and windows, and took refuge in the innermost recesses of his mansion, that he might not hear the ignoble rejoicings of the rabble.

Commissioners were now appointed on both sides, and a capitulation was speedily arranged; all that was wanting to ratify it was that it should be signed by the governor. When the commissioners waited upon him for this purpose, they were received with grim and bitter courtesy. His warlike accoutrements were laid aside—an old Indian night-gown was wrapped about his rugged limbs, a red night-cap overshadowed his frowning brow, an iron-gray beard of three days' growth gave additional grimness to his visage. Thrice did he seize a worn-out stump of a pen, and essay to sign the loathsome paper —thrice did he clinch his teeth, and make a horrible countenance, as though a dose of rhubarb, senna, and ipecacuanha, had been offered to his lips; at length, dashing it from him, he seized his brass-hilted sword, and jerking it from the scabbard, swore by St. Nicholas, to sooner die than yield to any power under heaven.

For two whole days did he persist in this magnanimous resolution, during which his house was besieged by the rabble, and menaces and clamorous revilings exhausted to no purpose. And now another course was adopted to soothe, if possible, his mighty ire. A procession was formed by the burgomasters and schepens, followed by the populace, to bear the capitulation in state to the governor's dwelling. They found the castle strongly barricadoed, and the old hero in full regimentals, with his cocked hat on his head, posted with a blunderbuss at the garret window.

There was something in this formidable position that struck even the ignoble vulgar with awe and admiration. The brawling multitude could not but reflect with self-abasement upon their own pusillanimous conduct, when they beheld their hardy but deserted old governor, thus faithful to his post, like a forlorn hope, and fully prepared to defend his ungrateful city to the last. These compunctions, however, were soon overwhelmed by the recurring tide of public apprehension. The populace arranged themselves before the house, taking off their hats with most respectful humility—Burgomaster Roerback, who was of that popular class of orators described by Sallust, as being "talkative rather than eloquent," stepped forth and addressed the governor in a speech of three hours' length, detailing, in the most pathetic terms, the calamitous situation of the province, and urging him in a constant repetition of the same arguments and words to sign the capitulation.

The mighty Peter eyed him from his garret window in grim silence—now and then his eye would glance over the surrounding rabble, and an indignant grin, like that of an angry mastiff, would mark his iron visage. But though a man of most undaunted mettle—though he had a heart as big as an ox, and a head that would have set adamant to scorn—yet after all he was a mere mortal. Wearied out by these repeated oppositions, and this eternal haranguing, and perceiving that unless he complied, the inhabitants would follow their own inclination, or rather their fears, without waiting for his consent; or, what was still worse, the Yankees would have time to pour in their forces and claim a share in the conquest, he testily ordered them to hand up the paper. It was accordingly hoisted to him on the end of a pole, and having scrawled his name at the bottom of it, he anathematized them all for a set of cowardly, mutinous, degenerate poltroons—threw the capitulation at their heads, slammed down the window, and was heard stumping down stairs with vehement indignation. The rabble incontinently took to their heels; even the burgomasters were not slow in evacuating the premises, fearing lest the sturdy Peter might issue from his den, and greet them with some unwelcome testimonial of his displeasure.

Within three hours after the surrender, a legion of British beef-fed warriors poured into New Amsterdam, taking possession of the fort and batteries. And now might be heard, from all quarters, the sound of hammers made by the old Dutch burghers, in nailing up their doors and windows, to protect their vrouws from these fierce barbarians, whom they contemplated in silent sullenness from the garret windows as they paraded through the streets.

Thus did Colonel Richard Nichols, the commander of the British forces, enter into quiet possession of the conquered realm as *locum tenens* for the Duke of York. The victory was attended with no other outrage than that of changing the name of the province and its metropolis, which thenceforth were denominated NEW YORK, and so have continued to be called unto the present day. The inhabitants, according to treaty, were allowed to maintain quiet possession of their property; but so inveterately did they retain their abhorrence of the British nation, that in a private meeting of the leading citizens, it was unanimously determined never to ask any of their conquerors to dinner.[34]

CHAPTER XII

CONTAINING THE DIGNIFIED RETIREMENT, AND MORTAL SURRENDER OF PETER THE HEADSTRONG

Thus, then, have I concluded this great historical enterprise; but before I lay aside my weary pen, there yet remains to be performed one pious duty. If among the variety of readers who may peruse this book, there should haply be found any of those souls of true nobility, which glow with celestial fire at the history of the generous and the brave, they will doubtless be anxious to know the fate of the gallant Peter Stuyvesant. To gratify one such sterling heart of gold I would go more lengths than to instruct the cold-blooded curiosity of a whole fraternity of philosophers.

No sooner had that high-mettled cavalier signed the articles of capitulation, than, determined not to witness the humiliation of his favorite city, he turned his back on its walls and made a growling retreat to his *bouwery*, or country-seat, which was situated about two miles off; where he passed the remainder of his days in patriarchal retirement. There he enjoyed that tranquillity of mind, which he had never known amid the distracting cares of government; and tasted the sweets of absolute and uncontrolled authority, which his factious subjects had so often dashed with the bitterness of opposition.

No persuasions could ever induce him to revisit the city— on the contrary, he would always have his great arm-chair placed with its back to the windows which looked in that direction; until a thick grove of trees planted by his own hand grew up and formed a screen that effectually excluded it from the prospect. He railed continually at the degenerate innovations and improvements introduced by the conquerors—forbade a word of their detested language to be spoken in his family, a prohibition readily obeyed, since none of the household could speak any thing but Dutch—and even ordered a fine avenue to be cut down in front of his house because it consisted of English cherry trees.

The same incessant vigilance, which blazed forth when he had a vast province under his care, now showed itself with equal vigor, though in narrower limits. He patrolled with unceasing watchfulness the boundaries of his little territory; repelled every encroachment with intrepid promptness; punished every vagrant depredation upon his orchard or his farm-yard with inflexible severity; and conducted every stray hog or cow in triumph to the pound. But to the indigent neighbor, the friendless stranger, or the weary wanderer, his spacious doors were ever open, and his capacious fire-place, that emblem of his own warm and generous heart, had always a corner to receive and cherish them. There was an exception to this, I must confess, in case the ill-starred applicant were an Englishman or a Yankee; to whom, though he might extend the hand of assistance, he could never be brought to yield the rites of hospitality. Nay, if peradventure some straggling merchant of the East should stop at his door, with his cart-load of tin ware or wooden bowls, the fiery Peter would issue forth like a giant from his castle, and make such a furious clattering among his pots and kettles, that the vender of *"notions"* was fain to betake himself to instant flight.

His suit of regimentals, worn threadbare by the brush, were carefully hung up in the state bed-chamber, and regularly aired the first fair day of every month; and his cocked hat and trusty sword were suspended in grim repose over the parlor mantelpiece, forming supporters to a full length portrait of the renowned Admiral Van Tromp. In his domestic empire he maintained strict discipline, and a well-organized despotic government; but though his own will was the supreme law, yet the good of his subjects was his constant object. He watched over, not merely their immediate comforts, but their morals, and their ultimate welfare; for he gave them abundance of excellent admonition, nor could any of them complain, that, when occasion required, he was by any means niggardly in bestowing wholesome correction.

The good old Dutch festivals, those periodical demonstrations of an overflowing heart and a thankful spirit, which are falling into sad disuse among my fellow-citizens, were faithfully observed in the mansion of Governor Stuyvesant. New-Year was truly a day of open-handed liberality, of jocund revelry, and warm-hearted congratulation, when the bosom swelled with genial good fellowship, and the plenteous table was attended with an unceremonious freedom, and honest broad-mouthed merriment, unknown in these days of degeneracy and refinement. Paas and Pinxter were scrupulously observed throughout his dominions; nor was the day of St. Nicholas suffered to pass by, without making presents, hanging the stocking in the chimney, and complying with all its other ceremonies.

Once a year, on the first day of April, he used to array himself in full regimentals, being the anniversary of his triumphal entry into New Amsterdam, after the conquest of New Sweden. This was always a kind of saturnalia among the domestics, when they considered themselves at liberty, in some measure, to say and do what they pleased; for on this day their master was always observed to unbend, and become exceeding pleasant and jocose, sending the old gray-headed negroes on April-fool's errands for pigeon's milk; not one of whom but allowed himself to be taken in, and humored his old master's jokes, as became a faithful and well-disciplined dependant. Thus did he reign, happily and peacefully on his own land—injuring no man—envying no man—molested by no outward strifes; perplexed by no internal commotions—and the mighty monarchs of the earth, who were vainly seeking to maintain peace, and promote the welfare of mankind, by war and desolation, would have done well to have made a voyage to the little island of Manna-hata, and learned a lesson in government from the domestic economy of Peter Stuyvesant.

In process of time, however, the old governor, like all other children of mortality, began to exhibit evident tokens of decay. Like an aged oak, which, though it long has braved the fury of the elements, and still retains its gigantic proportions, begins to shake and groan with every blast—so was it with the gallant Peter; for though he still bore the port and semblance of what he was, in the days of his hardihood and chivalry, yet did age and infirmity begin to sap the vigor of his frame—but his heart, that unconquerable citadel, still triumphed unsubdued. With matchless avidity would he listen to every article of intelligence concerning the battles between the English and Dutch—still would his pulse beat high, whenever he heard of the victories of De Ruyter—and his countenance lower, and his eyebrows knit, when fortune turned in favor of the English. At length, as on a certain day he had just smoked his fifth pipe, and was napping after dinner, in his arm-chair, conquering the whole British nation in his dreams, he was suddenly aroused by a ringing of bells, rattling of drums, and roaring of cannon, that put all his blood in a ferment. But when he learnt that these rejoicings were in honor of a great victory obtained by the combined English and French fleets over the brave De Ruyter, and the younger Van Tromp, it went so much to his heart, that he took to his bed, and, in less than three days, was brought to death's door, by a violent cholera morbus! Even in this extremity he still displayed the unconquerable spirit of Peter *the Headstrong;* holding out to the last gasp, with inflexible obstinacy, against a whole army of old women who were bent upon driving the enemy out of his bowels, in the true Dutch mode of defence, by inundation.

While he thus lay, lingering on the verge of dissolution, news was brought him, that the brave De Ruyter had made good his retreat, with little loss, and meant once more to meet the enemy in battle. The closing eye of the old warrior kindled with martial fire at the words—he partly raised himself in bed—clinched his withered hand, as if he felt within his gripe that sword which waved in triumph before the walls of Fort Christina, and giving a grim smile of exultation, sank back upon his pillow, and expired.

Thus died Peter Stuyvesant, a valiant soldier—a loyal subject—an upright governor, and an honest Dutchman—who wanted only a few empires to desolate, to have been immortalized as a hero!

His funeral obsequies were celebrated with the utmost grandeur and solemnity. The town was perfectly emptied of its inhabitants, who crowded in throngs to pay the last sad honors to their good old governor. All his sterling qualities rushed in full tide upon their recollection, while the memory of his foibles and his faults had expired with him. The ancient burghers contended who should have the privilege of bearing the pall; the populace strove who should walk nearest to the bier, and the melancholy procession was closed by a number of gray-headed negroes, who had wintered and summered in the household of their departed master for the greater part of a century.

With sad and gloomy countenances, the multitude gathered round the grave. They dwelt with mournful hearts on the sturdy virtues, the signal services, and the gallant exploits of the brave old worthy. They recalled, with secret upbraidings, their own factious oppositions to his government, and many an ancient burgher, whose phlegmatic features had never been known to relax, nor his eyes to moisten, was now observed to puff a pensive pipe, and the big drop to steal down his cheek; while he muttered, with affectionate accent, and melancholy shake of the head—"Well, den!—Hardkoppig Peter ben gone at last!"

His remains were deposited in the family vault, under a chapel which he had piously erected on his estate, and dedicated to St. Nicholas—and which stood on the identical spot at present occupied by St. Mark's church, where his tombstone is still to be seen. His estate, or *bouwery*, as it was called, has ever continued in the possession of his descendants, who, by the uniform integrity of their conduct, and their strict adherence to the customs and manners that prevailed in the *"good old times,"* have proved themselves worthy of their illustrious ancestor. Many a time and oft has the farm been haunted at night by enterprising money-diggers, in quest of pots of gold, said to have been buried by the old governor—though I cannot learn that any of them have ever been enriched by their researches—and who is there, among my native-born fellow-citizens, that does not remember when, in the mischievous days of his boyhood, he conceived it a great exploit to rob "Stuyvesant's orchard" on a holiday afternoon?

At this strong-hold of the family may still be seen certain memorials of the immortal Peter. His full-length portrait frowns in martial terrors from the parlor wall—his cocked hat and sword still hang up in the best bedroom—his brimstone-colored breeches were for a long while suspended in the hall, until some years since they occasioned a dispute between a new-married couple—and his silver-mounted wooden leg is still treasured up in the store-room, as an invaluable relique.

THE AUTHOR'S ACCOUNT OF HIMSELF [36]

I am of this mind with Homer, that as the snaile that crept out of her shel was turned eftsoons into a toad, and thereby was forced to make a stoole to sit on; so the traveller that stragleth from his owne country is in a short time transformed into so monstrous a shape, that he is faine to alter his mansion with his manners, and to live where he can, not where he would.   LYLY'S EUPHUES.

I was always fond of visiting new scenes, and observing strange characters and manners. Even when a mere child I began my travels, and made many tours of discovery into foreign parts and unknown regions of my native city, to the frequent alarm of my parents, and the emolument of the town-crier. As I grew into boyhood, I extended the range of my observations. My holiday afternoons were spent in rambles about the surrounding country. I made myself familiar with all its places famous in history or fable. I knew every spot where a murder or robbery had been committed, or a ghost seen. I visited the neighboring villages, and added greatly to my stock of knowledge, by noting their habits and customs, and conversing with their sages and great men. I even journeyed one long summer's day to the summit of the most distant hill, whence I stretched my eye over many a mile of terra incognita, and was astonished to find how vast a globe I inhabited.

This rambling propensity strengthened with my years. Books of voyages and travels became my passion, and in devouring their contents, I neglected the regular exercises of the school. How wistfully would I wander about the pier-heads in fine weather, and watch the parting ships, bound to distant climes—with what longing eyes would I gaze after their lessening sails, and waft myself in imagination to the ends of the earth!

Further reading and thinking, though they brought this

vague inclination into more reasonable bounds, only served to make it more decided. I visited various parts of my own country; and had I been merely a lover of fine scenery, I should have felt little desire to seek elsewhere its gratification, for on no country have the charms of nature been more prodigally lavished. Her mighty lakes, like oceans of liquid silver; her mountains, with their bright aerial tints; her valleys, teeming with wild fertility; her tremendous cataracts, thundering in their solitudes; her boundless plains, waving with spontaneous verdure; her broad deep rivers, rolling in solemn silence to the ocean; her trackless forests, where vegetation puts forth all its magnificence; her skies, kindling with the magic of summer clouds and glorious sunshine;—no, never need an American look beyond his own country for the sublime and beautiful of natural scenery.

But Europe held forth the charms of storied and poetical association. There were to be seen the masterpieces of art, the refinements of highly-cultivated society, the quaint peculiarities of ancient and local custom. My native country was full of youthful promise: Europe was rich in the accumulated treasures of age. Her very ruins told the history of times gone by, and every mouldering stone was a chronicle. I longed to wander over the scenes of renowned achievement—to tread, as it were, in the footsteps of antiquity—to loiter about the ruined castle—to meditate on the falling tower—to escape, in short, from the common-place realities of the present, and lose myself among the shadowy grandeurs of the past.

I had, beside all this, an earnest desire to see the great men of the earth. We have, it is true, our great men in America: not a city but has an ample share of them. I have mingled among them in my time, and been almost withered by the shade into which they cast me; for there is nothing so baleful to a small man as the shade of a great one, particularly the great man of a city. But I was anxious to see the great men of Europe; for I had read in the works of various philosophers, that all animals degenerated in America, and man among the number. A great man of Europe, thought I, must therefore be as superior to a

great man of America, as a peak of the Alps to a highland of
the Hudson; and in this idea I was confirmed, by observing the
comparative importance and swelling magnitude of many English travellers among us, who, I was assured, were very little
people in their own country. I will visit this land of wonders,
thought I, and see the gigantic race from which I am degenerated.

It has been either my good or evil lot to have my roving
passion gratified. I have wandered through different countries,
and witnessed many of the shifting scenes of life. I cannot say
that I have studied them with the eye of a philosopher; but
rather with the sauntering gaze with which humble lovers of
the picturesque stroll from the window of one print-shop to
another; caught sometimes by the delineations of beauty, sometimes by the distortions of caricature, and sometimes by the
loveliness of landscape. As it is the fashion for modern tourists
to travel pencil in hand, and bring home their portfolios filled
with sketches, I am disposed to get up a few for the entertainment of my friends. When, however, I look over the hints and
memorandums I have taken down for the purpose, my heart
almost fails me at finding how my idle humor has led me aside
from the great objects studied by every regular traveller who
would make a book. I fear I shall give equal disappointment
with an unlucky landscape painter, who had travelled on the
continent, but, following the bent of his vagrant inclination,
had sketched in nooks, and corners, and by-places. His sketch-
book was accordingly crowded with cottages, and landscapes,
and obscure ruins; but he had neglected to paint St. Peter's, or
the Coliseum; the cascade of Terni, or the bay of Naples; and
had not a single glacier or volcano in his whole collection.

RIP VAN WINKLE[37]

A POSTHUMOUS WRITING OF DIEDRICH KNICKERBOCKER

By Woden, God of Saxons,
From whence comes Wensday, that is Wodensday.
Truth is a thing that ever I will keep
Unto thylke day in which I creep into
My sepulchre—

CARTWRIGHT.

(The following Tale was found among the papers of the late Diedrich Knickerbocker, an old gentleman of New York, who was very curious in the Dutch history of the province, and the manners of the descendants from its primitive settlers. His historical researches, however, did not lie so much among books as among men; for the former are lamentably scanty on his favorite topics; whereas he found the old burghers, and still more their wives, rich in that legendary lore, so invaluable to true history. Whenever, therefore, he happened upon a genuine Dutch family, snugly shut up in its low-roofed farmhouse, under a spreading sycamore, he looked upon it as a little clasped volume of black-letter, and studied it with the zeal of a book-worm.

The result of all these researches was a history of the province during the reign of the Dutch governors, which he published some years since. There have been various opinions as to the literary character of his work, and, to tell the truth, it is not a whit better than it should be. Its chief merit is its scrupulous accuracy, which indeed was a little questioned on its first appearance, but has since been completely established; and it is now admitted into all historical collections, as a book of unquestionable authority.

The old gentleman died shortly after the publication of his work, and now that he is dead and gone, it cannot do much harm to his memory to say that his time might have been much better employed in weightier labors. He, however, was apt to ride his hobby his own way; and though it did now and then kick up the dust a little in the eyes of his neighbors, and grieve the spirit of some friends, for whom he felt the truest deference and affection; yet his errors and follies are remembered "more in sorrow than in anger," and it begins to be suspected, that he never intended to injure or offend. But however his memory may be appreciated by critics, it is still held dear by many folk, whose good opinion is well worth having; particularly by certain biscuit-bakers, who have gone so far as to imprint his likeness on their new-year cakes; and have thus given him a chance for immortality, almost equal to the being stamped on a Waterloo Medal, or a Queen Anne's Farthing.)

Whoever has made a voyage up the Hudson must remember the Kaatskill mountains. They are a dismembered branch of the great Appalachian family, and are seen away to the west of the river, swelling up to a noble height, and lording it over the surrounding country. Every change of season, every change of weather, indeed, every hour of the day, produces some change in the magical hues and shapes of these mountains, and they are regarded by all the good wives, far and near, as perfect barometers. When the weather is fair and settled, they are clothed in blue and purple, and print their bold outlines on the clear evening sky; but, sometimes, when the rest of the landscape is cloudless, they will gather a hood of gray vapors about their summits, which, in the last rays of the setting sun, will glow and light up like a crown of glory.

At the foot of these fairy mountains, the voyager may have descried the light smoke curling up from a village, whose shingle-roofs gleam among the trees, just where the blue tints of the upland melt away into the fresh green of the nearer landscape. It is a little village, of great antiquity, having been founded by some of the Dutch colonists, in the early times of the province, just about the beginning of the government of the good Peter Stuyvesant, (may he rest in peace!) and there were some of the houses of the original settlers standing within a few years, built of small yellow bricks brought from Holland, having latticed windows and gable fronts, surmounted with weather-cocks.

In that same village, and in one of these very houses (which, to tell the precise truth, was sadly time-worn and weather-beaten), there lived many years since, while the country was yet a province of Great Britain, a simple good-natured fellow, of the name of Rip Van Winkle. He was a descendant of the Van Winkles who figured so gallantly in the chivalrous days of Peter Stuyvesant, and accompanied him to the siege of Fort Christina. He inherited, however, but little of the martial character of his ancestors. I have observed that he was a simple good-natured man; he was, moreover, a kind neighbor, and an obedient hen-pecked husband. Indeed, to the latter circumstance might be owing that meekness of spirit which gained him such universal popularity; for those men are most apt to be obsequious and conciliating abroad, who are under the discipline of shrews at home. Their tempers, doubtless, are rendered pliant and malleable in the fiery furnace of domestic tribulation; and a curtain lecture is worth all the sermons in the world for teaching the virtues of patience and long-suffering. A termagant wife may, therefore, in some respects, be considered a tolerable blessing; and if so, Rip Van Winkle was thrice blessed.

Certain it is, that he was a great favorite among all the good wives of the village, who, as usual, with the amiable sex, took his part in all family squabbles; and never failed, whenever they talked those matters over in their evening gossipings, to lay all the blame on Dame Van Winkle. The children of the village, too, would shout with joy whenever he approached. He assisted at their sports, made their playthings, taught them to fly kites and shoot marbles, and told them long stories of ghosts, witches, and Indians. Whenever he went dodging about the village, he was surrounded by a troop of them, hanging on his skirts, clambering on his back, and playing a thousand tricks on him with impunity; and not a dog would bark at him throughout the neighborhood.

The great error in Rip's composition was an insuperable aversion to all kinds of profitable labor. It could not be from the want of assiduity or perseverance; for he would sit on a wet rock, with a rod as long and heavy as a Tartar's lance, and fish all day without a murmur, even though he should not be encouraged by a single nibble. He would carry a fowling-piece on his shoulder for hours together, trudging through woods and swamps, and up hill and down dale, to shoot a few squirrels or wild pigeons. He would never refuse to assist a neighbor even in the roughest toil, and was a foremost man at all country frolics for husking Indian corn, or building stone-fences; the women of the village, too, used to employ him to run their errands, and to do such little odd jobs as their less obliging husbands would not do for them. In a word Rip was ready to attend to anybody's business but his own; but as to doing family duty, and keeping his farm in order, he found it impossible.

In fact, he declared it was of no use to work on his farm; it was the most pestilent little piece of ground in the whole country; every thing about it went wrong, and would go wrong, in spite of him. His fences were continually falling to pieces; his cow would either go astray, or get among the cabbages; weeds were sure to grow quicker in his fields than anywhere else; the rain always made a point of setting in just as he had some outdoor work to do; so that though his patrimonial estate had dwindled away under his management, acre by acre, until there was little more left than a mere patch of Indian corn and potatoes, yet it was the worst conditioned farm in the neighborhood.

His children, too, were as ragged and wild as if they belonged to nobody. His son Rip, an urchin begotten in his own likeness, promised to inherit the habits, with the old clothes of his father. He was generally seen trooping like a colt at his mother's heels, equipped in a pair of his father's cast-off galligaskins, which he had much ado to hold up with one hand, as a fine lady does her train in bad weather.

Rip Van Winkle, however, was one of those happy mortals, of foolish, well-oiled dispositions, who take the world easy, eat white bread or brown, whichever can be got with least thought or trouble, and would rather starve on a penny than work for a pound. If left to himself, he would have whistled life away in perfect contentment; but his wife kept continually dinning in his ears about his idleness, his carelessness, and the ruin he was bringing on his family. Morning, noon, and night, her tongue was incessantly going, and every thing he said or did was sure to produce a torrent of household eloquence. Rip had but one way of replying to all lectures of the kind, and that, by frequent use, had grown into a habit. He shrugged his shoulders, shook his head, cast up his eyes, but said nothing. This, however, always provoked a fresh volley from his wife; so that he was fain to draw off his forces, and take to the outside of the house—the only side which, in truth, belongs to a hen-pecked husband.

Rip's sole domestic adherent was his dog Wolf, who was as much hen-pecked as his master; for Dame Van Winkle regarded them as companions in idleness, and even looked upon Wolf with an evil eye, as the cause of his master's going so often astray. True it is, in all points of spirit befitting an honorable dog, he was as courageous an animal as ever scoured the woods —but what courage can withstand the ever-during and all-besetting terrors of a woman's tongue? The moment Wolf entered the house his crest fell, his tail drooped to the ground, or curled between his legs, he sneaked about with a gallows air, casting many a sidelong glance at Dame Van Winkle, and at the least flourish of a broomstick or ladle, he would fly to the door with yelping precipitation.

Times grew worse and worse with Rip Van Winkle as years of matrimony rolled on; a tart temper never mellows with age, and a sharp tongue is the only edged tool that grows keener with constant use. For a long while he used to console himself, when driven from home, by frequenting a kind of perpetual club of the sages, philosophers, and other idle personages of the village; which held its sessions on a bench before a small inn, designated by a rubicund portrait of His Majesty George the Third. Here they used to sit in the shade through a long lazy summer's day, talking listlessly over village gossip, or telling endless sleepy stories about nothing. But it would have been worth any statesman's money to have heard the profound discussions that sometimes took place, when by chance an old newspaper fell into their hands from some passing traveller. How solemnly they would listen to the contents, as drawled

out by Derrick Van Bummel, the schoolmaster, a dapper
learned little man, who was not to be daunted by the most
gigantic word in the dictionary; and how sagely they would
deliberate upon public events some months after they had taken
place.

The opinions of this junto were completely controlled by
Nicholas Vedder, a patriarch of the village, and landlord of the
inn, at the door of which he took his seat from morning till
night, just moving sufficiently to avoid the sun and keep in the
shade of a large tree; so that the neighbors could tell the hour
by his movements as accurately as by a sun-dial. It is true he
was rarely heard to speak, but smoked his pipe incessantly. His
adherents, however (for every great man has his adherents),
perfectly understood him, and knew how to gather his opinions.
When any thing that was read or related displeased him, he was
observed to smoke his pipe vehemently, and to send forth
short, frequent and angry puffs; but when pleased, he would inhale the smoke slowly and tranquilly, and emit it in light and
placid clouds; and sometimes, taking the pipe from his mouth,
and letting the fragrant vapor curl about his nose, would
gravely nod his head in token of perfect approbation.

From even this stronghold the unlucky Rip was at length
routed by his termagant wife, who would suddenly break in
upon the tranquillity of the assemblage and call the members
all to naught; nor was that august personage, Nicholas Vedder
himself, sacred from the daring tongue of this terrible virago,
who charged him outright with encouraging her husband in
habits of idleness.

Poor Rip was at last reduced almost to despair; and his only
alternative, to escape from the labor of the farm and clamor of
his wife, was to take gun in hand and stroll away into the woods.
Here he would sometimes seat himself at the foot of a tree, and
share the contents of his wallet with Wolf, with whom he
sympathized as a fellow-sufferer in persecution. "Poor Wolf,"
he would say, "thy mistress leads thee a dog's life of it; but
never mind, my lad, whilst I live thou shalt never want a friend
to stand by thee!" Wolf would wag his tail, look wistfully in

his master's face, and if dogs can feel pity I verily believe he reciprocated the sentiment with all his heart.

In a long ramble of the kind on a fine autumnal day, Rip had unconsciously scrambled to one of the highest parts of the Kaatskill mountains. He was after his favorite sport of squirrel shooting, and the still solitudes had echoed and re-echoed with the reports of his gun. Panting and fatigued, he threw himself, late in the afternoon, on a green knoll, covered with mountain herbage, that crowned the brow of a precipice. From an opening between the trees he could overlook all the lower country for many a mile of rich woodland. He saw at a distance the lordly Hudson, far, far below him, moving on its silent but majestic course, with the reflection of a purple cloud, or the sail of a lagging bark, here and there sleeping on its glassy bosom, and at last losing itself in the blue highlands.

On the other side he looked down into a deep mountain glen, wild, lonely, and shagged, the bottom filled with fragments from the impending cliffs, and scarcely lighted by the reflected rays of the setting sun. For some time Rip lay musing on this scene; evening was gradually advancing; the mountains began to throw their long blue shadows over the valleys; he saw that it would be dark long before he could reach the village, and he heaved a heavy sigh when he thought of encountering the terrors of Dame Van Winkle.

As he was about to descend, he heard a voice from a distance, hallooing, "Rip Van Winkle! Rip Van Winkle!" He looked round, but could see nothing but a crow winging its solitary flight across the mountain. He thought his fancy must have deceived him, and turned again to descend, when he heard the same cry ring through the still evening air; "Rip Van Winkle! Rip Van Winkle!"—at the same time Wolf bristled up his back, and giving a low growl, skulked to his master's side, looking fearfully down into the glen. Rip now felt a vague apprehension stealing over him; he looked anxiously in the same direction, and perceived a strange figure slowly toiling up the rocks, and bending under the weight of something he carried on his back. He was surprised to see any human being in this lonely and unfrequented place, but supposing it to be some one of the neighborhood in need of his assistance, he hastened down to yield it.

On nearer approach he was still more surprised at the singularity of the stranger's appearance. He was a short square-built old fellow, with thick bushy hair, and a grizzled beard. His dress was of the antique Dutch fashion—a cloth jerkin strapped round the waist—several pair of breeches, the outer one of ample volume, decorated with rows of buttons down the sides, and bunches at the knees. He bore on his shoulder a stout keg, that seemed full of liquor, and made signs for Rip to approach and assist him with the load. Though rather shy and distrustful of this new acquaintance, Rip complied with his usual alacrity; and mutually relieving one another, they clambered up a narrow gully, apparently the dry bed of a mountain torrent. As they ascended, Rip every now and then heard long rolling peals, like distant thunder, that seemed to issue out of a deep ravine, or rather cleft, between lofty rocks, toward which their rugged path conducted. He paused for an instant, but supposing it to be the muttering of one of those transient thunder-showers which often take place in mountain heights, he proceeded. Passing through the ravine, they came to a hollow, like a small amphitheatre, surrounded by perpendicular precipices, over the brinks of which impending trees shot their branches, so that you only caught glimpses of the azure sky and the bright evening cloud. During the whole time Rip and his companion had labored on in silence; for though the former marvelled greatly what could be the object of carrying a keg of liquor up this wild mountain, yet there was something strange and incomprehensible about the unknown, that inspired awe and checked familiarity.

On entering the amphitheatre, new objects of wonder presented themselves. On a level spot in the centre was a company of odd-looking personages playing at nine-pins. They were dressed in a quaint outlandish fashion; some wore short doublets, others jerkins, with long knives in their belts, and most of them had enormous breeches, of similar style with that of the guide's. Their visages, too, were peculiar: one had a large beard, broad face, and small piggish eyes: the face of another seemed to consist entirely of nose, and was surmounted by a white sugar-loaf hat, set off with a little red cock's tail. They all had beards, of various shapes and colors. There was one who seemed to be the commander. He was a stout old gentleman, with a weather-beaten countenance; he wore a laced doublet, broad belt and hanger, high crowned hat and feather, red stockings, and high-heeled shoes, with roses in them. The whole group reminded Rip of the figures in an old Flemish painting, in the parlor of Dominie Van Shaick, the village parson, and which had been brought over from Holland at the time of the settlement.

What seemed particularly odd to Rip was, that though these folks were evidently amusing themselves, yet they maintained the gravest faces, the most mysterious silence, and were, withal, the most melancholy party of pleasure he had ever witnessed. Nothing interrupted the stillness of the scene but the noise of the balls, which, whenever they were rolled, echoed along the mountains like rumbling peals of thunder.

As Rip and his companion approached them, they suddenly desisted from their play, and stared at him with such fixed statue-like gaze, and such strange, uncouth, lack-lustre countenances, that his heart turned within him, and his knees smote together. His companion now emptied the contents of the keg into large flagons, and made signs to him to wait upon the company. He obeyed with fear and trembling; they quaffed the liquor in profound silence, and then returned to their game.

By degrees Rip's awe and apprehension subsided. He even ventured, when no eye was fixed upon him, to taste the beverage, which he found had much of the flavor of excellent Hollands. He was naturally a thirsty soul, and was soon tempted to repeat the draught. One taste provoked another; and he reiterated his visits to the flagon so often that at length his senses were overpowered, his eyes swam in his head, his head gradually declined, and he fell into a deep sleep.

On waking, he found himself on the green knoll whence he had first seen the old man of the glen. He rubbed his eyes—it was a bright sunny morning. The birds were hopping and twittering among the bushes, and the eagle was wheeling aloft, and breasting the pure mountain breeze. "Surely," thought Rip, "I have not slept here all night." He recalled the occurrences before he fell asleep. The strange man with a keg of liquor—the mountain ravine—the wild retreat among the rocks—the wobegone party at nine-pins—the flagon—"Oh! that flagon! that wicked flagon!" thought Rip—"what excuse shall I make to Dame Van Winkle!"

He looked round for his gun, but in place of the clean well-oiled fowling-piece, he found an old firelock lying by him, the barrel incrusted with rust, the lock falling off, and the stock worm-eaten. He now suspected that the grave roysters of the mountain had put a trick upon him, and, having dosed him with liquor, had robbed him of his gun. Wolf, too, had disappeared, but he might have strayed away after a squirrel or partridge. He whistled after him and shouted his name, but all in vain; the echoes repeated his whistle and shout, but no dog was to be seen.

He determined to revisit the scene of the last evening's gambol, and if he met with any of the party, to demand his dog and gun. As he rose to walk, he found himself stiff in the joints, and wanting in his usual activity. "These mountain beds do not agree with me," thought Rip, "and if this frolic should lay me up with a fit of the rheumatism, I shall have a blessed time with Dame Van Winkle." With some difficulty he got down into the glen: he found the gully up which he and his companion had ascended the preceding evening; but to his astonishment a mountain stream was now foaming down it, leaping from rock to rock, and filling the glen with babbling murmurs. He, however, made shift to scramble up its sides, working his toilsome way through thickets of birch, sassafras, and witch-hazel, and sometimes tripped up or entangled by the wild grapevines that twisted their coils or tendrils from tree to tree, and spread a kind of network in his path.

At length he reached to where the ravine had opened through the cliffs to the amphitheatre; but no traces of such opening remained. The rocks presented a high impenetrable wall over which the torrent came tumbling in a sheet of feathery foam, and fell into a broad deep basin, black from the shadows of the surrounding forest. Here, then, poor Rip was brought to a stand. He again called and whistled after his dog; he was only answered by the cawing of a flock of idle crows, sporting high in air about a dry tree that overhung a sunny precipice; and who, secure in their elevation, seemed to look down and scoff at the poor man's perplexities. What was to be done? the morning was passing away, and Rip felt famished for want of his breakfast. He grieved to give up his dog and gun; he dreaded to meet his wife; but it would not do to starve among the mountains. He shook his head, shouldered the rusty firelock, and, with a heart full of trouble and anxiety, turned his steps homeward.

As he approached the village he met a number of people, but none whom he knew, which somewhat surprised him, for he had thought himself acquainted with every one in the country round. Their dress, too, was of a different fashion from that to which he was accustomed. They all stared at him with equal marks of surprise, and whenever they cast their eyes upon him, invariably stroked their chins. The constant recurrence of this gesture induced Rip, involuntarily, to do the same, when, to his astonishment, he found his beard had grown a foot long!

He had now entered the skirts of the village. A troop of strange children ran at his heels, hooting after him, and pointing at his gray beard. The dogs, too, not one of which he recognized for an old acquaintance, barked at him as he passed. The very village was altered; it was larger and more populous. There were rows of houses which he had never seen before, and those which had been his familiar haunts had disappeared. Strange names were over the doors—strange faces at the windows—every thing was strange. His mind now misgave him; he began to doubt whether both he and the world around him were not bewitched. Surely this was his native village, which he had left but the day before. There stood the Kaatskill mountains—there ran the silver Hudson at a distance—there was every hill and dale precisely as it had always been—Rip was sorely perplexed—"That flagon last night," thought he, "has addled my poor head sadly!"

It was with some difficulty that he found the way to his own house, which he approached with silent awe, expecting every moment to hear the shrill voice of Dame Van Winkle. He found the house gone to decay—the roof fallen in, the windows shattered, and the doors off the hinges. A half-starved dog that looked like Wolf was skulking about it. Rip called him by name, but the cur snarled, showed his teeth, and passed on. This was an unkind cut indeed—"My very dog," sighed poor Rip, "has forgotten me!"

He entered the house, which, to tell the truth, Dame Van Winkle had always kept in neat order. It was empty, forlorn, and apparently abandoned. This desolateness overcame all his connubial fears—he called loudly for his wife and children—the lonely chambers rang for a moment with his voice, and then all again was silence.

He now hurried forth, and hastened to his old resort, the village inn—but it too was gone. A large rickety wooden building stood in its place, with great gaping windows, some of them broken and mended with old hats and petticoats, and over the door was painted, "the Union Hotel, by Jonathan Doolittle." Instead of the great tree that used to shelter the quiet little Dutch inn of yore, there now was reared a tall naked pole, with something on the top that looked like a red night-cap, and from it was fluttering a flag, on which was a singular assemblage of stars and stripes—all this was strange and incomprehensible. He recognized on the sign, however, the ruby face of King George, under which he had smoked so many a peaceful pipe; but even this was singularly metamorphosed. The red coat was changed for one of blue and buff, a sword was held in the hand instead of a sceptre, the head was decorated with a cocked hat, and underneath was painted in large characters, GENERAL WASHINGTON.

There was, as usual, a crowd of folk about the door, but none that Rip recollected. The very character of the people seemed changed. There was a busy, bustling, disputatious tone about it, instead of the accustomed phlegm and drowsy tranquillity. He looked in vain for the sage Nicholas Vedder, with his broad face, double chin, and fair long pipe, uttering clouds of tobacco-smoke instead of idle speeches; or Van Bummel, the schoolmaster, doling forth the contents of an ancient newspaper. In place of these, a lean, bilious-looking fellow, with his pockets full of handbills, was haranguing vehemently about rights of citizens—elections—members of congress—liberty—Bunker's Hill—heroes of seventy-six—and other words, which were a perfect Babylonish jargon to the bewildered Van Winkle.

The appearance of Rip, with his long grizzled beard, his rusty fowling-piece, his uncouth dress, and an army of women and children at his heels, soon attracted the attention of the tavern politicians. They crowded round him, eyeing him from head to foot with great curiosity. The orator bustled up to him, and, drawing him partly aside, inquired "on which side he voted?" Rip stared in vacant stupidity. Another short but busy little fellow pulled him by the arm, and, rising on tiptoe, inquired in his ear, "Whether he was Federal or Democrat?" Rip was equally at a loss to comprehend the question; when a knowing, self-important old gentleman, in a sharp cocked hat, made his way through the crowd, putting them to the right and left with his elbows as he passed, and planting himself before Van Winkle, with one arm akimbo, the other resting on his cane, his keen eyes and sharp hat penetrating, as it were, into his very soul, demanded in an austere tone, "what brought him to the election with a gun on his shoulder, and a mob at his heels, and whether he meant to breed a riot in the village?"—"Alas! gentlemen," cried Rip, somewhat dismayed, "I am a poor quiet man, a native of the place, and a loyal subject of the king, God bless him!"

Here a general shout burst from the by-standers—"A tory! a tory! a spy! a refugee! hustle him! away with him!" It was with great difficulty that the self-important man in the cocked hat restored order; and, having assumed a tenfold austerity of brow, demanded again of the unknown culprit, what he came there for, and whom he was seeking? The poor man humbly assured him that he meant no harm, but merely came there in search of some of his neighbors, who used to keep about the tavern.

"Well—who are they?—name them."

Rip bethought himself a moment, and inquired, "Where's Nicholas Vedder?"

There was a silence for a little while, when an old man replied, in a thin piping voice, "Nicholas Vedder! why, he is dead and gone these eighteen years! There was a wooden tombstone in the church-yard that used to tell all about him, but that's rotten and gone too."

"Where's Brom Dutcher?"

"Oh, he went off to the army in the beginning of the war; some say he was killed at the storming of Stony Point—others say he was drowned in a squall at the foot of Antony's Nose. I don't know—he never came back again."

"Where's Van Bummel, the schoolmaster?"

"He went off to the wars too, was a great militia general, and is now in congress."

Rip's heart died away at hearing of these sad changes in his home and friends, and finding himself thus alone in the world. Every answer puzzled him too, by treating of such enormous lapses of time, and of matters which he could not understand: war—congress—Stony Point;—he had no courage to ask after any more friends, but cried out in despair, "Does nobody here know Rip Van Winkle?"

"Oh, Rip Van Winkle!" exclaimed two or three, "Oh, to be sure! that's Rip Van Winkle yonder, leaning against the tree."

Rip looked, and beheld a precise counterpart of himself, as he went up the mountain: apparently as lazy, and certainly as ragged. The poor fellow was now completely confounded. He doubted his own identity, and whether he was himself or another man. In the midst of his bewilderment, the man in the cocked hat demanded who he was, and what was his name?

"God knows," exclaimed he, at his wit's end; "I'm not myself—I'm somebody else—that's me yonder—no—that's somebody else got into my shoes—I was myself last night, but I fell asleep on the mountain, and they've changed my gun, and every thing's changed, and I'm changed, and I can't tell what's my name, or who I am!"

The by-standers began now to look at each other, nod, wink significantly, and tap their fingers against their foreheads. There was a whisper, also, about securing the gun, and keeping the old fellow from doing mischief, at the very suggestion of which the self-important man in the cocked hat retired with some precipitation. At this critical moment a fresh comely woman pressed through the throng to get a peep at the gray-bearded man. She had a chubby child in her arms, which, frightened at his looks, began to cry. "Hush, Rip," cried she, "hush, you little fool; the old man won't hurt you." The name of the child, the air of the mother, the tone of her voice, all awakened a train of recollections in his mind. "What is your name, my good woman?" asked he.

"Judith Gardenier."

"And your father's name?"

"Ah, poor man, Rip Van Winkle was his name, but it's twenty years since he went away from home with his gun, and never has been heard of since—his dog came home without him; but whether he shot himself, or was carried away by the Indians, nobody can tell. I was then but a little girl."

Rip had but one question more to ask; but he put it with a faltering voice:

"Where's your mother?"

"Oh, she too had died but a short time since; she broke a blood-vessel in a fit of passion at a New-England peddler."

There was a drop of comfort, at least, in this intelligence. The honest man could contain himself no longer. He caught his daughter and her child in his arms. "I am your father!" cried he—"Young Rip Van Winkle once—old Rip Van Winkle now!—Does nobody know poor Rip Van Winkle?"

All stood amazed, until an old woman, tottering out from

among the crowd, put her hand to her brow, and peering under it in his face for a moment, exclaimed, "Sure enough! it is Rip Van Winkle—it is himself! Welcome home again, old neighbor —Why, where have you been these twenty long years?"

Rip's story was soon told, for the whole twenty years had been to him but as one night. The neighbors stared when they heard it; some were seen to wink at each other, and put their tongues in their cheeks: and the self-important man in the cocked hat, who, when the alarm was over, had returned to the field, screwed down the corners of his mouth, and shook his head—upon which there was a general shaking of the head throughout the assemblage.

It was determined, however, to take the opinion of old Peter Vanderdonk, who was seen slowly advancing up the road. He was a descendant of the historian of that name, who wrote one of the earliest accounts of the province. Peter was the most ancient inhabitant of the village, and well versed in all the wonderful events and traditions of the neighborhood. He recollected Rip at once, and corroborated his story in the most satisfactory manner. He assured the company that it was a fact, handed down from his ancestor the historian, that the Kaatskill mountains had always been haunted by strange beings. That it was affirmed that the great Hendrick Hudson, the first discoverer of the river and country, kept a kind of vigil there every twenty years, with his crew of the Half-moon; being permitted in this way to revisit the scenes of his enterprise, and keep a guardian eye upon the river, and the great city called by his name. That his father had once seen them in their old Dutch dresses playing at nine-pins in a hollow of the mountain; and that he himself had heard, one summer afternoon, the sound of their balls, like distant peals of thunder.

To make a long story short, the company broke up, and returned to the more important concerns of the election. Rip's daughter took him home to live with her; she had a snug, well-furnished house, and a stout cheery farmer for a husband, whom Rip recollected for one of the urchins that used to climb. upon his back. As to Rip's son and heir, who was the ditto of himself, seen leaning against the tree, he was employed to work on the farm; but evinced an hereditary disposition to attend to any thing else but his business.

Rip now resumed his old walks and habits; he soon found many of his former cronies, though all rather the worse for the wear and tear of time; and preferred making friends among the rising generation, with whom he soon grew into great favor.

Having nothing to do at home, and being arrived at that happy age when a man can be idle with impunity, he took his place once more on the bench at the inn door, and was reverenced as one of the patriarchs of the village, and a chronicle of the old times "before the war." It was some time before he could get into the regular track of gossip, or could be made to comprehend the strange events that had taken place during his torpor. How that there had been a revolutionary war—that the country had thrown off the yoke of old England—and that, instead of being a subject of His Majesty George the Third, he was now a free citizen of the United States. Rip, in fact, was no politician; the changes of states and empires made but little impression on him; but there was one species of despotism under which he had long groaned, and that was—petticoat government. Happily that was at an end; he had got his neck out of the yoke of matrimony, and could go in and out whenever he pleased, without dreading the tyranny of Dame Van Winkle. Whenever her name was mentioned, however, he shook his head, shrugged his shoulders, and cast up his eyes; which might pass either for an expression of resignation to his fate, or joy at his deliverance.

He used to tell his story to every stranger that arrived at Mr. Doolittle's hotel. He was observed, at first, to vary on some points every time he told it, which was, doubtless, owing to his having so recently awaked. It at last settled down precisely to the tale I have related, and not a man, woman, or child in the neighborhood, but knew it by heart. Some always pretended to doubt the reality of it, and insisted that Rip had been out of his head, and that this was one point on which he always remained flighty. The old Dutch inhabitants, however, almost universally gave it full credit. Even to this day they never hear a thunderstorm of a summer afternoon about the Kaatskill, but they say Hendrick Hudson and his crew are at their game of nine-pins; and it is a common wish of all henpecked husbands in the neighborhood, when life hangs heavy on their hands, that they might have a quieting draught out of Rip Van Winkle's flagon.[38]

THE SPECTRE BRIDEGROOM [39]

A TRAVELLER'S TALE [40]

He that supper for is dight,
He lyes full cold, I trow, this night!
Yestreen to chamber I him led,
This night Gray-Steel has made his bed.
        SIR EGER, SIR GRAHAME, AND SIR GRAY-STEEL.

On the summit of one of the heights of the Odenwald, a wild and romantic tract of Upper Germany, that lies not far from the confluence of the Main and the Rhine, there stood, many, many years since, the Castle of the Baron Von Landshort. It is now quite fallen to decay, and almost buried among beech trees and dark firs; above which, however, its old watch-tower may still be seen, struggling, like the former possessor I have mentioned, to carry a high head, and look down upon the neighboring country.

The baron was a dry branch of the great family of Katzenellenbogen,[41] and inherited the relics of the property, and all the pride of his ancestors. Though the warlike disposition of his predecessors had much impaired the family possessions, yet the baron still endeavored to keep up some show of former state. The times were peaceable, and the German nobles, in general, had abandoned their inconvenient old castles, perched like eagles' nests among the mountains, and had built more convenient residences in the valleys: still the baron remained proudly drawn up in his little fortress, cherishing, with hereditary inveteracy, all the old family feuds; so that he was on ill terms with some of his nearest neighbors, on account of disputes that had happened between their great-great-grandfathers.

The baron had but one child, a daughter; but nature, when she grants but one child, always compensates by making it a prodigy; and so it was with the daughter of the baron. All the nurses, gossips, and country cousins, assured her father that she had not her equal for beauty in all Germany; and who should know better than they? She had, moreover, been brought up with great care under the superintendence of two maiden aunts, who had spent some years of their early life at one of the little German courts, and were skilled in all the branches of knowledge necessary to the education of a fine lady. Under their instructions she became a miracle of accomplishments. By the time she was eighteen, she could embroider to admiration, and had worked whole histories of the saints in tapestry, with such strength of expression in their countenances, that they looked like so many souls in purgatory. She could read without great difficulty, and had spelled her way through several church legends, and almost all the chivalric wonders of the Heldenbuch. She had even made considerable proficiency in writing; could sign her own name without missing a letter, and so legibly, that her aunts could read it without spectacles. She excelled in making little elegant good-for-nothing lady-like nicknacks of all kinds; was versed in the most abstruse dancing of the day; played a number of airs on the harp and guitar; and knew all the tender ballads of the Minnie-lieders by heart.

Her aunts, too, having been great flirts and coquettes in their younger days, were admirably calculated to be vigilant guardians and strict censors of the conduct of their niece; for there is no duenna so rigidly prudent, and inexorably decorous, as a superannuated coquette. She was rarely suffered out of their sight; never went beyond the domains of the castle, unless well attended, or rather well watched; had continual lectures read to her about strict decorum and implicit obedience; and, as to the men—pah!—she was taught to hold them at such a distance, and in such absolute distrust, that, unless properly authorized, she would not have cast a glance upon the handsomest cavalier in the world—no, not if he were even dying at her feet.

The good effects of this system were wonderfully apparent.

The young lady was a pattern of docility and correctness. While others were wasting their sweetness in the glare of the world, and liable to be plucked and thrown aside by every hand, she was coyly blooming into fresh and lovely womanhood under the protection of those immaculate spinsters, like a rose-bud blushing forth among guardian thorns. Her aunts looked upon her with pride and exultation, and vaunted that though all the other young ladies in the world might go astray, yet, thank Heaven, nothing of the kind could happen to the heiress of Katzenellenbogen.

But, however scantily the Baron Von Landshort might be provided with children, his household was by no means a small one; for Providence had enriched him with abundance of poor relations. They, one and all, possessed the affectionate disposition common to humble relatives; were wonderfully attached to the baron, and took every possible occasion to come in swarms and enliven the castle. All family festivals were commemorated by these good people at the baron's expense; and when they were filled with good cheer, they would declare that there was nothing on earth so delightful as these family meetings, these jubilees of the heart.

The baron, though a small man, had a large soul, and it swelled with satisfaction at the consciousness of being the greatest man in the little world about him. He loved to tell long stories about the dark old warriors whose portraits looked grimly down from the walls around, and he found no listeners equal to those who fed at his expense. He was much given to the marvellous, and a firm believer in all those supernatural tales with which every mountain and valley in Germany abounds. The faith of his guests exceeded even his own: they listened to every tale of wonder with open eyes and mouth, and never failed to be astonished, even though repeated for the hundredth time. Thus lived the Baron Von Landshort, the oracle of his table, the absolute monarch of his little territory, and happy, above all things, in the persuasion that he was the wisest man of the age.

At the time of which my story treats, there was a great family gathering at the castle, on an affair of the utmost importance: it was to receive the destined bridegroom of the baron's daughter. A negotiation had been carried on between the father and an old nobleman of Bavaria, to unite the dignity of their houses by the marriage of their children. The preliminaries had been conducted with proper punctilio. The young people were betrothed without seeing each other; and the time was appointed for the marriage ceremony. The young Count Von Altenburg had been recalled from the army for the purpose, and was actually on his way to the baron's to receive his bride. Missives had even been received from him, from Wurtzburg, where he was accidentally detained, mentioning the day and hour when he might be expected to arrive.

The castle was in a tumult of preparation to give him a suitable welcome. The fair bride had been decked out with uncommon care. The two aunts had superintended her toilet, and quarrelled the whole morning about every article of her dress. The young lady had taken advantage of their contest to follow the bent of her own taste; and fortunately it was a good one. She looked as lovely as youthful bridegroom could desire; and the flutter of expectation heightened the lustre of her charms.

The suffusions that mantled her face and neck, the gentle heaving of the bosom, the eye now and then lost in reverie, all betrayed the soft tumult that was going on in her little heart. The aunts were continually hovering around her; for maiden aunts are apt to take great interest in affairs of this nature. They were giving her a world of staid counsel how to deport herself, what to say, and in what manner to receive the expected lover.

The baron was no less busied in preparations. He had, in truth, nothing exactly to do: but he was naturally a fuming bustling little man, and could not remain passive when all the world was in a hurry. He worried from top to bottom of the castle with an air of infinite anxiety; he continually called the servants from their work to exhort them to be diligent; and buzzed about every hall and chamber, as idly restless and importunate as a blue-bottle fly on a warm summer's day.

In the mean time the fatted calf had been killed; the forests had rung with the clamor of the huntsmen; the kitchen was

crowded with good cheer; the cellars had yielded up whole
oceans of *Rhein-wein* and *Ferne-wein;* and even the great Heidel-
burg tun had been laid under contribution. Every thing was
ready to receive the distinguished guest with *Saus und Braus* in
the true spirit of German hospitality—but the guest delayed to
make his appearance. Hour rolled after hour. The sun, that
had poured his downward rays upon the rich forest of the Odenwald, now just gleamed along the summits of the mountains.
The baron mounted the highest tower, and strained his eyes in
hope of catching a distant sight of the count and his attendants.
Once he thought he beheld them; the sound of horns came floating from the valley, prolonged by the mountain echoes. A
number of horsemen were seen far below, slowly advancing
along the road; but when they had nearly reached the foot of
the mountain, they suddenly struck off in a different direction.
The last ray of sunshine departed—the bats began to flit by in
the twilight—the road grew dimmer and dimmer to the view;
and nothing appeared stirring in it but now and then a peasant
lagging homeward from his labor.

While the old castle of Landshort was in this state of perplexity, a very interesting scene was transacting in a different
part of the Odenwald.

The young Count Von Altenburg was tranquilly pursuing
his route in that sober jog-trot way, in which a man travels
toward matrimony when his friends have taken all the trouble
and uncertainty of courtship off his hands, and a bride is waiting for him, as certainly as a dinner at the end of his journey.
He had encountered at Wurtzburg, a youthful companion in
arms, with whom he had seen some service on the frontiers;
Herman Von Starkenfaust, one of the stoutest hands, and wor-
thiest hearts, of German chivalry, who was now returning from
the army. His father's castle was not far distant from the old
fortress of Landshort, although an hereditary feud rendered the
families hostile, and strangers to each other.

In the warm-hearted moment of recognition, the young
friends related all their past adventures and fortunes, and the
count gave the whole history of his intended nuptials with a

young lady whom he had never seen, but of whose charms he had received the most enrapturing descriptions.

As the route of the friends lay in the same direction, they agreed to perform the rest of their journey together; and, that they might do it the more leisurely, set off from Wurtzburg at an early hour, the count having given directions for his retinue to follow and overtake him.

They beguiled their wayfaring with recollections of their military scenes and adventures; but the count was apt to be a little tedious, now and then, about the reputed charms of his bride, and the felicity that awaited him.

In this way they had entered among the mountains of the Odenwald, and were traversing one of its most lonely and thickly-wooded passes. It is well known that the forests of Germany have always been as much infested by robbers as its castles by spectres; and, at this time, the former were particularly numerous, from the hordes of disbanded soldiers wandering about the country. It will not appear extraordinary, therefore, that the cavaliers were attacked by a gang of these stragglers, in the midst of the forest. They defended themselves with bravery, but were nearly overpowered, when the count's retinue arrived to their assistance. At sight of them the robbers fled, but not until the count had received a mortal wound. He was slowly and carefully conveyed back to the city of Wurtzburg, and a friar summoned from a neighboring convent, who was famous for his skill in administering to both soul and body; but half of his skill was superfluous; the moments of the unfortunate count were numbered.

With his dying breath he entreated his friend to repair instantly to the castle of Landshort, and explain the fatal cause of his not keeping his appointment with his bride. Though not the most ardent of lovers, he was one of the most punctilious of men, and appeared earnestly solicitous that his mission should be speedily and courteously executed. "Unless this is done," said he, "I shall not sleep quietly in my grave!" He repeated these last words with peculiar solemnity. A request, at a moment so impressive, admitted no hesitation. Starkenfaust endeavored to soothe him to calmness; promised faithfully to execute his wish, and gave him his hand in solemn pledge. The dying man pressed it in acknowledgment, but soon lapsed into delirium—raved about his bride—his engagements—his plighted word; ordered his horse, that he might ride to the castle of Landshort; and expired in the fancied act of vaulting into the saddle.

Starkenfaust bestowed a sigh and a soldier's tear on the untimely fate of his comrade; and then pondered on the awkward mission he had undertaken. His heart was heavy, and his head perplexed; for he was to present himself an unbidden guest among hostile people, and to damp their festivity with tidings fatal to their hopes. Still there were certain whisperings of curiosity in his bosom to see this far-famed beauty of Katzenellenbogen, so cautiously shut up from the world; for he was a passionate admirer of the sex, and there was a dash of eccentricity and enterprise in his character that made him fond of all singular adventure.

Previous to his departure he made all due arrangements with the holy fraternity of the convent for the funeral solemnities of his friend, who was to be buried in the cathedral of Wurtzburg, near some of his illustrious relatives; and the mourning retinue of the count took charge of his remains.

It is now high time that we should return to the ancient family of Katzenellenbogen, who were impatient for their guest, and still more for their dinner; and to the worthy little baron, whom we left airing himself on the watch-tower.

Night closed in, but still no guest arrived. The baron descended from the tower in despair. The banquet, which had been delayed from hour to hour, could no longer be postponed. The meats were already overdone; the cook in an agony; and the whole household had the look of a garrison that had been reduced by famine. The baron was obliged reluctantly to give orders for the feast without the presence of the guest. All were seated at table, and just on the point of commencing, when the sound of a horn from without the gate gave notice of the approach of a stranger. Another long blast filled the old courts of the castle with its echoes, and was answered by the warder from the walls. The baron hastened to receive his future son-in-law.

The drawbridge had been let down, and the stranger was before the gate. He was a tall, gallant cavalier, mounted on a black steed. His countenance was pale, but he had a beaming, romantic eye, and an air of stately melancholy. The baron was a little mortified that he should have come in this simple, solitary style. His dignity for a moment was ruffled, and he felt disposed to consider it a want of proper respect for the important occasion, and the important family with which he was to be connected. He pacified himself, however, with the conclusion, that it must have been youthful impatience which had induced him thus to spur on sooner than his attendants.

"I am sorry," said the stranger, "to break in upon you thus unseasonably——"

Here the baron interrupted him with a world of compliments and greetings; for, to tell the truth, he prided himself upon his courtesy and eloquence. The stranger attempted, once or twice, to stem the torrent of words, but in vain, so he bowed his head and suffered it to flow on. By the time the baron had come to a pause, they had reached the inner court of the castle; and the stranger was again about to speak, when he was once more interrupted by the appearance of the female part of the family, leading forth the shrinking and blushing bride. He gazed on her for a moment as one entranced; it seemed as if his whole soul beamed forth in the gaze, and rested upon that lovely form. One of the maiden aunts whispered something in her ear; she made an effort to speak; her moist blue eye was timidly raised; gave a shy glance of inquiry on the stranger; and was cast again to the ground. The words died away; but there was a sweet smile playing about her lips, and a soft dimpling of the cheek that showed her glance had not been unsatisfactory. It was impossible for a girl of the fond age of eighteen, highly predisposed for love and matrimony, not to be pleased with so gallant a cavalier.

The late hour at which the guest had arrived left no time for parley. The baron was peremptory, and deferred all particular conversation until the morning, and led the way to the untasted banquet.

It was served up in the great hall of the castle. Around the walls hung the hard-favored portraits of the heroes of the house of Katzenellenbogen, and the trophies which they had gained in the field and in the chase. Hacked corslets, splintered jousting spears, and tattered banners, were mingled with the spoils of sylvan warfare; the jaws of the wolf, and the tusks of the boar, grinned horribly among cross-bows and battle-axes, and a huge pair of antlers branched immediately over the head of the youthful bridegroom.

The cavalier took but little notice of the company or the entertainment. He scarcely tasted the banquet, but seemed absorbed in admiration of his bride. He conversed in a low tone that could not be overheard—for the language of love is never loud; but where is the female ear so dull that it cannot catch the softest whisper of the lover? There was a mingled tenderness and gravity in his manner, that appeared to have a powerful effect upon the young lady. Her color came and went as she listened with deep attention. Now and then she made some blushing reply, and when his eye was turned away, she would steal a sidelong glance at his romantic countenance, and heave a gentle sigh of tender happiness. It was evident that the young couple were completely enamored. The aunts, who were deeply versed in the mysteries of the heart, declared that they had fallen in love with each other at first sight.

The feast went on merrily, or at least noisily, for the guests were all blessed with those keen appetites that attend upon light purses and mountain air. The baron told his best and longest stories, and never had he told them so well, or with such great effect. If there was any thing marvellous, his auditors were lost in astonishment; and if any thing facetious, they were sure to laugh exactly in the right place. The baron, it is true, like most great men, was too dignified to utter any joke but a dull one; it was always enforced, however, by a bumper of excellent Hockheimer; and even a dull joke, at one's own table, served up with jolly old wine, is irresistible. Many good things were said by poorer and keener wits, that would not bear repeating, except on similar occasions; many sly speeches whispered in ladies' ears, that almost convulsed them with suppressed laughter; and a song or two roared out by a poor, but merry and broad-faced cousin of the baron, that absolutely made the maiden aunts hold up their fans.

Amidst all this revelry, the stranger guest maintained a most singular and unseasonable gravity. His countenance assumed a deeper cast of dejection as the evening advanced; and, strange as it may appear, even the baron's jokes seemed only to render him the more melancholy. At times he was lost in thought, and at times there was a perturbed and restless wandering of the eye that bespoke a mind but ill at ease. His conversations with the bride became more and more earnest and mysterious. Lowering clouds began to steal over the fair serenity of her brow, and tremors to run through her tender frame.

All this could not escape the notice of the company. Their gayety was chilled by the unaccountable gloom of the bridegroom; their spirits were infected; whispers and glances were interchanged, accompanied by shrugs and dubious shakes of the head. The song and the laugh grew less and less frequent; there were dreary pauses in the conversation, which were at length succeeded by wild tales and supernatural legends. One dismal story produced another still more dismal, and the baron nearly frightened some of the ladies into hysterics with the history of the goblin horseman that carried away the fair Leonora; a dreadful story, which has since been put into excellent verse, and is read and believed by all the world.

The bridegroom listened to this tale with profound attention. He kept his eyes steadily fixed on the baron, and, as the story drew to a close, began gradually to rise from his seat, growing taller and taller, until, in the baron's entranced eye, he seemed almost to tower into a giant. The moment the tale was finished, he heaved a deep sigh, and took a solemn farewell of the company. They were all amazement. The baron was perfectly thunder-struck.

"What! going to leave the castle at midnight? why, every

thing was prepared for his reception; a chamber was ready for him if he wished to retire."

The stranger shook his head mournfully and mysteriously; "I must lay my head in a different chamber to-night!"

There was something in this reply, and the tone in which it was uttered, that made the baron's heart misgive him; but he rallied his forces, and repeated his hospitable entreaties.

The stranger shook his head silently, but positively, at every offer; and, waving his farewell to the company, stalked slowly out of the hall. The maiden aunts were absolutely petrified—the bride hung her head, and a tear stole to her eye.

The baron followed the stranger to the great court of the castle, where the black charger stood pawing the earth, and snorting with impatience.—When they had reached the portal, whose deep archway was dimly lighted by a cresset, the stranger paused, and addressed the baron in a hollow tone of voice, which the vaulted roof rendered still more sepulchral.

"Now that we are alone," said he, "I will impart to you the reason of my going. I have a solemn, an indispensable engagement—"

"Why," said the baron, "cannot you send some one in your place?"

"It admits of no substitute—I must attend it in person—I must away to Wurtzburg cathedral—"

"Ay," said the baron, plucking up spirit, "but not until to-morrow—to-morrow you shall take your bride there."

"No! no!" replied the stranger, with tenfold solemnity, "my engagement is with no bride—the worms! the worms expect me! I am a dead man—I have been slain by robbers—my body lies at Wurtzburg—at midnight I am to be buried—the grave is waiting for me—I must keep my appointment!"

He sprang on his black charger, dashed over the drawbridge, and the clattering of his horse's hoofs was lost in the whistling of the night blast.

The baron returned to the hall in the utmost consternation, and related what had passed. Two ladies fainted outright, others sickened at the idea of having banqueted with a spectre. It was the opinion of some, that this might be the wild huntsman, famous in German legend. Some talked of mountain sprites, of wood-demons, and of other supernatural beings, with which the good people of Germany have been so grievously harassed since time immemorial. One of the poor relations ventured to suggest that it might be some sportive evasion of the young cavalier, and that the very gloominess of the caprice seemed to accord with so melancholy a personage. This, however, drew on him the indignation of the whole company, and especially of the baron, who looked upon him as little better than an infidel; so that he was fain to abjure his heresy as speedily as possible, and come into the faith of the true believers.

But whatever may have been the doubts entertained, they were completely put to an end by the arrival, next day, of regular missives, confirming the intelligence of the young count's murder, and his interment in Wurtzburg cathedral.

The dismay at the castle may well be imagined. The baron shut himself up in his chamber. The guests, who had come to rejoice with him, could not think of abandoning him in his distress. They wandered about the courts, or collected in groups in the hall, shaking their heads and shrugging their shoulders, at the troubles of so good a man; and sat longer than ever at table, and ate and drank more stoutly than ever, by way of keeping up their spirits. But the situation of the widowed bride was the most pitiable. To have lost a husband before she had even embraced him—and such a husband! if the very spectre could be so gracious and noble, what must have been the living man. She filled the house with lamentations.

On the night of the second day of her widowhood, she had retired to chamber, accompanied by one of her aunts, who insisted on sleeping with her. The aunt, who was one of the best tellers of ghost stories in all Germany, had just been recounting one of her longest, and had fallen asleep in the very midst of it. The chamber was remote, and overlooked a small garden. The niece lay pensively gazing at the beams of the rising moon, as they trembled on the leaves of an aspen-tree before the lattice. The castle clock had just tolled midnight, when a soft strain of music stole up from the garden. She rose hastily from her bed, and stepped lightly to the window. A tall figure stood among the shadows of the trees. As it raised its head, a beam of moonlight fell upon the countenance. Heaven and earth! she beheld the Spectre Bridegroom! A loud shriek at that moment burst upon her ear, and her aunt, who had been awakened by the music, and had followed her silently to the window, fell into her arms. When she looked again, the spectre had disappeared.

Of the two females, the aunt now required the most soothing, for she was perfectly beside herself with terror. As to the young lady, there was something, even in the spectre of her lover, that seemed endearing. There was still the semblance of manly beauty; and though the shadow of a man is but little calculated to satisfy the affections of a love-sick girl, yet, where the substance is not to be had, even that is consoling. The aunt declared she would never sleep in that chamber again; the niece, for once, was refractory, and declared as strongly that she would sleep in no other in the castle: the consequence was, that she had to sleep in it alone: but she drew a promise from her aunt not to relate the story of the spectre, lest she should be denied the only melancholy pleasure left her on earth—that of inhabiting the chamber over which the guardian shade of her lover kept its nightly vigils.

How long the good old lady would have observed this promise is uncertain, for she dearly loved to talk of the marvellous, and there is a triumph in being the first to tell a frightful story; it is, however, still quoted in the neighborhood, as a memorable instance of female secrecy, that she kept it to herself for a whole week; when she was suddenly absolved from all further restraint, by intelligence brought to the breakfast table one morning that the young lady was not to be found. Her room was empty— the bed had not been slept in—the window was open, and the bird had flown!

The astonishment and concern with which the intelligence was received, can only be imagined by those who have witnessed the agitation which the mishaps of a great man cause among his friends. Even the poor relations paused for a moment from the indefatigable labors of the trencher; when the aunt, who had at first been struck speechless, wrung her hands, and shrieked out, "The goblin! the goblin! she's carried away by the goblin."

In a few words she related the fearful scene of the garden, and concluded that the spectre must have carried off his bride. Two of the domestics corroborated the opinion, for they had heard the clattering of a horse's hoofs down the mountain about midnight, and had no doubt that it was the spectre on his black charger, bearing her away to the tomb. All present were struck with the direful probability; for events of the kind are extremely common in Germany, as many well authenticated histories bear witness.

What a lamentable situation was that of the poor baron! What a heart-rending dilemma for a fond father, and a member of the great family of Katzenellenbogen! His only daughter had either been rapt away to the grave, or he was to have some wood-demon for a son-in-law, and, perchance, a troop of goblin grandchildren. As usual, he was completely bewildered, and all the castle in an uproar. The men were ordered to take horse, and scour every road and path and glen of the Odenwald. The baron himself had just drawn on his jack-boots, girded on his sword, and was about to mount his steed to sally forth on the doubtful quest, when he was brought to a pause by a new apparition. A lady was seen approaching the castle, mounted on a palfrey, attended by a cavalier on horseback. She galloped up to the gate, sprang from her horse, and falling at the baron's feet, embraced his knees. It was his lost daughter, and her companion—the Spectre Bridegroom! The baron was astounded. He looked at his daughter, then at the spectre, and almost doubted the evidence of his senses. The latter, too, was wonderfully improved in his appearance since his visit to the world of spirits. His dress was splendid, and set off a noble figure of manly symmetry. He was no longer pale and melancholy. His fine countenance was flushed with the glow of youth, and joy rioted in his large dark eye.

The mystery was soon cleared up. The cavalier (for, in truth, as you must have known all the while, he was no goblin) announced himself as Sir Herman Von Starkenfaust. He related his adventure with the young count. He told how he had hastened to the castle to deliver the unwelcome tidings, but that the eloquence of the baron had interrupted him in every attempt to tell his tale. How the sight of the bride had completely captivated him, and that to pass a few hours near her, he had tacitly suffered the mistake to continue. How he had been sorely perplexed in what way to make a decent retreat, until the baron's goblin stories had suggested his eccentric exit. How, fearing the feudal hostility of the family, he had repeated his visits by stealth—had haunted the garden beneath the young lady's window—had wooed—had won—had borne away in triumph—and, in a word, had wedded the fair.

Under any other circumstances the baron would have been inflexible, for he was tenacious of paternal authority, and devoutly obstinate in all family feuds, but he loved his daughter; he had lamented her as lost; he rejoiced to find her still alive; and, though her husband was of a hostile house, yet, thank Heaven, he was not a goblin. There was something, it must be acknowledged, that did not exactly accord with his notions of strict veracity, in the joke the knight had passed upon him of his being a dead man; but several old friends present, who had served in the wars, assured him that every stratagem was excusable in love, and that the cavalier was entitled to especial privilege, having lately served as a trooper.

Matters, therefore, were happily arranged. The baron pardoned the young couple on the spot. The revels at the castle were resumed. The poor relations overwhelmed this new member of the family with loving kindness; he was so gallant, so generous—and so rich. The aunts, it is true, were somewhat scandalized that their system of strict seclusion, and passive obedience should be so badly exemplified, but attributed it all to their negligence in not having the windows grated. One of them was particularly mortified at having her marvellous story marred, and that the only spectre she had ever seen should turn out a counterfeit; but the niece seemed perfectly happy at having found him substantial flesh and blood—and so the story ends.

TRAITS OF INDIAN CHARACTER [42]

"I appeal to any white man if ever he entered Logan's cabin hungry, and he gave him not to eat; if ever he came cold and naked, and he clothed him not."

SPEECH OF AN INDIAN CHIEF.

There is something in the character and habits of the North American savage, taken in connection with the scenery over which he is accustomed to range, its vast lakes, boundless forests, majestic rivers, and trackless plains, that is, to my mind, wonderfully striking and sublime. He is formed for the wilderness, as the Arab is for the desert. His nature is stern, simple, and enduring; fitted to grapple with difficulties, and to support privations. There seems but little soil in his heart for the support of the kindly virtues; and yet, if we would but take the trouble to penetrate through that proud stoicism and habitual taciturnity, which lock up his character from casual observation, we should find him linked to his fellow-man of civilized life by more of those sympathies and affections than are usually ascribed to him.

It has been the lot of the unfortunate aborigines of America, in the early periods of colonization, to be doubly wronged by the white men. They have been dispossessed of their hereditary possessions by mercenary and frequently wanton warfare: and their characters have been traduced by bigoted and interested writers. The colonist often treated them like beasts of the forest; and the author has endeavored to justify him in his outrages. The former found it easier to exterminate than to civilize; the latter to vilify than to discriminate. The appellations of savage and pagan were deemed sufficient to sanction the hostilities of both; and thus the poor wanderers of the forest were persecuted and defamed, not because they were guilty, but because they were ignorant.

The rights of the savage have seldom been properly appreciated or respected by the white man. In peace he has too often been the dupe of artful traffic; in war he has been regarded as a ferocious animal, whose life or death was a question of mere precaution and convenience. Man is cruelly wasteful of life when his own safety is endangered, and he is sheltered by impunity; and little mercy is to be expected from him, when he feels the sting of the reptile and is conscious of the power to destroy.

The same prejudices, which were indulged thus early, exist in common circulation at the present day. Certain learned societies have, it is true, with laudable diligence, endeavored to investigate and record the real characters and manners of the Indian tribes; the American government, too, has wisely and humanely exerted itself to inculcate a friendly and forbearing spirit towards them, and to protect them from fraud and injustice.[43] The current opinion of the Indian character, however, is too apt to be formed from the miserable hordes which infest the frontiers, and hang on the skirts of the settlements. These are too commonly composed of degenerate beings, corrupted and enfeebled by the vices of society, without being benefited by its civilization. That proud independence, which formed the main pillar of savage virtue, has been shaken down, and the whole moral fabric lies in ruins. Their spirits are humiliated and debased by a sense of inferiority, and their native courage cowed and daunted by the superior knowledge and power of their enlightened neighbors. Society has advanced upon them like one of those withering airs that will sometimes breed desolation over a whole region of fertility. It has enervated their strength, multiplied their diseases, and superinduced upon their original barbarity the low vices of artificial life. It has given them a thousand superfluous wants, whilst it has diminished their means of mere existence. It has driven before it the animals of the chase, who fly from the sound of the axe and the smoke of the settlement, and seek refuge in the depths of remoter forests and yet untrodden wilds. Thus do we too often find the Indians on our frontiers to be the mere wrecks and remnants of once powerful tribes, who have lingered in the vicinity of the settlements, and sunk into precarious and vagabond existence. Poverty, repining and hopeless poverty, a canker of the mind unknown in savage life, corrodes their spirits, and blights every free and noble quality of their natures. They become drunken, indolent, feeble, thievish, and pusillanimous. They loiter like vagrants about the settlements, among spacious dwellings replete with elaborate comforts, which only render them sensible of the comparative wretchedness of their own condition. Luxury spreads its ample board before their eyes; but they are excluded from the banquet. Plenty revels over the fields; but they are starving in the midst of its abundance: the whole wilderness has blossomed into a garden; but they feel as reptiles that infest it.

How different was their state while yet the undisputed lords of the soil! Their wants were few, and the means of gratification within their reach. They saw every one around them sharing the same lot, enduring the same hardships, feeding on the same aliments, arrayed in the same rude garments. No roof then rose, but was open to the homeless stranger; no smoke curled among the trees, but he was welcome to sit down by its fire, and join the hunter in his repast. "For," says an old historian of New England, "their life is so void of care, and they are so loving also, that they make use of those things they enjoy as common goods, and are therein so compassionate, that rather than one should starve through want, they would starve all; thus they pass their time merrily, not regarding our pomp, but are better content with their own, which some men esteem so meanly of." Such were the Indians, whilst in the pride and energy of their primitive natures: they resembled those wild plants, which thrive best in the shades of the forest, but shrink from the hand of cultivation, and perish beneath the influence of the sun.

In discussing the savage character, writers have been too prone to indulge in vulgar prejudice and passionate exaggeration, instead of the candid temper of true philosophy. They have not sufficiently considered the peculiar circumstances in which the Indians have been placed, and the peculiar principles

under which they have been educated. No being acts more
rigidly from rule than the Indian. His whole conduct is regulated according to some general maxims early implanted in his
mind. The moral laws that govern him are, to be sure, but few;
but then he conforms to them all;—the white man abounds in
laws of religion, morals, and manners, but how many does he
violate?

A frequent ground of accusation against the Indians is their
disregard of treaties, and the treachery and wantonness with
which, in time of apparent peace, they will suddenly fly to hostilities. The intercourse of the white men with the Indians,
however, is too apt to be cold, distrustful, oppressive, and insulting. They seldom treat them with that confidence and frank-
ness which are indispensable to real friendship; nor is sufficient
caution observed not to offend against those feelings of pride
or superstition, which often prompts the Indian to hostility
quicker than mere considerations of interest. The solitary
savage feels silently, but acutely. His sensibilities are not diffused over so wide a surface as those of the white man; but they
run in steadier and deeper channels. His pride, his affections,
his superstitions, are all directed towards fewer objects; but
the wounds inflicted on them are proportionably severe, and
furnish motives of hostility which we cannot sufficiently appreciate. Where a community is also limited in number, and forms
one great patriarchal family, as in an Indian tribe, the injury of
an individual is the injury of the whole; and the sentiment of
vengeance is almost instantaneously diffused. One council fire
is sufficient for the discussion and arrangement of a plan of hostilities. Here all the fighting men and sages assemble. Eloquence
and superstition combine to inflame the minds of the warriors.
The orator awakens their martial ardor, and they are wrought
up to a kind of religious desperation, by the visions of the
prophet and the dreamer.

An instance of one of those sudden exasperations, arising
from a motive peculiar to the Indian character, is extant in an
old record of the early settlement of Massachusetts. The
planters of Plymouth had defaced the monuments of the dead

at Passonagessit, and had plundered the grave of the Sachem's mother of some skins with which it had been decorated. The Indians are remarkable for the reverence which they entertain for the sepulchres of their kindred. Tribes that have passed generations exiled from the abodes of their ancestors, when by chance they have been travelling in the vicinity, have been known to turn aside from the highway, and, guided by wonderfully accurate tradition, have crossed the country for miles to some tumulus, buried perhaps in woods, where the bones of their tribe were anciently deposited; and there have passed hours in silent meditation. Influenced by this sublime and holy feeling, the Sachem, whose mother's tomb had been violated, gathered his men together, and addressed them in the following beautifully simple and pathetic harangue; a curious specimen of Indian eloquence, and an affecting instance of filial piety in a savage.

"When last the glorious light of all the sky was underneath this globe, and birds grew silent, I began to settle, as my custom is, to take repose. Before mine eyes were fast closed, methought I saw a vision, at which my spirit was much troubled; and trembling at that doleful sight, a spirit cried aloud, 'Behold, my son, whom I have cherished, see the breasts that gave thee suck, the hands that lapped thee warm, and fed thee oft. Canst thou forget to take revenge of those wild people who have defaced my monument in a despiteful manner, disdaining our antiquities and honorable customs? See, now, the Sachem's grave lies like the common people, defaced by an ignoble race. Thy mother doth complain, and implores thy aid against this thievish people, who have newly intruded on our land. If this be suffered, I shall not rest quiet in my everlasting habitation.' This said, the spirit vanished, and I, all in a sweat, not able scarce to speak, began to get some strength, and recollect my spirits that were fled, and determined to demand your counsel and assistance."

I have adduced this anecdote at some length, as it tends to show how these sudden acts of hostility, which have been attributed to caprice and perfidy, may often arise from deep and

generous motives, which our inattention to Indian character
and customs prevents our properly appreciating.

Another ground of violent outcry against the Indians is their
barbarity to the vanquished. This had its origin partly in policy
and partly in superstition. The tribes, though sometimes called
nations, were never so formidable in their numbers, but that the
loss of several warriors was sensibly felt; this was particularly
the case when they had been frequently engaged in warfare; and
many an instance occurs in Indian history, where a tribe, that
had long been formidable to its neighbors, has been broken up
and driven away, by the capture and massacre of its principal
fighting men. There was a strong temptation, therefore, to the
victor to be merciless; not so much to gratify any cruel revenge,
as to provide for future security. The Indians had also the superstitious belief, frequent among barbarous nations, and prevalent
also among the ancients, that the manes of their friends who had
fallen in battle were soothed by the blood of the captives. The
prisoners, however, who are not thus sacrificed, are adopted into their families in the place of the slain, and are treated with the
confidence and affection of relatives and friends; nay, so hospitable and tender is their entertainment, that when the alternative is offered them, they will often prefer to remain with their
adopted brethren, rather than return to the home and the friends
of their youth.

The cruelty of the Indians towards their prisoners has been
heightened since the colonization of the whites. What was
formerly a compliance with policy and superstition, has been
exasperated into a gratification of vengeance. They cannot but
be sensible that the white men are the usurpers of their ancient
dominion, the cause of their degradation, and the gradual
destroyers of their race. They go forth to battle, smarting with
injuries and indignities which they have individually suffered,
and they are driven to madness and despair by the wide-spread-
ing desolation, and the overwhelming ruin of European warfare. The whites have too frequently set them an example of
violence, by burning their villages, and laying waste their slender means of subsistence: and yet they wonder that savages do

not show moderation and magnanimity towards those who have left them nothing but mere existence and wretchedness.

We stigmatize the Indians, also, as cowardly and treacherous, because they use stratagem in warfare, in preference to open force; but in this they are fully justified by their rude code of honor. They are early taught that stratagem is praiseworthy; the bravest warrior thinks it no disgrace to lurk in silence, and take every advantage of his foe: he triumphs in the superior craft and sagacity by which he has been enabled to surprise and destroy an enemy. Indeed, man is naturally more prone to subtilty than open valor, owing to his physical weakness in comparison with other animals. They are endowed with natural weapons of defence: with horns, with tusks, with hoofs, and talons; but man has to depend on his superior sagacity. In all his encounters with these, his proper enemies, he resorts to stratagem; and when he perversely turns his hostility against his fellow-man, he at first continues the same subtle mode of warfare.

The natural principle of war is to do the most harm to our enemy with the least harm to ourselves; and this of course is to be effected by stratagem. That chivalrous courage which induces us to despise the suggestions of prudence, and to rush in the face of certain danger, is the offspring of society, and produced by education. It is honorable, because it is in fact the ' triumph of lofty sentiment over an instinctive repugnance to pain, and over those yearnings after personal ease and security, which society has condemned as ignoble. It is kept alive by pride and the fear of shame; and thus the dread of real evil is overcome by the superior dread of an evil which exists but in the imagination. It has been cherished and stimulated also by various means. It has been the theme of spirit-stirring song and chivalrous story. The poet and minstrel have delighted to shed round it the splendors of fiction; and even the historian has forgotten the sober gravity of narration, and broken forth into enthusiasm and rhapsody in its praise. Triumphs and gorgeous pageants have been its reward: monuments, on which art has exhausted its skill, and opulence its treasures, have been erected

to perpetuate a nation's gratitude and admiration. Thus artificially excited, courage has risen to an extraordinary and facti-
tious degree of heroism: and arrayed in all the glorious "pomp
and circumstance of war," this turbulent quality has even been
able to eclipse many of those quiet, but invaluable virtues, which
silently ennoble the human character, and swell the tide of
human happiness.

But if courage intrinsically consists in the defiance of danger
and pain, the life of the Indian is a continual exhibition of it. He
lives in a state of perpetual hostility and risk. Peril and adventure are congenial to his nature; or rather seem necessary to
arouse his faculties and to give an interest to his existence. Surrounded by hostile tribes, whose mode of warfare is by ambush
and surprisal, he is always prepared for fight, and lives with his
weapons in his hands. As the ship careers in fearful singleness
through the solitudes of ocean;—as the bird mingles among
clouds and storms, and wings its way, a mere speck, across the
pathless fields of air;—so the Indian holds his course, silent,
solitary, but undaunted, through the boundless bosom of the
wilderness. His expeditions may vie in distance and danger with
the pilgrimage of the devotee, or the crusade of the knight-
errant. He traverses vast forests, exposed to the hazards of
lonely sickness, of lurking enemies, and pining famine. Stormy
lakes, those great inland seas, are no obstacles to his wanderings:
in his light canoe of bark he sports, like a feather, on their
waves, and darts, with the swiftness of an arrow, down the
roaring rapids of the rivers. His very subsistence is snatched
from the midst of toil and peril. He gains his food by the hardships and dangers of the chase: he wraps himself in the spoils of
the bear, the panther, and the buffalo, and sleeps among the
thunders of the cataract.

No hero of ancient or modern days can surpass the Indian in
his lofty contempt of death, and the fortitude with which he
sustains its cruellest infliction. Indeed we here behold him rising
superior to the white man, in consequence of his peculiar education. The latter rushes to glorious death at the cannon's
mouth; the former calmly contemplates its approach, and tri-

umphantly endures it, amidst the varied torments of surrounding foes and the protracted agonies of fire. He even takes a pride in taunting his persecutors, and provoking their ingenuity of torture; and as the devouring flames prey on his very vitals, and the flesh shrinks from the sinews, he raises his last song of triumph, breathing the defiance of an unconquered heart, and invoking the spirits of his fathers to witness that he dies without a groan.

Notwithstanding the obloquy with which the early historians have overshadowed the characters of the unfortunate natives, some bright gleams occasionally break through, which throw a degree of melancholy lustre on their memories. Facts are occasionally to be met with in the rude annals of the eastern provinces, which, though recorded with the coloring of prejudice and bigotry, yet speak for themselves; and will be dwelt on with applause and sympathy, when prejudice shall have passed away.

In one of the homely narratives of the Indian wars in New England, there is a touching account of the desolation carried into the tribe of the Pequod Indians. Humanity shrinks from the cold-blooded detail of indiscriminate butchery. In one place we read of the surprisal of an Indian fort in the night, when the wigwams were wrapped in flames, and the miserable inhabitants shot down and slain in attempting to escape, "all being despatched and ended in the course of an hour." After a series of similar transactions, "our soldiers," as the historian piously observes, "being resolved by God's assistance to make a final destruction of them," the unhappy savages being hunted from their homes and fortresses, and pursued with fire and sword, a scanty, but gallant band, the sad remnant of the Pequod warriors, with their wives and children, took refuge in a swamp.

Burning with indignation, and rendered sullen by despair; with hearts bursting with grief at the destruction of their tribe, and spirits galled and sore at the fancied ignominy of their defeat, they refused to ask their lives at the hands of an insulting foe, and preferred death to submission.

As the night drew on they were surrounded in their dismal

retreat, so as to render escape impracticable. Thus situated, their enemy "plied them with shot all the time, by which means many were killed and buried in the mire." In the darkness and fog that preceded the dawn of day some few broke through the besiegers and escaped into the woods: "the rest were left to the conquerors, of which many were killed in the swamp, like sullen dogs who would rather, in their self-willedness and madness, sit still and be shot through, or cut to pieces," than implore for mercy. When the day broke upon this handful of forlorn but dauntless spirits, the soldiers, we are told, entering the swamp, "saw several heaps of them sitting close together, upon whom they discharged their pieces, laden with ten or twelve pistol bullets at a time, putting the muzzles of the pieces under the boughs, within a few yards of them; so as, besides those that were found dead, many more were killed and sunk into the mire, and never were minded more by friend or foe."

Can any one read this plain unvarnished tale, without admiring the stern resolution, the unbending pride, the loftiness of spirit, that seemed to nerve the hearts of these self-taught heroes, and to raise them above the instinctive feelings of human nature? When the Gauls laid waste the city of Rome, they found the senators clothed in their robes, and seated with stern tranquillity in their curule chairs; in this manner they suffered death without resistance or even supplication. Such conduct was, in them, applauded as noble and magnanimous; in the hapless Indian it was reviled as obstinate and sullen! How truly are we the dupes of show and circumstance! How different is virtue, clothed in purple and enthroned in state, from virtue, naked and destitute, and perishing obscurely in a wilderness!

But I forbear to dwell on these gloomy pictures. The eastern tribes have long since disappeared; the forests that sheltered them have been laid low, and scarce any traces remain of them in the thickly-settled states of New England, excepting here and there the Indian name of a village or a stream. And such must, sooner or later, be the fate of those other tribes which skirt the frontiers, and have occasionally been inveigled from their forests to mingle in the wars of white men. In a little while, and they will go the way that their brethren have gone before. The few hordes which still linger about the shores of Huron and Superior, and the tributary streams of the Mississippi, will share the fate of those tribes that once spread over Massachusetts and Connecticut, and lorded it along the proud banks of the Hudson; of that gigantic race said to have existed on the borders of the Susquehanna; and of those various nations that flourished about the Potomac and the Rappahannock, and that peopled the forests of the vast valley of Shenandoah. They will vanish like a vapor from the face of the earth; their very history will be lost in forgetfulness; and "the places that now know them will know them no more for ever." Or if, perchance, some dubious memorial of them should survive, it may be in the romantic dreams of the poet, to people in imagination his glades and groves, like the fauns and satyrs and sylvan deities of antiquity. But should he venture upon the dark story of their wrongs and wretchedness; should he tell how they were invaded, corrupted, despoiled, driven from their native abodes and the sepulchres of their fathers, hunted like wild beasts about the earth, and sent down with violence and butchery to the grave, posterity will either turn with horror and incredulity from the tale, or blush with indignation at the inhumanity of their forefathers.—"We are driven back," said an old warrior, "until we can retreat no farther—our hatchets are broken, our bows are snapped, our fires are nearly extinguished:—a little longer, and the white man will cease to persecute us—for we shall cease to exist!"

JOHN BULL[44]

An old song, made by an aged old pate,
Of an old worshipful gentleman who had a great estate,
That kept a brave old house at a bountiful rate,
And an old porter to relieve the poor at his gate.
With an old study fill'd full of learned old books,
With an old reverend chaplain, you might know him by his looks,
With an old buttery hatch worn quite off the hooks,
And an old kitchen that maintained half-a-dozen old cooks.
            Like an old courtier, etc.
                                            OLD SONG.

There is no species of humor in which the English more excel, than that which consists in caricaturing and giving ludicrous appellations, or nicknames. In this way they have whimsically designated, not merely individuals, but nations; and, in their fondness for pushing a joke, they have not spared even themselves. One would think that, in personifying itself, a nation would be apt to picture something grand, heroic, and imposing; but it is characteristic of the peculiar humor of the English, and of their love for what is blunt, comic, and familiar, that they have embodied their national oddities in the figure of a sturdy, corpulent old fellow, with a three-cornered hat, red waistcoat, leather breeches, and stout oaken cudgel. Thus they have taken a singular delight in exhibiting their most private foibles in a laughable point of view; and have been so successful in their delineations, that there is scarcely a being in actual existence more absolutely present to the public mind than that eccentric personage, John Bull.

Perhaps the continual contemplation of the character thus drawn of them has contributed to fix it upon the nation; and thus to give reality to what at first may have been painted in a great measure from the imagination. Men are apt to acquire peculiarities that are continually ascribed to them. The common orders of English seem wonderfully captivated with the *beau ideal* which they have formed of John Bull, and endeavor to act up to the broad caricature that is perpetually before their eyes. Unluckily, they sometimes make their boasted Bull-ism an apology for their prejudice or grossness; and this I have especially noticed among those truly homebred and genuine sons of the soil who have never migrated beyond the sound of Bow-bells. If one of these should be a little uncouth in speech, and apt to utter impertinent truths, he confesses that he is a real John Bull, and always speaks his mind. If he now and then flies into an unreasonable burst of passion about trifles, he observes, that John Bull is a choleric old blade, but then his passion is over in a moment, and he bears no malice. If he betrays a coarseness of taste, and an insensibility to foreign refinements, he thanks heaven for his ignorance—he is a plain John Bull, and has no relish for frippery and nicknacks. His very proneness to be gulled by strangers, and to pay extravagantly for absurdities, is excused under the plea of munificence —for John is always more generous than wise.

Thus, under the name of John Bull, he will contrive to argue every fault into a merit, and will frankly convict himself of being the honestest fellow in existence.

However little, therefore, the character may have suited in the first instance, it has gradually adapted itself to the nation, or rather they have adapted themselves to each other; and a stranger who wishes to study English peculiarities, may gather much valuable information from the innumerable portraits of John Bull, as exhibited in the windows of the caricature-shops. Still, however, he is one of those fertile humorists, that are continually throwing out new portraits, and presenting different aspects from different points of view; and, often as he has been described, I cannot resist the temptation to give a slight sketch of him, such as he has met my eye.

John Bull, to all appearance, is a plain downright matter-of-fact fellow, with much less of poetry about him than rich prose. There is little of romance in his nature, but a vast deal of strong natural feeling. He excels in humor more than in wit; is jolly rather than gay; melancholy rather than morose; can easily be moved to a sudden tear, or surprised into a broad laugh; but he loathes sentiment, and has no turn for light pleasantry. He is a boon companion, if you allow him to have his humor, and to talk about himself; and he will stand by a friend in a quarrel, with life and purse, however soundly he may be cudgelled.

In this last respect, to tell the truth, he has a propensity to be somewhat too ready. He is a busy-minded personage, who thinks not merely for himself and family, but for all the country round, and is most generously disposed to be everybody's champion. He is continually volunteering his services to settle his neighbors' affairs, and takes it in great dudgeon if they engage in any matter of consequence without asking his advice; though he seldom engages in any friendly office of the kind without finishing by getting into a squabble with all parties, and then railing bitterly at their ingratitude. He unluckily took lessons in his youth in the noble science of defence, and having accomplished himself in the use of his limbs and his weapons, and become a perfect master at boxing and cudgel-play, he has had a troublesome life of it ever since. He cannot hear of a quarrel between the most distant of his neighbors, but he begins incontinently to fumble with the head of his cudgel, and consider whether his interest or honor does not require that he should meddle in the broil. Indeed he has extended his relations of pride and policy so completely over the whole country, that no event can take place, without infringing some of his finely-spun rights and dignities. Couched in his little domain, with these filaments stretching forth in every direction, he is like some choleric, bottle-bellied old spider, who has woven his web over a whole chamber, so that a fly cannot buzz, nor a breeze blow, without startling his repose, and causing him to sally forth wrathfully from his den.

Though really a good-hearted, good-tempered old fellow at bottom, yet he is singularly fond of being in the midst of contention. It is one of his peculiarities, however, that he only relishes the beginning of an affray; he always goes into a fight with alacrity, but comes out of it grumbling even when victorious; and though no one fights with more obstinacy to carry a contested point, yet, when the battle is over, and he comes to the reconciliation, he is so much taken up with the mere shaking of hands, that he is apt to let his antagonist pocket all that they have been quarrelling about. It is not, therefore, fighting that he ought so much to be on his guard against, as making friends. It is difficult to cudgel him out of a farthing; but put him in a good humor, and you may bargain him out of all the money in his pocket. He is like a stout ship, which will weather the roughest storm uninjured, but roll its masts overboard in the succeeding calm.

He is a little fond of playing the magnifico abroad; of pulling out a long purse; flinging his money bravely about at boxing matches, horse races, cock fights, and carrying a high head among "gentlemen of the fancy:" but immediately after one of these fits of extravagance, he will be taken with violent qualms of economy; stop short at the most trivial expenditure; talk desperately of being ruined and brought upon the parish; and, in such moods, will not pay the smallest tradesman's bill, without violent altercation. He is in fact the most punctual and discontented paymaster in the world; drawing his coin out of his breeches pocket with infinite reluctance; paying to the uttermost farthing, but accompanying every guinea with a growl.

With all his talk of economy, however, he is a bountiful provider, and a hospitable housekeeper. His economy is of a whimsical kind, its chief object being to devise how he may afford to be extravagant; for he will begrudge himself a beef-steak and pint of port one day, that he may roast an ox whole, broach a hogshead of ale, and treat all his neighbors on the next.

His domestic establishment is enormously expensive: not so much from any great outward parade, as from the great consumption of solid beef and pudding; the vast number of followers he feeds and clothes; and his singular disposition to pay hugely for small services. He is a most kind and indulgent master, and, provided his servants humor his peculiarities, flatter his vanity a little now and then, and do not peculate grossly on him before his face, they may manage him to perfection. Every thing that lives on him seems to thrive and grow fat. His house-servants are well paid, and pampered, and have little to do. His horses are sleek and lazy, and prance slowly before his state carriage; and his house-dogs sleep quietly about the door, and will hardly bark at a house-breaker.

His family mansion is an old castellated manor-house, gray with age, and of a most venerable, though weather-beaten appearance. It has been built upon no regular plan, but is a vast accumulation of parts, erected in various tastes and ages. The centre bears evident traces of Saxon architecture, and is as solid as ponderous stone and old English oak can make it. Like all the relics of that style, it is full of obscure passages, intricate mazes, and dusky chambers; and though these have been partially lighted up in modern days, yet there are many places where you must still grope in the dark. Additions have been made to the original edifice from time to time, and great alterations have taken place; towers and battlements have been erected during wars and tumults: wings built in time of peace; and out-houses, lodges, and offices, run up according to the whim or convenience of different generations, until it has become one of the most spacious, rambling tenements imaginable. An entire wing is taken up with the family chapel, a reverend pile, that must have been exceedingly sumptuous, and, indeed, in spite of having been altered and simplified at various periods, has still a look of solemn religious pomp. Its walls within are storied with the monuments of John's ancestors; and it is snugly fitted up with soft cushions and well-lined chairs, where such of his family as are inclined to church services, may doze comfortably in the discharge of their duties.

To keep up this chapel has cost John much money; but he is stanch in his religion, and piqued in his zeal, from the circumstance that many dissenting chapels have been erected in his vicinity, and several of his neighbors, with whom he has had quarrels, are strong papists.

To do the duties of the chapel he maintains, at a large expense, a pious and portly family chaplain. He is a most learned and decorous personage, and a truly well-bred Christian, who always backs the old gentleman in his opinions, winks discreetly at his little peccadilloes, rebukes the children when refractory, and is of great use in exhorting the tenants to read their Bibles, say their prayers, and, above all, to pay their rents punctually, and without grumbling.

The family apartments are in a very antiquated taste, somewhat heavy, and often inconvenient, but full of the solemn magnificence of former times; fitted up with rich, though faded tapestry, unwieldy furniture, and loads of massy gorgeous old plate. The vast fireplaces, ample kitchens, extensive cellars, and sumptuous banqueting halls, all speak of the roaring hospitality of days of yore, of which the modern festivity at the manor-house is but a shadow. There are, however, complete suites of rooms apparently deserted and time-worn; and towers and turrets that are tottering to decay; so that in high winds there is danger of their tumbling about the ears of the household.

John has frequently been advised to have the old edifice thoroughly overhauled; and to have some of the useless parts pulled down, and the others strengthened with their materials; but the old gentleman always grows testy on this subject. He swears the house is an excellent house—that it is tight and weather proof, and not to be shaken by tempests—that it has stood for several hundred years, and, therefore, is not likely to tumble down now—that as to its being inconvenient, his family is accustomed to the inconveniences, and would not be comfortable without them—that as to its unwieldy size and irregular construction, these result from its being the growth of centuries, and being improved by the wisdom of every generation —that an old family, like his, requires a large house to dwell in; new, upstart families may live in modern cottages and snug boxes; but an old English family should inhabit an old English manor-house. If you point out any part of the building as superfluous, he insists that it is material to the strength or decoration of the rest, and the harmony of the whole; and swears that the parts are so built into each other, that if you pull down one, you run the risk of having the whole about your ears.

The secret of the matter is, that John has a great disposition to protect and patronize. He thinks it indispensable to the dignity of an ancient and honorable family, to be bounteous in its appointments, and to be eaten up by dependents; and so, partly from pride, and partly from kind-heartedness, he makes it a rule always to give shelter and maintenance to his super-annuated servants.

The consequence is, that, like many other venerable family establishments, his manor is encumbered by old retainers whom he cannot turn off, and an old style which he cannot lay down. His mansion is like a great hospital of invalids, and, with all its magnitude, is not a whit too large for its inhabitants. Not a nook or corner but is of use in housing some useless personage. Groups of veteran beef-eaters, gouty pensioners, and retired heroes of the buttery and the larder, are seen lolling about its walls, crawling over its lawns, dozing under its trees, or sunning themselves upon the benches at its doors. Every office and out-house is garrisoned by these supernumeraries and their families; for they are amazingly prolific, and when they die off, are sure to leave John a legacy of hungry mouths to be provided for. A mattock cannot be struck against the most mouldering tumble-down tower, but out pops, from some cranny or loop-hole, the gray pate of some superannuated hanger-on, who has lived at John's expense all his life, and makes the most grievous outcry at their pulling down the roof from over the head of a worn-out servant of the family. This is an appeal that John's honest heart never can withstand; so that a man, who has faithfully eaten his beef and pudding all his life, is sure to be rewarded with a pipe and tankard in his old days.

A great part of his park, also, is turned into paddocks, where his broken-down chargers are turned loose to graze undisturbed for the remainder of their existence—a worthy example of grateful recollection, which if some of his neighbors were to imitate, would not be to their discredit. Indeed, it is one of his great pleasures to point out these old steeds to his visitors, to dwell on their good qualities, extol their past services, and boast, with some little vainglory, of the perilous adventures and hardy exploits through which they have carried him.

He is given, however, to indulge his veneration for family usages, and family incumbrances, to a whimsical extent. His manor is infested by gangs of gipsies; yet he will not suffer them to be driven off, because they have infested the place time out of mind, and been regular poachers upon every generation of the family. He will scarcely permit a dry branch to be lopped from the great trees that surround the house, lest it should molest the rooks, that have bred there for centuries. Owls have taken possession of the dovecote; but they are hereditary owls, and must not be disturbed. Swallows have nearly choked up every chimney with their nests; martins build in every frieze and cornice; crows flutter about the towers, and perch on every weather-cock; and old gray-headed rats may be seen in every quarter of the house, running in and out of their holes undauntedly in broad daylight. In short, John has such a reverence for every thing that has been long in the family, that he will not hear even of abuses being reformed, because they are good old family abuses.

All these whims and habits have concurred wofully to drain the old gentleman's purse; and as he prides himself on punctuality in money matters, and wishes to maintain his credit in the neighborhood, they have caused him great perplexity in meeting his engagements. This, too, has been increased by the altercations and heart-burnings which are continually taking place in his family. His children have been brought up to different callings, and are of different ways of thinking; and as they have always been allowed to speak their minds freely, they do not fail to exercise the privilege most clamorously in the present posture of his affairs. Some stand up for the honor of the race, and are clear that the old establishment should be kept up in all its state, whatever maybe the cost; others, who are more prudent and considerate, entreat the old gentleman to retrench his expenses, and to put his whole system of housekeeping on a more moderate footing. He has, indeed, at times, seemed inclined to listen to their opinions, but their wholesome advice has been completely defeated by the obstreperous conduct of one of his sons. This is a noisy, rattle-pated fellow, of rather low habits, who neglects his business to frequent alehouses—is the orator of village clubs, and a complete oracle among the poorest of his father's tenants. No sooner does he hear any of his brothers mention reform or retrenchment, than up he jumps, takes the words out of their mouths, and roars out for an overturn. When his tongue is once going nothing can stop it. He rants about the room; hectors the old man about his spendthrift practices; ridicules his tastes and pursuits; insists that he shall turn the old servants out of doors; give the broken-down horses to the hounds; send the fat chaplain packing, and take a field-preacher in his place—nay, that the whole family mansion shall be levelled with the ground, and a plain one of brick and mortar built in its place. He rails at every social entertainment and family festivity, and skulks away growling to the ale-house whenever an equipage drives up to the door. Though constantly complaining of the emptiness of his purse, yet he scruples not to spend all his pocket-money in these tavern convocations, and even runs up scores for the liquor over which he preaches about his father's extravagance.

It may readily be imagined how little such thwarting agrees with the old cavalier's fiery temperament. He has become so irritable, from repeated crossings, that the mere mention of retrenchment or reform is a signal for a brawl between him and the tavern oracle. As the latter is too sturdy and refractory for paternal discipline, having grown out of all fear of the cudgel, they have frequent scenes of wordy warfare, which at times run so high, that John is fain to call in the aid of his son Tom, an officer who has served abroad, but is at present living at home, on half-pay. This last is sure to stand by the old gentleman, right or wrong; likes nothing so much as a racketing, roystering life; and is ready at a wink or nod, to out sabre, and flourish it over the orator's head, if he dares to array himself against paternal authority.

These family dissensions, as usual, have got abroad, and are rare food for scandal in John's neighborhood. People begin to look wise, and shake their heads, whenever his affairs are mentioned. They all "hope that matters are not so bad with him as represented; but when a man's own children begin to rail at his extravagance, things must be badly managed. They understand he is mortgaged over head and ears, and is continually dabbling with money lenders. He is certainly an open-handed old gentleman, but they fear he has lived too fast; indeed, they never knew any good come of this fondness for hunting, racing, revelling and prize-fighting. In short, Mr. Bull's estate is a very fine one, and has been in the family a long time; but, for all that, they have known many finer estates come to the hammer."

What is worst of all, is the effect which these pecuniary embarrassments and domestic feuds have had on the poor man himself. Instead of that jolly round corporation, and smug rosy face, which he used to present, he has of late become as shrivelled and shrunk as a frost-bitten apple. His scarlet gold-laced waistcoat, which bellied out so bravely in those prosperous days when he sailed before the wind, now hangs loosely about him like a mainsail in a calm. His leather breeches are all in folds and wrinkles, and apparently have much ado to hold up the boots that yawn on both sides of his once sturdy legs.

Instead of strutting about as formerly, with his three-cornered hat on one side; flourishing his cudgel, and bringing it down every moment with a hearty thump upon the ground; looking every one sturdily in the face, and trolling out a stave of a catch or a drinking song; he now goes about whistling thoughtfully to himself, with his head drooping down, his cudgel tucked under his arm, and his hands thrust to the bottom of his breeches pockets, which are evidently empty.

Such is the plight of honest John Bull at present; yet for all this the old fellow's spirit is as tall and as gallant as ever. If you drop the least expression of sympathy or concern, he takes fire in an instant; swears that he is the richest and stoutest fellow in the country; talks of laying out large sums to adorn his house or buy another estate; and with a valiant swagger and grasping of his cudgel, longs exceedingly to have another bout at quarter-staff.

Though there may be something rather whimsical in all this, yet I confess I cannot look upon John's situation without strong feelings of interest. With all his odd humors and obstinate prejudices, he is a sterling-hearted old blade. He may not be so wonderfully fine a fellow as he thinks himself, but he is at least twice as good as his neighbors represent him. His virtues are all his own; all plain, homebred, and unaffected. His very faults smack of the raciness of his good qualities. His extravagance savors of his generosity; his quarrelsomeness of his courage; his credulity of his open faith; his vanity of his pride; and his bluntness of his sincerity. They are all the redundancies of a rich and liberal character. He is like his own oak, rough without, but sound and solid within; whose bark abounds with excrescences in proportion to the growth and grandeur of the timber; and whose branches make a fearful groaning and murmuring in the least storm, from their very magnitude and luxuriance. There is something, too, in the appearance of his old family mansion that is extremely poetical and picturesque; and, as long as it can be rendered comfortably habitable, I should almost tremble to see it meddled with, during the present conflict of tastes and opinions. Some of his advisers are no doubt good architects, that might be of service; but many, I fear, are mere levellers, who, when they had once got to work with their mattocks on this venerable edifice, would never stop until they had brought it to the ground, and perhaps buried themselves among the ruins. All that I wish is, that John's present troubles may teach him more prudence in future. That he may cease to distress his mind about other people's affairs; that he may give up the fruitless attempt to promote the good of his neighbors, and the peace and happiness of the world, by dint of the cudgel; that he may remain quietly at home; gradually get his house into repair; cultivate his rich estate according to his fancy; husband his income—if he thinks proper; bring his unruly children into order—if he can; renew the jovial scenes of ancient prosperity; and long enjoy, on his paternal lands, a green, an honorable, and a merry old age.

THE PRIDE OF THE VILLAGE[45]

May no wolfe howle; no screech owle stir
A wing about thy sepulchre!
No boysterous winds or stormes come hither,
   To starve or wither
Thy soft sweet earth! but, like a spring,
Love keep it ever flourishing.

HERRICK.

In the course of an excursion through one of the remote counties of England, I had struck into one of those cross-roads that lead through the more secluded parts of the country, and stopped one afternoon at a village, the situation of which was beautifully rural and retired. There was an air of primitive simplicity about its inhabitants, not to be found in the villages which lie on the great coach-roads. I determined to pass the night there, and, having taken an early dinner, strolled out to enjoy the neighboring scenery.

My ramble, as is usually the case with travellers, soon led me to the church, which stood at a little distance from the village. Indeed, it was an object of some curiosity, its old tower being completely overrun with ivy, so that only here and there a jutting buttress, an angle of gray wall, or a fantastically carved ornament, peered through the verdant covering. It was a lovely evening. The early part of the day had been dark and showery, but in the afternoon it had cleared up; and though sullen clouds still hung overhead, yet there was a broad tract of golden sky in the west, from which the setting sun gleamed through the dripping leaves, and lit up all nature with a melancholy smile. It seemed like the parting hour of a good Christian, smiling on the sins and sorrows of the world, and giving, in the serenity of his decline, an assurance that he will rise again in glory.

I had seated myself on a half-sunken tombstone, and was musing, as one is apt to do at this sober-thoughted hour, on past scenes and early friends—on those who were distant and those who were dead—and indulging in that kind of melancholy fancying, which has in it something sweeter even than pleasure. Every now and then, the stroke of a bell from the neighboring tower fell on my ear; its tones were in unison with the scene, and, instead of jarring, chimed in with my feelings; and it was some time before I recollected that it must be tolling the knell of some new tenant of the tomb.

Presently I saw a funeral train moving across the village green; it wound slowly along a lane; was lost, and reappeared through the breaks of the hedges, until it passed the place where I was sitting. The pall was supported by young girls, dressed in white; and another, about the age of seventeen, walked before, bearing a chaplet of white flowers; a token that the deceased was a young and unmarried female. The corpse was followed by the parents. They were a venerable couple of the better order of peasantry. The father seemed to repress his feelings; but his fixed eye, contracted brow, and deeply-furrowed face, showed the struggle that was passing within. His wife hung on his arm, and wept aloud with the convulsive bursts of a mother's sorrow.

I followed the funeral into the church. The bier was placed in the centre aisle, and the chaplet of white flowers, with a pair of white gloves, were hung over the seat which the deceased had occupied.

Every one knows the soul-subduing pathos of the funeral service; for who is so fortunate as never to have followed some one he has loved to the tomb? but when performed over the remains of innocence and beauty, thus laid low in the bloom of existence—what can be more affecting? At that simple, but most solemn consignment of the body to the grave—"Earth to earth—ashes to ashes—dust to dust!"—the tears of the youthful companions of the deceased flowed unrestrained. The father still seemed to struggle with his feelings, and to comfort himself with the assurance, that the dead are blessed which die in the Lord; but the mother only thought of her child as a flower of the field cut down and withered in the midst of its sweetness; she was like Rachel, "mourning over her children, and would not be comforted."

On returning to the inn, I learned the whole story of the deceased. It was a simple one, and such as has often been told. She had been the beauty and pride of the village. Her father had once been an opulent farmer, but was reduced in circumstances. This was an only child, and brought up entirely at home, in the simplicity of rural life. She had been the pupil of the village pastor, the favorite lamb of his little flock. The good man watched over her education with paternal care; it was limited, and suitable to the sphere in which she was to move; for he only sought to make her an ornament to her station in life, not to raise her above it. The tenderness and indulgence of her parents, and the exemption from all ordinary occupations, had fostered a natural grace and delicacy of character, that accorded with the fragile loveliness of her form. She appeared like some tender plant of the garden, blooming accidentally amid the hardier natives of the fields.

The superiority of her charms was felt and acknowledged by her companions, but without envy; for it was surpassed by the unassuming gentleness and winning kindness of her manners. It might be truly said of her:

> "This is the prettiest low-born lass, that ever
> Ran on the green-sward; nothing she does or seems,
> But smacks of something greater than herself;
> Too noble for this place."

The village was one of those sequestered spots, which still retain some vestiges of old English customs. It had its rural festivals and holiday pastimes, and still kept up some faint observance of the once popular rites of May. These, indeed, had been promoted by its present pastor, who was a lover of old customs, and one of those simple Christians that think their mission fulfilled by promoting joy on earth and good-will among mankind. Under his auspices the May-pole stood from year to year in the centre of the village green; on May-day it was decorated with garlands and streamers; and a queen or lady of the May was appointed, as in former times, to preside at the sports, and distribute the prizes and rewards. The picturesque situation of the village, and the fancifulness of its rustic fêtes, would often attract the notice of casual visitors. Among these, on one May-day, was a young officer, whose regiment had been recently quartered in the neighborhood. He was charmed with the native taste that pervaded this village pageant; but, above all, with the dawning loveliness of the queen of May. It was the village favorite, who was crowned with flowers, and blushing and smiling in all the beautiful confusion of girlish diffidence and delight. The artlessness of rural habits enabled him readily to make her acquaintance; he gradually won his way into her intimacy; and paid his court to her in that unthinking way in which young officers are too apt to trifle with rustic simplicity.

There was nothing in his advances to startle or alarm. He never even talked of love: but there are modes of making it more eloquent than language, and which convey it subtilely and irresistibly to the heart. The beam of the eye, the tone of voice, the thousand tendernesses which emanate from every word, and look, and action—these form the true eloquence of love, and can always be felt and understood, but never described. Can we wonder that they should readily win a heart, young, guileless, and susceptible? As to her, she loved almost unconsciously; she scarcely inquired what was the growing passion that was absorbing every thought and feeling, or what were to be its consequences. She, indeed, looked not to the future. When present, his looks and words occupied her whole attention; when absent, she thought but of what had passed at their recent interview. She would wander with him through the green lanes and rural scenes of the vicinity. He taught her to see new beauties in nature; he talked in the language of polite and cultivated life, and breathed into her ear the witcheries of romance and poetry.

Perhaps there could not have been a passion, between the sexes, more pure than this innocent girl's. The gallant figure of her youthful admirer, and the splendor of his military attire, might at first have charmed her eye; but it was not these that had captivated her heart. Her attachment had something in it of idolatry. She looked up to him as to a being of a superior order. She felt in his society the enthusiasm of a mind naturally delicate and poetical, and now first awakened to a keen perception of the beautiful and grand. Of the sordid distinctions of rank and fortune she thought nothing; it was the difference of intellect, of demeanor, of manners, from those of the rustic society to which she had been accustomed, that elevated him in her opinion. She would listen to him with charmed ear and downcast look of mute delight, and her cheek would mantle with enthusiasm; or if ever she ventured a shy glance of timid admiration, it was as quickly withdrawn, and she would sigh and blush at the idea of her comparative unworthiness.

Her lover was equally impassioned; but his passion was mingled with feelings of a coarser nature. He had begun the connection in levity; for he had often heard his brother officers boast of their village conquests, and thought some triumph of the kind necessary to his reputation as a man of spirit. But he was too full of youthful fervor. His heart had not yet been rendered sufficiently cold and selfish by a wandering and a dissipated life: it caught fire from the very flame it sought to kindle; and before he was aware of the nature of his situation, he became really in love.

What was he to do? There were the old obstacles which so incessantly occur in these heedless attachments. His rank in life—the prejudices of titled connections—his dependence upon a proud and unyielding father—all forbad him to think of matrimony:—but when he looked down upon this innocent being, so tender and confiding, there was a purity in her manners, a blamelessness in her life, and a beseeching modesty in her looks that awed down every licentious feeling. In vain did he try to fortify himself by a thousand heartless examples of men of fashion; and to chill the glow of generous sentiment with that cold derisive levity with which he had heard them talk of female virtue: whenever he came into her presence, she was still surrounded by that mysterious but impassive charm of virgin purity in whose hallowed sphere no guilty thought can live.

The sudden arrival of orders for the regiment to repair to the continent completed the confusion of his mind. He remained for a short time in a state of the most painful irresolution; he hesitated to communicate the tidings, until the day for marching was at hand; when he gave her the intelligence in the course of an evening ramble.

The idea of parting had never before occurred to her. It broke in at once upon her dream of felicity; she looked upon it as a sudden and insurmountable evil, and wept with the guileless simplicity of a child. He drew her to his bosom, and kissed the tears from her soft cheek; nor did he meet with a repulse, for there are moments of mingled sorrow and tenderness, which hallow the caresses of affection. He was naturally impetuous; and the sight of beauty, apparently yielding in his arms, the confidence of his power over her, and the dread of losing her for ever, all conspired to overwhelm his better feelings—he ventured to propose that she should leave her home, and be the companion of his fortunes.

He was quite a novice in seduction, and blushed and faltered at his own baseness; but so innocent of mind was his intended victim, that she was at first at a loss to comprehend his meaning; and why she should leave her native village, and the humble roof of her parents. When at last the nature of his proposal flashed upon her pure mind, the effect was withering. She did not weep—she did not break forth into reproach—she said not a word—but she shrunk back aghast as from a viper; gave him a look of anguish that pierced to his very soul; and, clasping her hands in agony, fled, as if for refuge, to her father's cottage.

The officer retired, confounded, humiliated, and repentant. It is uncertain what might have been the result of the conflict of his feelings, had not his thoughts been diverted by the bustle of departure. New scenes, new pleasures, and new companions, soon dissipated his self-reproach, and stifled his tenderness; yet, amidst the stir of camps, the revelries of garrisons, the array of armies, and even the din of battles, his thoughts would sometimes steal back to the scenes of rural quiet and village simplicity—the white cottage—the footpath along the silver brook and up the hawthorn hedge, and the little village maid loitering along it, leaning on his arm, and listening to him with eyes beaming with unconscious affection.

The shock which the poor girl had received, in the destruction of all her ideal world, had indeed been cruel. Faintings and hysterics had at first shaken her tender frame, and were succeeded by a settled and pining melancholy. She had beheld from her window the march of the departing troops. She had seen her faithless lover borne off, as if in triumph, amidst the sound of drum and trumpet, and the pomp of arms. She strained a last aching gaze after him, as the morning sun glittered about his figure, and his plume waved in the breeze; he passed away like a bright vision from her sight, and left her all in darkness.

It would be trite to dwell on the particulars of her after story. It was, like other tales of love, melancholy. She avoided society, and wandered out alone in the walks she had most frequented with her lover. She sought, like the stricken deer, to weep in silence and loneliness, and brood over the barbed sorrow that rankled in her soul. Sometimes she would be seen late of an evening sitting in the porch of the village church; and the milkmaids, returning from the fields, would now and then overhear her singing some plaintive ditty in the hawthorn walk. She became fervent in her devotions at church; and as the old people saw her approach, so wasted away, yet with a hectic gloom, and that hallowed air which melancholy diffuses round the form, they would make way for her, as for something spiritual, and, looking after her, would shake their heads in gloomy foreboding.

She felt a conviction that she was hastening to the tomb, but looked forward to it as a place of rest. The silver cord that had bound her to existence was loosed, and there seemed to be no more pleasure under the sun. If ever her gentle bosom had entertained resentment against her lover, it was extinguished. She was incapable of angry passions; and in a moment of saddened tenderness, she penned him a farewell letter. It was couched in the simplest language, but touching from its very simplicity. She told him that she was dying, and did not conceal from him that his conduct was the cause. She even depicted the sufferings which she had experienced; but concluded with saying, that she could not die in peace, until she had sent him her forgiveness and her blessing.

By degrees her strength declined, that she could no longer leave the cottage. She could only totter to the window, where, propped up in her chair, it was her enjoyment to sit all day and look out upon the landscape. Still she uttered no complaint, nor imparted to any one the malady that was preying on her heart. She never even mentioned her lover's name; but would lay her head on her mother's bosom and weep in silence. Her poor parents hung, in mute anxiety, over this fading blossom of their hopes, still flattering themselves that it might again revive to freshness, and that the bright unearthly bloom which sometimes flushed her cheek might be the promise of returning health.

In this way she was seated between them one Sunday afternoon; her hands were clasped in theirs, the lattice was thrown open, and the soft air that stole in brought with it the fragrance of the clustering honeysuckle which her own hands had trained round the window.

Her father had just been reading a chapter in the Bible: it spoke of the vanity of worldly things, and of the joys of heaven: it seemed to have diffused comfort and serenity through her bosom. Her eye was fixed on the distant village church; the bell had tolled for the evening service; the last villager was lagging into the porch; and every thing had sunk into that hallowed stillness peculiar to the day of rest. Her parents were gazing on her with yearning hearts. Sickness and sorrow, which pass so roughly over some faces, had given to hers the expression of a seraph's. A tear trembled in her soft blue eye.— Was she thinking of her faithless lover?—or were her thoughts wandering to that distant church-yard, into whose bosom she might soon be gathered?

Suddenly the clang of hoofs was heard—a horseman galloped to the cottage—he dismounted before the window—the poor girl gave a faint exclamation, and sunk back in her chair: it was her repentant lover! He rushed into the house, and flew to clasp her to his bosom; but her wasted form—her deathlike countenance—so wan, yet so lovely in its desolation,—smote him to the soul, and he threw himself in agony at her feet. She was too faint to rise—she attempted to extend her trembling hand—her lips moved as if she spoke, but no word was articulated—she looked down upon him with a smile of unutterable tenderness,—and closed her eyes for ever!

Such are the particulars which I gathered of this village story. They are but scanty, and I am conscious have little novelty to recommend them. In the present rage also for strange incident and high-seasoned narrative, they may appear trite and insignificant, but they interested me strongly at the time; and, taken in connection with the affecting ceremony which I had just witnessed, left a deeper impression on my mind than many circumstances of a more striking nature. I have passed through the place since, and visited the church again, from a better motive than mere curiosity. It was a wintry evening; the trees were stripped of their foliage; the church-yard looked naked and mournful, and the wind rustled coldly through the dry grass. Evergreens, however, had been planted about the grave of the village favorite, and osiers were bent over it to keep the turf uninjured.

The church door was open, and I stepped in. There hung the chaplet of flowers and the gloves, as on the day of the funeral: the flowers were withered, it is true, but care seemed to have been taken that no dust should soil their whiteness. I have seen many monuments, where art has exhausted its powers to awaken the sympathy of the spectator, but I have met with none that spoke more touchingly to my heart, than this simple but delicate memento of departed innocence.

THE LEGEND OF SLEEPY HOLLOW [46]

FOUND AMONG THE PAPERS OF THE LATE DIEDRICH KNICKER-
BOCKER

> A pleasing land of drowsy head it was,
>   Of dreams that wave before the half-shut eye;
> And of gay castles in the clouds that pass,
>   For ever flushing round a summer sky.
>   CASTLE OF INDOLENCE.

In the bosom of one of those spacious coves which indent
the eastern shore of the Hudson, at that broad expansion of
the river denominated by the ancient Dutch navigators the
Tappan Zee, and where they always prudently shortened sail,
and implored the protection of St. Nicholas when they crossed,
there lies a small market-town or rural port, which by some is
called Greensburgh, but which is more generally and properly
known by the name of Tarry Town. This name was given,
we are told, in former days, by the good housewives of the
adjacent country, from the inveterate propensity of their husbands to linger about the village tavern on market days. Be
that as it may, I do not vouch for the fact, but merely advert
to it, for the sake of being precise and authentic. Not far from
this village, perhaps about two miles, there is a little valley, or
rather lap of land, among high hills, which is one of the quietest
places in the whole world. A small brook glides through it,
with just murmur enough to lull one to repose; and the occasional whistle of a quail, or tapping of a woodpecker, is almost
the only sound that ever breaks in upon the uniform tranquillity.

I recollect that, when a stripling, my first exploit in squirrel-
shooting was in a grove of tall walnut-trees that shades one
side of the valley. I had wandered into it at noon time, when
all nature is peculiarly quiet, and was startled by the roar of my
own gun, as it broke the Sabbath stillness around, and was
prolonged and reverberated by the angry echoes. If ever I
should wish for a retreat, whither I might steal from the world

and its distractions, and dream quietly away the remnant of a troubled life, I know of none more promising than this little valley.

From the listless repose of the place, and the peculiar character of its inhabitants, who are descendants from the original Dutch settlers, this sequestered glen has long been known by the name of SLEEPY HOLLOW, and its rustic lads are called the Sleepy Hollow Boys throughout all the neighboring country. A drowsy, dreamy influence seems to hang over the land, and to pervade the very atmosphere. Some say that the place was bewitched by a high German doctor, during the early days of the settlement; others, that an old Indian chief, the prophet or wizard of his tribe, held his powwows there before the country was discovered by Master Hendrick Hudson. Certain it is, the place still continues under the sway of some witching power, that holds a spell over the minds of the good people, causing them to walk in a continual reverie. They are given to all kinds of marvellous beliefs; are subject to trances and visions; and frequently see strange sights, and hear music and voices in the air. The whole neighborhood abounds with local tales, haunted spots, and twilight superstitions; stars shoot and meteors glare oftener across the valley than in any other part of the country, and the nightmare, with her whole nine fold, seems to make it the favorite scene of her gambols.

The dominant spirit, however, that haunts this enchanted region, and seems to be commander-in-chief of all the powers of the air, is the apparition of a figure on horseback without a head. It is said by some to be the ghost of a Hessian trooper, whose head had been carried away by a cannon-ball, in some nameless battle during the revolutionary war; and who is ever and anon seen by the country folk, hurrying along in the gloom of night, as if on the wings of the wind. His haunts are not confined to the valley, but extend at times to the adjacent roads, and especially to the vicinity of a church at no great distance. Indeed, certain of the most authentic historians of those parts, who have been careful in collecting and collating the floating facts concerning this spectre, allege that the body of the trooper,

having been buried in the church-yard, the ghost rides forth
to the scene of battle in nightly quest of his head; and that the
rushing speed with which he sometimes passes along the
Hollow, like a midnight blast, is owing to his being belated,
and in a hurry to get back to the church-yard before daybreak.

Such is the general purport of this legendary superstition,
which has furnished materials for many a wild story in that
region of shadows; and the spectre is known, at all the country
firesides, by the name of the Headless Horseman of Sleepy
Hollow.

It is remarkable that the visionary propensity I have mentioned is not confined to the native inhabitants of the valley,
but is unconsciously imbibed by every one who resides there
for a time. However wide awake they may have been before
they entered that sleepy region, they are sure, in a little time,
to inhale the witching influence of the air, and begin to grow
imaginative—to dream dreams, and see apparitions.

I mention this peaceful spot with all possible laud; for it is
in such little retired Dutch valleys, found here and there
embosomed in the great State of New-York, that population,
manners, and customs, remain fixed; while the great torrent of
migration and improvement, which is making such incessant
changes in other parts of this restless country, sweeps by them
unobserved. They are like those little nooks of still water
which border a rapid stream; where we may see the straw and
bubble riding quietly at anchor, or slowly revolving in their
mimic harbor, undisturbed by the rush of the passing current.
Though many years have elapsed since I trod the drowsy
shades of Sleepy Hollow, yet I question whether I should not
still find the same trees and the same families vegetating in its
sheltered bosom.

In this by-place of nature, there abode, in a remote period
of American history, that is to say, some thirty years since, a
worthy wight of the name of Ichabod Crane; who sojourned,
or, as he expressed it, "tarried," in Sleepy Hollow, for the
purpose of instructing the children of the vicinity. He was a
native of Connecticut; a State which supplies the Union with

pioneers for the mind as well as for the forest, and sends forth yearly its legions of frontier woodsmen and country school-masters. The cognomen of Crane was not inapplicable to his person. He was tall, but exceedingly lank, with narrow shoulders, long arms and legs, hands that dangled a mile out of his sleeves, feet that might have served for shovels, and his whole frame most loosely hung together. His head was small, and flat at top, with huge ears, large green glassy eyes, and a long snipe nose, so that it looked like a weather-cock, perched upon his spindle neck, to tell which way the wind blew. To see him striding along the profile of a hill on a windy day, with his clothes bagging and fluttering about him, óne might have mistaken him for the genius of famine descending upon the earth, or some scarecrow eloped from a córnfield.

His school-house was a low building of one large room, rudely constructed of logs; the windows partly glazed, and partly patched with leaves of old copy-books. It was most ingeniously secured at vacant hours, by a withe twisted in the handle of the door, and stakes set against the window shutters; so that, though a thief might get in with perfect ease, he would find some embarrassment in getting out; an idea most probably borrowed by the architect, Yost Van Houten, from the mystery of an eel-pot. The school-house stood in a rather lonely but pleasant situation, just at the foot of a woody hill, with a brook running close by, and a formidable birch tree growing àt one end of it. From hence the low murmur of his pupils' voices, conning over their lessons, might be heard in a drowsy summer's day, like the hum of a bee-hive; interrupted now and then by the authoritative voice of the master, in the tone of menace or command; or, peradventure, by the appalling sound of the birch, as he urged some tardy loiterer along the flowery path of knowledge. Truth to say, he was a conscientious man, and ever bore in mind the golden maxim, "Spare the rod and spoil the child."—Ichabod Crane's scholars certainly were not spoiled.

I would not have it imagined, however, that he was one of those cruel potentates of the school, who joy in the smart of their subjects; on the contrary, he administered justice with discrimination rather than severity; taking the burthen off the backs of the weak, and laying it on those of the strong. Your mere puny stripling, that winced at the least flourish of the rod, was passed by with indulgence; but the claims of justice were satisfied by inflicting a double portion on some little, tough, wrong-headed, broad-skirted Dutch urchin, who sulked and swelled and grew dogged and sullen beneath the birch. All this he called "doing his duty by their parents;" and he never inflicted a chastisement without following it by the assurance, so consolatory to the smarting urchin, that "he would remember it, and thank him for it the longest day he had to live."

When school hours were over, he was even the companion and playmate of the larger boys; and on holiday afternoons would convoy some of the smaller ones home, who happened to have pretty sisters, or good housewives for mothers, noted for the comforts of the cupboard. Indeed it behooved him to keep on good terms with his pupils. The revenue arising from his school was small, and would have been scarcely sufficient to furnish him with daily bread, for he was a huge feeder, and though lank, had the dilating powers of an anaconda; but to help out his maintenance, he was, according to country custom in those parts, boarded and lodged at the houses of the farmers, whose children he instructed. With these he lived successively a week at a time; thus going the rounds of the neighborhood, with all his worldly effects tied up in a cotton handkerchief.

That all this might not be too onerous on the purses of his rustic patrons, who are apt to consider the costs of schooling a grievous burden, and schoolmasters as mere drones, he had various ways of rendering himself both useful and agreeable. He assisted the farmers occasionally in the lighter labors of their farms; helped to make hay; mended the fences; took the horses to water; drove the cows from pasture; and cut wood for the winter fire. He laid aside, too, all the dominant dignity and absolute sway with which he lorded it in his little empire, the school, and became wonderfully gentle and ingratiating. He found favor in the eyes of the mothers, by petting the children, particularly the youngest; and like the lion bold, which whilom so magnanimously the lamb did hold, he would sit with a child on one knee, and rock a cradle with his foot for whole hours together.

In addition to his other vocations, he was the singing-master of the neighborhood, and picked up many bright shillings by instructing the young folks in psalmody. It was a matter of no little vanity to him, on Sundays, to take his station in front of the church gallery, with a band of chosen singers; where, in his own mind, he completely carried away the palm from the parson. Certain it is, his voice resounded far above all the rest of the congregation; and there are peculiar quavers still to be heard in that church, and which may even be heard half a mile off, quite to the opposite side of the mill-pond, on a still Sunday morning, which are said to be legitimately descended from the nose of Ichabod Crane. Thus, by divers little make-shifts in that ingenious way which is commonly denominated "by hook and by crook," the worthy pedagogue got on tolerably enough, and was thought, by all who understood nothing of the labor of headwork, to have a wonderfully easy life of it.

The schoolmaster is generally a man of some importance in the female circle of a rural neighborhood; being considered a kind of idle gentlemanlike personage, of vastly superior taste and accomplishments to the rough country swains, and, indeed, inferior in learning only to the parson. His appearance, therefore, is apt to occasion some little stir at the tea-table of a farmhouse, and the addition of a supernumerary dish of cakes or sweetmeats, or, peradventure, the parade of a silver tea-pot. Our man of letters, therefore, was peculiarly happy in the smiles of all the country damsels. How he would figure among them in the churchyard, between services on Sundays! gathering grapes for them from the wild vines that overrun the surrounding trees; reciting for their amusement all the epitaphs on the tombstones; or sauntering, with a whole bevy of them, along the banks of the adjacent mill-pond; while the more bashful country bumpkins hung sheepishly back, envying his superior elegance and address.

From his half itinerant life, also, he was a kind of travelling gazette, carrying the whole budget of local gossip from house to house; so that his appearance was always greeted with satisfaction. He was, moreover, esteemed by the women as a man of great erudition, for he had read several books quite through, and was a perfect master of Cotton Mather's history of New England Witchcraft, in which, by the way, he most firmly and potently believed.

He was, in fact, an odd mixture of small shrewdness and simple credulity. His appetite for the marvellous, and his powers of digesting it, were equally extraordinary; and both had been increased by his residence in this spellbound region. No tale was too gross or monstrous for his capacious swallow. It was often his delight, after his school was dismissed in the afternoon, to stretch himself on the rich bed of clover, bordering the little brook that whimpered by his school-house, and there con over old Mather's direful tales, until the gathering dusk of the evening made the printed page a mere mist before his eyes. Then, as he wended his way, by swamp and stream and awful woodland, to the farmhouse where he happened to be quartered, every sound of nature, at that witching hour, fluttered his excited imagination: the moan of the whip-poor-will [47] from the hill-side; the boding cry of the tree-toad, that harbinger of storm; the dreary hooting of the screech-owl, or the sudden rustling in the thicket of birds frightened from their roost. The fire-flies, too, which sparkled most vividly in the darkest places, now and then startled him, as one of uncommon brightness would stream across his path; and if, by chance, a huge blockhead of a beetle came winging his blundering flight against him, the poor varlet was ready to give up the ghost, with the idea that he was struck with a witch's token. His only resource on such occasions, either to drown thought, or drive away evil spirits, was to sing psalm tunes;—and the good people of Sleepy Hollow, as they sat by their doors of an evening, were often filled with awe, at hearing his nasal melody, "in linked sweetness long drawn out," floating from the distant hill, or along the dusky road.

Another of his sources of fearful pleasure was, to pass long winter evenings with the old Dutch wives, as they sat spinning by the fire, with a row of apples roasting and spluttering along the hearth, and listen to their marvellous tales of ghosts and goblins, and haunted fields, and haunted brooks, and haunted bridges, and haunted houses, and particularly of the headless horseman, or galloping Hessian of the Hollow, as they sometimes called him. He would delight them equally by his anecdotes of witchcraft, and of the direful omens and portentous sights and sounds in the air, which prevailed in the earlier times of Connecticut; and would frighten them wofully with speculations upon comets and shooting stars; and with the alarming fact that the world did absolutely turn round, and that they were half the time topsy-turvy!

But if there was a pleasure in all this, while snugly cuddling in the chimney corner of a chamber that was all of a ruddy glow from the crackling wood fire, and where, of course, no spectre dared to show his face, it was dearly purchased by the terrors of his subsequent walk homewards. What fearful shapes and shadows beset his path amidst the dim and ghastly glare of a snowy night!—With what wistful look did he eye every trembling ray of light streaming across the waste fields from some distant window!—How often was he appalled by some shrub covered with snow, which, like a sheeted spectre, beset his very path!—How often did he shrink with curdling awe at the sound of his own steps on the frosty crust beneath his feet; and dread to look over his shoulder, lest he should behold some uncouth being tramping close behind him!—and how often was he thrown into complete dismay by some rushing blast, howling among the trees, in the idea that it was the Galloping Hessian on one of his nightly scourings!

All these, however, were mere terrors of the night, phantoms of the mind that walk in darkness; and though he had seen many spectres in his time, and been more than once beset by Satan in divers shapes, in his lonely perambulations, yet daylight put an end to all these evils; and he would have passed a pleasant life of it, in despite of the devil and all his works, if

his path had not been crossed by a being that causes more perplexity to mortal man than ghosts, goblins, and the whole race
of witches put together, and that was—a woman.

Among the musical disciples who assembled, one evening in
each week, to receive his instructions in psalmody, was Katrina
Van Tassel, the daughter and only child of a substantial Dutch
farmer. She was a blooming lass of fresh eighteen; plump as a
partridge; ripe and melting and rosy cheeked as one of her
father's peaches, and universally famed, not merely for her
beauty, but her vast expectations. She was withal a little of a
coquette, as might be perceived even in her dress, which was a
mixture of ancient and modern fashions, as most suited to set
off her charms. She wore the ornaments of pure yellow gold,
which her great-great-grandmother had brought over from
Saardam; the tempting stomacher of the olden time; and withal
a provokingly short petticoat, to display the prettiest foot and
ankle in the country round.

Ichabod Crane had a soft and foolish heart towards the sex;
and it is not to be wondered at, that so tempting a morsel soon
found favor in his eyes; more especially after he had visited her
in her paternal mansion. Old Baltus Van Tassel was a perfect
picture of a thriving, contented, liberal-hearted farmer. He
seldom, it is true, sent either his eyes or his thoughts beyond
the boundaries of his own farm; but within those every thing
was snug, happy, and well-conditioned. He was satisfied with
his wealth, but not proud of it; and piqued himself upon the
hearty abundance, rather than the style in which he lived. His
stronghold was situated on the banks of the Hudson, in one of
those green, sheltered, fertile nooks, in which the Dutch farmers
are so fond of nestling. A great elm-tree spread its broad
branches over it; at the foot of which bubbled up a spring of
the softest and sweetest water, in a little well, formed of a barrel;
and then stole sparkling away through the grass, to a neighboring brook, that bubbled along among alders and dwarf willows.
Hard by the farmhouse was a vast barn, that might have served
for a church; every window and crevice of which seemed bursting forth with the treasures of the farm; the flail was busily

resounding within it from morning to night; swallows and martins skimmed twittering about the eaves; and rows of pigeons, some with one eye turned up, as if watching the weather, some with their heads under their wings, or buried in their bosoms, and others swelling, and cooing, and bowing about their dames, were enjoying the sunshine on the roof. Sleek unwieldy porkers were grunting in the repose and abundance of their pens; whence sallied forth, now and then, troops of sucking pigs, as if to snuff the air. A stately squadron of snowy geese were riding in an adjoining pond, convoying whole fleets of ducks; regiments of turkeys were gobbling through the farmyard, and guinea fowls fretting about it, like ill-tempered housewives, with their peevish discontented cry. Before the barn door strutted the gallant cock, that pattern of a husband, a warrior, and a fine gentleman, clapping his burnished wings, and crowing in the pride and gladness of his heart—sometimes tearing up the earth with his feet, and then generously calling his ever-hungry family of wives and children to enjoy the rich morsel which he had discovered.

The pedagogue's mouth watered, as he looked upon this sumptuous promise of luxurious winter fare. In his devouring mind's eye, he pictured to himself every roasting-pig running about with a pudding in his belly, and an apple in his mouth; the pigeons were snugly put to bed in a comfortable pie, and tucked in with a coverlet of crust; the geese were swimming in their own gravy; and the ducks pairing cosily in dishes, like snug married couples, with a decent competency of onion sauce. In the porkers he saw carved out the future sleek side of bacon, and juicy relishing ham; not a turkey but he beheld daintily trussed up, with its gizzard under its wing, and, peradventure, a necklace of savory sausages; and even bright chanticleer himself lay sprawling on his back, in a side-dish, with uplifted claws, as if craving that quarter which his chivalrous spirit disdained to ask while living.

As the enraptured Ichabod fancied all this, and as he rolled his great green eyes over the fat meadow-lands, the rich fields of wheat, of rye, of buckwheat, and Indian corn, and the

orchards burthened with ruddy fruit, which surrounded the
warm tenement of Van Tassel, his heart yearned after the damsel who was to inherit these domains, and his imagination
expanded with the idea, how they might be readily turned into
cash, and the money invested in immense tracts of wild land,
and shingle palaces in the wilderness. Nay, his busy fancy
already realized his hopes, and presented to him the blooming
Katrina, with a whole family of children, mounted on the top
of a wagon loaded with household trumpery, with pots and
kettles dangling beneath; and he beheld himself bestriding a
pacing mare, with a colt at her heels, setting out for Kentucky,
Tennessee, or the Lord knows where.

When he entered the house the conquest of his heart was
complete. It was one of those spacious farmhouses, with high-
ridged, but lowly-sloping roofs, built in the style handed down
from the first Dutch settlers; the low projecting eaves forming
a piazza along the front, capable of being closed up in bad
weather. Under this were hung flails, harness, various utensils
of husbandry, and nets for fishing in the neighboring river.
Benches were built along the sides for summer use; and a great
spinning-wheel at one end, and a churn at the other, showed
the various uses to which this important porch might be devoted. From this piazza the wondering Ichabod entered the
hall, which formed the centre of the mansion and the place of
usual residence. Here, rows of resplendent pewter, ranged on
a long dresser, dazzled his eyes. In one corner stood a huge bag
of wool ready to be spun; in another a quantity of linsey-
woolsey just from the loom; ears of Indian corn, and strings of
dried apples and peaches, hung in gay festoons along the walls,
mingled with the gaud of red peppers; and a door left ajar gave
him a peep into the best parlor, where the claw-footed chairs,
and dark mahogany tables, shone like mirrors; and irons, with
their accompanying shovel and tongs, glistened from their
covert of asparagus tops; mock-oranges and conch-shells
decorated the mantel-piece; strings of various colored birds'
eggs were suspended above it: a great ostrich egg was hung
from the centre of the room, and a corner cupboard, knowingly

left open, displayed immense treasures of old silver and well-mended china.

From the moment Ichabod laid his eyes upon these regions of delight, the peace of his mind was at an end, and his only study was how to gain the affections of the peerless daughter of Van Tassel. In this enterprise, however, he had more real difficulties than generally fell to the lot of a knight-errant of yore, who seldom had any thing but giants, enchanters, fiery dragons, and such like easily-conquered adversaries, to contend with; and had to make his way merely through gates of iron and brass, and walls of adamant, to the castle keep, where the lady of his heart was confined; all which he achieved as easily as a man would carve his way to the centre of a Christmas pie; and then the lady gave him her hand as a matter of course. Ichabod, on the contrary, had to win his way to the heart of a country coquette, beset with a labyrinth of whims and caprices, which were for ever presenting new difficulties and impediments; and he had to encounter a host of fearful adversaries of real flesh and blood, the numerous rustic admirers, who beset every portal to her heart; keeping a watchful and angry eye upon each other, but ready to fly out in the common cause against any new competitor.

Among these the most formidable was a burly, roaring, roystering blade, of the name of Abraham, or, according to the Dutch abbreviation, Brom Van Brunt, the hero of the country round, which rang with his feats of strength and hardihood. He was broad-shouldered and double-jointed, with short curly black hair, and a bluff, but not unpleasant countenance, having a mingled air of fun and arrogance. From his Herculean frame and great powers of limb, he had received the nickname of BROM BONES, by which he was universally known. He was famed for great knowledge and skill in horsemanship, being as dexterous on horseback as a Tartar. He was foremost at all races and cock-fights; and, with the ascendency which bodily strength acquires in rustic life, was the umpire in all disputes, setting his hat on one side, and giving his decisions with an air and tone admitting of no gainsay or appeal. He was always ready for either a fight or a frolic; but had more mischief than ill-will in his composition; and, with all his overbearing roughness, there was a strong dash of waggish good humor at bottom. He had three or four boon companions, who regarded him as their model, and at the head of whom he scoured the country, attending every scene of feud or merriment for miles round. In cold weather he was distinguished by a fur cap, surmounted with a flaunting fox's tail; and when the folks at a country gathering descried this well-known crest at a distance, whisking about among a squad of hard riders, they always stood by for a squall. Sometimes his crew would be heard dashing along past the farmhouses at midnight, with whoop and halloo, like a troop of Don Cossacks; and the old dames, startled out of their sleep, would listen for a moment till the hurry-scurry had clattered by, and then exclaim, "Ay, there goes Brom Bones and his gang!" The neighbors looked upon him with a mixture of awe, admiration, and good will; and when any madcap prank, or rustic brawl, occurred in the vicinity, always shook their heads, and warranted Brom Bones was at the bottom of it.

This rantipole hero had for some time singled out the blooming Katrina for the object of his uncouth gallantries, and though his amorous toyings were something like the gentle caresses and endearments of a bear, yet it was whispered that she did not altogether discourage his hopes. Certain it is, his advances were signals for rival candidates to retire, who felt no inclination to cross a lion in his amours; insomuch, that when his horse was seen tied to Van Tassel's paling, on a Sunday night, a sure sign that his master was courting, or, as it is termed, "sparking," within, all other suitors passed by in despair, and carried the war into other quarters.

Such was the formidable rival with whom Ichabod Crane had to contend, and, considering all things, a stouter man than he would have shrunk from the competition, and a wiser man would have despaired. He had, however, a happy mixture of pliability and perseverance in his nature; he was in form and spirit like a supple-jack—yielding, but tough; though he bent, he never broke; and though he bowed beneath the slightest pressure, yet, the moment it was away—jerk! he was as erect, and carried his head as high as ever.

To have taken the field openly against his rival would have been madness; for he was not a man to be thwarted in his amours, any more than that stormy lover, Achilles. Ichabod, therefore, made his advances in a quiet and gently-insinuating manner. Under cover of his character of singing-master, he made frequent visits at the farmhouse; not that he had any thing to apprehend from the meddlesome interference of parents, which is so often a stumbling-block in the path of lovers. Balt Van Tassel was an easy indulgent soul; he loved his daughter better even than his pipe, and, like a reasonable man and an excellent father, let her have her way in every thing. His notable little wife, too, had enough to do to attend to her house-keeping and manage her poultry; for, as she sagely observed, ducks and geese are foolish things, and must be looked after, but girls can take care of themselves. Thus while the busy dame bustled about the house, or plied her spinning-wheel at one end of the piazza, honest Balt would sit smoking his evening pipe at the other, watching the achievements of a little wooden warrior, who, armed with a sword in each hand, was most valiantly fighting the wind on the pinnacle of the barn. In the mean time, Ichabod would carry on his suit with the daughter by the side of the spring under the great elm, or sauntering along in the twilight, that hour so favorable to the lover's eloquence.

I profess not to know how women's hearts are wooed and won. To me they have always been matters of riddle and admiration. Some seem to have but one vulnerable point, or door of access; while others have a thousand avenues, and may be captured in a thousand different ways. It is a great triumph of skill to gain the former, but a still greater proof of general-ship to maintain possession of the latter, for the man must battle for his fortress at every door and window. He who wins a thousand common hearts is therefore entitled to some renown; but he who keeps undisputed sway over the heart of a coquette, is indeed a hero. Certain it is, this was not the case with the

redoubtable Brom Bones; and from the moment Ichabod Crane
made his advances, the interests of the former evidently declined; his horse was no longer seen tied at the palings on Sunday nights, and a deadly feud gradually arose between him
and the preceptor of Sleepy Hollow.

Brom, who had a degree of rough chivalry in his nature,
would fain have carried matters to open warfare, and have settled their pretensions to the lady, according to the mode of
those most concise and simple reasoners, the knights-errant of
yore—by single combat; but Ichabod was too conscious of the
superior might of his adversary to enter the lists against him:
he had overheard a boast of Bones, that he would "double the
schoolmaster up, and lay him on a shelf of his own school-
house;" and he was too wary to give him an opportunity.
There was something extremely provoking in this obstinately
pacific system; it left Brom no alternative but to draw upon the
funds of rustic waggery in his disposition, and to play off boor-
ish practical jokes upon his rival. Ichabod became the object
of whimsical persecution to Bones, and his gang of rough
riders. They harried his hitherto peaceful domains; smoked
out his singing school, by stopping up the chimney; broke into
the school-house at night, in spite of its formidable fastenings
of withe and window stakes, and turned every thing topsy-
turvy: so that the poor schoolmaster began to think all the
witches in the country held their meetings there. But what was
still more annoying, Brom took all opportunities of turning
him into ridicule in presence of his mistress, and had a scoundrel
dog whom he taught to whine in the most ludicrous manner, and introduced as a rival of Ichabod's to instruct her in
psalmody.

In this way matters went on for some time, without producing any material effect on the relative situation of the contending powers. On a fine autumnal afternoon, Ichabod, in pensive mood, sat enthroned on the lofty stool whence he usually
watched all the concerns of his little literary realm. In his hand
he swayed a ferule, that sceptre of despotic power; the birch of
justice reposed on three nails, behind the throne, a constant

terror to evil doers; while on the desk before him might be seen sundry contraband articles and prohibited weapons, detected upon the persons of idle urchins; such as half-munched apples, popguns, whirligigs, fly-cages, and whole legions of rampant little paper game-cocks. Apparently there had been some appalling act of justice recently inflicted, for his scholars were all busily intent upon their books, or slyly whispering behind them with one eye kept upon the master; and a kind of buzzing stillness reigned throughout the schoolroom. It was suddenly interrupted by the appearance of a negro, in tow-cloth jacket and trowsers, a round-crowned fragment of a hat, like the cap of Mercury, and mounted on the back of a ragged, wild, half-broken colt, which he managed with a rope by way of halter. He came clattering up to the school door with an invitation to Ichabod to attend a merry-making or "quilting frolic," to be held that evening at Mynheer Van Tassel's; and having delivered his message with that air of importance, and effort at fine language, which a negro is apt to display on petty embassies of the kind, he dashed over the brook, and was seen scampering away up the hollow, full of the importance and hurry of his mission.

All was now bustle and hubbub in the late quiet schoolroom. The scholars were hurried through their lessons, without stopping at trifles; those who were nimble skipped over half with impunity, and those who were tardy, had a smart application now and then in the rear, to quicken their speed, or help them over a tall word. Books were flung aside without being put away on the shelves, inkstands were overturned, benches thrown down, and the whole school was turned loose an hour before the usual time, bursting forth like a legion of young imps, yelping and racketing about the green, in joy at their early emancipation.

The gallant Ichabod now spent at least an extra half hour at his toilet, brushing and furbishing up his best, and indeed only suit of rusty black, and arranging his looks by a bit of broken looking-glass, that hung up in the school-house. That he might make his appearance before his mistress in the true style of a cavalier, he borrowed a horse from the farmer with whom he was domiciliated, a choleric old Dutchman, of the name of Hans Van Ripper, and, thus gallantly mounted, issued forth, like a knight-errant in quest of adventures. But it is meet I should, in the true spirit of romantic story, give some account of the looks and equipments of my hero and his steed. The animal he bestrode was a broken-down plough-horse, that had outlived almost every thing but his viciousness. He was gaunt and shagged, with a ewe neck and a head like a hammer; his rusty mane and tail were tangled and knotted with burrs; one eye had lost its pupil, and was glaring and spectral; but the other had the gleam of a genuine devil in it. Still he must have had fire and mettle in his day, if we may judge from the name he bore of Gunpowder. He had, in fact, been a favorite steed of his master's, the choleric Van Ripper, who was a furious rider, and had infused, very probably, some of his own spirit into the animal; for, old and broken-down as he looked, there was more of the lurking devil in him than in any young filly in the country.

Ichabod was a suitable figure for such a steed. He rode with short stirrups, which brought his knees nearly up to the pommel of the saddle; his sharp elbows stuck out like grasshoppers'; he carried his whip perpendicularly in his hand, like a sceptre, and, as his horse jogged on, the motion of his arms was not unlike the flapping of a pair of wings. A small wool hat rested on the top of his nose, for so his scanty strip of forehead might be called; and the skirts of his black coat fluttered out almost to the horse's tail. Such was the appearance of Ichabod and his steed, as they shambled out of the gate of Hans Van Ripper, and it was altogether such an apparition as is seldom to be met with in broad daylight.

It was, as I have said, a fine autumnal day, the sky was clear and serene, and nature wore that rich and golden livery which we always associate with the idea of abundance. The forests had put on their sober brown and yellow, while some trees of the tenderer kind had been nipped by the frosts into brilliant dyes of orange, purple, and scarlet. Streaming files of wild ducks began to make their appearance high in the air; the bark of the squirrel might be heard from the groves of beech and hickory nuts, and the pensive whistle of the quail at intervals from the neighboring stubble-field.

The small birds were taking their farewell banquets. In the fulness of their revelry, they fluttered, chirping and frolicking, from bush to bush, and tree to tree, capricious from the very profusion and variety around them. There was the honest cock-robin, the favorite game of stripling sportsmen, with its loud querulous note; and the twittering blackbirds flying in sable clouds; and the golden-winged woodpecker, with his crimson crest, his broad black gorget, and splendid plumage; and the cedar bird, with its red-tipt wings and yellow-tipt tail, and its little monteiro cap of feathers; and the blue jay, that noisy coxcomb, in his gay light-blue coat and white under-clothes; screaming and chattering, nodding and bobbing and bowing, and pretending to be on good terms with every songster of the grove.

As Ichabod jogged slowly on his way, his eye, ever open to every symptom of culinary abundance, ranged with delight over the treasures of jolly autumn. On all sides he beheld vast store of apples; some hanging in oppressive opulence on the trees; some gathered into baskets and barrels for the market; others heaped up in rich piles for the cider-press. Farther on he beheld great fields of Indian corn, with its golden ears peeping from their leafy coverts, and holding out the promise of cakes and hasty pudding; and the yellow pumpkins lying beneath them, turning up their fair round bellies to the sun, and giving ample prospects of the most luxurious of pies; and anon he passed the fragrant buckwheat fields, breathing the odor of the bee-hive, and as he beheld them, soft anticipations stole over his mind of dainty slapjacks, well buttered, and garnished with honey or treacle, by the delicate little dimpled hand of Katrina Van Tassel.

Thus feeding his mind with many sweet thoughts and "sugared suppositions," he journeyed along the sides of a range of hills which look out upon some of the goodliest scenes of the mighty Hudson. The sun gradually wheeled his broad disk down into the west. The wide bosom of the Tappan Zee lay motionless and glassy, excepting that here and there a gentle undulation waved and prolonged the blue shadow of the dis-. tant mountain. A few amber clouds floated in the sky, without a breath of air to move them. The horizon was of a fine golden tint, changing gradually into a pure apple green, and from that into the deep blue of the mid-heaven. A slanting ray lingered on the woody crests of the precipices that overhung some parts of the river, giving greater depth to the dark-gray and purple of their rocky sides. A sloop was loitering in the distance, dropping slowly down with the tide, her sail hanging uselessly against the mast; and as the reflection of the sky gleamed along the still water, it seemed as if the vessel was suspended in the air.

It was toward evening that Ichabod arrived at the castle of the Heer Van Tassel, which he found thronged with the pride and flower of the adjacent country. Old farmers, a spare leathern-faced race, in homespun coats and breeches, blue stockings, huge shoes, and magnificent pewter buckles. Their brisk withered little dames, in close crimped caps, long-waisted shortgowns, homespun petticoats, with scissors and pin-cushions, and gay calico pockets hanging on the outside. Buxom lasses, almost as antiquated as their mothers, excepting where a straw hat, a fine ribbon, or perhaps a white frock, gave symptoms of city innovation. The sons, in short square-skirted coats with rows of stupendous brass buttons, and their hair generally queued in the fashion of the times, especially if they could procure an eel-skin for the purpose, it being esteemed, throughout the country, as a potent nourisher and strengthener of the hair.

Brom Bones, however, was the hero of the scene, having come to the gathering on his favorite steed Daredevil, a crea-ture, like himself, full of mettle and mischief, and which no one but himself could manage. He was, in fact, noted for preferring vicious animals, given to all kinds of tricks, which kept the rider in constant risk of his neck, for he held a tractable well-broken horse as unworthy of a lad of spirit.

Fain would I pause to dwell upon the world of charms that burst upon the enraptured gaze of my hero, as he entered the state parlor of Van Tassel's mansion. Not those of the bevy of buxom lasses, with their luxurious display of red and white; but the ample charms of a genuine Dutch country tea-table, in the sumptuous time of autumn. Such heaped-up platters of cakes of various and almost indescribable kinds, known only to experienced Dutch housewives! There was the doughty dough-nut, the tenderer oly koek, and the crisp and crumbling cruller; sweet cakes and short cakes, ginger cakes and honey cakes, and the whole family of cakes. And then there were apple pies and peach pies and pumpkin pies; besides slices of ham and smoked beef; and moreover delectable dishes of preserved plums, and peaches, and pears, and quinces; not to mention broiled shad and roasted chickens; together with bowls of milk and cream, all mingled higgledy-piggledy, pretty much as I have enumerated them, with the motherly tea-pot sending up its clouds of vapor from the midst—Heaven bless the mark! I want breath and time to discuss this banquet as it deserves, and am too eager to get on with my story. Happily, Ichabod Crane was not in so great a hurry as his historian, but did ample justice to every dainty.

He was a kind and thankful creature, whose heart dilated in proportion as his skin was filled with good cheer; and whose spirits rose with eating as some men's do with drink. He could not help, too, rolling his large eyes round him as he ate, and chuckling with the possibility that he might one day be lord of all this scene of almost unimaginable luxury and splendor. Then, he thought, how soon he'd turn his back upon the old school-house; snap his fingers in the face of Hans Van Ripper, and every other niggardly patron, and kick any itinerant pedagogue out of doors that should dare to call him comrade!

Old Baltus Van Tassel moved about among his guests with a face dilated with content and good humor, round and jolly as the harvest moon. His hospitable attentions were brief, but expressive, being confined to a shake of the hand, a slap on the shoulder, a loud laugh, and a pressing invitation to "fall to, and help themselves."

And now the sound of the music from the common room, or hall, summoned to the dance. The musician was an old grayheaded negro, who had been the itinerant orchestra of the neighborhood for more than half a century. His instrument was as old and battered as himself. The greater part of the time he scraped on two or three strings, accompanying every movement of the bow with a motion of the head; bowing almost to the ground, and stamping with his foot whenever a fresh couple were to start.

Ichabod prided himself upon his dancing as much as upon his vocal powers. Not a limb, not a fibre about him was idle; and to have seen his loosely hung frame in full motion, and clattering about the room, you would have thought Saint Vitus himself, that blessed patron of the dance, was figuring before you in person. He was the admiration of all the negroes; who, having gathered, of all ages and sizes, from the farm and the neighborhood, stood forming a pyramid of shining black faces at every door and window, gazing with delight at the scene, rolling their white eye-balls, and showing grinning rows of ivory from ear to ear. How could the flogger of urchins be otherwise than animated and joyous? the lady of his heart was his partner in the dance, and smiling graciously in reply to all his amorous oglings; while Brom Bones, sorely smitten with love and jealousy, sat brooding by himself in one corner.

When the dance was at an end, Ichabod was attracted to a knot of the sager folks, who, with old Van Tassel, sat smoking at one end of the piazza, gossiping over former times, and drawing out long stories about the war.

This neighborhood, at the time of which I am speaking, was one of those highly-favored places which abound with chronicle and great men. The British and American line had run near it during the war; it had, therefore, been the scene of marauding, and infested with refugees, cow-boys, and all kinds of border chivalry. Just sufficient time had elapsed to enable each storyteller to dress up his tale with a little becoming fiction, and, in the indistinctness of his recollection, to make himself the hero of every exploit.

There was the story of Doffue Martling, a large blue-bearded Dutchman, who had nearly taken a British frigate with an old iron nine-pounder from a mud breastwork, only that his gun burst at the sixth discharge. And there was an old gentleman who shall be nameless, being too rich a mynheer to be lightly mentioned, who, in the battle of Whiteplains, being an excellent master of defence, parried a musket ball with a small sword, insomuch that he absolutely felt it whiz round the blade, and glance off at the hilt: in proof of which, he was ready at any time to show the sword, with the hilt a little bent. There were several more that had been equally great in the field, not one of whom but was persuaded that he had a considerable hand in bringing the war to a happy termination.

But all these were nothing to the tales of ghosts and apparitions that succeeded. The neighborhood is rich in legendary treasures of the kind. Local tales and superstitions thrive best in these sheltered long-settled retreats; but are trampled under foot by the shifting throng that forms the population of most of our country places. Besides, there is no encouragement for ghosts in most of our villages, for they have scarcely had time to finish their first nap, and turn themselves in their graves, before their surviving friends have travelled away from the neighborhood; so that when they turn out at night to walk their rounds, they have no acquaintance left to call upon. This is perhaps the reason why we so seldom hear of ghosts except in our long-established Dutch communities.

The immediate cause, however, of the prevalence of supernatural stories in these parts, was doubtless owing to the vicinity of Sleepy Hollow. There was a contagion in the very air that blew from that haunted region; it breathed forth an atmosphere of dreams and fancies infecting all the land. Several of the Sleepy Hollow people were present at Van Tassel's, and, as usual, were doling out their wild and wonderful legends. Many dismal tales were told about funeral trains, and mourning cries and wailings heard and seen about the great tree where the unfortunate Major André was taken, and which stood in the neighborhood. Some mention was made also of the woman in white, that haunted the dark glen at Raven Rock, and was often heard to shriek on winter nights before a storm, having perished there in the snow. The chief part of the stories, however, turned upon the favorite spectre of Sleepy Hollow, the headless horseman, who had been heard several times of late, patrolling the country; and, it was said, tethered his horse nightly among the graves in the churchyard.

The sequestered situation of this church seems always to have made it a favorite haunt of troubled spirits. It stands on a knoll, surrounded by locust-trees and lofty elms, from among which its decent whitewashed walls shine modestly forth, like Christian purity beaming through the shades of retirement. A gentle slope descends from it to a silver sheet of water, bordered by high trees, between which, peeps may be caught at the blue hills of the Hudson. To look upon its grass-grown yard, where the sunbeams seem to sleep so quietly, one would think that there at least the dead might rest in peace. On one side of the church extends a wide woody dell, along which raves a large brook among broken rocks and trunks of fallen trees. Over a deep black part of the stream, not far from the church, was formerly thrown a wooden bridge; the road that led to it, and the bridge itself, were thickly shaded by over-hanging trees, which cast a gloom about it, even in the day-time; but occasioned a fearful darkness at night. This was one of the favorite haunts of the headless horseman; and the place where he was most frequently encountered. The tale was told of old Brouwer, a most heretical disbeliever in ghosts, how he met the horseman returning from his foray into Sleepy Hollow, and was obliged to get up behind him; how they galloped over bush and brake, over hill and swamp, until they reached the bridge; when the horseman suddenly turned into a skeleton, threw old Brouwer into the brook, and sprang away over the tree-tops with a clap of thunder.

This story was immediately matched by a thrice marvellous adventure of Brom Bones, who made light of the galloping

Hessian as an arrant jockey. He affirmed that, on returning one night from the neighboring village of Sing Sing, he had been overtaken by this midnight trooper; that he had offered to race with him for a bowl of punch, and should have won it too, for Daredevil beat the goblin horse all hollow, but, just as they came to the church-bridge, the Hessian bolted, and vanished in a flash of fire.

All these tales, told in that drowsy undertone with which men talk in the dark, the countenances of the listeners only now and then receiving a casual gleam from the glare of a pipe, sank deep in the mind of Ichabod. He repaid them in kind with large extracts from his invaluable author, Cotton Mather, and added many marvellous events that had taken place in his native State of Connecticut, and fearful sights which he had seen in his nightly walks about Sleepy Hollow.

The revel now gradually broke up. The old farmers gathered together their families in their wagons, and were heard for some time rattling along the hollow roads, and over the distant hills. Some of the damsels mounted on pillions behind their favorite swains, and their light-hearted laughter, mingling with the clatter of hoofs, echoed along the silent woodlands, sounding fainter and fainter until they gradually died away—and the late scene of noise and frolic was all silent and deserted. Ichabod only lingered behind, according to the custom of country lovers, to have a tête-à-tête with the heiress, fully convinced that he was now on the high road to success. What passed at this interview I will not pretend to say, for in fact I do not know. Something, however, I fear me, must have gone wrong, for he certainly sallied forth, after no very great interval, with an air quite desolate and chop-fallen.—Oh these women! these women! Could that girl have been playing off any of her coquettish tricks?—Was her encouragement of the poor pedagogue all a mere sham to secure her conquest of his rival?— Heaven only knows, not I!—Let it suffice to say, Ichabod stole forth with the air of one who had been sacking a hen-roost, rather than a fair lady's heart. Without looking to the right or left to notice the scene of rural wealth, on which he had so often gloated, he went straight to the stable, and with several hearty cuffs and kicks, roused his steed most uncourteously from the comfortable quarters in which he was soundly sleeping, dreaming of mountains of corn and oats, and whole valleys of timothy and clover.

It was the very witching time of night that Ichabod, heavy-hearted and crest-fallen, pursued his travel homewards, along the sides of the lofty hills which rise above Tarry Town, and which he had traversed so cheerily in the afternoon. The hour was as dismal as himself. Far below him, the Tappan Zee spread its dusky and indistinct waste of waters, with here and there the tall mast of a sloop, riding quietly at anchor under the land. In the dead hush of midnight, he could even hear the barking of the watch dog from the opposite shore of the Hudson; but it was so vague and faint as only to give an idea of his distance from this faithful companion of man. Now and then, too, the long-drawn crowing of a cock, accidentally awakened, would sound far, far off, from some farmhouse away among the hills— but it was like a dreaming sound in his ear. No signs of life occurred near him, but occasionally the melancholy chirp of a cricket, or perhaps the guttural twang of a bull-frog, from a neighboring marsh, as if sleeping uncomfortably, and turning suddenly in his bed.

All the stories of ghosts and goblins that he had heard in the afternoon, now came crowding upon his recollection. The night grew darker and darker; the stars seemed to sink deeper in the sky, and driving clouds occasionally hid them from his sight. He had never felt so lonely and dismal. He was, more-over, approaching the very place where many of the scenes of the ghost stories had been laid. In the centre of the road stood an enormous tulip-tree, which towered like a giant above all the other trees of the neighborhood, and formed a kind of landmark. Its limbs were gnarled, and fantastic, large enough to form trunks for ordinary trees, twisting down almost to the earth, and rising again into the air. It was connected with the tragical story of the unfortunate André, who had been taken prisoner hard by; and was universally known by the name of

Major André's tree. The common people regarded it with a mixture of respect and superstition, partly out of sympathy for the fate of its ill-starred namesake, and partly from the tales of strange sights and doleful lamentations told concerning it.

As Ichabod approached this fearful tree, he began to whistle: he thought his whistle was answered—it was but a blast sweeping sharply through the dry branches. As he approached a little nearer, he thought he saw something white, hanging in the midst of the tree—he paused and ceased whistling; but on looking more narrowly, perceived that it was a place where the tree had been scathed by lightning, and the white wood laid bare. Suddenly he heard a groan—his teeth chattered and his knees smote against the saddle: it was but the rubbing of one huge bough upon another, as they were swayed about by the breeze. He passed the tree in safety, but new perils lay before him.

About two hundred yards from the tree a small brook crossed the road, and ran into a marshy and thickly-wooded glen, known by the name of Wiley's swamp. A few rough logs, laid side by side, served for a bridge over this stream. On that side of the road where the brook entered the wood, a group of oaks and chestnuts, matted thick with wild grapevines, threw a cavernous gloom over it. To pass this bridge was the severest trial. It was at this identical spot that the unfortunate André was captured, and under the covert of those chestnuts and vines were the sturdy yeomen concealed who surprised him. This has ever since been considered a haunted stream, and fearful are the feelings of the schoolboy who has to pass it alone after dark.

As he approached the stream his heart began to thump; he summoned up, however, all his resolution, gave his horse half a score of kicks in the ribs, and attempted to dash briskly across the bridge; but instead of starting forward, the perverse old animal made a lateral movement, and ran broadside against the fence. Ichabod, whose fears increased with the delay, jerked the reins on the other side, and kicked lustily with the contrary foot: it was all in vain; his steed started, it is true, but it was only to plunge to the opposite side of the road into a thicket of brambles and alder bushes. The schoolmaster now bestowed both whip and heel upon the starveling ribs of old Gunpowder, who dashed forward, snuffling and snorting, but came to a stand just by the bridge, with a suddenness that had nearly sent his rider sprawling over his head. Just at this moment a plashy tramp by the side of the bridge caught the sensitive ear of Ichabod. In the dark shadow of the grove, on the margin of the brook, he beheld something huge, misshapen, black and towering. It stirred not, but seemed gathered up in the gloom, like some gigantic monster ready to spring upon the traveller.

The hair of the affrighted pedagogue rose upon his head with terror. What was to be done? To turn and fly was now too late; and besides, what chance was there of escaping ghost or goblin, if such it was, which could ride upon the wings of the wind? Summoning up, therefore, a show of courage, he demanded in stammering accents—"Who are you?" He received no reply. He repeated his demand in a still more agitated voice. Still there was no answer. Once more he cudgelled the sides of the inflexible Gunpowder, and, shutting his eyes, broke forth with involuntary fervor into a psalm tune. Just then the shadowy object of alarm put itself in motion, and, with a scramble and a bound, stood at once in the middle of the road. Though the night was dark and dismal, yet the form of the unknown might now in some degree be ascertained. He appeared to be a horseman of large dimensions, and mounted on a black horse of powerful frame. He made no offer of molestation or sociability, but kept aloof on one side of the road, jogging along on the blind side of old Gunpowder, who had now got over his fright and waywardness.

Ichabod, who had no relish for this strange midnight companion, and bethought himself of the adventure of Brom Bones with the Galloping Hessian, now quickened his steed, in hopes of leaving him behind. The stranger, however, quickened his horse to an equal pace. Ichabod pulled up, and fell into a walk, thinking to lag behind—the other did the same. His heart began to sink within him; he endeavored to resume his psalm tune, but his parched tongue clove to the roof of his mouth, and he could not utter a stave. There was something in the moody and dogged silence of this pertinacious companion, that was mysterious and appalling. It was soon fearfully accounted for. On mounting a rising ground, which brought the figure of his fellow-traveller in relief against the sky, gigantic in height, and muffled in a cloak, Ichabod was horror-struck, on perceiving that he was headless!—but his horror was still more increased, on observing that the head, which should have rested on his shoulders, was carried before him on the pommel of the saddle: his terror rose to desperation; he rained a shower of kicks and blows upon Gunpowder, hoping, by a sudden movement, to give his companion the slip—but the spectre started full jump with him. Away then they dashed, through thick and thin; stones flying, and sparks flashing at every bound. Ichabod's flimsy garments fluttered in the air, as he stretched his long lank body away over his horse's head, in the eagerness of his flight.

They had now reached the road which turns off to Sleepy Hollow; but Gunpowder, who seemed possessed with a demon, instead of keeping up it, made an opposite turn, and plunged headlong down hill to the left. This road leads through a sandy hollow, shaded by trees for about a quarter of a mile, where it crosses the bridge famous in goblin story, and just beyond swells the green knoll on which stands the whitewashed church.

As yet the panic of the steed had given his unskilful rider an apparent advantage in the chase; but just as he had got half way through the hollow, the girths of the saddle gave way, and he felt it slipping from under him. He seized it by the pommel, and endeavored to hold it firm, but in vain; and had just time to save himself by clasping old Gunpowder round the neck, when the saddle fell to the earth, and he heard it trampled under foot by his pursuer. For a moment the terror of Hans Van Ripper's wrath passed across his mind—for it was his Sunday saddle; but this was no time for petty fears; the goblin was hard on his haunches; and (unskilful rider that he was!) he had much ado to maintain his seat; sometimes slipping on one side, sometimes on another, and sometimes jolted on the high ridge of his horse's back-bone, with a violence that he verily feared would cleave him asunder.

An opening in the trees now cheered him with the hopes that the church bridge was at hand. The wavering reflection of a silver star in the bosom of the brook told him that he was not mistaken. He saw the walls of the church dimly glaring under the trees beyond. He recollected the place where Brom Bones's ghostly competitor had disappeared. "If I can but reach that bridge," thought Ichabod, "I am safe." Just then he heard the black steed panting and blowing close behind him; he even fancied that he felt his hot breath. Another convulsive kick in the ribs and old Gunpowder sprang upon the bridge; he thundered over the resounding planks; he gained the opposite side; and now Ichabod cast a look behind to see if his pursuer should vanish, according to rule, in a flash of fire and brimstone. Just then he saw the goblin rising in his stirrups, and in the very act of hurling his head at him. Ichabod endeavored to dodge the horrible missile, but too late. It encountered his cranium with a tremendous crash—he was tumbled headlong into the dust, and Gunpowder, the black steed, and the goblin rider, passed by like a whirlwind.

The next morning the old horse was found without his saddle, and with the bridle under his feet, soberly cropping the grass at his master's gate. Ichabod did not make his appearance at breakfast—dinner-hour came, but no Ichabod. The boys assembled at the school-house, and strolled idly about the banks of the brook; but no schoolmaster. Hans Van Ripper now began to feel some uneasiness about the fate of poor Ichabod, and his saddle. An inquiry was set on foot, and after diligent investigation they came upon his traces. In one part of the road leading to the church was found the saddle trampled in the dirt; the tracks of horses' hoofs deeply dented in the road, and evidently at furious speed, were traced to the bridge, beyond which, on the bank of a broad part of the brook, where the water ran deep and black, was found the hat of the unfortunate Ichabod, and close beside it a shattered pumpkin.

The brook was searched, but the body of the schoolmaster

was not to be discovered. Hans Van Ripper, as executor of his estate, examined the bundle which contained all his worldly effects. They consisted of two shirts and a half; two stocks for the neck; a pair or two of worsted stockings; an old pair of corduroy small-clothes; a rusty razor; a book of psalm tunes, full of dogs' ears; and a broken pitchpipe. As to the books and furniture of the school-house, they belonged to the community, excepting Cotton Mather's History of Witchcraft, a New England Almanac, and a book of dreams and fortune-telling; in which last was a sheet of foolscap much scribbled and blotted in several fruitless attempts to make a copy of verses in honor of the heiress of Van Tassel. These magic books and the poetic scrawl were forthwith consigned to the flames by Hans Van Ripper; who from that time forward determined to send his children no more to school; observing, that he never knew any good come of this same reading and writing. Whatever money the schoolmaster possessed, and he had received his quarter's pay but a day or two before, he must have had about his person at the time of his disappearance.

The mysterious event caused much speculation at the church on the following Sunday. Knots of gazers and gossips were collected in the churchyard, at the bridge, and at the spot where the hat and pumpkin had been found. The stories of Brouwer, of Bones, and a whole budget of others, were called to mind; and when they had diligently considered them all, and compared them with the symptoms of the present case, they shook their heads, and came to the conclusion that Ichabod had been carried off by the galloping Hessian. As he was a bachelor, and in nobody's debt, nobody troubled his head any more about him. The school was removed to a different quarter of the hollow, and another pedagogue reigned in his stead.

It is true, an old farmer, who had been down to New York on a visit several years after, and from whom this account of the ghostly adventure was received, brought home the intelligence that Ichabod Crane was still alive; that he had left the neighborhood, partly through fear of the goblin and Hans Van Ripper, and partly in mortification at having been suddenly dismissed by the heiress; that he had changed his quarters to a distant part of the country; had kept school and studied law at the same time, had been admitted to the bar, turned politician, electioneered, written for the newspapers, and finally had been made a justice of the Ten Pound Court. Brom Bones too, who shortly after his rival's disappearance conducted the blooming Katrina in triumph to the altar, was observed to look exceedingly knowing whenever the story of Ichabod was related, and always burst into a hearty laugh at the mention of the pumpkin; which led some to suspect that he knew more about the matter than he chose to tell.

The old country wives, however, who are the best judges of these matters, maintain to this day that Ichabod was spirited away by supernatural means; and it is a favorite story often told about the neighborhood round the winter evening fire. The bridge became more than ever an object of superstitious awe, and that may be the reason why the road has been altered of late years, so as to approach the church by the border of the mill-pond. The school-house being deserted, soon fell to decay, and was reported to be haunted by the ghost of the unfortunate pedagogue; and the ploughboy, loitering homeward of a still summer evening, has often fancied his voice at a distance, chanting a melancholy psalm tune among the tranquil solitudes of Sleepy Hollow.[48]

From BRACEBRIDGE HALL [49]

THE HALL

The ancientest house, and the best for housekeeping, in this county or the next; and though the master of it write but squire, I know no lord like him.   MERRY BEGGARS.

The reader, if he has perused the volumes of the Sketch-Book, will probably recollect something of the Bracebridge family, with which I once passed a Christmas. I am now on another visit at the Hall, having been invited to a wedding which is shortly to take place. The Squire's second son, Guy, a fine, spirited young captain in the army, is about to be married to his father's ward, the fair Julia Templeton. A gathering of relations and friends has already commenced, to celebrate the joyful occasion; for the old gentleman is an enemy to quiet, private weddings. "There is nothing," he says, "like launching a young couple gayly, and cheering them from the shore; a good outset is half the voyage."

Before proceeding any farther, I would beg that the Squire might not be confounded with that class of hard-riding, fox-hunting gentlemen, so often described, and, in fact, so nearly extinct in England. I use this rural title partly because it is his universal appellation throughout the neighborhood, and partly because it saves me the frequent repetition of his name, which is one of those rough old English names at which Frenchmen exclaim in despair.

The Squire is, in fact, a lingering specimen of the old English country gentleman; rusticated a little by living almost entirely on his estate, and something of a humorist, as Englishmen are apt to become when they have an opportunity of living in their own way. I like his hobby passing well, however, which is, a bigoted devotion to old English manners and customs; it jumps a little with my own humor, having as yet a lively and unsated curiosity about the ancient and genuine characteristics of my "father land."

There are some traits about the Squire's family, also, which appear to me to be national. It is one of those old aristocratical families, which, I believe, are peculiar to England, and scarcely understood in other countries; that is to say, families of the ancient gentry, who, though destitute of titled rank, maintain a high ancestral pride: who look down upon all nobility of recent creation, and would consider it a sacrifice of dignity to merge the venerable name of their house in a modern title.

This feeling is very much fostered by the importance which they enjoy on their hereditary domains. The family mansion is an old manor-house, standing in a retired and beautiful part of Yorkshire. Its inhabitants have been always regarded, through the surrounding country, as "the great ones of the earth;" and the little village near the Hall looks up to the Squire with almost feudal homage. An old manor-house, and an old family of this kind, are rarely to be met with at the present day; and it is probably the peculiar humor of the Squire that has retained this secluded specimen of English housekeeping in something like the genuine old style.

I am again quartered in the panelled chamber, in the antique wing of the house. The prospect from my window, however, has quite a different aspect from that which it wore on my winter visit. Though early in the month of April, yet a few warm, sunshiny days have drawn forth the beauties of the spring, which, I think, are always most captivating on their first opening. The parterres of the old-fashioned garden are gay with flowers; and the gardener has brought out his exotics, and placed them along the stone balustrades. The trees are clothed with green buds and tender leaves. When I throw open my jingling casement, I smell the odor of mignonette, and hear the hum of the bees from the flowers against the sunny wall, with the varied song of the throstle, and the cheerful notes of the tuneful little wren.

While sojourning in this stronghold of old fashions, it is my intention to make occasional sketches of the scenes and characters before me. I would have it understood, however, that I am not writing a novel, and have nothing of intricate plot nor marvellous adventure to promise the reader. The Hall of which I treat has, for aught I know, neither trap-door, nor sliding-panel, nor donjon-keep; and indeed appears to have no mystery about it. The family is a worthy, well-meaning family, that, in all probability, will eat and drink, and go to bed, and get up regularly, from one end of my work to the other; and the Squire is so kind-hearted, that I see no likelihood of his throwing any kind of distress in the way of the approaching nuptials. In a word, I cannot foresee a single extraordinary event that is likely to occur in the whole term of my sojourn at the Hall.

I tell this honestly to the reader, lest, when he finds me dallying along, through every-day English scenes, he may hurry ahead, in hopes of meeting with some marvellous adventure further on. I invite him, on the contrary, to ramble gently on with me, as he would saunter out into the fields, stopping occasionally to gather a flower, or listen to a bird, or admire a prospect, without any anxiety to arrive at the end of his career. Should I, however, in the course of my wanderings about this old mansion, see or hear any thing curious, that might serve to vary the monotony of this every-day life, I shall not fail to report it for the reader's entertainment:

> For freshest wits I know will soon be wearie,
> Of any book, how grave soe'er it be,
> Except it have odd matter, strange and merrie,
> Well sauc'd with lies, and glared all with glee.[50]

THE BUSY MAN

A decayed gentleman, who lives most upon his own mirth and my master's means, and much good do him with it. He does hold my master up with his stories, and songs, and catches, and such tricks and jigs, you would admire—he is with him now.

JOVIAL CREW.

By no one has my return to the Hall been more heartily greeted than by Mr. Simon Bracebridge, or Master Simon, as the

Squire most commonly calls him. I encountered him just as I entered the park, where he was breaking a pointer, and he received me with all the hospitable cordiality with which a man welcomes a friend to another one's house. I have already introduced him to the reader as a brisk old bachelor-looking little man; the wit and superannuated beau of a large family connection, and the Squire's factotum. I found him, as usual, full of bustle; with a thousand petty things to do, and persons to attend to, and in chirping good-humor; for there are few happier beings than a busy idler; that is to say, a man who is eternally busy about nothing.

I visited him, the morning after my arrival, in his chamber, which is in a remote corner of the mansion, as he says he likes to be to himself, and out of the way. He has fitted it up in his own taste, so that it is a perfect epitome of an old bachelor's notions of convenience and arrangement. The furniture is made up of odd pieces from all parts of the house, chosen on account of their suiting his notions, or fitting some corner of his apartment; and he is very eloquent in praise of an ancient elbow-chair, from which he takes occasion to digress into a censure on modern chairs, as having degenerated from the dignity and comfort of high-backed antiquity.

Adjoining to his room is a small cabinet, which he calls his study. Here are some hanging shelves, of his own construction, on which are several old works on hawking, hunting, and farriery, and a collection or two of poems and songs of the reign of Elizabeth, which he studies out of compliment to the Squire; together with the Novelist's Magazine, the Sporting Magazine, the Racing Calendar, a volume or two of the Newgate Calendar, a book of peerage, and another of heraldry.

His sporting dresses hang on pegs in a small closet; and about the walls of his apartment are hooks to hold his fishing-tackle, whips, spurs, and a favorite fowling-piece, curiously wrought and inlaid, which he inherits from his grandfather. He has, also, a couple of old single-keyed flutes, and a fiddle which he has repeatedly patched and mended himself, affirming it to be a veritable Cremona; though I have never heard him extract a single note from it that was not enough to make one's blood run cold.

From this little nest his fiddle will often be heard, in the stillness of mid-day, drowsily sawing some long-forgotten tune; for he prides himself on having a choice collection of good old English music, and will scarcely have any thing to do with modern composers. The time, however, at which his musical powers are of most use, is now and then of an evening, when he plays for the children to dance in the hall, and he passes among them and the servants for a perfect Orpheus.

His chamber also bears evidence of his various avocations: there are half-copied sheets of music; designs for needle-work; sketches of landscapes, very indifferently executed; a camera lucida; a magic lantern, for which he is endeavoring to paint glasses; in a word, it is the cabinet of a man of many accomplishments, who knows a little of every thing, and does nothing well.

After I had spent some time in his apartment, admiring the ingenuity of his small inventions, he took me about the establishment, to visit the stables, dog-kennel, and other dependencies, in which he appeared like a general visiting the different quarters of his camp; as the Squire leaves the control of all these matters to him, when he is at the Hall. He inquired into the state of the horses; examined their feet; prescribed a drench for one, and bleeding for another; and then took me to look at his own horse, on the merits of which he dwelt with great prolixity, and which, I noticed, had the best stall in the stable.

After this I was taken to a new toy of his and the Squire's, which he termed the falconry, where there were several unhappy birds in durance, completing their education. Among the number was a fine falcon, which Master Simon had in especial training, and he told me that he would show me, in a few days, some rare sport of the good old-fashioned kind. In the course of our round, I noticed that the grooms, gamekeeper, whippers-in, and other retainers, seemed all to be on somewhat of a familiar footing with Master Simon, and fond of having a joke with him, though it was evident they had great deference for his opinion in matters relating to their functions,

There was one exception, however, in a testy old huntsman, as hot as a pepper-corn; a meagre, wiry old fellow, in a thread-bare velvet jockey-cap, and a pair of leather breeches, that, from much wear, shone as though they had been japanned. He was very contradictory and pragmatical, and apt, as I thought, to differ from Master Simon now and then, out of mere captious-ness. This was particularly the case with respect to the treatment of the hawk, which the old man seemed to have under his peculiar care, and, according to Master Simon, was in a fair way to ruin: the latter had a vast deal to say about *casting*, and *imping*, and *gleaming*, and *enseaming*, and giving the hawk the *rangle*, which I saw was all heathen Greek to old Christy; but he main-tained his point notwithstanding, and seemed to hold all this technical lore in utter disrespect.

I was surprised at the good humor with which Master Simon bore his contradictions, till he explained the matter to me after-wards. Old Christy is the most ancient servant in the place, having lived among dogs and horses the greater part of a century, and been in the service of Mr. Bracebridge's father. He knows the pedigree of every horse on the place, and has bestrode the great-great grandsires of most of them. He can give a circum-stantial detail of every fox-hunt for the last sixty or seventy years, and has a history for every stag's head about the house, and every hunting trophy nailed to the door of the dog-kennel.

All the present race have grown up under his eye, and humor him in his old age. He once attended the Squire to Oxford, when he was student there, and enlightened the whole university with his hunting lore. All this is enough to make the old man opin-ionated, since he finds, on all these matters of first-rate impor-tance, he knows more than the rest of the world. Indeed, Master Simon had been his pupil, and acknowledges that he derived his first knowledge in hunting from the instructions of Christy; and I much question whether the old man does not still look upon him as rather a greenhorn.

On our return homewards, as we were crossing the lawn in front of the house, we heard the porter's bell ring at the lodge, and shortly afterwards, a kind of cavalcade advanced slowly up the avenue. At sight of it my companion paused, considered it for a moment, and then, making a sudden exclamation, hurried away to meet it. As it approached I discovered a fair, fresh-looking elderly lady, dressed in an old-fashioned riding-habit, with a broad-brimmed white beaver hat, such as may be seen in Sir Joshua Reynolds' paintings. She rode a sleek white pony, and was followed by a footman in rich livery, mounted on an over-fed hunter. At a little distance in the rear came an ancient cumbrous chariot drawn by two very corpulent horses, driven by as corpulent a coachman, beside whom sat a page dressed in a fanciful green livery. Inside of the chariot was a starched prim personage, with a look somewhat between a lady's companion and a lady's maid, and two pampered curs, that showed their ugly faces, and barked out of each window.

There was a general turning out of the garrison to receive this new-comer. The Squire assisted her to alight, and saluted her affectionately; the fair Julia flew into her arms, and they embraced with the romantic fervor of boarding-school friends: she was escorted into the house by Julia's lover, towards whom she showed distinguished favor; and a line of the old servants, who had collected in the Hall, bowed most profoundly as she passed.

I observed·that Master Simon was most assiduous and devout in his attentions upon this old lady. He walked by the side of her pony up the avenue; and, while she was receiving the salutations of the rest of the family, he took occasion to notice the fat coachman; to pat the sleek carriage horses, and, above all, to say a civil word to my lady's gentlewoman, the prim, sour-looking vestal in the chariot.

I had no more of his company for the rest of the morning. He was swept off in the vortex that followed in the wake of this lady. Once indeed he paused for a moment, as he was hurrying on some errand of the good lady's, to let me know that this was Lady Lillycraft, a sister of the Squire's, of large fortune, which the captain would inherit, and that her estate lay in one of the best sporting counties in all England.

STORY-TELLING

A favorite evening pastime at the Hall, and one which the worthy Squire is fond of promoting, is story-telling, "a good old-fashioned fireside amusement," as he terms it. Indeed, I believe he promotes it chiefly because it was one of the choice recreations in those days of yore, when ladies and gentlemen were not much in the habit of reading. Be this as it may, he will often, at supper table, when conversation flags, call on some one or other of the company for a story, as it was formerly the custom to call for a song; and it is edifying to see the exemplary patience, and even satisfaction, with which the good old gentleman will sit and listen to some hackneyed tale that he has heard for at least a hundred times.

In this way one evening the current of anecdotes and stories ran upon mysterious personages that have figured at different times, and filled the world with doubts and conjecture; such as the Wandering Jew, the Man with the Iron Mask, who tormented the curiosity of all Europe; the Invisible Girl, and last, though not least, the Pigfaced Lady.

At length one of the company was called upon who had the most unpromising physiognomy for a story-teller that ever I had seen. He was a thin, pale, weazen-faced man, extremely nervous, who had sat at one corner of the table, shrunk up, as it were, into himself, and almost swallowed up in the cape of his coat, as a turtle in its shell.

The very demand seemed to throw him into a nervous agitation, yet he did not refuse. He emerged his head out of his shell, made a few odd grimaces and gesticulations, before he could get his muscles into order, or his voice under command, and then offered to give some account of a mysterious personage whom he had recently encountered in the course of his travels, and one whom he thought fully entitled of being classed with the Man with the Iron Mask.

I was so much struck with his extraordinary narrative, that I have written it out to the best of my recollection, for the amusement of the reader. I think it has in it all the elements of that mysterious and romantic narrative, so greedily sought after at the present day.

THE STOUT GENTLEMAN

A STAGE-COACH ROMANCE

I'll cross it, though it blast me!
HAMLET.

It was a rainy Sunday in the gloomy month of November. I had been detained, in the course of a journey, by a slight indisposition, from which I was recovering; but was still feverish, and obliged to keep within doors all day, in an inn of the small town of Derby. A wet Sunday in a country inn!—whoever has had the luck to experience one can alone judge of my situation. The rain pattered against the casements; the bells tolled for church with a melancholy sound. I went to the windows in quest of something to amuse the eye; but it seemed as if I had been placed completely out of the reach of all amusement. The windows of my bedroom looked out among tiled roofs and stacks of chimneys, while those of my sitting-room commanded a full view of the stable-yard. I know of nothing more calculated to make a man sick of this world than a stable-yard on a rainy day. The place was littered with wet straw that had been kicked about by travellers and stable-boys. In one corner was a stagnant pool of water, surrounding an island of muck; there were several half-drowned fowls crowded together under a cart, among which was a miserable, crest-fallen cock, drenched out of all life and spirit, his drooping tail matted, as it were, into a single feather, along which the water trickled from his back; near the cart was a half-dozing cow, chewing the cud, and standing patiently to be rained on, with wreaths of vapor rising from her reeking hide; a wall-eyed horse, tired of the loneliness of the stable, was poking his spectral head out of a window, with the rain dripping on it from the eaves; an unhappy cur, chained to a doghouse hard by, uttered something every now and then, between a bark and a yelp; a drab of a kitchen wench tramped backwards and forwards through the yard in pattens, looking as sulky as the weather itself; every thing, in short, was comfortless and forlorn, excepting a crew of hardened ducks, assembled like boon companions round a puddle, and making a riotous noise over their liquor.

I was lonely and listless, and wanted amusement. My room soon became insupportable. I abandoned it, and sought what is technically called the travellers'-room. This is a public room set apart at most inns for the accommodation of a class of wayfarers, called travellers, or riders; a kind of commercial knights-errant, who are incessantly scouring the kingdom in gigs, on horseback, or by coach. They are the only successors that I know of at the present day to the knights-errant of yore. They lead the same kind of roving, adventurous life, only changing the lance for a driving-whip, the buckler for a pattern-card, and the coat of mail for an upper Benjamin. Instead of vindicating the charms of peerless beauty, they rove about, spreading the fame and standing of some substantial tradesman, or manufacturer, and are ready at any time to bargain in his name; it being the fashion nowadays to trade, instead of fight, with one another. As the room of the hostel, in the good old fighting times, would be hung round at night with the armor of way-worn warriors, such as coats of mail, falchions, and yawning helmets; so the travellers'-room is garnished with the harnessing of their successors, with box-coats, whips of all kinds, spurs, gaiters, and oil-cloth covered hats.

I was in hopes of finding some of these worthies to talk with, but was disappointed. There were, indeed, two or three in the room; but I could make nothing of them. One was just finishing his breakfast, quarrelling with his bread and butter, and huffing the waiter; another buttoned on a pair of gaiters, with many execrations at Boots for not having cleaned his shoes well; a third sat drumming on the table with his fingers and looking at the rain as it streamed down the window-glass; they all appeared infected by the weather, and disappeared, one after the other, without exchanging a word.

I sauntered to the window, and stood gazing at the people,

picking their way to church, with petticoats hoisted midleg high, and dripping umbrellas. The bell ceased to toll, and the streets became silent. I then amused myself with watching the daughters of a tradesman opposite; who, being confined to the house for fear of wetting their Sunday finery, played off their charms at the front windows, to fascinate the chance tenants of the inn. They at length were summoned away by a vigilant vinegar-faced mother, and I had nothing further from without to amuse me.

What was I to do to pass away the long-lived day? I was sadly nervous and lonely; and every thing about an inn seems calculated to make a dull day ten times duller. Old newspapers, smelling of beer and tobacco smoke, and which I had already read half a dozen times. Good-for-nothing books, that were worse than rainy weather. I bored myself to death with an old volume of the Lady's Magazine. I read all the commonplace names of ambitious travellers scrawled on the panes of glass; the eternal families of the Smiths, and the Browns, and the Jacksons, and the Johnsons, and all the other sons; and I deciphered several scraps of fatiguing in-window poetry which I have met with in all parts of the world.

The day continued lowering and gloomy; the slovenly, ragged, spongy clouds drifted heavily along; there was no variety even in the rain: it was one dull, continued, monotonous patter —patter—patter, excepting that now and then I was enlivened by the idea of a brisk shower, from the rattling of the drops upon a passing umbrella.

It was quite *refreshing* (if I may be allowed a hackneyed phrase of the day) when, in the course of the morning, a horn blew, and a stage-coach whirled through the street, with outside passengers stuck all over it, cowering under cotton umbrellas, and seethed together, and reeking with the steams of wet box-coats and upper Benjamins.

The sound brought out from their lurking-places a crew of vagabond boys, and vagabond dogs, and the carroty-headed hostler, and that nondescript animal ycleped Boots, and all the other vagabond race that infest the purlieus of an inn; but the bustle was transient; the coach again whirled on its way; and boy and dog, and hostler and Boots, all slunk back again to their holes; the street again became silent, and the rain continued to rain on. In fact, there was no hope of its clearing up; the barometer pointed to rainy weather; mine hostess' tortoise-shell cat sat by the fire washing her face, and rubbing her paws over her ears; and, on referring to the Almanac, I found a direful prediction stretching from the top of the page to the bottom through the whole month, "expect—much—rain—about—this—time!"

I was dreadfully hipped. The hours seemed as if they would never creep by. The very ticking of the clock became irksome. At length the stillness of the house was interrupted by the ringing of a bell. Shortly after I heard the voice of a waiter at the bar: "The stout gentleman in No. 13, wants his breakfast. Tea and bread and butter, with ham and eggs; the eggs not to be too much done."

In such a situation as mine, every incident is of importance. Here was a subject of speculation presented to my mind, and ample exercise for my imagination. I am prone to paint pictures to myself, and on this occasion I had some materials to work upon. Had the guest up stairs been mentioned as Mr. Smith, or Mr. Brown, or Mr. Jackson, or Mr. Johnson, or merely as "the gentleman in No. 13," it would have been a perfect blank to me. I should have thought nothing of it; but "The stout gentleman!" —the very name had something in it of the picturesque. It at once gave the size; it embodied the personage to my mind's eye, and my fancy did the rest.

He was stout, or, as some term it, lusty; in all probability, therefore, he was advanced in life, some people expanding as they grow old. By his breakfasting rather late, and in his own room, he must be a man accustomed to live at his ease, and above the necessity of early rising; no doubt a round, rosy, lusty old gentleman.

There was another violent ringing. The stout gentleman was impatient for his breakfast. He was evidently a man of importance; "well to do in the world;" accustomed to be promptly waited upon; of a keen appetite, and a little cross when hungry;

"perhaps," thought I, "he may be some London Alderman; or who knows but he may be a Member of Parliament?"

The breakfast was sent up, and there was a short interval of silence; he was, doubtless, making the tea. Presently there was a violent ringing; and before it could be answered, another ringing still more violent. "Bless me! what a choleric old gentleman!" The waiter came down in a huff. The butter was rancid, the eggs were over-done, the ham was too salt;—the stout gentleman was evidently nice in his eating; one of those who eat and growl, and keep the waiter on the trot, and live in a state militant with the household.

The hostess got into a fume. I should observe that she was a brisk, coquettish woman; a little of a shrew, and something of a slammerkin, but very pretty withal; with a nincompoop for a husband, as shrews are apt to have. She rated the servants roundly for their negligence in sending up so bad a breakfast, but said not a word against the stout gentleman; by which I clearly perceived that he must be a man of consequence, entitled to make a noise and to give trouble at a country inn. Other eggs, and ham, and bread and butter were sent up. They appeared to be more graciously received; at least there was no further complaint.

I had not made many turns about the travellers'-room, when there was another ringing. Shortly afterwards there was a stir and an inquest about the house. The stout gentleman wanted the Times or the Chronicle newspaper. I set him down, therefore, for a whig; or rather, from his being so absolute and lordly where he had a chance, I suspected him of being a radical. Hunt, I had heard, was a large man; "who knows," thought I, "but it is Hunt himself!"

My curiosity began to be awakened. I inquired of the waiter who was this stout gentleman that was making all this stir; but I could get no information: nobody seemed to know his name. The landlords of bustling inns seldom trouble their heads about the names or occupations of their transient guests. The color of a coat, the shape or size of the person, is enough to suggest a travelling name. It is either the tall gentleman, or the short gentleman, or the gentleman in black, or the gentleman in snuff-color; or, as in the present instance, the stout gentleman. A designation of the kind once hit on answers every purpose, and saves all further inquiry.

Rain—rain—rain! pitiless, ceaseless rain! No such thing as putting a foot out of doors, and no occupation nor amusement within. By and by I heard some one walking over head. It was in the stout gentleman's room. He evidently was a large man by the heaviness of his tread; and an old man from his wearing such creaking soles. "He is doubtless," thought I, "some rich old square-toes of regular habits, and is now taking exercise after breakfast."

I now read all the advertisement of coaches and hotels that were stuck about the mantelpiece. The Lady's Magazine had become an abomination to me; it was as tedious as the day itself. I wandered out, not knowing what to do, and ascended again to my room. I had not been there long, when there was a squall from a neighboring bedroom. A door opened and slammed violently; a chambermaid, that I had remarked for having a ruddy, good-humored face, went down stairs in a violent flurry. The stout gentleman had been rude to her!

This sent a whole host of my deductions to the deuce in a moment. This unknown personage could not be an old gentleman; for old gentlemen are not apt to be so obstreperous to chambermaids. He could not be a young gentleman; for young gentlemen are not apt to inspire such indignation. He must be a middle-aged man, and confounded ugly into the bargain, or the girl would not have taken the matter in such terrible dudgeon. I confess I was sorely puzzled.

In a few minutes I heard the voice of my landlady. I caught a glance of her as she came tramping up stairs; her face glowing, her cap flaring, her tongue wagging the whole way. "She'd have no such doings in her house, she'd warrant. If gentlemen did spend money freely, it was no rule. She'd have no servant maids of hers treated in that way, when they were about their work, that's what she wouldn't."

As I hate squabbles, particularly with women, and above all

with pretty women, I slunk back into my room, and partly closed the door; but my curiosity was too much excited not to listen. The landlady marched intrepidly to the enemy's citadel, and entered it with a storm: the door closed after her. I heard her voice in high windy clamor for a moment or two. Then it gradually subsided, like a gust of wind in a garret; then there was a laugh; then I heard nothing more.

After a little while my landlady came out with an odd smile on her face, adjusting her cap, which was a little on one side. As she went down stairs, I heard the landlord ask her what was the matter; she said, "Nothing at all, only the girl's a fool."—I was more than ever perplexed what to make of this unaccountable personage, who could put a good-natured chambermaid in a passion, and send away a termagant landlady in smiles. He could not be so old, nor cross, nor ugly either.

I had to go to work at his picture again, and to paint him entirely different. I now set him down for one of those stout gentlemen that are frequently met with swaggering about the doors of country inns. Moist, merry fellows, in Belcher handkerchiefs, whose bulk is a little assisted by malt-liquors. Men who have seen the world, and been sworn at Highgate; who are used to tavern life; up to all the tricks of tapsters, and knowing in the ways of sinful publicans. Free-livers on a small scale; who are prodigal within the compass of a guinea; who call all the waiters by name, touzle the maids, gossip with the landlady at the bar, and prose over a pint of port, or a glass of negus, after dinner.

The morning wore away in forming these and similar surmises. As fast as I wove one system of belief, some movement of the unknown would completely overturn it, and throw all my thoughts again into confusion. Such are the solitary operations of a feverish mind. I was, as I have said, extremely nervous; and the continual meditation on the concerns of this invisible personage began to have its effect:—I was getting a fit of the fidgets.

Dinner-time came. I hoped the stout gentleman might dine in the travellers'-room, and that I might at length get a view of his person; but no—he had dinner served in his own room.

What could be the meaning of this solitude and mystery? He could not be a radical; there was something too aristocratical in thus keeping himself apart from the rest of the world, and condemning himself to his own dull company throughout a rainy day. And then, too, he lived too well for a discontented politician. He seemed to expatiate on a variety of dishes, and to sit over his wine like a jolly friend of good living. Indeed, my doubts on this head were soon at an end; for he could not have finished his first bottle before I could faintly hear him humming a tune; and on listening, I found it to be "God save the King." 'Twas plain, then, he was no radical, but a faithful subject; one who grew loyal over his bottle, and was ready to stand by king and constitution, when he could stand by nothing else. But who could he be? My conjectures began to run wild. Was he not some personage of distinction travelling incog.? "God knows!" said I, at my wit's end; "it may be one of the royal family for aught I know, for they are all stout gentlemen!"

The weather continued rainy. The mysterious unknown kept his room, and, as far as I could judge, his chair, for I did not hear him move. In the mean time, as the day advanced, the travellers'-room began to be frequented. Some, who had just arrived, came in buttoned-up in box-coats; others came home who had been dispersed about the town; some took their dinners, and some their tea. Had I been in a different mood, I should have found entertainment in studying this peculiar class of men. There were two especially, who were regular wags of the road, and up to all the standing jokes of travellers. They had a thousand sly things to say to the waiting-maid, whom they called Louisa, and Ethelinda, and a dozen other fine names, changing the name every time, and chuckling amazingly at their own waggery. My mind, however, had been completely engrossed by the stout gentleman. He had kept my fancy in chase during a long day, and it was not now to be diverted from the scent.

The evening gradually wore away. The travellers read the papers two or three times over. Some drew round the fire and told long stories about their horses, about their adventures, their overturns, and breakings down. They discussed the credit of different merchants and different inns; and the two wags told several choice anecdotes of pretty chambermaids, and kind landladies. All this passed as they were quietly taking what they called their night-caps, that is to say, strong glasses of brandy and water and sugar, or some other mixture of the kind; after which they one after another rang for "Boots" and the chambermaid, and walked off to bed in old shoes cut down into marvellously uncomfortable slippers.

There was now only one man left; a short-legged, long-bodied, plethoric fellow, with a very large, sandy head. He sat by himself, with a glass of port wine negus, and a spoon; sipping and stirring, and meditating and sipping, until nothing was left but the spoon. He gradually fell asleep bolt upright in his chair, with the empty glass standing before him; and the candle seemed to fall asleep too, for the wick grew long, and black, and cabbaged at the end, and dimmed the little light that remained in the chamber. The gloom that now prevailed was contagious. Around hung the shapeless, and almost spectral, box-coats of departed travellers, long since buried in deep sleep. I only heard the ticking of the clock, with the deep-drawn breathings of the sleeping topers, and the drippings of the rain, drop—drop—drop, from the eaves of the house. The church bells chimed midnight. All at once the stout gentleman began to walk over head, pacing slowly backwards and forwards. There was something extremely awful in all this, especially to one in my state of nerves. These ghastly great-coats, these guttural breathings, and the creaking footsteps of this mysterious being. His steps grew fainter and fainter, and at length died away. I could bear it no longer. I was wound up to the desperation of a hero of romance. "Be he who or what he may," said I to myself, "I'll have a sight of him!" I seized a chamber candle, and hurried up to No. 13. The door stood ajar. I hesitated—I entered: the room was deserted. There stood a large, broad-bottomed elbow-chair at a table, on which was an empty tumbler, and a "Times" newspaper, and the room smelt powerfully of Stilton cheese.

The mysterious stranger had evidently but just retired. I turned off, sorely disappointed, to my room, which had been changed to the front of the house. As I went along the corridor, I saw a large pair of boots, with dirty, waxed tops, standing at the door of a bedchamber. They doubtless belonged to the unknown; but it would not do to disturb so redoubtable a personage in his den; he might discharge a pistol, or something worse, at my head. I went to bed, therefore, and lay awake half the night in a terribly nervous state; and even when I fell asleep, I was still haunted in my dreams by the idea of the stout gentleman and his wax-topped boots.

I slept rather late the next morning, and was awakened by some stir and bustle in the house, which I could not at first comprehend; until getting more awake, I found there was a mail coach starting from the door. Suddenly there was a cry from below, "The gentleman has forgot his umbrella! look for the gentleman's umbrella in No. 13!" I heard an immediate scampering of a chambermaid along the passage, and a shrill reply as she ran, "Here it is! here's the gentleman's umbrella!"

The mysterious stranger then was on the point of setting off. This was the only chance I should ever have of knowing him. I sprang out of bed, scrambled to the window, snatched aside the curtains, and just caught a glimpse of the rear of a person getting in at the coach-door. The skirts of a brown coat parted behind, and gave me a full view of the broad disk of a pair of drab breeches. The door closed—"all right!" was the word—the coach whirled off:—and that was all I ever saw of the stout gentleman!

VILLAGE WORTHIES

Nay, I tell you, I am so well beloved in our town, that not the worst dog in the street will hurt my little finger.

COLLIER OF CROYDON.

As the neighboring village is one of those out-of-the-way, but gossiping little places where a small matter makes a great stir, it is not to be supposed that the approach of a festival like that of May-day can be regarded with indifference, especially since it is made a matter of such moment by the great folks at the Hall. Master Simon, who is the faithful factotum of the worthy Squire, and jumps with his humor in every thing, is frequent just now in his visits to the village, to give directions for the impending fête; and as I have taken the liberty occasionally of accompanying him, I have been enabled to get some insight into the characters and internal politics of this very sagacious little community.

Master Simon is in fact the Cæsar of the village. It is true the Squire is the protecting power, but his factotum is the active and busy agent. He intermeddles in all its concerns; is acquainted with all the inhabitants and their domestic history; gives counsel to the old folks in their business matters, and the young folks in their love affairs; and enjoys the proud satisfaction of being a great man in a little world.

He is the dispenser, too, of the Squire's charity, which is bounteous; and, to do Master Simon justice, he performs this part of his functions with great alacrity. Indeed, I have been entertained with the mixture of bustle, importance, and kindheartedness which he displays. He is of too vivacious a temperament to comfort the afflicted by sitting down moping and whining and blowing noses in concert; but goes whisking about like a sparrow, chirping consolation into every hole and corner of the village. I have seen an old woman, in a red cloak, hold him for half an hour together with some long phthisical tale of distress, which Master Simon listened to with many a bob of the head, smack of his dog-whip, and other symptoms of impatience, though he afterwards made a most faithful and circumstantial report of the case to the Squire. I have watched him, too, during one of his pop visits into the cottage of a superannuated villager, who is a pensioner of the Squire, where he fidgeted about the room without sitting down, made many excellent off-hand reflections with the old invalid, who was propped up in his chair, about the shortness of life, the certainty of death, and the necessity of preparing for "that awful change;" quoted several texts of Scripture very incorrectly, but much to the edification of the cottager's wife; and on coming out, pinched the daughter's rosy cheek, and wondered what was in the young men, that such a pretty face did not get a husband.

He has also his cabinet counsellors in the village, with whom he is very busy just now, preparing for the May-day ceremonies. Among these is the village tailor, a pale-faced fellow, who plays the clarinet in the church choir; and, being a great musical genius, has frequent meetings of the band at his house, where they "make night hideous" by their concerts. He is, in consequence, high in favor with Master Simon; and, through his influence, has the making, or rather marring, of all the liveries of the Hall; which generally look as though they had been cut out by one of those scientific tailors of the Flying Island of Laputa, who took measure of their customers with a quadrant. The tailor, in fact, might rise to be one of the moneyed men of the village, was he not rather too prone to gossip, and keep holidays, and give concerts, and blow all his substance, real and personal, through his clarinet; which literally keeps him poor both in body and estate. He has for the present thrown by all his regular work, and suffered the breeches of the village to go unmade and unmended, while he is occupied in making garlands of party-colored rags, in imitation of flowers, for the decoration of the May-pole.

Another of Master Simon's counsellors is the apothecary, a short, and rather fat man, with a pair of prominent eyes, that diverge like those of a lobster. He is the village wise man; very sententious, and full of profound remarks on shallow subjects. Master Simon often quotes his sayings, and mentions him as rather an extraordinary man; and even consults him occasionally in desperate cases of the dogs and horses. Indeed, he seems to have been overwhelmed by the apothecary's philosophy, which is exactly one observation deep, consisting of indisputable maxims, such as may be gathered from the mottoes of tobacco-boxes. I had a specimen of his philosophy in my very first conversation with him; in the course of which he observed, with great solemnity and emphasis, that "man is a compound of wisdom and folly;" upon which Master Simon, who had hold of my arm, pressed very hard upon it, and whispered in my ear, "That's a devilish shrewd remark."

THE SCHOOLMASTER

There will no mosse stick to the stone of Sisiphus, no grasse hang on the heeles of Mercury, no butter cleave on the bread of a traveller. For as the eagle at every flight loseth a feather, which maketh her bauld in her age, so the traveller in every country loseth some fleece, which maketh him a beggar in his youth, by buying that for a pound which he cannot sell again for a penny—repentance.

LILLY'S EUPHUES.

Among the worthies of the village, that enjoy the peculiar confidence of Master Simon, is one who has struck my fancy so much, that I have thought him worthy of a separate notice. It is Slingsby, the schoolmaster, a thin elderly man, rather threadbare and slovenly, somewhat indolent in manner, and with an easy, good-humored look, not often met with in his craft. I have been interested in his favor by a few anecdotes which I have picked up concerning him.

He is a native of the village, and was a contemporary and playmate of Ready-Money Jack in the days of their boyhood. Indeed, they carried on a kind of league of mutual good offices. Slingsby was rather puny, and withal somewhat of a coward, but very apt at his learning: Jack, on the contrary, was a bully-boy out of doors, but a sad laggard at his books. Slingsby helped Jack, therefore, to all his lessons; Jack fought all Slingsby's battles; and they were inseparable friends. This mutual kindness continued even after they left the school, notwithstanding the dissimilarity of their characters. Jack took to ploughing and reaping, and prepared himself to till his paternal acres; while the other loitered negligently on in the path of learning, until he penetrated even into the confines of Latin and Mathematics.

In an unlucky hour, however, he took to reading voyages and travels, and was smitten with a desire to see the world. This desire increased upon him as he grew up; so, early one bright sunny morning, he put all his effects in a knapsack, slung it on his back, took staff in hand, and called in his way to take leave of his early schoolmate. Jack was just going out with the plough; the friends shook hands over the farmhouse gate; Jack drove his team a-field, and Slingsby whistled "over the hills and far away," and sallied forth gayly to "seek his fortune."

Years and years passed away, and young Tom Slingsby was forgotten; when, one mellow Sunday afternoon in autumn, a thin man, somewhat advanced in life, with a coat out at elbows, a pair of old nankeen gaiters, and a few things tied in a hand-kerchief, and slung on the end of a stick, was seen loitering through the village. He appeared to regard several houses atten-tively, to peer into the windows that were open, to eye the vil-lagers wistfully as they returned from church, and then to pass some time in the church-yard, reading the tombstones.

At length he found his way to the farmhouse of Ready-Money Jack, but paused ere he attempted the wicket; contem-plating the picture of substantial independence before him. In the porch of the house sat Ready-Money Jack, in his Sunday dress; with his hat upon his head, his pipe in his mouth, and his tankard before him, the monarch of all he surveyed. Beside him lay his fat house-dog. The varied sounds of poultry were heard from the well-stocked farmyard; the bees hummed from their hives in the garden; the cattle lowed in the rich meadow; while the crammed barns and ample stacks bore proof of an abundant harvest.

The stranger opened the gate and advanced dubiously toward the house. The mastiff growled at the sight of the suspicious-looking intruder; but was immediately silenced by his master; who, taking his pipe from his mouth, awaited with inquiring aspect the address of this equivocal personage. The stranger eyed old Jack for a moment, so portly in his dimensions, and decked out in gorgeous apparel; then cast a glance upon his own threadbare and starveling condition, and the scanty bundle which he held in his hand; then giving his shrunk waistcoat a twitch to make it meet its receding waistband, and casting an-other look, half sad, half humorous, at the sturdy yeoman, "I suppose," said he, "Mr. Tibbets, you have forgot old times and old playmates."

The latter gazed at him with scrutinizing look, but acknowledged that he had no recollection of him.

"Like enough, like enough," said the stranger; "every body seems to have forgotten poor Slingsby!"

"Why no, sure! it can't be Tom Slingsby!"

"Yes, but it is though!" replied the stranger, shaking his head.

Ready-Money Jack was on his feet in a twinkling; thrust out his hand, gave his ancient crony the gripe of a giant, and slapping the other hand on a bench, "Sit down there," cried he, "Tom Slingsby!"

A long conversation ensued about old times, while Slingsby was regaled with the best cheer that the farmhouse afforded; for he was hungry as well as wayworn, and had the keen appetite of a poor pedestrian. The early playmates then talked over their subsequent lives and adventures. Jack had but little to relate, and was never good at a long story. A prosperous life, passed at home, has little incident for narrative; it is only poor devils, that are tossed about the world, that are the true heroes of story. Jack had stuck by the paternal farm, followed the same plough that his forefathers had driven, and had waxed richer and richer as he grew older. As to Tom Slingsby, he was an exemplification of the old proverb, "a rolling stone gathers no moss." He had sought his fortune about the world, without ever finding it; being a thing oftener found at home than abroad. He had been in all kinds of situations, and had learnt a dozen different modes of making a living; but had found his way back to his native village rather poorer than when he left it, his knapsack having dwindled down to a scanty bundle.

As luck would have it, the Squire was passing by the farmhouse that very evening, and called there, as is often his custom. He found the two schoolmates still gossiping in the porch, and, according to the good old Scottish song, "taking a cup of kindness yet, for auld lang syne." The Squire was struck by the contrast in appearance and fortunes of these early playmates.

Ready-Money Jack, seated in lordly state, surrounded by the good things of this life, with golden guineas hanging to his very watch-chain; and the poor pilgrim Slingsby, thin as a weasel, with all his worldly effects, his bundle, hat, and walking-staff, lying on the ground beside him.

The good Squire's heart warmed towards the luckless cosmopolite, for he is a little prone to like such half-vagrant characters. He cast about in his mind how he should contrive once more to anchor Slingsby in his native village. Honest Jack had already offered him a present shelter under his roof, in spite of the hints, and winks, and half remonstrances of the shrewd Dame Tibbets; but how to provide for his permanent maintenance, was the question. Luckily, the Squire bethought himself that the village school was without a teacher. A little further conversation convinced him that Slingsby was as fit for that as for any thing else, and in a day or two he was seen swaying the rod of empire in the very school-house where he had often been horsed in the days of his boyhood.

Here he has remained for several years, and, being honored by the countenance of the Squire, and the fast friendship of Mr. Tibbets, he has grown into much importance and consideration in the village. I am told, however, that he still shows, now and then, a degree of restlessness, and a disposition to rove abroad again, and see a little more of the world; an inclination which seems particularly to haunt him about spring-time. There is nothing so difficult to conquer as the vagrant humor, when once it has been fully indulged.

Since I have heard these anecdotes of poor Slingsby, I have more than once mused upon the picture presented by him and his schoolmate Ready-Money Jack, on their coming together again after so long a separation. It is difficult to determine between lots in life, where each is attended with its peculiar discontents. He who never leaves his home, repines at his monotonous existence, and envies the traveller, whose life is a constant tissue of wonder and adventure; while he who is tossed about the world, looks back with many a sigh to the safe and quiet shore which he has abandoned. I cannot help thinking, however, that the man who stays at home, and cultivates the comforts and pleasures daily springing up around him, stands the best chance for happiness. There is nothing so fascinating to a young mind as the idea of travelling; and there is very witchcraft in the old phrase found in every nursery tale, of "going to seek one's fortune." A continual change of place, and change of object, promises a continual succession of adventure and gratification of curiosity. But there is a limit to all our enjoyments, and every desire bears its death in its very gratification. Curiosity languishes under repeated stimulants; novelties cease to excite surprise; until at length we cannot wonder even at a miracle.

He who has sallied forth into the world, like poor Slingsby, full of sunny anticipations, finds too soon how different the distant scene becomes when visited. The smooth place roughens as he approaches; the wild place becomes tame and barren; the fairy tints which beguiled him on, still fly to the distant hill, or gather upon the land he has left behind; and every part of the landscape seems greener than the spot he stands on.

THE SCHOOL

But to come down from great men and higher matters to my little children and poor schoolhouse again; I will, God willing, go forward orderly, as I purposed, to instruct poor children and young men both for learning and manners.

ROGER ASCHAM.

Having given the reader a slight sketch of the village schoolmaster, he may be curious to learn something concerning his school. As the Squire takes much interest in the education of the neighboring children, he put into the hands of the teacher, on first installing him in office, a copy of Roger Ascham's Schoolmaster, and advised him, moreover, to con over that portion of old Peachem which treats of the duty of masters, and which condemns the favorite method of making boys wise by flagellation.

He exhorted Slingsby not to break down or depress the free spirit of the boys, by harshness and slavish fear, but to lead them freely and joyously on in the path of knowledge, making it pleasant and desirable in their eyes. He wished to see the youth trained up in the manners and habitudes of the peasantry of the good old times, and thus to lay a foundation for the accomplishment of his favorite object, the revival of old English customs and character. He recommended that all the ancient holidays should be observed, and the sports of the boys, in their hours of play, regulated according to the standard authorities laid down in Strutt; a copy of whose invaluable work, decorated with plates, was deposited in the school-house. Above all, he exhorted the pedagogue to abstain from the use of birch; an instrument of instruction which the good Squire regards as fit only for the coercion of brute natures, that cannot be reasoned with.

Mr. Slingsby has followed the Squire's instructions to the best of his disposition and ability. He never flogs the boys, because he is too easy, good-humored a creature to inflict pain on a worm. He is bountiful in holidays, because he loves holidays himself, and has a sympathy with the urchins' impatience of confinement, from having divers times experienced its irksomeness during the time that he was seeing the world. As to sports and pastimes, the boys are faithfully exercised in all that are on record; quoits, races, prison-bars, tipcat, trap-ball, bandy-ball, wrestling, leaping, and what not. The only misfortune is, that having banished the birch, honest Slingsby has not studied Roger Ascham sufficiently to find out a substitute; or rather, he has not the management in his nature to apply one; his school, therefore, though one of the happiest, is one of the most unruly in the country; and never was a pedagogue more liked, or less heeded, by his disciples than Slingsby.

He has lately taken a coadjutor worthy of himself; being another stray sheep returned to the village fold. This is no other than the son of the musical tailor, who had bestowed some cost upon his education, hoping one day to see him arrive at the dignity of an exciseman, or at least of a parish clerk. The lad grew up, however, as idle and musical as his father; and, being captivated by the drum and fife of a recruiting party, followed them off to the army. He returned not long since, out of money, and out at elbows, the prodigal son of the village. He remained for some time lounging about the place in half-tattered soldier's dress, with a foraging cap on one side of his head, jerking stones across the brook, or loitering about the tavern door, a burden to his father, and regarded with great coldness by all warm house-holders.

Something, however, drew honest Slingsby towards the youth. It might be the kindness he bore to his father, who is one of the schoolmaster's great cronies; it might be that secret sympathy which draws men of vagrant propensities toward each other; for there is something truly magnetic in the vagabond feeling; or it might be, that he remembered the time, when he himself had come back like this youngster, a wreck to his native place. At any rate, whatever the motive, Slingsby drew towards the youth. They had many conversations in the village tap-room about foreign parts, and the various scenes and places they had witnessed during their wayfaring about the world. The more Slingsby talked with him, the more he found him to his taste: and finding him almost as learned as himself, he forthwith engaged him as an assistant, or usher, in the school.

Under such admirable tuition, the school, as may be sup-posed, flourishes apace; and if the scholars do not become versed in all the holiday accomplishments of the good old times, to the Squire's heart's content, it will not be the fault of their teachers. The prodigal son has become almost as popular among the boys as the pedagogue himself. His instructions are not limited to school-hours; and having inherited the musical taste and talents of his father, he has bitten the whole school with the mania. He is a great hand at beating a drum, which is often heard rumbling from the rear of the school-house. He is teaching half the boys of the village, also, to play the fife, and the pandean pipes; and they weary the whole neighborhood with their vague pipings, as they sit perched on stiles, or loiter-ing about the barn-doors in the evenings. Among the other exercises of the school, also, he has introduced the ancient art of archery, one of the Squire's favorite themes, with such success,

that the whipsters roam in truant bands about the neighborhood, practising with their bows and arrows upon the birds of
the air, and the beasts of the field; and not unfrequently making
a foray into the Squire's domains, to the great indignation of
the gamekeepers. In a word, so completely are the ancient English customs and habits cultivated at this school, that I should
not be surprised if the Squire should live to see one of his poetic
visions realized, and a brood reared up, worthy successors to
Robin Hood, and his merry gang of outlaws.

A VILLAGE POLITICIAN

I am a rogue if I do not think I was designed for the helm of state; I am
so full of nimble stratagems, that I should have ordered affairs, and carried
it against the stream of a faction, with as much ease as a skipper would
laver against the wind.

THE GOBLINS.

In one of my visits to the village with Master Simon, he proposed that we should stop at the inn, which he wished to show
me, as a specimen of a real country inn, the head-quarters of
village gossip. I had remarked it before, in my perambulations
about the place. It has a deep old-fashioned porch, leading into
a large hall, which serves for tap-room and travellers'-room;
having a wide fireplace, with high-backed settles on each side,
where the wise men of the village gossip over their ale, and hold
their sessions during the long winter evenings. The landlord is
an easy, indolent fellow, shaped a little like one of his own beer-
barrels, and is apt to stand gossiping at his own door, with his
wig on one side, and his hands in his pockets, whilst his wife
and daughter attend to customers. His wife, however, is fully
competent to manage the establishment; and, indeed, from long
habitude, rules over all the frequenters of the tap-room as completely as if they were her dependents and not her patrons. Not
a veteran ale-bibber but pays homage to her, having, no doubt,
often been in her arrears. I have already hinted that she is on
very good terms with Ready-Money Jack. He was a sweetheart
of hers in early life, and has always countenanced the tavern on

her account. Indeed, he is quite a "cock of the walk" at the tap-room.

As we approached the inn, we heard some one talking with great volubility, and distinguished the ominous words, "taxes," "poor's rates," and "agricultural distress." It proved to be a thin, loquacious fellow, who had penned the landlord up in one corner of the porch, with his hands in his pockets, listening with an air of the most vacant acquiescence.

The sight seemed to have a curious effect on Master Simon, as he squeezed my arm, and altering his course, sheered wide of the porch, as though he had not had any idea of entering. This evident evasion induced me to notice the orator more particularly. He was meagre, but active in his make, with a long, pale, bilious face; a black beard, so ill-shaven as to leave marks of blood on his shirt-collar; a feverish eye, and a hat sharpened up at the sides, into a most pragmatical shape. He had a newspaper in his hand, and seemed to be commenting on its contents, to the thorough conviction of mine host.

At sight of Master Simon the landlord was evidently a little flurried, and began to rub his hands, edge away from his corner, and make several profound publican bows; while the orator took no other notice of my companion than to talk rather louder than before, and with, as I thought, something of an air of defiance. Master Simon, however, as I have before said, sheered off from the porch, and passed on, pressing my arm within his, and whispering as we got by, in a tone of awe and horror, "That's a radical! he reads Cobbett!"

I endeavored to get a more particular account of him from my companion, but he seemed unwilling even to talk about him, answering only in general terms, that he was "a cursed busy fellow, that had a confounded trick of talking, and was apt to bother one about the national debt, and such nonsense;" from which I suspected that Master Simon had been rendered wary of him by some accidental encounter on the field of argument; for these radicals are continually roving about in quest of wordy warfare, and never so happy as when they can tilt a gentleman logician out of his saddle.

On subsequent inquiry my suspicions have been confirmed.
I find the radical has but recently found his way into the village,
where he threatens to commit fearful devastations with his doctrines. He has already made two or three complete converts, or
new lights; has shaken the faith of several others; and has grievously puzzled the brains of many of the oldest villagers, who
had never thought about politics, nor scarce any thing else, during their whole lives.

He is lean and meagre from the constant restlessness of mind
and body; worrying about with newspapers and pamphlets in
his pockets, which he is ready to pull out on all occasions. He
has shocked several of the stanchest villagers, by talking lightly
of the Squire and his family; and hinting that it would be better
the park should be cut up into small farms and kitchen-gardens,
or feed good mutton instead of worthless deer.

He is a great thorn in the side of the Squire, who is sadly
afraid that he will introduce politics into the village, and turn it
into an unhappy, thinking community. He is a still greater
grievance to Master Simon, who has hitherto been able to sway
the political opinions of the place, without much cost of learning or logic; but has been much puzzled of late to weed out the
doubts and heresies already sown by this champion of reform.
Indeed, the latter has taken complete command at the tap-room
of the tavern, not so much because he has convinced, as because
he has out-talked all the old-established oracles. The apothecary, with all his philosophy, was as naught before him. He has
convinced and converted the landlord at least a dozen times;
who, however, is liable to be convinced and converted the other
way by the next person with whom he talks. It is true the radical
has a violent antagonist in the landlady, who is vehemently
loyal, and thoroughly devoted to the king, Master Simon, and
the Squire. She now and then comes out upon the reformer with
all the fierceness of a cat-o'-mountain, and does not spare her
own soft-headed husband, for listening to what she terms such
"low-lived politics." What makes the good woman the more
violent, is the perfect coolness with which the radical listens to
her attacks, drawing his face up into a provoking, supercilious

smile; and when she has talked herself out of breath, quietly asking her for a taste of her home-brewed.

The only person in any way a match for this redoubtable politician is Ready-Money Jack Tibbets; who maintains his stand in the tap-room, in defiance of the radical and all his works. Jack is one of the most loyal men in the country, without being able to reason about the matter. He has that admirable quality for a tough arguer, also, that he never knows when he is beat. He has half a dozen old maxims, which he advances on all occasions, and though his antagonist may overturn them ever so often, yet he always brings them anew to the field. He is like the robber in Ariosto, who, though his head might be cut off half a hundred times, yet whipped it on his shoulders again in a twinkling, and returned as sound a man as ever to the charge.

Whatever does not square with Jack's simple and obvious creed, he sets down for "French politics;" for, notwithstanding the peace, he cannot be persuaded that the French are not still laying plots to ruin the nation, and to get hold of the Bank of England. The radical attempted to overwhelm him one day by a long passage from a newspaper; but Jack neither reads nor believes in newspapers. In reply, he gave him one of the stanzas which he has by heart from his favorite, and indeed only author, old Tusser, and which he calls his Golden Rules:

> Leave princes' affairs undescanted on,
> And tend to such doings as stand thee upon;
> Fear God, and offend not the king nor his laws,
> And keep thyself out of the magistrate's claws.

When Tibbets had pronounced this with great emphasis, he pulled out a well-filled leathern purse, took out a handful of gold and silver, paid his score at the bar with great punctuality, returned his money, piece by piece, into his purse, his purse into his pocket, which he buttoned up; and then, giving his cudgel a stout thump upon the floor, and bidding the radical "good morning, sir!" with the tone of a man who conceives he has completely done for his antagonist, he walked with lionlike gravity out of the house. Two or three of Jack's admirers who were present, and had been afraid to take the field themselves, looked upon this as a perfect triumph, and winked at each other when the radical's back was turned. "Ay, ay!" said mine host, as soon as the radical was out of hearing, "let old Jack alone; I'll warrant he'll give him his own!"

From TALES OF A TRAVELLER[51]

TO THE READER

WORTHY AND DEAR READER!—Hast thou ever been waylaid
in the midst of a pleasant tour by some treacherous malady: thy
heels tripped up, and thou left to count the tedious minutes as
they passed, in the solitude of an inn chamber? If thou hast,
thou wilt be able to pity me. Behold me, interrupted in the
course of my journeying up the fair banks of the Rhine, and
laid up by indisposition in this old frontier town of Mentz. I
have worn out every source of amusement. I know the sound
of every clock that strikes, and bell that rings, in the place. I
know to a second when to listen for the first tap of the Prussian
drum, as it summons the garrison to parade, or at what hour
to expect the distant sound of the Austrian military band. All
these have grown wearisome to me; and even the well-known
step of my doctor, as he slowly paces the corridor, with healing
in the creak of his shoes, no longer affords an agreeable inter-
ruption to the monotony of my apartment.

For a time I attempted to beguile the weary hours, by studying German under the tuition of mine host's pretty little
daughter, Katrine; but I soon found even German had not
power to charm a languid ear, and that the conjugating of *ich
liebe* might be powerless, however rosy the lips which uttered it.

I tried to read, but my mind would not fix itself. I turned
over volume after volume, but threw them by with distaste:
"Well, then," said I at length, in despair, "if I cannot read a
book, I will write one." Never was there a more lucky idea; it
at once gave me occupation and amusement. The writing of a
book was considered in old times as an enterprise of toil and
difficulty, insomuch that the most trifling lucubration was
denominated a "work," and the world talked with awe and
reverence of "the labors of the learned."—These matters are
better understood nowadays.

Thanks to the improvements in all kind of manufactures, the art of book-making has been made familiar to the meanest capacity. Everybody is an author. The scribbling of a quarto is the mere pastime of the idle; the young gentleman throws off his brace of duodecimos in the intervals of the sporting season, and the young lady produces her set of volumes with the same facility that her great-grandmother worked a set of chair-bottoms.

The idea having struck me, therefore, to write a book, the reader will easily perceive that the execution of it was no difficult matter. I rummaged my portfolio, and cast about, in my recollection, for those floating materials which a man naturally collects in travelling; and here I have arranged them in this little work.

As I know this to be a story-telling and a story-reading age, and that the world is fond of being taught by apologue, I have digested the instruction I would convey into a number of tales. They may not possess the power of amusement, which the tales told by many of my contemporaries possess; but then I value myself on the sound moral which each of them contains.[52] This may not be apparent at first, but the reader will be sure to find it out in the end. I am for curing the world by gentle alteratives, not by violent doses; indeed, the patient should never be conscious that he is taking a dose. I have learnt this much from experience under the hands of the worthy Hippocrates of Mentz.

I am not, therefore, for those barefaced tales which carry their moral on the surface, staring one in the face; they are enough to deter the squeamish reader. On the contrary, I have often hid my moral from sight, and disguised it as much as possible by sweets and spices, so that while the simple reader is listening with open mouth to a ghost or a love story, he may have a bolus of sound morality popped down his throat, and be never the wiser for the fraud.

As the public is apt to be curious about the sources whence an author draws his stories, doubtless that it may know how far to put faith in them, I would observe, that the Adventure

of the German Student, or rather the latter part of it, is founded
on an anecdote related to me as existing somewhere in French;
and, indeed, I have been told, since writing it, that an ingenious
tale has been founded on it by an English writer; but I have
never met with either the former or the latter in print. Some
of the circumstances in the Adventure of the Mysterious Picture,
and in the Story of the Young Italian, are vague recollections of
anecdotes related to me some years since; but from what source
derived, I do not know. The Adventure of the Young Painter
among the banditti is taken almost entirely from an authentic
narrative in manuscript.

As to the other tales contained in this work, and indeed to
my tales generally, I can make but one observation; I am an
old traveller; I have read somewhat, heard and seen more, and
dreamt more than all. My brain is filled, therefore, with all
kinds of odds and ends. In travelling, these heterogeneous
matters have become shaken up in my mind, as the articles are
apt to be in an ill-packed travelling trunk; so that when I
attempt to draw forth a fact, I cannot determine whether I have
read, heard, or dreamt it; and I am always at a loss to know
how much to believe of my own stories.

These matters being premised, fall to, worthy reader, with
good appetite; and, above all, with good humor, to what is here
set before thee. If the tales I have furnished should prove to
be bad, they will at least be found short; so that no one will
be wearied long on the same theme. "Variety is charming," as
some poet observes.

There is a certain relief in change, even though it be from
bad to worse! As I have often found in travelling in a stage-
coach, that it is often a comfort to shift one's position, and be
bruised in a new place.

Ever thine,

GEOFFREY CRAYON.

Dated from the HOTEL DE DARMSTADT,
   ci-devant HOTEL DE PARIS,
      MENTZ, *otherwise called* MAYENCE.

From PART ONE: STRANGE STORIES
BY A NERVOUS GENTLEMAN

The Great Unknown

The following adventures were related to me by the same
nervous gentleman who told me the romantic tale of the Stout
Gentleman, published in Bracebridge Hall. It is very singular,
that although I expressly stated that story to have been told to
me, and described the very person who told it, still it has been
received as an adventure that happened to myself. Now I
protest I never met with any adventure of the kind. I should
not have grieved at this, had it not been intimated by the
author of Waverley, in an introduction to his novel of Peveril
of the Peak, that he was himself the stout gentleman alluded to.
I have ever since been importuned by questions and letters
from gentlemen, and particularly from ladies without number,
touching what I had seen of the Great Unknown.

Now all this is extremely tantalizing. It is like being con-
gratulated on the high prize when one has drawn a blank; for I
have just as great a desire as any one of the public to penetrate
the mystery of that very singular personage, whose voice fills
every corner of the world, without any one being able to tell
whence it comes.

My friend, the nervous gentleman, also, who is a man of
very shy, retired habits, complains that he has been excessively
annoyed in consequence of its getting about in his neighborhood that he is the fortunate personage. Insomuch, that he
has become a character of considerable notoriety in two or
three country towns, and has been repeatedly teased to exhibit
himself at blue-stocking parties, for no other reason than that
of being "the gentleman who has had a glimpse of the author
of Waverley."

Indeed the poor man has grown ten times as nervous as ever
since he has discovered, on such good authority, who the stout
gentleman was; and will never forgive himself for not having
made a more resolute effort to get a full sight of him. He has

anxiously endeavored to call up a recollection of what he saw of that portly personage; and has ever since kept a curious eye on all gentlemen of more than ordinary dimensions, whom he has seen getting into stage-coaches. All in vain! The features he had caught a glimpse of seem common to the whole race of stout gentlemen, and the Great Unknown remains as great an unknown as ever.

Having premised these circumstances, I will now let the nervous gentleman proceed with his stories.

The Hunting Dinner

I was once at a hunting-dinner, given by a worthy fox-hunting old Baronet, who kept bachelor's hall in jovial style in an ancient rook-haunted family mansion, in one of the middle counties. He had been a devoted admirer of the fair sex in his younger days; but, having travelled much, studied the sex in various countries with distinguished success, and returned home profoundly instructed, as he supposed, in the ways of woman, and a perfect master of the art of pleasing, had the mortification of being jilted by a little boarding-school girl, who was scarcely versed in the accidence of love.

The Baronet was completely overcome by such an incredible defeat; retired from the world in disgust; put himself under the government of his housekeeper; and took to fox-hunting like a perfect Nimrod. Whatever poets may say to the contrary, a man will grow out of love as he grows old; and a pack of fox-hounds may chase out of his heart even the memory of a boarding-school goddess. The Baronet was, when I saw him, as merry and mellow an old bachelor as ever followed a hound; and the love he had once felt for one woman had spread itself over the whole sex; so that there was not a pretty face in the whole country round but came in for a share.

The dinner was prolonged till a late hour; for our host having no ladies in his household to summon us to the drawing-room, the bottle maintained its true bachelor sway, unrivalled by its potent enemy, the tea-kettle. The old hall in which we dined echoed to bursts of robustious fox-hunting merriment, that made the ancient antlers shake on the walls. By degrees, however, the wine and the wassail of mine host began to operate upon bodies already a little jaded by the chase. The choice spirits which flashed up at the beginning of the dinner, sparkled for a time, then gradually went out one after another, or only emitted now and then a faint gleam from the socket. Some of the briskest talkers, who had given tongue so bravely at the first burst, fell fast asleep; and none kept on their way but certain of those long-winded prosers, who, like short-legged hounds, worry on unnoticed at the bottom of conversation, but are sure to be in at the death. Even these at length subsided into silence; and scarcely any thing was heard but the nasal communications of two or three veteran masticators, who having been silent while awake, were indemnifying the company in their sleep.

At length the announcement of tea and coffee in the cedar-parlor roused all hands from this temporary torpor. Every one awoke marvellously renovated, and while sipping the refreshing beverage out of the Baronet's old-fashioned hereditary china, began to think of departing for their several homes. But here a sudden difficulty arose. While we had been prolonging our repast, a heavy winter storm had set in, with snow, rain, and sleet, driven by such bitter blasts of wind, that they threatened to penetrate to the very bone.

"It's all in vain," said our hospitable host, "to think of putting one's head out of doors in such weather. So, gentlemen, I hold you my guests for this night at least, and will have your quarters prepared accordingly."

The unruly weather, which became more and more tempestuous, rendered the hospitable suggestion unanswerable. The only question was, whether such an unexpected accession of company to an already crowded house, would not put the housekeeper to her trumps to accommodate them.

"Pshaw," cried mine host; "did you ever know a bachelor's hall that was not elastic, and able to accommodate twice as many as it could hold?" So, out of a good-humored pique, the housekeeper was summoned to a consultation before us all. The old lady appeared in her gala suit of faded brocade, which rustled with flurry and agitation; for, in spite of our host's bravado, she was a little perplexed. But in a bachelor's house, and with bachelor guests, these matters are readily managed. There is no lady of the house to stand upon squeamish points about lodging gentlemen in odd holes and corners, and exposing the shabby parts of the establishment. A bachelor's housekeeper is used to shifts and emergencies; so, after much worrying to and fro, and divers consultations about the red-room, and the blue-room, and the chintz-room, and the damask-room, and the little room with the bow-window, the matter was finally arranged.

When all this was done, we were once more summoned to the standing rural amusement of eating. The time that had been consumed in dozing after dinner, and in the refreshment and consultation of the cedar-parlor, was sufficient, in the opinion of the rosy-faced butler, to engender a reasonable appetite for supper. A slight repast had, therefore, been tricked up from the residue of dinner, consisting of a cold sirloin of beef, hashed venison, a devilled leg of a turkey or so, and a few other of those light articles taken by country gentlemen to ensure sound sleep and heavy snoring.

The nap after dinner had brightened up every one's wit; and a great deal of excellent humor was expended upon the perplexities of mine host and his housekeeper, by certain married gentlemen of the company, who considered themselves privileged in joking with a bachelor's establishment. From this the banter turned as to what quarters each would find, on being thus suddenly billeted in so antiquated a mansion.

"By my soul," said an Irish captain of dragoons, one of the most merry and boisterous of the party, "by my soul, but I should not be surprised if some of those good-looking gentlefolks that hang along the walls should walk about the rooms of this stormy night; or if I should find the ghosts of one of those long-waisted ladies turning into my bed in mistake for her grave in the church-yard."

"Do you believe in ghosts, then?" said a thin, hatchet-faced gentleman, with projecting eyes like a lobster.

I had remarked this last personage during dinner-time for one of those incessant questioners, who have a craving, unhealthy appetite in conversation. He never seemed satisfied with the whole of a story; never laughed when others laughed; but always put the joke to the question. He never could enjoy the kernel of the nut, but pestered himself to get more out of the shell. "Do you believe in ghosts, then?" said the inquisitive gentleman.

"Faith, but I do," replied the jovial Irishman. "I was brought up in the fear and belief of them. We had a Benshee in our own family, honey."

"A Benshee, and what's that?" cried the questioner.

"Why, an old lady ghost that tends upon your real Milesian families, and waits at their window to let them know when some of them are to die."

"A mighty pleasant piece of information!" cried an elderly gentleman with a knowing look, and with a flexible nose, to which he could give a whimsical twist when he wished to be waggish.

"By my soul, but I'd have you to know it's a piece of distinction to be waited on by a Benshee. It's a proof that one has pure blood in one's veins. But i' faith, now we are talking of ghosts, there never was a house or a night better fitted than the present for a ghost adventure. Pray, Sir John, haven't you such a thing as a haunted chamber to put a guest in?"

"Perhaps," said the Baronet, smiling, "I might accommodate you even on that point."

"Oh, I should like it of all things, my jewel. Some dark oaken room, with ugly wobegone portraits, that stare dismally at one; and about which the housekeeper has a power of delightful stories of love and murder. And then a dim lamp, a table with a rusty sword across it, and a spectre all in white, to draw aside one's curtains at midnight—"

"In truth," said an old gentleman at one end of the table, "you put me in mind of an anecdote—"

"Oh, a ghost story! a ghost story!" was vociferated round the board, every one edging his chair a little nearer.

The attention of the whole company was now turned upon the speaker. He was an old gentleman, one side of whose face was no match for the other. The eye-lid drooped and hung down like an unhinged window-shutter. Indeed, the whole side of his head was dilapidated, and seemed like the wing of a house shut up and haunted. I'll warrant that side was well stuffed with ghost stories.

There was a universal demand for the tale.

"Nay," said the old gentleman, "it's a mere anecdote, and a very common-place one; but such as it is you shall have it. It is a story that I once heard my uncle tell as having happened to himself. He was a man very apt to meet with strange adventures. I have heard him tell of others much more singular."

"What kind of a man was your uncle?" said the questioning gentleman.

"Why, he was rather a dry, shrewd kind of body; a great traveller, and fond of telling his adventures."

"Pray, how old might he have been when that happened?"

"When what happened?" cried the gentleman with the flexible nose, impatiently. "Egad, you have not given any thing a chance to happen. Come, never mind our uncle's age; let us have his adventures."

[The old gentleman with the haunted head then relates "The Adventure of My Uncle," which puts "the knowing gentleman, with the flexible nose" in mind of a story that used to be told by his aunt, entitled by Irving "The Adventure of My Aunt." Upon the inquisitive gentleman's objection that the story contains no ghost, the Irish Captain of Dragoons cries, "Oh! If it's ghosts you want, you shall have a whole regiment of them"; whereupon he relates the following story:]

The Bold Dragoon

or the adventure of my grandfather

My grandfather was a bold dragoon, for it's a profession, d'ye see, that has run in the family. All my forefathers have been dragoons, and died on the field of honor, except myself, and I hope my posterity may be able to say the same; however, I don't mean to be vainglorious. Well, my grandfather, as I said, was a bold dragoon, and had served in the Low Countries. In fact, he was one of that very army, which, according to my uncle Toby, swore so terribly in Flanders. He could swear a good stick himself; and moreover was the very man that introduced the doctrine Corporal Trim mentions of radical heat and radical moisture; or, in other words, the mode of keeping out the damps of ditch-water by burnt brandy. Be that as it may, it's nothing to the purport of my story. I only tell it to show you that my grandfather was a man not easily to be humbugged. He had seen service, or, according to his own phrase, he had seen the devil—and that's saying every thing.

Well, gentlemen, my grandfather was on his way to England, for which he intended to embark from Ostend—bad luck to the place! for one where I was kept by storms and head-winds for three long days, and the devil of a jolly companion or pretty girl to comfort me. Well, as I was saying, my grandfather was on his way to England, or rather to Ostend—no matter which, it's all the same. So one evening, towards nightfall, he rode jollily into Bruges.—Very like you all know Bruges, gentlemen; a queer old-fashioned Flemish town, once, they say, a great place for trade and money-making in old times, when the Mynheers were in their glory; but almost as large and as empty as an Irishman's pocket at the present day.—Well, gentlemen, it was at the time of the annual fair. All Bruges was crowded; and the canals swarmed with Dutch boats, and the streets swarmed with Dutch merchants; and there was hardly any getting along for goods, wares, and merchandises, and peasants in big breeches, and women in half a score of petticoats.

My grandfather rode jollily along, in his easy, slashing way, for he was a saucy, sunshiny fellow—staring about him at the motley crowd, and the old houses with gable ends to the street, and storks' nests in the chimneys; winking at the yafrows who showed their faces at the windows, and joking the women right and left in the street; all of whom laughed, and took it in amazing good part; for though he did not know a word of the language, yet he had always a knack of making himself understood among the women.

Well, gentlemen, it being the time of the annual fair, all the town was crowded, every inn and tavern full, and my grandfather applied in vain from one to the other for admittance. At length he rode up to an old rickety inn, that looked ready to fall to pieces, and which all the rats would have run away from, if they could have found room in any other house to put their heads. It was just such a queer building as you see in Dutch pictures, with a tall roof that reached up into the clouds, and as many garrets, one over the other, as the seven heavens of Mahomet. Nothing had saved it from tumbling down but a stork's nest on the chimney, which always brings good luck to a house in the Low Countries; and at the very time of my grandfather's arrival, there were two of these long-legged birds of grace standing like ghosts on the chimney-top. Faith, but they've kept the house on its legs to this very day, for you may see it any time you pass through Bruges, as it stands there yet, only it is turned into a brewery of strong Flemish beer,—at least it was so when I came that way after the battle of Waterloo.

My grandfather eyed the house curiously as he approached. It might not have altogether struck his fancy, had he not seen in large letters over the door,

HEER VERKOOPT MAN GOEDEN DRANK.

My grandfather had learnt enough of the language to know that the sign promised good liquor. "This is the house for me," said he, stopping short before the door.

The sudden appearance of a dashing dragoon was an event in an old inn frequented only by the peaceful sons of traffic. A rich burgher of Antwerp, a stately ample man in a broad Flemish hat, and who was the great man and great patron of the establishment, sat smoking a clean long pipe on one side of the door; a fat little distiller of Geneva, from Schiedam, sat smoking on the other; and the bottle-nosed host stood in the door, and the comely hostess, in crimped cap, beside him; and the hostess's daughter, a plump Flanders lass, with long gold pendants in her ears, was at a side window.

"Humph!" said the rich burgher of Antwerp, with a sulky glance at the stranger.

"De duyvel!" said the fat little distiller of Schiedam.

The landlord saw, with the quick glance of a publican, that the new guest was not at all to the taste of the old ones; and, to tell the truth, he did not like my grandfather's saucy eye. He shook his head. "Not a garret in the house but was full."

"Not a garret!" echoed the landlady.

"Not a garret!" echoed the daughter.

The burgher of Antwerp, and the little distiller of Schiedam, continued to smoke their pipes sullenly, eyeing the enemy askance from under their broad hats, but said nothing.

My grandfather was not a man to be browbeaten. He threw the reins on his horse's neck, cocked his head on one side, stuck one arm akimbo,—"Faith and troth!" said he, "but I'll sleep in this house this very night."—As he said this he gave a slap on his thigh, by way of emphasis—the slap went to the landlady's heart.

He followed up the vow by jumping off his horse, and making his way past the staring Mynheers into the public room.— May be you've been in the bar-room of an old Flemish inn— faith, but a handsome chamber it was as you'd wish to see; with a brick floor, and a great fireplace, with the whole Bible history in glazed tiles; and then the mantelpiece, pitching itself head foremost out of the wall, with a whole regiment of cracked tea-pots and earthen jugs paraded on it; not to mention half a dozen great Delft platters, hung about the room by way of pictures; and the little bar in one corner, and the bouncing bar-maid inside of it, with a red calico cap, and yellow ear-drops.

My grandfather snapped his fingers over his head, as he cast an eye round the room—"Faith, this is the very house I've been looking after," said he.

There was some further show of resistance on the part of the garrison; but my grandfather was an old soldier, and an Irishman to boot, and not easily repulsed, especially after he had

got into the fortress. So he blarneyed the landlord, kissed the
landlord's wife, tickled the landlord's daughter, chucked the
bar-maid under the chin; and it was agreed on all hands that
it would be a thousand pities, and a burning shame into the bargain, to turn such a bold dragoon into the streets. So they laid
their heads together, that is to say, my grandfather and the
landlady, and it was at length agreed to accommodate him with
an old chamber, that had been for some time shut up.

"Some say it's haunted," whispered the landlord's daughter;
"but you are a bold dragoon, and I dare say don't fear ghosts."

"The devil a bit!" said my grandfather, pinching her plump
cheek. "But if I should be troubled by ghosts, I've been to the
Red Sea in my time, and have a pleasant way of laying them,
my darling."

And then he whispered something to the girl which made
her laugh, and give him a good-humored box on the ear. In
short, there was nobody knew better how to make his way
among the petticoats than my grandfather.

In a little while, as was his usual way, he took complete possession of the house, swaggering all over it; into the stable to
look after his horse, into the kitchen to look after his supper.
He had something to say or do with every one; smoked with
the Dutchmen, drank with the Germans, slapped the landlord
on the shoulder, romped with his daughter and the bar-maid:—
never, since the days of Alley Croaker, had such a rattling blade
been seen. The landlord stared at him with astonishment; the
landlord's daughter hung her head and giggled whenever he
came near; and as he swaggered along the corridor, with his
sword trailing by his side, the maids looked after him, and whispered to one another, "What a proper man!"

At supper, my grandfather took command of the table-d'hote
as though he had been at home; helped everybody, not forgetting himself; talked with every one, whether he understood
their language or not; and made his way into the intimacy of
the rich burgher of Antwerp, who had never been known to be
sociable with any one during his life. In fact, he revolutionized
the whole establishment, and gave it such a rouse, that the very

house reeled with it. He outsat every one at table, excepting the little fat distiller of Schiedam, who sat soaking a long time before he broke forth; but when he did, he was a very devil incarnate. He took a violent affection for my grandfather; so they sat drinking and smoking, and telling stories, and singing Dutch and Irish songs, without understanding a word each other said, until the little Hollander was fairly swamped with his own gin and water, and carried off to bed, whooping and hickuping, and trolling the burden of a Low Dutch love-song.

Well, gentlemen, my grandfather was shown to his quarters up a large staircase, composed of loads of hewn timber; and through long rigmarole passages, hung with blackened paintings of fish, and fruit, and game, and country frolics, and huge kitchens, and portly burgomasters, such as you see about old-fashioned Flemish inns, till at length he arrived at his room.

An old-times chamber it was, sure enough, and crowded with all kinds of trumpery. It looked like an infirmary for decayed and superannuated furniture, where every thing diseased or disabled was sent to nurse or to be forgotten. Or rather it might be taken for a general congress of old legitimate movables, where every kind and country had a representative. No two chairs were alike. Such high backs and low backs, and leather bottoms, and worsted bottoms, and straw bottoms, and no bottoms; and cracked marble tables with curiously carved legs, holding balls in their claws, as though they were going to play at nine-pins.

My grandfather made a bow to the motley assemblage as he entered, and, having undressed himself, placed his light in the fireplace, asking pardon of the tongs, which seemed to be making love to the shovel in the chimney-corner, and whispering soft nonsense in its ear.

The rest of the guests were by this time sound asleep, for your Mynheers are huge sleepers. The housemaids, one by one, crept up yawning to their attics; and not a female head in the inn was laid on a pillow that night without dreaming of the bold dragoon.

My grandfather, for his part, got into bed, and drew over

him one of those great bags of down, under which they smother a man in the Low Countries; and there he lay, melting between two feather beds, like an anchovy sandwich between two slices of toast and butter. He was a warm complexioned man, and this smothering played the very deuce with him. So, sure enough, in a little time it seemed as if a legion of imps were twitching at him, and all the blood in his veins was in a fever heat.

He lay still, however, until all the house was quiet, excepting the snoring of the Mynheers from the different chambers; who answered one another in all kinds of tones and cadences, like so many bull-frogs in a swamp. The quieter the house became, the more unquiet became my grandfather. He waxed warmer and warmer, until at length the bed became too hot to hold him.

"May be the maid had warmed it too much?" said the curious gentleman, inquiringly.

"I rather think the contrary," replied the Irishman. "But, be that as it may, it grew too hot for my grandfather."

"Faith, there's no standing this any longer," says he. So he jumped out of bed and went strolling about the house.

"What for?" said the inquisitive gentleman.

"Why to cool himself, to be sure—or perhaps to find a more comfortable bed—or perhaps—But no matter what he went for —he never mentioned—and there's no use in taking up our time in conjecturing."

Well, my grandfather had been for some time absent from his room, and was returning, perfectly cool, when just as he reached the door, he heard a strange noise within. He paused and listened. It seemed as if some one were trying to hum a tune in defiance of the asthma. He recollected the report of the room being haunted; but he was no believer in ghosts, so he pushed the door gently open and peeped in.

Egad, gentlemen, there was a gambol carrying on within enough to have astonished St. Anthony himself. By the light of the fire he saw a pale weazen-faced fellow, in a long flannel gown and a tall white night-cap with a tassel to it, who sat by the fire with a bellows under his arm by way of bagpipe, from

which he forced the asthmatical music that had bothered my
grandfather. As he played, too, he kept twitching about with
a thousand queer contortions, nodding his head, and bobbing
about his tasselled night-cap.

My grandfather thought this very odd and mighty presump-
tuous, and was about to demand what business he had to play
his wind instrument in another gentleman's quarters, when a
new cause of astonishment met his eye. From the opposite
side of the room a long-backed, bandy-legged chair covered
with leather, and studded all over in a coxcombical fashion with
little brass nails, got suddenly into motion, thrust out first a
claw-foot, then a crooked arm, and at length, making a leg,
sidled gracefully up to an easy chair of tarnished brocade, with
a hole in its bottom, and led it gallantly out in a ghostly minuet
about the floor.

The musician now played fiercer and fiercer, and bobbed his
head and his night-cap about like mad. By degrees the dancing
mania seemed to seize upon all the other pieces of furniture.
The antique, long-bodied chairs paired off in couples and led
down a country dance; a three-legged stool danced a hornpipe,
though horribly puzzled by its supernumerary limb; while the
amorous tongs seized the shovel round the waist, and whirled it
about the room in a German waltz. In short, all the movables
got in motion: pirouetting hands across, right and left, like so
many devils; all except a great clothes-press, which kept courtesying and courtesying in a corner, like a dowager, in exquisite
time to the music; being rather too corpulent to dance, or, perhaps at a loss for a partner.

My grandfather concluded the latter to be the reason; so
being, like a true Irishman, devoted to the sex, and at all times
ready for a frolic, he bounced into the room, called to the
musician to strike up Paddy O'Rafferty, capered up to the
clothes-press, and seized upon the two handles to lead her out:
——when——whirr! the whole revel was at an end. The chairs,
tables, tongs and shovel, slunk in an instant as quietly into their
places as if nothing had happened, and the musician vanished
up the chimney, leaving the bellows behind him in his hurry.

My grandfather found himself seated in the middle of the floor with the clothes-press sprawling before him, and the two handles jerked off, and in his hands.

"Then, after all, this was a mere dream!" said the inquisitive gentleman.

"The divil a bit of a dream!" replied the Irishman. "There never was a truer fact in this world. Faith, I should have liked to see any man tell my grandfather it was a dream."

Well, gentlemen, as the clothes-press was a mighty heavy body, and my grandfather likewise, particularly in rear, you may easily suppose that two such heavy bodies coming to the ground would make a bit of a noise. Faith, the old mansion shook as though it had mistaken it for an earthquake. The whole garrison was alarmed. The landlord, who slept below, hurried up with a candle to inquire the cause, but with all his haste his daughter had arrived at the scene of uproar before him. The landlord was followed by the landlady, who was followed by the bouncing bar-maid, who was followed by the simpering chambermaids, all holding together, as well as they could, such garments as they first laid hands on; but all in a terrible hurry to see what the deuce was to pay in the chamber of the bold dragoon. .

My grandfather related the marvellous scene he had witnessed, and the broken handles of the prostrate clothes-press bore testimony to the fact. There was no contesting such evidence; particularly with a lad of my grandfather's complexion, who seemed able to make good every word either with sword or shillelah. So the landlord scratched his head and looked silly, as he was apt to do when puzzled. The landlady scratched—no, she did not scratch her head, but she knit her brow, and did not seem half pleased with the explanation. But the landlady's daughter corroborated it by recollecting that the last person who had dwelt in that chamber was a famous juggler who died of St. Vitus's dance, and had no doubt infected all the furniture.

This set all things to rights, particularly when the chambermaids declared that they had all witnessed strange carryings on in that room; and as they declared this "upon their honors," there could not remain a doubt upon the subject.

"And did your grandfather go to bed again in that room?" said the inquisitive gentleman.

"That's more than I can tell. Where he passed the rest of the night was a secret he never disclosed. In fact, though he had seen much service, he was but indifferently acquainted with geography, and apt to make blunders in his travels about inns at night, which it would have puzzled him sadly to account for in the morning."

"Was he ever apt to walk in his sleep?" said the knowing old gentleman.

"Never that I heard of."

There was a little pause after this rigmarole Irish romance, when the old gentleman with the haunted head observed, that the stories hitherto related had rather a burlesque tendency. "I recollect an adventure, however," added he, "which I heard of during a residence at Paris, for the truth of which I can undertake to vouch, and which is of a very grave and singular nature."

ADVENTURE OF THE GERMAN STUDENT

On a stormy night, in the tempestuous times of the French revolution, a young German was returning to his lodgings, at a late hour, across the old part of Paris. The lightning gleamed, and the loud claps of thunder rattled through the lofty narrow streets—but I should first tell you something about this young German.

Gottfried Wolfgang was a young man of good family. He had studied for some time at Gottingen, but being of a visionary and enthusiastic character, he had wandered into those wild and speculative doctrines which have so often bewildered German students. His secluded life, his intense application, and the singular nature of his studies, had an effect on both mind and body. His health was impaired; his imagination diseased. He had been indulging in fanciful speculations on spiritual essences, until, like Swedenborg, he had an ideal world of his own around him. He took up a notion, I do not know from what cause, that there was an evil influence hanging over him; an evil genius or spirit seeking to ensnare him and ensure his perdition. Such an idea working on his melancholy temperament, produced the most gloomy effects. He became haggard and desponding. His friends discovered the mental malady preying upon him, and determined that the best cure was a change of scene; he was sent, therefore, to finish his studies amidst the splendors and gayeties of Paris.

Wolfgang arrived at Paris at the breaking out of the revolution. The popular delirium at first caught his enthusiastic mind, and he was captivated by the political and philosophical theories of the day: but the scenes of blood which followed shocked his sensitive nature, disgusted him with society and the world, and made him more than ever a recluse. He shut himself up in a solitary apartment in the *Pays Latin*, the quarter of students. There, in a gloomy street not far from the monastic walls of the Sorbonne, he pursued his favorite speculations. Sometimes he spent hours together in the great libraries of Paris, those catacombs of departed authors, rummaging among their hoards of dusty and obsolete works in quest of food for his unhealthy appetite. He was, in a manner, a literary ghoul, feeding in the charnel-house of decayed literature.

Wolfgang, though solitary and recluse, was of an ardent temperament, but for a time it operated merely upon his imagination. He was too shy and ignorant of the world to make any advances to the fair, but he was a passionate admirer of female beauty, and in his lonely chamber would often lose himself in reveries on forms and faces which he had seen, and his fancy would deck out images of loveliness far surpassing the reality.

While his mind was in this excited and sublimated state, a dream produced an extraordinary effect upon him. It was of a female face of transcendent beauty. So strong was the impression made, that he dreamt of it again and again. It haunted his thoughts by day, his slumbers by night; in fine, he became passionately enamoured of this shadow of a dream. This lasted so long that it became one of those fixed ideas which haunt the minds of melancholy men, and are at times mistaken for madness.

Such was Gottfried Wolfgang, and such his situation at the time I mentioned. He was returning home late one stormy night, through some of the old and gloomy streets of the *Marais*, the ancient part of Paris. The loud claps of thunder rattled among the high houses of the narrow streets. He came to the Place de Grève, the square where public executions are performed. The lightning quivered about the pinnacles of the ancient Hôtel de Ville, and shed flickering gleams over the open space in front. As Wolfgang was crossing the square, he shrank back with horror at finding himself close by the guillotine. It was the height of the reign of terror, when this dreadful instrument of death stood ever ready, and its scaffold was continually running with the blood of the virtuous and the brave. It had that very day been actively employed in the work of carnage, and there it stood in grim array, amidst a silent and sleeping city, waiting for fresh victims.

Wolfgang's heart sickened within him, and he was turning shuddering from the horrible engine, when he beheld a shadowy form, cowering as it were at the foot of the steps which led up to the scaffold. A succession of vivid flashes of lightning revealed it more distinctly. It was a female figure, dressed in black. She was seated on one of the lower steps of the scaffold, leaning forward, her face hid in her lap; and her long dishevelled tresses hanging to the ground, streaming with the rain which fell in torrents. Wolfgang paused. There was something awful in this solitary monument of woe. The female had the appearance of being above the common order. He knew the times to be full of vicissitude, and that many a fair head, which had once been pillowed on down, now wandered houseless. Perhaps this was some poor mourner whom the dreadful axe had rendered desolate, and who sat here heart-broken on the strand of existence, from which all that was dear to her had been launched into eternity.

He approached, and addressed her in the accents of sympathy. She raised her head and gazed wildly at him. What was his astonishment at beholding, by the bright glare of the lightning, the very face which had haunted him in his dreams. It was pale and disconsolate, but ravishingly beautiful.

Trembling with violent and conflicting emotions, Wolfgang again accosted her. He spoke something of her being exposed at such an hour of the night, and to the fury of such a storm, and offered to conduct her to her friends. She pointed to the guillotine with a gesture of dreadful signification.

"I have no friend on earth!" said she.

"But you have a home," said Wolfgang.

"Yes—in the grave!"

The heart of the student melted at the words.

"If a stranger dare make an offer," said he, "without danger of being misunderstood, I would offer my humble dwelling as a shelter; myself as a devoted friend. I am friendless myself in Paris, and a stranger in the land; but if my life could be of service, it is at your disposal, and should be sacrificed before harm or indignity should come to you."

There was an honest earnestness in the young man's manner that had its effect. His foreign accent, too, was in his favor; it showed him not to be a hackneyed inhabitant of Paris. Indeed, there is an eloquence in true enthusiasm that is not to be doubted. The homeless stranger confided herself implicitly to the protection of the student.

He supported her faltering steps across the Pont Neuf, and by the place where the statue of Henry the Fourth had been overthrown by the populace. The storm had abated, and the thunder rumbled at a distance. All Paris was quiet; that great volcano of human passion slumbered for a while, to gather fresh strength for the next day's eruption. The student conducted his charge through the ancient streets of the *Pays Latin*, and by the dusky walls of the Sorbonne, to the great dingy hotel which he inhabited. The old portress who admitted them stared with surprise at the unusual sight of the melancholy Wolfgang with a female companion.

On entering his apartment, the student, for the first time, blushed at the scantiness and indifference of his dwelling. He had but one chamber—an old-fashioned saloon—heavily carved, and fantastically furnished with the remains of former magnificence, for it was one of those hotels in the quarter of the Luxembourg palace, which had once belonged to nobility. It was lumbered with books and papers, and all the usual apparatus of a student, and his bed stood in a recess at one end.

When lights were brought, and Wolfgang had a better opportunity of contemplating the stranger, he was more than ever intoxicated by her beauty. Her face was pale, but of a dazzling fairness, set off by a profusion of raven hair that hung clustering about it. Her eyes were large and brilliant, with a singular expression approaching almost to wildness. As far as her black dress permitted her shape to be seen, it was of perfect symmetry. Her whole appearance was highly striking, though she was dressed in the simplest style. The only thing approaching to an ornament which she wore, was a broad black band round her neck, clasped by diamonds.

The perplexity now commenced with the student how to dispose of the helpless being thus thrown upon his protection. He thought of abandoning his chamber to her, and seeking shelter for himself elsewhere. Still he was so fascinated by her charms, there seemed to be such a spell upon his thoughts and senses, that he could not tear himself from her presence. Her manner, too, was singular and unaccountable. She spoke no more of the guillotine. Her grief had abated. The attentions of the student had first won her confidence, and then, apparently, her heart. She was evidently an enthusiast like himself, and enthusiasts soon understand each other.

In the infatuation of the moment, Wolfgang avowed his passion for her. He told her the story of his mysterious dream, and how she had possessed his heart before he had even seen her. She was strangely affected by his recital, and acknowledged to have felt an impulse towards him equally unaccountable. It was the time for wild theory and wild actions. Old prejudices and superstitions were done away; every thing was under the sway of the "Goddess of Reason." Among other rubbish of the old times, the forms and ceremonies of marriage began to be considered superfluous bonds for honorable minds. Social compacts were the vogue. Wolfgang was too much of a theorist not to be tainted by the liberal doctrines of the day.

"Why should we separate?" said he: "our hearts are united; in the eye of reason and honor we are as one. What need is there of sordid forms to bind high souls together?"

The stranger listened with emotion: she had evidently received illumination at the same school.

"You have no home nor family," continued he; "let me be every thing to you, or rather let us be every thing to one another. If form is necessary, form shall be observed—there is my hand. I pledge myself to you for ever."

"For ever?" said the stranger, solemnly.

"For ever!" repeated Wolfgang.

The stranger clasped the hand extended to her: "then I am yours," murmured she, and sank upon his bosom.

The next morning the student left his bride sleeping, and sallied forth at an early hour to seek more spacious apartments suitable to the change in his situation. When he returned, he found the stranger lying with her head hanging over the bed, and one arm thrown over it. He spoke to her, but received no reply. He advanced to awaken her from her uneasy posture. On taking her hand, it was cold—there was no pulsation—her face was pallid and ghastly.—In a word she was a corpse.

Horrified and frantic, he alarmed the house. A scene of confusion ensued. The police was summoned. As the officer of police entered the room, he started back on beholding the corpse.

"Great heaven!" cried he, "how did this woman come here?"

"Do you know any thing about her?" said Wolfgang, eagerly.

"Do I?" exclaimed the officer: "she was guillotined yesterday."

He stepped forward; undid the black collar round the neck of the corpse, and the head rolled on the floor!

The student burst into a frenzy. "The fiend! the fiend has gained possession of me!" shrieked he: "I am lost for ever."

They tried to soothe him, but in vain. He was possessed

with the frightful belief that an evil spirit had reanimated the dead body to ensnare him. He went distracted, and died in a mad-house.

Here the old gentleman with the haunted head finished his narrative.

"And is this really a fact?" said the inquisitive gentleman.

"A fact not to be doubted," replied the other. "I had it from the best authority. The student told it me himself. I saw him in a mad-house in Paris."⁵³

From PART THREE: THE ITALIAN BANDITTI

THE BELATED TRAVELLERS

[A group of travellers (French, Italian, and English) having gathered at the Inn at Terracina, an Italian improvisatore, to pass the time, entertains the assembled company with the following tale:]

It was late one evening that a carriage, drawn by mules, slowly toiled its way up one of the passes of the Apennines. It was through one of the wildest defiles, where a hamlet occurred only at distant intervals, perched on the summit of some rocky height, or the white towers of a convent peeped out from among the thick mountain foliage. The carriage was of ancient and ponderous construction. Its faded embellishments spoke of former splendor, but its crazy springs and axle-trees creaked out the tale of present decline. Within was seated a tall, thin old gentleman, in a kind of military travelling dress, and a foraging cap trimmed with fur, though the gray locks which stole from under it hinted that his fighting days were over. Beside him was a pale, beautiful girl of eighteen, dressed in something of a northern or Polish costume. One servant was seated in front, a rusty, crusty looking fellow, with a scar across his face, an orange-tawny *schnur-bart* or pair of mustaches, bristling from under his nose, and altogether the air of an old soldier.

It was, in fact, the equipage of a Polish nobleman; a wreck

of one of those princely families once of almost oriental magnificence, but broken down and impoverished by the disasters of
Poland. The Count, like many other generous spirits, had
been found guilty of the crime of patriotism, and was, in a
manner, an exile from his country. He had resided for some
time in the first cities of Italy, for the education of his daughter,
in whom all his cares and pleasures were now centred. He had
taken her into society, where her beauty and her accomplishments gained her many admirers; and had she not been the
daughter of a poor broken-down Polish nobleman, it is more
than probable many would have contended for her hand. Suddenly, however, her health became delicate and drooping; her
gayety fled with the roses of her cheek, and she sank into silence
and debility. The old Count saw the change with the solicitude
of a parent. "We must try a change of air and scene," said he;
and in a few days the old family carriage was rumbling among
the Apennines.

Their only attendant was the veteran Caspar, who had been
born in the family, and grown rusty in its service. He had
followed his master in all his fortunes; had fought by his side;
had stood over him when fallen in battle; and had received, in
his defence, the sabre-cut which added such grimness to his
countenance. He was now his valet, his steward, his butler, his
factotum. The only being that rivalled his master in his affections was his youthful mistress. She had grown up under his
eye, he had led her by the hand when she was a child, and he
now looked upon her with the fondness of a parent. Nay, he
even took the freedom of a parent in giving his blunt opinion
on all matters which he thought were for her good; and felt a
parent's vanity at seeing her gazed at and admired.

The evening was thickening; they had been for some time
passing through narrow gorges of the mountains, along the
edges of a tumbling stream. The scenery was lonely and savage.
The rocks often beetled over the road, with flocks of white
goats browsing on their brinks, and gazing down upon the
travellers. They had between two or three leagues yet to go
before they could reach any village; yet the muleteer, Pietro, a

tippling old fellow, who had refreshed himself at the last halting-place with a more than ordinary quantity of wine, sat singing and talking alternately to his mules, and suffering them to lag on at a snail's pace, in spite of the frequent entreaties of the Count and maledictions of Caspar.

The clouds began to roll in heavy masses along the mountains, shrouding their summits from view. The air was damp and chilly. The Count's solicitude on his daughter's account overcame his usual patience. He leaned from the carriage, and called to old Pietro in an angry tone:

"Forward!" said he. "It will be midnight before we arrive at our inn."

"Yonder it is, Signor," said the muleteer.

"Where?" demanded the Count.

"Yonder," said Pietro, pointing to a desolate pile about a quarter of a league distant.

"That the place?—why, it looks more like a ruin than an inn. I thought we were to put up for the night at a comfortable village."

Here Pietro uttered a string of piteous exclamations and ejaculations, such as are ever at the tip of the tongue of a delinquent muleteer. "Such roads! and such mountains! and then his poor animals were way-worn, and leg-weary; they would fall lame; they would never be able to reach the village. And then what could his Excellenza wish for better than the inn; a perfect castella—a palazza—and such people!—and such a larder!—and such beds!—His Excellenza might fare as sumptuously, and sleep as soundly there as a prince!"

The Count was easily persuaded, for he was anxious to get his daughter out of the night air; so in a little while the old carriage rattled and jingled into the great gateway of the inn.

The building did certainly in some measure answer to the muleteer's description. It was large enough for either castle or palace; built in a strong, but simple and almost rude style; with a great quantity of waste room. It had in fact been, in former times, a hunting-seat of one of the Italian princes. There was space enough within its walls and out-buildings to have accommodated a little army. A scanty household seemed now to people this dreary mansion. The faces that presented themselves on the arrival of the travellers were begrimed with dirt, and scowling in their expression. They all knew old Pietro, however, and gave him a welcome as he entered, singing and talking, and almost whooping, into the gateway.

The hostess of the inn waited, herself, on the Count and his daughter, to show them the apartments. They were conducted through a long gloomy corridor, and then through a suite of chambers opening into each other, with lofty ceilings, and great beams extending across them. Every thing, however, had a wretched, squalid look. The walls were damp and bare, excepting that here and there hung some great painting, large enough for a chapel, and blackened out of all distinction.

They chose two bedrooms, one within another; the inner one for the daughter. The bedsteads were massive and misshapen; but on examining the beds so vaunted by old Pietro they found them stuffed with fibres of hemp knotted in great lumps. The Count shrugged his shoulders, but there was no choice left.

The chilliness of the apartments crept to their bones; and they were glad to return to a common chamber or kind of hall, where was a fire burning in a huge cavern, miscalled a chimney. A quantity of green wood, just thrown on, puffed out volumes of smoke. The room corresponded to the rest of the mansion. The floor was paved and dirty. A great oaken table stood in the centre, immovable from its size and weight. The only thing that contradicted this prevalent air of indigence was the dress of the hostess. She was a slattern of course; yet her garments, though dirty and negligent, were of costly materials. She wore several rings of great value on her fingers, and jewels in her ears, and round her neck was a string of large pearls, to which was attached a sparkling crucifix. She had the remains of beauty, yet there was something in the expression of her countenance that inspired the young lady with singular aversion. She was officious and obsequious in her attentions, and both the Count and his daughter felt relieved, when she consigned them to the care of a dark, sullen-looking servant-maid, and went off to superintend the supper.

Caspar was indignant at the muleteer for having, either through negligence or design, subjected his master and mistress to such quarters; and vowed by his mustaches to have revenge on the old varlet the moment they were safe out from among the mountains. He kept up a continual quarrel with the sulky servant-maid, which only served to increase the sinister expression with which she regarded the travellers, from under her strong dark eyebrows.

As to the Count, he was a good-humored passive traveller. Perhaps real misfortunes had subdued his spirit, and rendered him tolerant of many of those petty evils which make prosperous men miserable. He drew a large broken arm-chair to the fireside for his daughter, and another for himself, and seizing an enormous pair of tongs, endeavored to rearrange the wood so as to produce a blaze. His efforts, however, were only repaid by thicker puffs of smoke, which almost overcame the good gentleman's patience. He would draw back, cast a look upon his delicate daughter, then upon the cheerless, squalid apartment, and, shrugging his shoulders, would give a fresh stir to the fire.

Of all the miseries of a comfortless inn, however, there is none greater than sulky attendance: the good Count for some time bore the smoke in silence, rather than address himself to the scowling servant-maid. At length he was compelled to beg for drier firewood. The woman retired muttering. On re-entering the room hastily, with an armful of fagots, her foot slipped; she fell, and striking her head against the corner of a chair, cut her temple severely.

The blow stunned her for a time, and the wound bled profusely. When she recovered, she found the Count's daughter administering to her wound, and binding it up with her own handkerchief. It was such an attention as any woman of ordinary feeling would have yielded; but perhaps there was something in the appearance of the lovely being who bent over her, or in the tones of her voice, that touched the heart of the woman, unused to be administered to by such hands. Certain it is, she was strongly affected. She caught the delicate hand of the Polonaise, and pressed it fervently to her lips:

"May San Francesco watch over you, Signora!" exclaimed she.

A new arrival broke the stillness of the inn. It was a Spanish princess with a numerous retinue. The court yard was in an uproar; the house in a bustle. The landlady hurried to attend such distinguished guests: and the poor Count and his daughter, and their supper, were for a moment forgotten. The veteran Caspar muttered Polish maledictions enough to agonize an Italian ear; but it was impossible to convince the hostess of the superiority of his old master and young mistress to the whole nobility of Spain.

The noise of the arrival had attracted the daughter to the window just as the new comers had alighted. A young cavalier sprang out of the carriage and handed out the Princess. The latter was a little shrivelled old lady, with a face of parchment and sparkling black eye; she was richly and gayly dressed, and walked with the assistance of a golden-headed cane as high as herself. The young man was tall and elegantly formed. The Count's daughter shrank back at the sight of him, though the deep frame of the window screened her from observation. She gave a heavy sigh as she closed the casement. What that sigh meant I cannot say. Perhaps it was at the contrast between the splendid equipage of the Princess, and the crazy rheumatic-looking old vehicle of her father, which stood hard by. Whatever might be the reason, the young lady closed the casement with a sigh. She returned to her chair,—a slight shivering passed over her delicate frame: she leaned her elbow on the arm of the chair, rested her pale cheek in the palm of her hand, and looked mournfully into the fire.

The Count thought she appeared paler than usual.

"Does anything ail thee, my child?" said he.

"Nothing, dear father!" replied she, laying her hand within his, and looking up smiling in his face; but as she said so, a treacherous tear rose suddenly to her eye, and she turned away her head.

"The air of the window has chilled thee," said the Count, fondly, "but a good night's rest will make all well again."

The supper table was at length laid, and the supper about to be served, when the hostess appeared, with her usual obsequiousness, apologizing for showing in the new-comers; but the night air was cold, and there was no other chamber in the inn with a fire in it. She had scarcely made the apology when the Princess entered, leaning on the arm of the elegant young man.

The Count immediately recognized her for a lady whom he had met frequently in society, both at Rome and Naples; and at whose conversaziones, in fact, he had been constantly invited. The cavalier, too, was her nephew and heir, who had been greatly admired in the gay circles both for his merits and prospects, and who had once been on a visit at the same time with his daughter and himself at the villa of a nobleman near Naples. Report had recently affianced him to a rich Spanish heiress.

The meeting was agreeable to both the Count and the Princess. The former was a gentleman of the old school, courteous in the extreme; the Princess had been a belle in her youth, and a woman of fashion all her life, and liked to be attended to.

The young man approached the daughter, and began something of a complimentary observation; but his manner was embarrassed, and his compliment ended in an indistinct murmur; while the daughter bowed without looking up, moved her lips without articulating a word, and sank again into her chair, where she sat gazing into the fire, with a thousand varying expressions passing over her countenance.

This singular greeting of the young people was not perceived by the old ones, who were occupied at the time with their own courteous salutations. It was arranged that they should sup together; and as the Princess travelled with her own cook, a very tolerable supper soon smoked upon the board. This, too, was assisted by choice wines, and liquors, and delicate confitures brought from one of her carriages; for she was a veteran epicure, and curious in her relish for the good things of this world. She was, in fact, a vivacious little old lady, who mingled the woman of dissipation with the devotee. She was actually on her way to Loretto to expiate a long life of gallantries and peccadilloes by a rich offering at the holy shrine. She was, to be sure, rather a luxurious penitent, and a contrast to the primitive pilgrims, with scrip and staff, and cockle-shell; but then it would be unreasonable to expect such self-denial from people of fashion; and there was not a doubt of the ample efficacy of the rich crucifixes, and golden vessels, and jeweled ornaments, which she was bearing to the treasury of the blessed Virgin.

The Princess and the Count chatted much during supper about the scenes and society in which they had mingled, and did not notice that they had all the conversation to themselves: the young people were silent and constrained. The daughter ate nothing in spite of the politeness of the Princess, who continually pressed her to taste of one or other of the delicacies. The Count shook his head.

"She is not well this evening," said he. "I thought she would have fainted just now as she was looking out of the window at your carriage on its arrival."

A crimson glow flushed to the very temples of the daughter; but she leaned over her plate, and her tresses cast a shade over her countenance.

When supper was over, they drew their chairs about the great fire-place. The flame and smoke had subsided, and a heap of glowing embers diffused a grateful warmth. A guitar, which had been brought from the Count's carriage, leaned against the wall; the Princess perceived it: "Can we not have a little music before parting for the night?" demanded she.

The Count was proud of his daughter's accomplishment, and joined in the request. The young man made an effort of politeness, and taking up the guitar, presented it, though in an embarrassed manner, to the fair musician. She would have declined it, but was too much confused to do so; indeed, she was so nervous and agitated, that she dared not trust her voice to make an excuse. She touched the instrument with a faltering hand, and, after preluding a little, accompanied herself in several Polish airs. Her father's eyes glistened as he sat gazing on her. Even the crusty Caspar lingered in the room, partly through a fondness for the music of his native country, but chiefly through his pride in the musician. Indeed the melody of the voice, and the delicacy of the touch, were enough to have charmed more fastidious ears. The little Princess nodded her head and tapped her hand to the music, though exceedingly out of time; while the nephew sat buried in profound contemplation of a black picture on the opposite wall.

"And now," said the Count, patting her cheek fondly, "one more favor. Let the Princess hear that little Spanish air you were so fond of. You can't think," added he, "what a proficiency she has made in your language; though she has been a sad girl and neglected it of late."

The color flushed the pale cheek of the daughter. She hesitated, murmured something; but with sudden effort, collected herself, struck the guitar boldly, and began. It was a Spanish romance, with something of love and melancholy in it. She gave the first stanza with great expression, for the tremulous melting tones of her voice went to the heart; but her articulation failed, her lips quivered, the song died away, and she burst into tears.

The Count folded her tenderly in his arms. "Thou art not well my child," said he, "and I am tasking thee cruelly. Retire to thy chamber, and God bless thee!" She bowed to the company without raising her eyes, and glided out of the room.

The Count shook his head as the door closed. "Something is the matter with that child," said he, "which I cannot divine. She has lost all health and spirits lately. She was always a tender flower, and I had much pains to rear her. Excuse a father's foolishness," continued he, "but I have seen much trouble in my family; and this poor girl is all that is now left to me; and she used to be so lively——"

"Maybe she's in love!" said the little Princess, with a shrewd nod of the head.

"Impossible!" replied the good Count artlessly. "She has never mentioned a word of such a thing to me."

How little did the worthy gentleman dream of the thousand cares, and griefs, and mighty love concerns which agitate a virgin heart, and which a timid girl scarcely breathes unto herself.

The nephew of the Princess rose abruptly and walked about the room.

When she found herself alone in her chamber, the feelings of the young lady, so long restrained, broke forth with violence. She opened the casement that the cool air might blow upon her throbbing temples. Perhaps there was some little pride or pique mingled with her emotions; though her gentle nature did not seem calculated to harbor any such angry inmate.

"He saw me weep!" said she, with a sudden mantling of the cheek, and a swelling of the throat,—"but no matter!—no matter!"

And so saying, she threw her white arms across the window frame, buried her face in them, and abandoned herself to an agony of tears. She remained lost in a reverie, until the sound of her father's and Caspar's voices in the adjoining room gave token that the party had retired for the night. The lights gleaming from window to window, showed that they were conducting the Princess to her apartments, which were in the opposite wing of the inn; and she distinctly saw the figure of the nephew as he passed one of the casements.

She heaved a deep heart-drawn sigh, and was about to close the lattice, when her attention was caught by words spoken below her window by two persons who had just turned an angle of the building.

"But what will become of the poor young lady?" said a voice, which she recognized for that of the servant-woman.

"Pooh! she must take her chance," was the reply from old Pietro.

"But cannot she be spared?" asked the other entreatingly; "she's so kind-hearted!"

"Cospetto! what has got into thee?" replied the other petulantly: "would you mar the whole business for the sake of a silly girl?" By this time they had got so far from the window that the Polonaise could hear nothing further. There was something in this fragment of conversation calculated to alarm. Did it relate to herself?—and if so, what was this impending danger from which it was entreated that she might be spared? She was several times on the point of tapping at her father's door, to tell him what she had heard, but she might have been mistaken; she might have heard indistinctly; the conversation might have alluded to some one else; at any rate, it was too indefinite to lead to any conclusion. While in this state of irresolution, she was startled by a low knock against the wainscot in a remote part of her gloomy chamber. On holding up the light, she beheld a small door there, which she had not before remarked. It was bolted on the inside. She advanced, and demanded who knocked, and was answered in a voice of the female domestic. On opening the door, the woman stood before it pale and agitated. She entered softly, laying her finger on her lips as in sign of caution and secrecy.

"Fly!" said she: "leave this house instantly, or you are lost!"

The young lady trembling with alarm, demanded an explanation.

"I have no time," replied the woman, "I dare not—I shall be missed if I linger here—but fly instantly, or you are lost."

"And leave my father?"

"Where is he?"

"In the adjoining chamber."

"Call him, then, but lose no time."

The young lady knocked at her father's door. He was not yet retired to bed. She hurried into his room, and told him of the fearful warnings she had received. The Count returned with her into the chamber, followed by Caspar. His questions soon drew the truth out of the embarrassed answers of the woman. The inn was beset by robbers. They were to be introduced after midnight, when the attendants of the Princess and the rest of the travellers were sleeping, and would be an easy prey.

"But we can barricade the inn, we can defend ourselves," said the Count.

"What! when the people of the inn are in league with the banditti?"

"How then are we to escape? Can we not order out the carriage and depart?"

"San Francesco! for what? to give the alarm that the plot is discovered? That would make the robbers desperate, and bring them on you at once. They have had notice of the rich booty in the inn, and will not easily let it escape them."

"But how else are we to get off?"

"There is a horse behind the inn," said the woman, "from which the man has just dismounted who has been to summon the aid of part of the band at a distance."

"One horse; and there are three of us!" said the Count.

"And the Spanish Princess!" cried the daughter anxiously—"How can she be extricated from the danger?"

"Diavolo! what is she to me?" said the woman in sudden passion. "It is *you* I come to save, and you will betray me, and we shall all be lost! Hark!" continued she, "I am called—I shall be discovered—one word more. This door leads by a staircase to the courtyard. Under the shed, in the rear of the yard, is a small door leading out to the fields. You will find a horse there; mount it; make a circuit under the shadow of a ridge of rocks that you will see; proceed cautiously and quietly until you cross a brook, and find yourself on the road just where there are three white crosses nailed against a tree; then put your horse to his speed, and make the best of your way to the village—but recollect, my life is in your hands—say nothing of what you have heard or seen, whatever may happen at this inn."

The woman hurried away. A short and agitated consultation took place between the Count, his daughter, and the veteran Caspar. The young lady seemed to have lost all apprehension for herself in her solicitude for the safety of the Princess. "To fly in selfish silence, and leave her to be massacred!"—A shuddering seized her at the very thought. The gallantry of the Count, too, revolted at the idea. He could not consent to turn his back upon a party of helpless travellers, and leave them in ignorance of the danger which hung over them.

"But what is to become of the young lady," said Caspar, "if the alarm is given, and the inn thrown in a tumult? What may happen to her in a chance-medley affray?"

Here the feelings of the father were aroused; he looked upon his lovely, helpless child, and trembled at the chance of her falling into the hands of ruffians.

The daughter, however, thought nothing of herself. "The Princess! the Princess!—only let the Princess know her danger." She was willing to share it with her.

At length Caspar interfered with the zeal of a faithful old servant. No time was to be lost—the first thing was to get the young lady out of danger. "Mount the horse," said he to the Count, "take her behind you, and fly! Make for the village, rouse the inhabitants, and send assistance. Leave me here to give the alarm to the Princess and her people. I am an old soldier, and I think we shall be able to stand siege until you send us aid."

The daughter would again have insisted on staying with the Princess—

"For what?" said old Caspar bluntly. "You could do no good—you would be in the way;—we should have to take care of you instead of ourselves."

There was no answering these objections; the Count seized his pistols, and taking his daughter under his arm, moved towards the staircase. The young lady paused, stepped back, and said, faltering with agitation—"There is a young cavalier with the Princess—her nephew—perhaps he may—"

"I understand you, Mademoiselle," replied old Caspar with a significant nod; "not a hair of his head shall suffer harm if I can help it."

The young lady blushed deeper than ever; she had not anticipated being so thoroughly understood by the blunt old servant.

"That is not what I mean," said she, hesitating. She would have added something, or made some explanation, but the moments were precious, and her father hurried her away.

They found their way through the courtyard to the small

postern gate where the horse stood, fastened to a ring in the wall. The Count mounted, took his daughter behind him, and they proceeded as quietly as possible in the direction which the woman had pointed out. Many a fearful and anxious look did the daughter cast back upon the gloomy pile; the lights which had feebly twinkled through the dusky casements were one by one disappearing, a sign that the inmates were gradually sinking to repose; and she trembled with impatience, lest succor should not arrive until that repose had been fatally interrupted.

They passed silently and safely along the skirts of the rocks, protected from observation by their overhanging shadows. They crossed the brook, and reached the place where three white crosses nailed against a tree told of some murder that had been committed there. Just as they had reached this ill-omened spot they beheld several men in the gloom coming down a craggy defile among the rocks.

"Who goes there?" exclaimed a voice. The Count put spurs to his horse, but one of the men sprang forward and seized the bridle. The horse started back, and reared, and had not the young lady clung to her father, she would have been thrown off. The Count leaned forward, put a pistol to the very head of the ruffian; and fired. The latter fell dead. The horse sprang forward. Two or three shots were fired which whistled by the fugitives, but only served to augment their speed. They reached the village in safety.

The whole place was soon roused; but such was the awe in which the banditti were held, that the inhabitants shrunk at the idea of encountering them. A desperate band had for some time infested that pass through the mountains, and the inn had long been suspected of being one of those horrible places where the unsuspicious wayfarer is entrapped and silently disposed of. The rich ornaments worn by the slattern hostess of the inn had excited heavy suspicions. Several instances had occurred of small parties of travellers disappearing mysteriously on that road, who, it was supposed at first, had been carried off by the robbers for the purpose of ransom, but who had never been heard of more. Such were the tales buzzed in the ears of the

Count by the villagers, as he endeavored to rouse them to the rescue of the Princess and her train from their perilous situation. The daughter seconded the exertions of her father with all the eloquence of prayers, and tears, and beauty. Every moment that elapsed increased her anxiety until it became agonizing. Fortunately there was a body of gendarmes resting at the village. A number of the young villagers volunteered to accompany them, and the little army was put in motion. The Count having deposited his daughter in a place of safety, was too much of the old soldier not to hasten to the scene of danger. It would be difficult to paint the anxious agitation of the young lady while awaiting the result.

The party arrived at the inn just in time. The robbers, finding their plans discovered, and the travellers prepared for their reception, had become open and furious in their attack. The Princess's party had barricaded themselves in one suite of apartments, and repulsed the robbers from the doors and windows. Caspar had shown the generalship of a veteran, and the nephew of the Princess, the dashing valor of a young soldier. Their ammunition, however, was nearly exhausted, and they would have found it difficult to hold out much longer, when a discharge from the musketry of the gendarmes gave them the joyful tidings of succor.

A fierce fight ensued, for part of the robbers were surprised in the inn, and had to stand siege in their turn; while their comrades made desperate attempts to relieve them from under cover of the neighboring rocks and thickets.

I cannot pretend to give a minute account of the fight, as I have heard it related in a variety of ways. Suffice it to say, the robbers were defeated; several of them killed, and several taken prisoners; which last, together with the people of the inn, were either executed or sent to the galleys.

I picked up these particulars in the course of a journey which I made some time after the event had taken place. I passed by the very inn. It was then dismantled, excepting one wing, in which a body of gendarmes was stationed. They pointed out to me the shot-holes in the window-frames, the walls, and the panels of the doors. There were a number of withered limbs dangling from the branches of a neighboring tree, and blackening in the air, which I was told were the limbs of the robbers who had been slain, and the culprits who had been executed. The whole place had a dismal, wild, forlorn look.

"Were any of the Princess's party killed?" inquired the Englishman.

"As far as I can recollect, there were two or three."

"Not the nephew, I trust?" said the fair Venetian.

"Oh no: he hastened with the Count to relieve the anxiety of the daughter by the assurances of victory. The young lady had been sustained through the interval of suspense by the very intensity of her feelings. The moment she saw her father returning in safety, accompanied by the nephew of the Princess, she uttered a cry of rapture, and fainted. Happily, however, she soon recovered, and what is more, was married shortly afterwards to the young cavalier, and the whole party accompanied the old Princess in her pilgrimage to Loretto, where her votive offerings may still be seen in the treasury of the Santa Casa."

From THE LIFE AND VOYAGES OF CHRISTOPHER COLUMBUS [54]

VOL. I, BK. III, CHAP. IV.——CONTINUATION OF THE VOYAGE——DISCOVERY OF LAND

[1492]

The situation of Columbus was daily becoming more and more critical. In proportion as he approached the regions where he expected to find land, the impatience of his crews augmented. The favorable signs which increased his confidence, were derided by them as delusive; and there was danger of their rebelling, and obliging him to turn back, when on the point of realizing the object of all his labors. They beheld themselves with dismay still wafted onward, over the boundless wastes of what appeared to them a mere watery desert, surrounding the habitable world. What was to become of them should their provisions fail? Their ships were too weak and defective even for the great voyage they had already made, but if they were still to press forward, adding at every moment to the immense expanse behind them, how should they ever be able to return, having no intervening port where they might victual and refit?

In this way they fed each other's discontents, gathering together in little knots, and fomenting a spirit of mutinous opposition: and when we consider the natural fire of the Spanish temperament and its impatience of control; and that a great part of these men were sailing on compulsion; we cannot wonder that there was imminent danger of their breaking forth into open rebellion and compelling Columbus to turn back. In their secret conferences they exclaimed against him as a desperado, bent, in a mad fantasy, upon doing something extravagant to render himself notorious. What were their sufferings and dangers to one evidently content to sacrifice his own life for the chance of distinction? What obligations bound them to continue on with him; or when were the terms of their agreement to be considered as fulfilled? They had already penetrated unknown seas, untraversed by a sail, far beyond where man had ever before ventured. They had done enough to gain themselves a character for courage and hardihood in undertaking such an enterprise and persisting in it so far. How much further were they to go in quest of a merely conjectured land? Were they to sail on until they perished, or until all return became impossible? In such case they would be the authors of their own destruction.

On the other hand, should they consult their safety, and turn back before too late, who would blame them? Any complaints made by Columbus would be of no weight; he was a foreigner without friends or influence; his schemes had been condemned by the learned, and discountenanced by people of all ranks. He had no party to uphold him, and a host of opponents whose pride of opinion would be gratified by his failure. Or, as an effectual means of preventing his complaints, they might throw him into the sea, and give out that he had fallen overboard while busy with his instruments contemplating the stars; a report which no one would have either the inclination or the means to controvert.[55]

Columbus was not ignorant of the mutinous disposition of his crew; but he still maintained a serene and steady countenance, soothing some with gentle words, endeavoring to stimulate the pride or avarice of others, and openly menacing the refractory with signal punishment, should they do any thing to impede the voyage.

On the 25th of September, the wind again became favorable, and they were able to resume their course directly to the west. The airs being light, and the sea calm, the vessels sailed near to each other, and Columbus had much conversation with Martin Alonzo Pinzon on the subject of a chart, which the former had sent three days before on board of the Pinta. Pinzon thought that, according to the indications of the map, they ought to be in the neighborhood of Cipango, and the other islands which the admiral had therein delineated. Columbus partly entertained the same idea, but thought it possible that the ships might have been borne out of their track by the prevalent currents, or that they had not come so far as the pilots had reckoned. He desired that the chart might be returned, and Pinzon tying it to the end of a cord, flung it on board to him. While Columbus, his pilot, and several of his experienced mariners were studying the map, and endeavoring to make out from it their actual position, they heard a shout from the Pinta, and looking up, beheld Martin Alonzo Pinzon mounted on the stern of his vessel, crying "Land! land! Señor, I claim my reward!" He pointed at the same time to the southwest, where there was indeed an appearance of land at about twenty-five leagues' distance. Upon this Columbus threw himself on his knees and returned thanks to God; and Martin Alonzo repeated the *Gloria in excelsis*, in which he was joined by his own crew and that of the admiral.[56]

The seamen now mounted to the mast-head or climbed about the rigging, straining their eyes in the direction pointed out. The conviction became so general of land in that quarter, and the joy of the people so ungovernable, that Columbus found it necessary to vary from his usual course, and stand all night to the southwest. The morning light, however, put an end to all their hopes, as to a dream. The fancied land proved to be nothing but an evening cloud, and had vanished in the night. With dejected hearts they once more resumed their western course, from which Columbus would never have varied, but in compliance with their clamorous wishes.

For several days they continued on with the same propitious breeze, tranquil sea, and mild, delightful weather. The water was so calm that the sailors amused themselves with swimming about the vessel. Dolphins began to abound, and flying fish, darting into the air, fell upon the decks. The continued signs of land diverted the attention of the crews, and insensibly beguiled them onward.

On the 1st of October, according to the reckoning of the pilot of the admiral's ship, they had come five hundred and eighty leagues west since leaving the Canary islands. The

reckoning which Columbus showed the crew, was five hundred
and eighty-four, but the reckoning which he kept privately, was
seven hundred and seven.[57] On the following day, the weeds
floated from east to west; and on the third day no birds were to
be seen.

The crews now began to fear that they had passed between
islands, from one to the other of which the birds had been flying. Columbus had also some doubts of the kind, but refused
to alter his westward course. The people again uttered murmurs and menaces; but on the following day they were visited
by such flights of birds, and the various indications of land became so numerous, that from a state of despondency they
passed to one of confident expectation.

Eager to obtain the promised pension, the seamen were continually giving the cry of land, on the least appearance of the
kind. To put a stop to these false alarms, which produced continual disappointments, Columbus declared that should any
one give such notice, and land not be discovered within three
days afterwards, he should thenceforth forfeit all claim to the
reward.

On the evening of the 6th of October, Martin Alonzo Pinzon
began to lose confidence in their present course, and proposed
that they should stand more to the southward. Columbus,
however, still persisted in steering directly west.[58] Observing
this difference of opinion in a person so important in his
squadron as Pinzon, and fearing that chance or design might
scatter the ships, he ordered that, should either of the caravels
be separated from him, it should stand to the west, and endeavor
as soon as possible to join company again: he directed, also,
that the vessels should keep near to him at sunrise and sunset,
as at these times the state of the atmosphere is most favorable
to the discovery of distant land.

On the morning of the 7th of October, at sunrise, several
of the admiral's crew thought they beheld land in the west, but
so indistinctly that no one ventured to proclaim it, lest he should
be mistaken, and forfeit all chance of the reward: the Niña,
however, being a good sailer, pressed forward to ascertain the

fact. In a little while a flag was hoisted at her mast-head, and a gun discharged, being the preconcerted signals for land. New joy was awakened throughout the little squadron, and every eye was turned to the west. As they advanced, however, their cloud-built hopes faded away, and before evening the fancied land had again melted into air.[59]

The crews now sank into a degree of dejection proportioned to their recent excitement; but new circumstances occurred to arouse them. Columbus, having observed great flights of small field-birds going towards the southwest, concluded they must be secure of some neighboring land, where they would find food and a resting-place. He knew the importance which the Portuguese voyagers attached to the flight of birds, by following which they had discovered most of their islands. He had now come seven hundred and fifty leagues, the distance at which he had computed to find the island of Cipango; as there was no appearance of it, he might have missed it through some mistake in the latitude. He determined, therefore, on the evening of the 7th of October to alter his course to the west-southwest, the direction in which the birds generally flew, and continue that direction for at least two days. After all, it was no great deviation from his main course, and would meet the wishes of the Pinzons, as well as be inspiriting to his followers generally.

For three days they stood in this direction, and the further they went the more frequent and encouraging were the signs of land. Flights of small birds of various colors, some of them such as sing in the fields, came flying about the ships, and then continued towards the southwest, and others were heard also flying by in the night. Tunny fish played about the smooth sea, and a heron, a pelican, and a duck, were seen, all bound in the same direction. The herbage which floated by was fresh and green, as if recently from land, and the air, Columbus observes, was sweet and fragrant as April breezes in Seville.

All these, however, were regarded by the crews as so many delusions beguiling them on to destruction; and when on the evening of the third day they beheld the sun go down upon a shoreless ocean, they broke forth into turbulent clamor. They exclaimed against this obstinacy in tempting fate by continuing on into a boundless sea. They insisted upon turning homeward, and abandoning the voyage as hopeless. Columbus endeavored to pacify them by gentle words and promises of large rewards; but finding that they only increased in clamor, he assumed a decided tone. He told them it was useless to murmur; the expedition had been sent by the sovereigns to seek the Indies, and, happen what might, he was determined to persevere, until, by the blessing of God, he should accomplish the enterprise.[60]

Columbus was now at open defiance with his crew, and his situation became desperate. Fortunately the manifestations of the vicinity of land were such on the following day as no longer to admit a doubt. Beside a quantity of fresh weeds, such as grow in rivers, they saw a green fish of a kind which keeps about rocks; then a branch of thorn with berries on it, and recently separated from the tree, floated by them; then they picked up a reed, a small board, and, above all, a staff artificially carved. All gloom and mutiny now gave way to sanguine expectation; and throughout the day each one was eagerly on the watch, in hopes of being the first to discover the long-sought-for land.

In the evening, when, according to invariable custom on board of the admiral's ship, the mariners had sung the *salve regina*, or vesper hymn to the Virgin, he made an impressive address to his crew. He pointed out the goodness of God in thus conducting them by soft and favoring breezes across a tranquil ocean, cheering their hopes continually with fresh signs, increasing as their fears augmented, and thus leading and guiding them to a promised land. He now reminded them of the orders he had given on leaving the Canaries, that, after sailing westward seven hundred leagues, they should not make sail after midnight. Present appearances authorized such a precaution. He thought it probable they would make land that very night; he ordered, therefore, a vigilant lookout to be kept from the forecastle, promising to whomsoever should make the discovery, a doublet of velvet, in addition to the pension to be given by the sovereigns.[61]

The breeze had been fresh all day, with more sea than usual, and they had made great progress. At sunset they had stood again to the west, and were ploughing the waves at a rapid rate, the Pinta keeping the lead, from her superior sailing. The greatest animation prevailed throughout the ships; not an eye was closed that night. As the evening darkened, Columbus took his station on the top of the castle or cabin on the high poop of his vessel, ranging his eye along the dusky horizon, and maintaining an intense and unremitting watch. About ten o'clock, he thought he beheld a light glimmering at a great distance. Fearing his eager hopes might deceive him, he called to Pedro Gutierrez, gentleman of the king's bed-chamber, and inquired whether he saw such a light; the latter replied in the affirmative. Doubtful whether it might not yet be some delusion of the fancy, Columbus called Rodrigo Sanchez of Segovia, and made the same inquiry. By the time the latter had ascended the round-house, the light had disappeared. They saw it once or twice afterwards in sudden and passing gleams; as if it were a torch in the bark of a fisherman, rising and sinking with the waves; or in the hand of some person on shore, borne up and down as he walked from house to house. So transient and uncertain were these gleams, that few attached any importance to them; Columbus, however, considered them as certain signs of land, and, moreover, that the land was inhabited.

They continued their course until two in the morning, when a gun from the Pinta gave the joyful signal of land. It was first descried by a mariner named Rodrigo de Triana; but the reward was afterwards adjudged to the admiral, for having previously perceived the light. The land was now clearly seen about two leagues distant, whereupon they took in sail, and laid to, waiting impatiently for the dawn.

The thoughts and feelings of Columbus in this little space of time must have been tumultuous and intense. At length in spite of every difficulty and danger, he had accomplished his object. The great mystery of the ocean was revealed; his theory, which had been the scoff of sages, was triumphantly established; he had secured to himself a glory durable as the world itself.

It is difficult to conceive the feelings of such a man, at such a moment; or the conjectures which must have thronged upon his mind, as to the land before him, covered with darkness. That it was fruitful, was evident from the vegetables which floated from its shores. He thought, too, that he perceived the fragrance of aromatic groves. The moving light he had beheld proved it the residence of man. But what were its inhabitants? Were they like those of the other parts of the globe; or were they some strange and monstrous race, such as the imagination was prone in those times to give to all remote and unknown regions? Had he come upon some wild island far in the Indian sea; or was this the famed Cipango itself, the object of his golden fancies? A thousand speculations of the kind must have swarmed upon him, as, with his anxious crews, he waited for the night to pass away; wondering whether the morning light would reveal a savage wilderness, or dawn upon spicy groves, and glittering fanes, and gilded cities, and all the splendor of oriental civilization.

From A CHRONICLE OF THE CONQUEST
OF GRANADA

CHAPTER XCVI. FAMINE AND DISCORD
IN THE CITY

The besieged city now began to suffer the distress of famine. Its supplies were all cut off; a cavalgada of flocks and herds, and mules laden with money, coming to the relief of the city from the mountains of the Alpuxarras, was taken by the marques of Cadiz, and led in triumph to the camp, in sight of the suffering Moors. Autumn arrived; but the harvests had been swept from the face of the country; a rigorous winter was approaching, and the city was almost destitute of provisions. The people sank into deep despondency. They called to mind all that had been predicted by astrologers at the birth of their ill-starred sovereign, and all that had been foretold of the fate of Granada at the time of the capture of Zahara.

Boabdil was alarmed by the gathering dangers from without, and by the clamors of his starving people. He summoned a council, composed of the principal officers of the army, the alcaydes of the fortresses, the xequis or sages of the city, and the alfaquis or doctors of the faith. They assembled in the great hall of audience of the Alhambra, and despair was painted in their countenances. Boabdil demanded of them, what was to be done in the present extremity; and their answer was, "Surrender." The venerable Abul Cazim, governor of the city, represented its unhappy state: "Our granaries are nearly exhausted, and no further supplies are to be expected. The provender for the war-horses is required as sustenance for the soldiery; the very horses themselves are killed for food; of seven thousand steeds which once could be sent into the field, three hundred only remain. Our city contains two hundred thousand inhabitants, old and young, with each a mouth that calls piteously for bread."

The xequis and principal citizens declared that the people could no longer sustain the labors and sufferings of a defence: "And of what avail is our defence," said they, "when the enemy is determined to persist in the siege?—what alternative remains, but to surrender or to die?"

The heart of Boabdil was touched by this appeal, and he maintained a gloomy silence. He had cherished some faint hope of relief from the soldan of Egypt or the Barbary powers; but it was now at an end; even if such assistance were to be sent, he had no longer a seaport where it might debark. The counsellors saw that the resolution of the king was shaken, and they united their voices in urging him to capitulate.

Muza alone rose in opposition: "It is yet too early," said he, "to talk of a surrender. Our means are not exhausted; we have yet one source of strength remaining, terrible in its effects, and which often has achieved the most signal victories—it is our despair. Let us rouse the mass of the people—let us put weapons in their hands—let us fight the enemy to the very utmost, until we rush upon the points of their lances. I am ready to lead the way into the thickest of their squadrons; and much rather would I be numbered among those who fell in the defence of Granada, than of those who survived to capitulate for her surrender!"

The words of Muza were without effect, for they were addressed to broken-spirited and heartless men, or men, perhaps, to whom sad experience had taught discretion. They were arrived at that state of public depression, when heroes and heroism are no longer regarded, and when old men and their counsels rise into importance. Boabdil el Chico yielded to the general voice; it was determined to capitulate with the Christian sovereigns; and the venerable Abul Cazim was sent forth to the camp, empowered to treat for terms.

CHAPTER XCVII. CAPITULATION OF GRANADA

The old governor Abul Cazim was received with great courtesy by Ferdinand and Isabella, who being informed of the purport of his embassy, granted the besieged a truce of sixty days from the 5th of October, and appointed Gonsalvo of Cordova, and Fernando de Zafra, the secretary of the king, to treat about the terms of surrender with such commissioners as might be named by Boabdil. The latter on his part named Abul Cazim, Aben Comixa the vizier, and the grand cadi. As a pledge of good faith, Boabdil gave his son in hostage, who was taken to Moclin, where he was treated with the greatest respect and attention by the good count de Tendilla, as general of the frontier.

The commissioners on both parts, held repeated conferences in secret in the dead of the night, at the village of Churriana; those who first arrived at the place of meeting giving notice to the others by signal-fires, or by means of spies. After many debates and much difficulty, the capitulation was signed on the 25th of November. According to this, the city was to be delivered up, with all its gates, towers and fortresses, within sixty days.

All Christian captives should be liberated, without ransom.

Boabdil and his principal cavaliers should perform the act of homage, and take an oath of fealty to the Castilian crown.

The Moors of Granada should become subjects of the Spanish sovereigns, retaining their possessions, their arms and horses, and yielding up nothing but their artillery. They should be protected in the exercise of their religion, and governed by their own laws, administered by cadis of their own faith, under governors appointed by the sovereigns. They should be exempted from tribute for three years, after which term they should pay the same that they had been accustomed to render to their native monarchs.

Those who chose to depart for Africa within three years, should be provided with a passage for themselves and their effects, free of charge, from whatever port they should prefer.

For the fulfilment of these articles, five hundred hostages from the principal families were required, previous to the surrender, who should be treated with great respect and distinction by the Christians, and subsequently restored. The son of the king of Granada, and all other hostages in possession of the Castilian sovereigns, were to be restored at the same time.

Such are the main articles affecting the public weal, which were agreed upon after much discussion, by the mixed commission. There were other articles, however, secretly arranged, which concerned the royal family. These secured to Boabdil, to his wife Morayma, his mother Ayxa, his brothers, and to Zoraya, the widow of Muley Abul Hassan, all the landed possessions, houses, mills, baths, and other hereditaments which formed the royal patrimony, with the power of selling them, personally or by agent, at any and all times. To Boabdil was secured, moreover, his wealthy estates, both in and out of Granada, and to him and his descendants in. perpetuity, the lordships of various towns and lands and fertile valleys in the Alpuxarras, forming a petty sovereignty. In addition to all which it was stipulated, that, on the day of surrender, he should receive thirty thousand castellanos of gold.[63]

The conditions of surrender being finally agreed upon by the commissioners, Abul Cazim proceeded to the royal camp at Santa Fé, where they were signed by Ferdinand and Isabella; he then returned to Granada, accompanied by Fernando de Zafra, the royal secretary, to have the same ratified also by the Moorish king. Boabdil assembled his council, and with a dejected countenance laid before it the articles of capitulation as the best that could be obtained from the besieging foe.

When the members of the council found the awful moment arrived when they were to sign and seal the perdition of their empire, and blot themselves out as a nation, all firmness deserted them, and many gave way to tears. Muza alone retained an unaltered mien: "Leave, Señors," cried he, "this idle lamentation to helpless women and children: we are men—we have hearts, not to shed tender tears, but drops of blood. I see the spirit of the people so cast down, that it is impossible to save the kingdom. Yet there still remains an alternative for noble minds— a glorious death! Let us die defending our liberty, and avenging the woes of Granada. Our mother earth will receive her children into her bosom, safe from the chains and oppressions of the conqueror; or, should any fail a sepulchre to hide his remains, he will not want a sky to cover him. Allah forbid it should be said the nobles of Granada feared to die in her defence!"

Muza ceased to speak, and a dead silence reigned in the assembly. Boabdil looked anxiously round, and scanned every face; but he read in all the anxiety of care-worn men, in whose hearts enthusiasm was dead, and who had grown callous to every chivalrous appeal. "Allah Achbar!" exclaimed he; "there is no God but God, and Mahomet is his prophet! We have no longer forces in the city and the kingdom to resist our powerful enemies. It is in vain to struggle against the will of Heaven. Too surely was it written in the book of fate, that I should be unfortunate, and the kingdom expire under my rule."

"Allah Achbar!" echoed the viziers and alfaquis; "the will of God be done!" So they all agreed with the king, that these evils were pre-ordained; that it was hopeless to contend with them; and that the terms offered by the Castilian monarchs were as favorable as could be expected.

When Muza heard them assent to the treaty of surrender, he rose in violent indignation: "Do not deceive yourselves," cried he, "nor think the Christians will be faithful to their promises, or their king as magnanimous in conquest as he has been victorious in war. Death is the least we have to fear. It is the plundering and sacking of our city, the profanation of our mosques, the ruin of our homes, the violation of our wives and daughters, cruel oppression, bigoted intolerance, whips and chains, the dungeon, the fagot, and the stake—such are the miseries and indignities we shall see and suffer; at least, those grovelling souls will see and suffer them, who now shrink from an honorable death. For my part, by Allah, I will never witness them!"

With these words he left the council-chamber, and passed gloomily through the Court of Lions, and the outer halls of the Alhambra, without deigning to speak to the obsequious courtiers who attended in them. He repaired to his dwelling, armed himself at all points, mounted his favorite war-horse, and, issuing from the city by the gate of Elvira, was never seen or heard of more.[64]

CHAPTER XCVIII. COMMOTIONS IN GRANADA

The capitulation for the surrender of Granada was signed on the 25th of November, 1491, and produced a sudden cessation of those hostilities which had raged for so many years. Christian and Moor might now be seen mingling courteously on the banks of the Xenel and the Darro, where to have met a few days previous would have produced a scene of sanguinary contest. Still, as the Moors might be suddenly roused to defence, if, within the allotted term of sixty days, succors should arrive from abroad; and as they were at all times a rash, inflammable people, the wary Ferdinand maintained a vigilant watch upon the city, and permitted no supplies of any kind to enter. His garrisons in the sea-ports, and his cruisers in the Straits of Gibraltar, were ordered likewise to guard against any relief from the grand soldan of Egypt, or the princes of Barbary. There was no need of such precautions. Those powers were either too much engrossed by their own wars, or too much daunted by the success of the Spanish arms, to interfere in a desperate cause; and the unfortunate Moors of Granada were abandoned to their fate.

The month of December had nearly passed away; the famine became extreme, and there was no hope of any favorable event within the term specified in the capitulation. Boabdil saw, that to hold out to the end of the allotted time would but be to protract the miseries of his people. With the consent of his council, he determined to surrender the city on the sixth of January. He accordingly sent his grand vizier, Yusef Aben Comixa, to King Ferdinand, to make known his intention; bearing him, at the same time, a present of a magnificent scimitar, and two Arabian steeds superbly caparisoned.

The unfortunate Boabdil was doomed to meet with trouble, to the end of his career. The very next day, the santon or dervise, Hamet Aben Zarrax, the same who had uttered prophecies and excited commotions on former occasions, suddenly made his appearance. Whence he came no one knew; it was rumored that he had been in the mountains of the Alpuxarras, and on the coast of Barbary, endeavoring to rouse the Moslems to the relief of Granada. He was reduced to a skeleton; his eyes glowed like coals in their sockets, and his speech was little better than frantic raving. He harangued the populace, in the streets and squares; inveighed against the capitulation, denounced the king and nobles as Moslems only in name, and called upon the people to sally forth against the unbelievers, for that Allah had decreed them a signal victory.

Upwards of twenty thousand of the populace seized their arms, and paraded the streets with shouts and outcries. The shops and houses were shut up; the king himself did not dare to venture forth, but remained a kind of prisoner in the Alhambra.

The turbulent multitude continued roaming and shouting and howling about the city, during the day and a part of the night. Hunger, and a wintry tempest, tamed their frenzy; and when morning came, the enthusiast who had led them on had disappeared. Whether he had been disposed of by the emissaries of the king, or by the leading men of the city, is not known: his disappearance remains a mystery.[65]

Boabdil now issued from the Alhambra, attended by his principal nobles, and harangued the populace. He set forth the necessity of complying with the capitulation, from the famine that reigned in the city, the futility of defence, and from the hostages having already been delivered into the hands of the besiegers.

In the dejection of his spirits, the unfortunate Boabdil attributed to himself the miseries of the country. "It was my crime in ascending the throne in rebellion against my father," said he mournfully, "which has brought these woes upon the kingdom; but Allah has grievously visited my sins upon my head. For your sake, my people, I have now made this treaty, to protect you from the sword, your little ones from famine, your wives and daughters from outrage; and to secure you in the enjoyment of your properties, your liberties, your laws, and your religion, under a sovereign of happier destinies than the ill-starred Boabdil."

The versatile population were touched by the humility of their sovereign—they agreed to adhere to the capitulation, and there was even a faint shout of "Long live Boabdil the unfortunate!" and they all returned to their homes in perfect tranquillity.

Boabdil immediately sent missives to king Ferdinand, apprising him of these events, and of his fears lest further delay should produce new tumults. The vizier Yusef Aben Comixa was again the agent between the monarchs. He was received with unusual courtesy and attention by Ferdinand and Isabella, and it was arranged between them that the surrender should take place on the second day of January instead of the sixth. A new difficulty now arose in regard to the ceremonial of surrender. The haughty Ayxa la Horra, whose pride rose with the decline of her fortunes, declared that, as sultana mother, she would never consent that her son should stoop to the humiliation of kissing the hand of his conquerors, and, unless this part of the ceremonial were modified, she would find means to resist a surrender accompanied by such indignities.

Aben Comixa was sorely troubled by this opposition. He knew the high spirit of the indomitable Ayxa, and her influence over her less heroic son, and wrote an urgent letter on the subject to his friend, the count de Tendilla. The latter imparted the circumstance to the Christian sovereigns; a council was called on the matter. Spanish pride and etiquette were obliged to bend in some degree to the haughty spirit of a woman. It was agreed that Boabdil should sally forth on horseback, that on approaching the Spanish sovereigns he should make a slight movement as if about to draw his foot from the stirrup and dismount, but would be prevented from doing so by Ferdinand, who should treat him with a respect due to his dignity and elevated birth. The count de Tendilla dispatched a messenger with this arrangement; and the haughty scruples of Ayxa la Horra were satisfied.[66]

CHAPTER XCIX.   SURRENDER OF GRANADA

The night preceding the surrender was a night of doleful lamentings, within the walls of the Alhambra; for the household of Boabdil were preparing to take a last farewell of that delightful abode. All the royal treasures, and most precious effects, were hastily packed upon mules; the beautiful apartments were despoiled, with tears and wailings, by their own inhabitants. Before the dawn of day, a mournful cavalcade moved obscurely out of a postern-gate of the Alhambra, and departed through one of the most retired quarters of the city. It was composed of the family of the unfortunate Boabdil, which he sent off thus privately, that they might not be exposed to the eyes of scoffers, or the exultation of the enemy. The mother of Boabdil, the sultana Ayxa la Horra, rode on in silence, with dejected yet dignified demeanor; but his wife Zorayma, and all the females of his household, gave way to loud lamentations, as they looked back upon their favorite abode, now a mass of gloomy towers behind them. They were attended by the ancient domestics of the household, and by a small guard of veteran Moors, loyally attached to the fallen monarch, and who would have sold their lives dearly in defence of his family. The city was yet buried in sleep, as they passed through its silent streets. The guards at the gate shed tears, as they opened it for their departure. They paused not, but proceeded along the banks of the Xenel on the road that leads to the Alpuxarras, until they arrived at a hamlet at some distance from the city, where they halted, and waited until they should be joined by king Boabdil.

The night which had passed so gloomily in the sumptuous halls of the Alhambra, had been one of joyful anticipation in the Christian camp. In the evening proclamation had been made that Granada was to be surrendered on the following day, and the troops were all ordered to assemble at an early hour under their several banners. The cavaliers, pages, and esquires were all charged to array themselves in their richest and most splendid style, for the occasion; and even the royal family determined to lay by the mourning they had recently assumed for the sudden death of the prince of Portugal, the husband of the princess Isabella. In a clause of the capitulation it had been stipulated that the troops destined to take possession, should not traverse the city, but should ascend to the Alhambra by a road opened for the purpose outside of the walls. This was to spare the feelings of the afflicted inhabitants, and to prevent any angry collision between them and their conquerors. So rigorous was Ferdinand in enforcing this precaution, that the soldiers were prohibited under pain of death from leaving the ranks to enter into the city.

The rising sun had scarce shed his rosy beams upon the snowy summits of the Sierra Nevada, when three signal guns boomed heavily from the lofty fortress of the Alhambra. It was the concerted sign that all was ready for the surrender. The Christian army forthwith poured out of the city, or rather camp of Santa Fé, and advanced across the vega. The king and queen, with the prince and princess, the dignitaries and ladies of the court, took the lead, accompanied by the different orders of monks and friars, and surrounded by the royal guards splendidly arrayed. The procession moved slowly forward, and paused at the village of Armilla, at the distance of half a league from the city.

In the mean time, the grand cardinal of Spain, Don Pedro Gonzalez de Mendoza, escorted by three thousand foot and a troop of cavalry, and accompanied by the commander Don Gutierrez de Cardenas, and a number of prelates and hidalgos, crossed the Xenel and proceeded in the advance, to ascend to the Alhambra and take possession of that royal palace and fortress. The road which had been opened for the purpose led by the Puerta de los Molinos, or gate of mills, up a defile to the esplanade on the summit of the Hill of Martyrs. At the approach of this detachment, the Moorish king sallied forth from a postern gate of the Alhambra, having left his vizier Yusef Aben Comixa to deliver up the palace. The gate by which he sallied passed through a lofty tower of the outer wall, called the tower of the seven floors (de los siete suelos). He was accompanied by fifty cavaliers, and approached the grand cardinal on foot. The latter immediately alighted, and advanced to meet him with the utmost respect. They stepped aside a few paces, and held a brief conversation in an under tone, when Boabdil, raising his voice, exclaimed, "Go, Señor, and take possession of those fortresses in the name of the powerful sovereigns, to whom God has been pleased to deliver them in reward of their great merits, and in punishment of the sins of the Moors." The grand cardinal sought to console him in his reverses, and offered him the use of his own tent during any time he might sojourn in the camp. Boabdil thanked him for the courteous offer, adding some words of melancholy import, and then taking leave of him gracefully, passed mournfully on to meet the Catholic sovereigns, descending to the vega by the same road by which the cardinal had come. The latter, with the prelates and cavaliers who attended him, entered the Alhambra, the gates of which were thrown wide open by the alcayde Aben Comixa. At the same time the Moorish guards yielded up their arms, and the towers and battlements were taken possession of by the Christian troops.

While these transactions were passing in the Alhambra and its vicinity, the sovereigns remained with their retinue and guards near the village of Armilla, their eyes fixed on the towers of the royal fortress, watching for the appointed signal of possession. The time that had elapsed since the departure of the detachment seemed to them more than necessary for the purpose, and the anxious mind of Ferdinand began to entertain doubts of some commotion in the city. At length they saw the silver cross, the great standard of this crusade, elevated on the Torre de la Vela, or Great Watch-Tower, and sparkling in the sunbeams. This was done by Hernando de Talavera, bishop of Avila. Beside it was planted the pennon of the glorious apostle St. James, and a great shout of "Santiago! Santiago!" rose throughout the army. Lastly was reared the royal standard by the king of arms, with the shout of "Castile! Castile! For king Ferdinand and queen Isabella!" The words were echoed by the whole army, with acclamations that resounded across the vega. At sight of these signals of possession, the sovereigns sank upon their knees, giving thanks to God for this great triumph; the whole assembled host followed their example, and the choristers of the royal chapel broke forth into the solemn anthem of *"Te Deum laudamus."*

‹ The king now advanced with a splendid escort of cavalry and the sound of trumpets, until he came to a small mosque near the banks of the Xenel, and not far from the foot of the Hill of Martyrs, which edifice remains to the present day consecrated as the hermitage of St. Sebastian. Here he beheld the unfortunate king of Granada approaching on horseback, at the head of his slender retinue. Boabdil, as he drew near made a movement to dismount, but, as had previously been concerted, Ferdinand prevented him. He then offered to kiss the king's hand, which according to arrangement was likewise declined, whereupon he leaned forward and kissed the king's right arm; at the same time he delivered the keys of the city with an air of mingled melancholy and resignation: "These keys," said he, "are the last relics of the Arabian empire in Spain: thine, oh king, are our trophies, our kingdom, and our person. Such is the will of God! Receive them with the clemency thou hast promised, and which we look for at thy hands."[67]

King Ferdinand restrained his exultation into an air of serene magnanimity. "Doubt not our promises," replied he, "nor that thou shalt regain from our friendship the prosperity of which the fortune of war has deprived thee."

Being informed that Don Inigo Lopez de Mendoza, the good count of Tendilla, was to be governor of the city, Boabdil drew from his finger a gold ring set with a precious stone, and presented it to the count. "With this ring," said he, "Granada has been governed; take it and govern with it, and God make you more fortunate than I."[68]

He then proceeded to the village of Armilla, where the queen Isabella remained with her escort and attendants. The queen, like her husband, declined all act of homage, and received him with her accustomed grace and benignity. She at the same time delivered to him his son, who had been held as a hostage for the fulfilment of the capitulation. Boabdil pressed his child to his bosom with tender emotion, and they seemed mutually endeared to each other by their misfortunes.[69]

Having rejoined his family, the unfortunate Boabdil continued on towards the Alpuxarras, that he might not behold the entrance of the Christians into his capital. His devoted band of cavaliers followed him in gloomy silence; but heavy sighs burst from their bosoms, as shouts of joy and strains of triumphant music were borne on the breeze from the victorious army.

Having rejoined his family, Boabdil set forward with a heavy heart for his allotted residence in the valley of Purchena. At two leagues' distance, the cavalcade, winding into the skirts of the Alpuxarras, ascended an eminence commanding the last view of Granada. As they arrived at this spot, the Moors paused involuntarily, to take a farewell gaze at their beloved city, which a few steps more would shut from their sight for ever. Never had it appeared so lovely in their eyes. The sunshine, so bright in that transparent climate, lit up each tower and minaret, and rested gloriously upon the crowning battlements of the Alhambra; while the vega spread its enamelled bosom of verdure below, glistening with the silver windings of the Xenel. The Moorish cavaliers gazed with a silent agony of tenderness and grief upon that delicious abode, the scene of their loves and pleasures. While they yet looked, a light cloud of smoke burst forth from the citadel, and presently a peal of artillery, faintly heard, told that the city was taken possession of, and the throne of the Moslem kings was lost for ever. The heart of Boabdil, softened by misfortunes and overcharged with grief, could no longer contain itself: "Allah Achbar! God is great!" said he; but the words of resignation died upon his lips, and he burst into tears.

His mother, the intrepid Ayxa, was indignant at his weakness: "You do well," said she, "to weep like a woman, for what you failed to defend like a man!"

The vizier Aben Comixa endeavored to console his royal master. "Consider, Señor," said he, "that the most signal misfortunes often render men as renowned as the most prosperous achievements, provided they sustain them with magnanimity."

The unhappy monarch, however, was not to be consoled; his tears continued to flow. "Allah Achbar!" exclaimed he; "when did misfortunes ever equal mine?"

From this circumstance, the hill, which is not far from Padul, took the name of Feg Allah Achbar: but the point of view commanding the last prospect of Granada, is known among Spaniards by the name of *El ultimo suspiro del Moro;* or, "The last sigh of the Moor."

CHAPTER C. HOW THE CASTILIAN SOVEREIGNS
TOOK POSSESSION OF GRANADA

Queen Isabella having joined the king, the royal pair, followed by a triumphant host, passed up the road by the Hill of Martyrs, and thence to the main entrance of the Alhambra. The grand cardinal awaited them under the lofty arch of the great gate of justice, accompanied by Don Gutierrez de Cardenas and Aben Comixa. Here king Ferdinand gave the keys which had been delivered up to him into the hands of the queen; they were passed successively into the hands of the prince Juan, the grand cardinal, and finally into those of the count de Tendilla, in whose custody they remained, that brave cavalier having been named alcayde of the Alhambra, and captain-general of Granada.

The sovereigns did not remain long in the Alhambra on this first visit, but leaving a strong garrison there under the count de Tendilla, to maintain tranquillity in the palace and the subjacent city, returned to the camp at Santa Fé.

We must not omit to mention a circumstance attending the surrender of the city, which spoke eloquently to the hearts of the victors. As the royal army had advanced in all the pomp of courtly and chivalrous array, a procession of a different kind came forth to meet it. This was composed of more than five hundred Christian captives, many of whom had languished for years in Moorish dungeons. Pale and emaciated, they came clanking their chains in triumph, and shedding tears of joy. They were received with tenderness by the sovereigns. The king hailed them as good Spaniards, as men loyal and brave, as martyrs to the holy cause; the queen distributed liberal relief among them with her own hands, and they passed on before the squadrons of the army, singing hymns of jubilee.[70]

The sovereigns forbore to enter the city until it should be fully occupied by their troops, and public tranquillity insured. All this was done under the vigilant superintendence of the count de Tendilla, assisted by the marques of Villena; and the glistening of Christian helms and lances along the walls and bulwarks, and the standards of the faith and of the realm flaunting from the towers, told that the subjugation of the city was complete. The proselyte prince, Cid Hiaya, now known by the Christian appellation of Don Pedro de Granada Vanegas,[71] was appointed chief alguazil of the city, and had charge of the Moorish inhabitants; and his son, lately the prince Alnayer, now Alonzo de Granada Vanegas, was appointed admiral of the fleets.

It was on the sixth of January, the day of kings and festival of the Epiphany, that the sovereigns made their triumphal entry with grand military parade. First advanced, we are told, a splendid escort of cavaliers in burnished armor, and superbly mounted. Then followed the prince Juan, glittering with jewels and diamonds; on each side of him, mounted on mules, rode the grand cardinal, clothed in purple, Fray Hernando de Talavero, bishop of Airla, and the archbishop elect of Granada. To these succeeded the queen and her ladies, and the king, managing in galliard style, say the Spanish chroniclers, a proud and mettlesome steed (un caballo arrogante). Then followed the army in shining columns, with flaunting banners and the inspiring clamor of military music. The king and queen (says the worthy Fray Antonio Agapida) looked, on this occasion, as more than mortal: the venerable ecclesiastics, to whose advice and zeal this glorious conquest ought in a great measure to be attributed, moved along with hearts swelling with holy exultation, but with chastened and downcast looks of edifying humility; while the hardy warriors, in tossing plumes and shining steel, seemed elevated with a stern joy, at finding themselves in possession of this object of so many toils and perils. As the streets resounded with the tramp of steeds and swelling peals of music, the Moors buried themselves in the deepest recesses of their dwellings. There they bewailed in secret the fallen glory of their race, but suppressed their groans, lest they should be heard by their enemies and increase their triumph.

The royal procession advanced to the principal mosque, which had been consecrated as a cathedral. Here the sovereigns offered up prayers and thanksgivings, and the choir of the royal chapel chanted a triumphant anthem, in which they were joined by all the courtiers and cavaliers. Nothing (says Fray Antonio Agapida) could exceed the thankfulness to God of the pious king Ferdinand, for having enabled him to eradicate from Spain the empire and name of that accursed heathen race, and for the elevation of the cross in that city wherein the impious doctrines of Mahomet had so long been cherished. In the fervor of his spirit, he supplicated from Heaven a continuance of its grace, and that this glorious triumph might be perpetuated.[72] The prayer of the pious monarch was responded by the people, and even his enemies were for once convinced of his sincerity.

When the religious ceremonies were concluded, the court ascended to the stately palace of the Alhambra, and entered by the great gate of justice. The halls lately occupied by turbaned infidels now rustled with stately dames and Christian courtiers, who wandered with eager curiosity over this far-famed palace, admiring its verdant courts and gushing fountains, its halls decorated with elegant arabesques, and storied with inscriptions, and the splendor of its gilded and brilliantly painted ceilings.

It had been a last request of the unfortunate Boabdil, and one which showed how deeply he felt the transition of his fate, that no person might be permitted to enter or depart by the gate of the Alhambra, through which he had sallied forth to surrender his capital. His request was granted; the portal was closed up and remains so to the present day—a mute memorial of that event.[73]

The Spanish sovereigns fixed their throne in the presence-chamber of the palace, so long the seat of Moorish royalty. Hither the principal inhabitants of Granada repaired, to pay them homage and kiss their hands in token of vassalage; and their example was followed by deputies from all the towns and fortresses of the Alpuxarras, which had not hitherto submitted.

Thus terminated the war of Granada, after ten years of incessant fighting; equalling (says Fray Antonio Agapida) the far-famed siege of Troy in duration, and ending, like that, in the capture of the city. Thus ended also the dominion of the

Moors in Spain, having endured seven hundred and seventy-eight years, from the memorable defeat of Roderick, the last of the Goths, on the banks of the Guadalete. The authentic Agapida is uncommonly particular in fixing the epoch of this event. This great triumph of our holy Catholic faith, according to his computation, took place in the beginning of January, in the year of our Lord 1492, being 3655 years from the population of Spain by the patriarch Tubal; 3797 from the general deluge; 5453 from the creation of the world, according to Hebrew calculation; and in the month Rabic, in the eight hundred and ninety-seventh year of the Hegira, or flight of Mahomet; whom may God confound! saith the pious Agapida!

LEGEND OF THE ARABIAN ASTROLOGER

In old times, many hundred years ago, there was a Moorish king named Aben Habuz, who reigned over the kingdom of Granada. He was a retired conqueror, that is to say, one who having in his more youthful days led a life of constant foray and depredation, now that he was grown feeble and superannuated, "languished for repose," and desired nothing more than to live at peace with all the world, to husband his laurels, and to enjoy in quiet the possessions he had wrested from his neighbors.

It so happened, however, that this most reasonable and pacific old monarch had young rivals to deal with; princes full of his early passion for fame and fighting, and who were disposed to call him to account for the scores he had run up with their fathers. Certain distant districts of his own territories, also, which during the days of his vigor he had treated with a high hand, were prone, now that he languished for repose, to rise in rebellion and threaten to invest him in his capital. Thus he had foes on every side; and as Granada is surrounded by wild and craggy mountains, which hide the approach of an enemy, the unfortunate Aben Habuz was kept in a constant state of vigilance and alarm, not knowing in what quarter hostilities might break out.

It was in vain that he built watchtowers on the mountains, and stationed guards at every pass with orders to make fires by night and smoke by day, on the approach of an enemy. His alert foes, baffling every precaution, would break out of some unthought-of defile, ravage his lands beneath his very nose, and then make off with prisoners and booty to the mountains. Was ever peaceable and retired conqueror in a more uncomfortable predicament?

While Aben Habuz was harassed by these perplexities and

molestations, an ancient Arabian physician arrived at his court. His gray beard descended to his girdle, and he had every mark of extreme age, yet he had travelled almost the whole way from Egypt on foot, with no other aid than a staff, marked with hieroglyphics. His fame had preceded him. His name was Ibrahim Ebn Abu Ayub, he was said to have lived ever since the days of Mahomet, and to be son of Abu Ayub, the last of the companions of the Prophet. He had, when a child, followed the conquering army of Amru into Egypt, where he had remained many years studying the dark sciences, and particularly magic, among the Egyptian priests.

It was, moreover, said that he had found out the secret of prolonging life, by means of which he had arrived to the great age of upwards of two centuries, though, as he did not discover the secret until well stricken in years, he could only perpetuate his gray hairs and wrinkles.

This wonderful old man was honorably entertained by the king; who, like most superannuated monarchs, began to take physicians into great favor. He would have assigned him an apartment in his palace, but the astrologer preferred a cave in the side of the hill which rises above the city of Granada, being the same on which the Alhambra has since been built. He caused the cave to be enlarged so as to form a spacious and lofty hall, with a circular hole at the top, through which, as through a well, he could see the heavens and behold the stars even at mid-day. The walls of this hall were covered with Egyptian hieroglyphics with cabalistic symbols, and with the figures of the stars in their signs. This hall he furnished with many implements, fabricated under his directions by cunning artificers of Granada, but the occult properties of which were known only to himself.

In a little while the sage Ibrahim became the bosom counsellor of the king, who applied to him for advice in every emergency. Aben Habuz was once inveighing against the injustice of his neighbors, and bewailing the restless vigilance he had to observe to guard himself against their invasions; when he had finished, the astrologer remained silent for a moment, and then replied, "Know, O King, that when I was in Egypt I beheld a great marvel devised by a pagan priestess of old. On a mountain, above the city of Borsa, and overlooking the great valley of the Nile, was a figure of a ram, and above it a figure of a cock, both of molten brass, and turning upon a pivot. Whenever the country was threatened with invasion, the ram would turn in the direction of the enemy, and the cock would crow; upon this the inhabitants of the city knew of the danger, and of the quarter from which it was approaching, and could take timely means to guard against it."

"God is great!" exclaimed the pacific Aben Habuz, "what a treasure would be such a ram to keep an eye upon these mountains around me; and then such a cock, to crow in time of danger! Allah Akbar! how securely I might sleep in my palace with such sentinels on the top!"

The astrologer waited until the ecstasies of the king had subsided, and then proceeded.

"After the victorious Amru (may he rest in peace!) had finished his conquest of Egypt, I remained among the priests of the land, studying the rites and ceremonies of their idolatrous faith, and seeking to make myself master of the hidden knowledge for which they are renowned. I was one day seated on the banks of the Nile, conversing with an ancient priest, when he pointed to the mighty pyramids which rose like mountains out of the neighboring desert. 'All that we can teach thee,' said he, 'is nothing to the knowledge locked up in those mighty piles. In the centre of the central pyramid is a sepulchral chamber, in which is inclosed the mummy of the high-priest, who aided in rearing that stupendous pile; and with him is buried a wondrous book of knowledge containing all the secrets of magic and art. This book was given to Adam after his fall, and was handed down from generation to generation to King Solomon the wise, and by its aid he built the temple of Jerusalem. How it came into the possession of the builder of the pyramids, is known to him alone who knows all things.'

"When I heard these words of the Egyptian priest, my heart burned to get possession of that book. I could command the services of many of the soldiers of our conquering army, and of a number of the native Egyptians: with these I set to work, and pierced the solid mass of the pyramid, until, after great toil, I came upon one of its interior and hidden passages. Following this up, and threading a fearful labyrinth, I penetrated into the very heart of the pyramid, even to the sepulchral chamber, where the mummy of the high-priest had lain for ages. I broke through the outer cases of the mummy, unfolded its many wrappers and bandages, and at length found the precious volume on its bosom. I seized it with a trembling hand, and groped my way out of the pyramid, leaving the mummy in its dark and silent sepulchre, there to await the final day of resurrection and judgment."

"Son of Abu Ayub," exclaimed Aben Habuz, "thou hast been a great traveller, and seen marvellous things; but of what avail to me is the secret of the pyramid, and the volume of knowledge of the wise Solomon?"

"This it is, O king! By the study of that book I am instructed in all magic arts, and can command the assistance of genii to accomplish my plans. The mystery of the Talisman of Borsa is therefore familiar to me, and such a talisman can I make; nay, one of greater virtues."

"O wise son of Abu Ayub," cried Aben Habuz, "better were such a talisman, than all the watchtowers on the hills, and sentinels upon the borders. Give me such a safeguard, and the riches of my treasury are at thy command."

The astrologer immediately set to work to gratify the wishes of the monarch. He caused a great tower to be erected upon the top of the royal palace, which stood on the brow of the hill of the Albaycin. The tower was built of stones brought from Egypt, and taken, it is said, from one of the pyramids. In the upper part of the tower was a circular hall, with windows looking towards every point of the compass, and before each window was a table, on which was arranged, as on a chess-board, a mimic army of horse and foot, with the effigy of the potentate that ruled in that direction, all carved of wood. To each of these tables there was a small lance, no bigger than a bodkin, on which were engraved certain Chaldaic characters. This hall was kept constantly closed, by a gate of brass, with a great lock of steel, the key of which was in possession of the king.

On the top of the tower was a bronze figure of a Moorish horseman, fixed on a pivot, with a shield on one arm, and his lance elevated perpendicularly. The face of this horseman was towards the city, as if keeping guard over it; but if any foe were at hand, the figure would turn in that direction, and would level the lance as if for action.

When this talisman was finished, Aben Habuz was all impatient to try its virtues; and longed as ardently for an invasion as he had ever sighed after repose. His desire was soon gratified. Tidings were brought, early one morning, by the sentinel appointed to watch the tower, that the face of the bronze horseman was turned towards the mountains of Elvira, and that his lance pointed directly against the Pass of Lope.

"Let the drums and trumpets sound to arms, and all Granada be put on the alert," said Aben Habuz.

"O king," said the astrologer, "let not your city be disquieted, nor your warriors called to arms; we need no aid of force to deliver you from your enemies. Dismiss your attendants, and let us proceed alone to the secret hall of the tower."

The ancient Aben Habuz mounted the staircase of the tower, leaning on the arm of the still more ancient Ibrahim Ebn Abu Ayub. They unlocked the brazen door and entered. The window that looked towards the Pass of Lope was open. "In this direction," said the astrologer, "lies the danger; approach, O king, and behold the mystery of the table."

King Aben Habuz approached the seeming chess-board, on which were arranged the small wooden effigies, when, to his surprise, he perceived that they were all in motion. The horses pranced and curveted, the warriors brandished their weapons, and there was a faint sound of drums and trumpets, and the clang of arms, and neighing of steeds; but all no louder, nor more distinct, than the hum of the bee, or the summer-fly, in the drowsy ear of him who lies at noontide in the shade.

"Behold, O king," said the astrologer, "a proof that thy enemies are even now in the field. They must be advancing

through yonder mountains, by the Pass of Lope. Would you
produce a panic and confusion amongst them, and cause them
to retreat without loss of life, strike these effigies with the but-
end of this magic lance; would you cause bloody feud and
carnage, strike with the point."

A livid streak passed across the countenance of Aben Habuz;
he seized the lance with trembling eagerness; his gray beard
wagged with exultation as he tottered toward the table: "Son of
Abu Ayub," exclaimed he, in chuckling tone, "I think we will
have a little blood!"

So saying, he thrust the magic lance into some of the pigmy
effigies, and belabored others with the but-end, upon which the
former fell as dead upon the board, and the rest turning upon
each other began, pell-mell, a chance-medley fight.

It was with difficulty the astrologer could stay the hand of the
most pacific of monarchs, and prevent him from absolutely ex-
terminating his foes; at length he prevailed upon him to leave
the tower, and to send out scouts to the mountains by the Pass
of Lope.

They returned with the intelligence, that a Christian army
had advanced through the heart of the Sierra, almost within
sight of Granada, where a dissension had broken out among
them; they had turned their weapons against each other, and
after much slaughter had retreated over the border.

Aben Habuz was transported with joy on thus proving the
efficacy of the talisman. "At length," said he, "I shall lead a
life of tranquillity, and have all my enemies in my power. O
wise son of Abu Ayub, what can I bestow on thee in reward for
such a blessing?"

"The wants of an old man and a philosopher, O king, are
few and simple; grant me but the means of fitting up my cave as
a suitable hermitage, and I am content."

"How noble is the moderation of the truly wise!" exclaimed
Aben Habuz, secretly pleased at the cheapness of the recom-
pense. He summoned his treasurer, and bade him dispense
whatever sums might be required by Ibrahim to complete and
furnish his hermitage.

The astrologer now gave orders to have various chambers hewn out of the solid rock, so as to form ranges of apartments connected with his astrological hall; these he caused to be furnished with luxurious ottomans and divans, and the walls to be hung with the richest silks of Damascus. "I am an old man," said he, "and can no longer rest my bones on stone couches, and these damp walls require covering."

He had baths too constructed, and provided with all kinds of perfumes and aromatic oils: "For a bath," said he, "is necessary to counteract the rigidity of age, and to restore freshness and suppleness to the frame withered by study."

He caused the apartments to be hung with innumerable silver and crystal lamps, which he filled with a fragrant oil, prepared according to a receipt discovered by him in the tombs of Egypt. This oil was perpetual in its nature, and diffused a soft radiance like the tempered light of day. "The light of the sun," said he, "is too gairish and violent for the eyes of an old man, and the light of the lamp is more congenial to the studies of a philosopher."

The treasurer of king Aben Habuz groaned at the sums daily demanded to fit up this hermitage, and he carried his complaints to the king. The royal word, however, had been given; Aben Habuz shrugged his shoulders: "We must have patience," said he, "this old man has taken his idea of a philosophic retreat from the interior of the pyramids, and of the vast ruins of Egypt; but all things have an end, and so will the furnishing of his cavern."

The king was in the right; the hermitage was at length complete, and formed a sumptuous subterranean palace. The astrologer expressed himself perfectly content, and, shutting himself up, remained for three whole days buried in study. At the end of that time he appeared again before the treasurer. "One thing more is necessary," said he, "one trifling solace for the intervals of mental labor."

"O wise Ibrahim, I am bound to furnish every thing necessary for thy solitude; what more dost thou require?"

"I would fain have a few dancing women."

"Dancing women!" echoed the treasurer, with surprise.

"Dancing women," replied the sage, gravely; "and let them be young and fair to look upon; for the sight of youth and beauty is refreshing. A few will suffice, for I am a philosopher of simple habits and easily satisfied."

While the philosophic Ibrahim Ebn Abu Ayub passed his time thus sagely in his hermitage, the pacific Aben Habuz carried on furious campaigns in effigy in his tower. It was a glorious thing for an old man, like himself, of quiet habits, to have war made easy, and to be enabled to amuse himself in his chamber by brushing away whole armies like so many swarms of flies.

For a time he rioted in the indulgence of his humors, and even taunted and insulted his neighbors, to induce them to make incursions; but by degrees they grew wary from repeated disasters until no one ventured to invade his territories. For many months the bronze horseman remained on the peace establishment with his lance elevated in the air, and the worthy old monarch began to repine at the want of his accustomed sport, and to grow peevish at his monotonous tranquillity.

At length, one day, the talismanic horseman veered suddenly round, and lowering his lance, made a dead point towards the mountains of Guadix. Aben Habuz hastened to his tower, but the magic table in that direction remained quiet; not a single warrior was in motion. Perplexed at the circumstance, he sent forth a troop of horse to scour the mountains and reconnoitre. They returned after three days' absence.

"We have searched every mountain pass," said they, "but not a helm nor spear was stirring. All that we have found in the course of our foray, was a Christian damsel of surpassing beauty, sleeping at noontide beside a fountain, whom we have brought away captive."

"A damsel of surpassing beauty!" exclaimed Aben Habuz, his eyes gleaming with animation; "let her be conducted into my presence."

The beautiful damsel was accordingly conducted into his presence. She was arrayed with all the luxury of ornament that had prevailed among the Gothic Spaniards at the time of the Arabian conquest. Pearls of dazzling whiteness were entwined with her raven tresses; and jewels sparkled on her forehead, rivalling the lustre of her eyes. Around her neck was a golden chain, to which was suspended a silver lyre, which hung by her side.

The flashes of her dark refulgent eye were like sparks of fire on the withered, yet combustible, heart of Aben Habuz; the swimming voluptuousness of her gait made his senses reel. "Fairest of women," cried he, with rapture, "who and what art thou?"

"The daughter of one of the Gothic princes, who but lately ruled over this land. The armies of my father have been destroyed, as if by magic, among these mountains; he has been driven into exile, and his daughter is a captive."

"Beware, O king!" whispered Ibrahim Ebn Abu Ayub, "this may be one of these northern sorceresses of whom we have heard, who assume the most seductive forms to beguile the unwary. Methinks I read witchcraft in her eye, and sorcery in every movement. Doubtless this is the enemy pointed out by the talisman."

"Son of Abu Ayub," replied the king, "thou art a wise man, I grant, a conjuror for aught I know; but thou art little versed in the ways of woman. In that knowledge will I yield to no man; no, not to the wise Solomon himself, notwithstanding the number of his wives and concubines. As to this damsel, I see no harm in her; she is fair to look upon, and finds favor in my eyes."

"Hearken, O king!" replied the astrologer. "I have given thee many victories by means of my talisman, but have never shared any of the spoil. Give me then this stray captive, to solace me in my solitude with her silver lyre. If she be indeed a sorceress, I have counter spells that set her charms at defiance."

"What! more women!" cried Aben Habuz. "Hast thou not already dancing women enough to solace thee?"

"Dancing women have I, it is true, but no singing women.

I would fain have a little minstrelsy to refresh my mind when weary with the toils of study."

"A truce with thy hermit cravings," said the king, impatiently. "This damsel have I marked for my own. I see much comfort in her; even such comfort as David, the father of Solomon the wise, found in the society of Abishag the Shunamite."

Further solicitations and remonstrances of the astrologer only provoked a more peremptory reply from the monarch, and they parted in high displeasure. The sage shut himself up in his hermitage to brood over his disappointment; ere he departed, however, he gave the king one more warning to beware of his dangerous captive. But where is the old man in love that will listen to council? Aben Habuz resigned himself to the full sway of his passion. His only study was how to render himself amiable in the eyes of the Gothic beauty. He had not youth to recommend him, it is true, but then he had riches; and when a lover is old, he is generally generous. The Zacatin of Granada was ransacked for the most precious merchandise of the East; silks, jewels, precious gems, exquisite perfumes, all that Asia and Africa yielded of rich and rare, were lavished upon the princess. All kinds of spectacles and festivities were devised for her entertainment: minstrelsy, dancing, tournaments, bull-fights:—Granada for a time was a scene of perpetual pageant. The Gothic princess regarded all this splendor with the air of one accustomed to magnificence. She received every thing as a homage due to her rank, or rather to her beauty; for beauty is more lofty in its exactions even than rank. Nay, she seemed to take a secret pleasure in exciting the monarch to expenses that made his treasury shrink, and then treating his extravagant generosity as a mere matter of course. With all his assiduity and munificence, also, the venerable lover could not flatter himself that he had made any impression on her heart. She never frowned on him, it is true, but then she never smiled. Whenever he began to plead his passion, she struck her silver lyre. There was a mystic charm in the sound. In an instant the monarch began to nod; a drowsiness stole over him, and he gradually sank into a sleep, from which he awoke wonderfully refreshed, but perfectly cooled for the time of his passion. This was very baffling to his suit; but then these slumbers were accompanied by agreeable dreams, which completely inthralled the senses of the drowsy lover; so he continued to dream on, while all Granada scoffed at his infatuation, and groaned at the treasures lavished for a song.

At length a danger burst on the head of Aben Habuz, against which his talisman yielded him no warning. An insurrection broke out in his very capital; his palace was surrounded by an armed rabble, who menaced his life and the life of his Christian paramour. A spark of his ancient warlike spirit was awakened in the breast of the monarch. At the head of a handful of his guards he sallied forth, put the rebels to flight, and crushed the insurrection in the bud.

When quiet was again restored, he sought the astrologer, who still remained shut up in his hermitage, chewing the bitter cud of resentment.

Aben Habuz approached him with a conciliatory tone. "O wise son of Abu Ayub," said he, "well didst thou predict dangers to me from this captive beauty: tell me then, thou who art so quick at foreseeing peril, what I should do to avert it."

"Put from thee the infidel damsel who is the cause."

"Sooner would I part with my kingdom," cried Aben Habuz.

"Thou art in danger of losing both," replied the astrologer.

"Be not harsh and angry, O most profound of philosophers; consider the double distress of a monarch and a lover, and devise some means of protecting me from the evils by which I am menaced. I care not for grandeur, I care not for power, I languish only for repose; would that I had some quiet retreat where I might take refuge from the world, and all its cares, and pomps, and troubles, and devote the remainder of my days to tranquillity and love."

The astrologer regarded him for a moment, from under his bushy eyebrows.

"And what wouldst thou give, if I could provide thee such a retreat?"

"Thou shouldst name thy own reward, and whatever it might be, if within the scope of my power, as my soul liveth, it should be thine."

"Thou hast heard, O king, of the garden of Irem, one of the prodigies of Arabia the happy."

"I have heard of that garden; it is recorded in the Koran, even in the chapter entitled 'The Dawn of Day.' I have, moreover, heard marvellous things related of it by pilgrims who had been to Mecca; but I considered them wild fables, such as travellers are wont to tell who have visited remote countries."

"Discredit not, O king, the tales of travellers," rejoined the astrologer, gravely, "for they contain precious rarities of knowledge brought from the ends of the earth. As to the palace and garden of Irem, what is generally told of them is true; I have seen them with mine own eyes—listen to my adventure; for it has a bearing upon the object of your request.

"In my younger days, when a mere Arab of the desert, I tended my father's camels. In traversing the desert of Aden, one of them strayed from the rest, and was lost. I searched after it for several days, but in vain, until, wearied and faint, I laid myself down at noontide, and slept under a palm-tree by the side of a scanty well. When I awoke, I found myself at the gate of a city. I entered, and beheld noble streets, and squares, and market-places; but all were silent and without an inhabitant. I wandered on until I came to a sumptuous palace with a garden adorned with fountains and fishponds, and groves and flowers, and orchards laden with delicious fruit; but still no one was to be seen. Upon which, appalled at this loneliness, I hastened to depart; and, after issuing forth at the gate of the city, I turned to look upon the place, but it was no longer to be seen; nothing but the silent desert extended before my eyes.

"In the neighborhood I met with an aged dervise, learned in the traditions and secrets of the land, and related to him what had befallen me. 'This,' said he, 'is the far-famed garden of Irem, one of the wonders of the desert. It only appears at times to some wanderer like thyself, gladdening him with the sight of towers and palaces and garden walls overhung with richly-laden fruit-trees, and then vanishes, leaving nothing but a lonely desert. And this is the story of it. In old times, when this country was inhabited by the Addites, King Sheddad, the son of Ad, the great grandson of Noah, founded here a splendid city. When it was finished, and he saw its grandeur, his heart was puffed up with pride and arrogance, and he determined to build a royal palace, with gardens which should rival all related in the Koran of the celestial paradise. But the curse of heaven fell upon him for his presumption. He and his subjects were swept from the earth, and his splendid city, and palace, and gardens, were laid under a perpetual spell, which hides them from human sight, excepting that they are seen at intervals, by way of keeping his sin in perpetual remembrance.'

"This story, O king, and the wonders I had seen, ever dwelt in my mind; and in after years, when I had been in Egypt, and was possessed of the book of knowledge of Solomon the wise, I determined to return and revisit the garden of Irem. I did so, and found it revealed to my instructed sight. I took possession of the palace of Sheddad, and passed several days in his mock paradise. The genii who watch over the place, were obedient to my magic power, and revealed to me the spells by which the whole garden had been, as it were, conjured into existence, and by which it was rendered invisible. Such a palace and garden, O king, can I make for thee, even here, on the mountain above thy city. Do I not know all the secret spells? and am I not in possession of the book of knowledge of Solomon the wise?"

"O wise son of Abu Ayub!" exclaimed Aben Habuz, trembling with eagerness, "thou art a traveller indeed, and hast seen and learned marvellous things! Contrive me such a paradise, and ask any reward, even to the half of my kingdom."

"Alas!" replied the other, "thou knowest I am an old man, and a philosopher, and easily satisfied; all the reward I ask is the first beast of burden, with its load, which shall enter the magic portal of the palace."

The monarch gladly agreed to so moderate a stipulation, and the astrologer began his work. On the summit of the hill, immediately above his subterranean hermitage, he caused a great

gateway or barbican to be erected, opening through the centre of
a strong tower.

There was an outer vestibule or porch, with a lofty arch, and
within it a portal secured by massive gates. On the key-stone
of the portal the astrologer, with his own hand, wrought the
figure of a huge key; and on the key-stone of the outer arch of
the vestibule, which was loftier than that of the portal, he carved
a gigantic hand. These were potent talismans, over which he
repeated many sentences in an unknown tongue.

When this gateway was finished he shut himself up for two
days in his astrological hall, engaged in secret incantations; on
the third he ascended the hill, and passed the whole day on its
summit. At a late hour of the night he came down, and presented himself before Aben Habuz. "At length, O king," said
he, "my labor is accomplished. On the summit of the hill
stands one of the most delectable palaces that ever the head of
man devised, or the heart of man desired. It contains sumptuous halls and galleries, delicious gardens, cool fountains, and
fragrant baths; in a word, the whole mountain is converted into
a paradise. Like the garden of Irem, it is protected by a mighty
charm, which hides it from the view and search of mortals, excepting such as possess the secret of its talismans."

"Enough!" cried Aben Habuz, joyfully, "to-morrow morning with the first light we will ascend and take possession."
The happy monarch slept but little that night. Scarcely had the
rays of the sun begun to play about the snowy summit of the
Sierra Nevada, when he mounted his steed, and, accompanied
only by a few chosen attendants, ascended a steep and narrow
road leading up the hill. Beside him, on a white palfrey, rode
the Gothic princess, her whole dress sparkling with jewels, while
round her neck was suspended her silver lyre. The astrologer
walked on the other side of the king, assisting his steps with his
hieroglyphic staff, for he never mounted steed of any kind.

Aben Habuz looked to see the towers of the palace brighten-
ing above him, and the imbowered terraces of its gardens stretching along the heights; but as yet nothing of the kind was to be
descried. "That is the mystery and safeguard of the place,"

said the astrologer, "nothing can be discerned until you have passed the spell-bound gateway, and been put in possession of the place."

As they approached the gateway, the astrologer paused, and pointed out to the king the mystic hand and key carved upon the portal of the arch. "These," said he, "are the talismans which guard the entrance to this paradise. Until yonder hand shall reach down and seize that key, neither mortal power nor magic artifice can prevail against the lord of this mountain."

While Aben Habuz was gazing, with open mouth and silent wonder, at these mystic talismans, the palfrey of the princess proceeded, and bore her in at the portal, to the very centre of the barbican.

"Behold," cried the astrologer, "my promised reward; the first animal with its burden which should enter the magic gateway."

Aben Habuz smiled at what he considered a pleasantry of the ancient man; but when he found him to be in earnest, his gray beard trembled with indignation.

"Son of Abu Ayub," said he, sternly, "what equivocation is this? Thou knowest the meaning of my promise: the first beast of burden, with its load, that should enter this portal. Take the strongest mule in my stables, load it with the most precious things of my treasury, and it is thine; but dare not raise thy thoughts to her who is the delight of my heart."

"What need I of wealth," cried the astrologer, scornfully; "have I not the book of knowledge of Solomon the wise, and through it the command of the secret treasures of the earth? The princess is mine by right; thy royal word is pledged; I claim her as my own."

The princess looked down haughtily from her palfrey, and a light smile of scorn curled her rosy lip at this dispute between two gray-beards, for the possession of youth and beauty. The wrath of the monarch got the better of his discretion. "Base son of the desert," cried he, "thou may'st be master of many arts, but know me for thy master, and presume not to juggle with thy king."

"My master! my king!" echoed the astrologer—"The monarch of a mole-hill to claim sway over him who possesses the talismans of Solomon! Farewell, Aben Habuz; reign over thy petty kingdom, and revel in thy paradise of fools; for me, I will laugh at thee in my philosophic retirement."

So saying he seized the bridle of the palfrey, smote the earth with his staff, and sank with the Gothic princess through the centre of the barbican. The earth closed over them, and no trace remained of the opening by which they had descended.

Aben Habuz was struck dumb for a time with astonishment. Recovering himself, he ordered a thousand workmen to dig, with pickaxe and spade, into the ground where the astrologer had disappeared. They digged and digged, but in vain; the flinty bosom of the hill resisted their implements; or if they did penetrate a little way, the earth filled in again as fast as they threw it out. Aben Habuz sought the mouth of the cavern at the foot of the hill, leading to the subterranean palace of the astrologer; but it was nowhere to be found. Where once had been an entrance, was now a solid surface of primeval rock. With the disappearance of Ibrahim Ebn Abu Ayub ceased the benefit of his talismans. The bronze horseman remained fixed, with his face turned toward the hill, and his spear pointed to the spot where the astrologer had descended, as if there still lurked the deadliest foe of Aben Habuz.

From time to time the sound of music, and the tones of a female voice, could be faintly heard from the bosom of the hill; and a peasant one day brought word to the king, that in the preceding night he had found a fissure in the rock, by which he had crept in, until he looked down into a subterranean hall, in which sat the astrologer, on a magnificent divan, slumbering and nodding to the silver lyre of the princess, which seemed to hold a magic sway over his senses.

Aben Habuz sought the fissure in the rock, but it was again closed. He renewed the attempt to unearth his rival, but all in vain. The spell of the hand and key was too potent to be counteracted by human power. As to the summit of the mountain, the site of the promised palace and garden, it remained a naked waste; either the boasted elysium was hidden from sight by enchantment, or was a mere fable of the astrologer. The world charitably supposed the latter, and some used to call the place "The King's Folly;" while others named it "The Fool's Paradise."

To add to the chagrin of Aben Habuz, the neighbors whom he had defied and taunted, and cut up at his leisure while master of the talismanic horseman, finding him no longer protected by magic spell, made inroads into his territories from all sides, and the remainder of the life of the most pacific of monarchs was a tissue of turmoils.

At length Aben Habuz died, and was buried. Ages have since rolled away. The Alhambra has been built on the eventful mountain, and in some measure realizes the fabled delights of the garden of Irem. The spell-bound gateway still exists entire, protected no doubt by the mystic hand and key, and now forms the Gate of Justice, the grand entrance to the fortress. Under that gateway, it is said, the old astrologer remains in his subterranean hall, nodding on his divan, lulled by the silver lyre of the princess.

The old invalid sentinels who mount guard at the gate hear the strains occasionally in the summer nights; and, yielding to their soporific power, doze quietly at their posts. Nay, so drowsy an influence pervades the place, that even those who watch by day may generally be seen nodding on the stone benches of the barbican, or sleeping under the neighboring trees; so that in fact it is the drowsiest military post in all Christendom. All this, say the ancient legends, will endure from age to age. The princess will remain captive to the astrologer; and the astrologer, bound up in magic slumber by the princess, until the last day, unless the mystic hand shall grasp the fated key, and dispel the whole charm of this enchanted mountain.[75]

LEGEND OF THE TWO DISCREET STATUES

There lived once in a waste apartment of the Alhambra, a merry little fellow, named Lope Sanchez, who worked in the gardens, and was as brisk and blithe as a grasshopper, singing all day long. He was the life and soul of the fortress; when his work was over, he would sit on one of the stone benches of the esplanade, strum his guitar, and sing long ditties about the Cid, and Bernardo del Carpio, and Fernando del Pulgar, and other Spanish heroes, for the amusement of the old soldiers of the fortress, or would strike up a merrier tune, and set the girls dancing boleros and fandangos.

Like most little men, Lope Sanchez had a strapping buxom dame for a wife, who could almost have put him in her pocket; but he lacked the usual poor man's lot—instead of ten children he had but one. This was a little black-eyed girl about twelve years of age, named Sanchica, who was as merry as himself, and the delight of his heart. She played about him as he worked in the gardens, danced to his guitar as he sat in the shade, and ran as wild as a young fawn about the groves and alleys and ruined halls of the Alhambra.

It was now the eve of the blessed St. John, and the holiday-loving gossips of the Alhambra, men, women, and children, went up at night to the mountain of the sun, which rises above the Generalife, to keep their midsummer vigil on its level summit. It was a bright moonlight night, and all the mountains were gray and silvery, and the city, with its domes and spires, lay in shadows below, and the Vega was like a fairy land, with haunted streams gleaming among its dusky groves. On the highest part of the mountain they lit up a bonfire, according to an old custom of the country handed down from the Moors. The inhabitants of the surrounding country were keeping a similar vigil, and bonfires, here and there in the Vega, and along the folds of the mountains, blazed up palely in the moonlight.

The evening was gayly passed in dancing to the guitar of Lope Sanchez, who was never so joyous as when on a holiday revel of the kind. While the dance was going on, the little Sanchica with some of her playmates sported among the ruins of an old Moorish fort that crowns the mountain, when, in gathering pebbles in the fosse, she found a small hand curiously carved of jet, the fingers closed, and the thumb firmly clasped upon them.

Overjoyed with her good fortune, she ran to her mother with her prize. It immediately became a subject of sage speculation, and was eyed by some with superstitious distrust. "Throw it away," said one; "it's Moorish—depend upon it there's mischief and witchcraft in it." "By no means," said another; "you may sell it for something to the jewellers of the Zacatin." In the midst of this discussion an old tawny soldier drew near, who had served in Africa, and was as swarthy as a Moor. He examined the hand with a knowing look. "I have seen things of this kind," said he, "among the Moors of Barbary. It is a great virtue to guard against the evil eye, and all kinds of spells and enchantments. I give you joy, friend Lope, this bodes good luck to your child."

Upon hearing this, the wife of Lope Sanchez tied the little hand of jet to a ribbon, and hung it round the neck of her daughter.

The sight of this talisman called up all the favorite superstitions about the Moors. The dance was neglected, and they sat in groups on the ground, telling old legendary tales handed down from their ancestors. Some of their stories turned upon the wonders of the very mountain upon which they were seated, which is a famous hobgoblin region. One ancient crone gave a long account of the subterranean palace in the bowels of that mountain where Boabdil and all his Moslem court are said to remain enchanted. "Among yonder ruins," said she, pointing to some crumbling walls and mounds of earth on a distant part of the mountain, "there is a deep black pit that goes down, down into the very heart of the mountain. For all the money in Granada I would not look down into it. Once upon a time a poor man of the Alhambra, who tended goats upon this mountain, scrambled down into that pit after a kid that had fallen in. He came out again all wild and staring, and told such things of what he had seen, that every one thought his brain was turned. He raved for a day or two about the hobgoblin Moors that had pursued him in the cavern, and could hardly be persuaded to drive his goats up again to the mountain. He did so at last, but, poor man, he never came down again. The neighbors found his goats browsing about the Moorish ruins, and his hat and mantle lying near the mouth of the pit, but he was never more heard of."

The little Sanchica listened with breathless attention to this story. She was of a curious nature, and felt immediately a great hankering to peep into this dangerous pit. Stealing away from her companions she sought the distant ruins, and after groping for some time among them came to a small hollow, or basin, near the brow of the mountain, where it swept steeply down into the valley of the Darro. In the centre of this basin yawned the mouth of the pit. Sanchica ventured to the verge, and peeped in. All was as black as pitch, and gave an idea of immeasurable depth. Her blood ran cold; she drew back, then peeped in again, then would have run away, then took another peep—the very horror of the thing was delightful to her. At length she rolled a large stone, and pushed it over the brink. For some time it fell in silence; then struck some rocky projection with a violent crash, then rebounded from side to side, rumbling and tumbling, with a noise like thunder, then made a final splash into water, far, far below—and all was again silent.

The silence, however, did not long continue. It seemed as if something had been awakened within this dreary abyss. A murmuring sound gradually rose out of the pit like the hum and buzz of a beehive. It grew louder and louder; there was the confusion of voices as of a distant multitude, together with the faint din of arms, clash of cymbals and clangor of trumpets, as if some army were marshalling for battle in the very bowels of the mountain.

The child drew off with silent awe, and hastened back to the place where she had left her parents and their companions. All were gone. The bonfire was expiring, and its last wreath of smoke curling up in the moonshine. The distant fires that had blazed along the mountains and in the Vega were all extinguished, and every thing seemed to have sunk to repose. Sanchica called her parents and some of her companions by name, but received no reply. She ran down the side of the mountain, and by the gardens of the Generalife, until she arrived in the alley of trees leading to the Alhambra, when she seated herself on a bench of a woody recess to recover breath. The bell from the watchtower of the Alhambra tolled midnight. There was a deep tranquillity as if all nature slept; excepting the low tinkling sound of an unseen stream that ran under the covert of the bushes. The breathing sweetness of the atmosphere was lulling her to sleep, when her eye was caught by something glittering at a distance, and to her surprise she beheld a long cavalcade of Moorish warriors pouring down the mountain side and along the leafy avenues. Some were armed with lances and shields; others with cimeters and battle-axes, and with polished cuirasses that flashed in the moonbeams. Their horses pranced proudly and champed upon their bits, but their tramp caused no more sound than if they had been shod with felt, and the riders were all as pale as death. Among them rode a beautiful lady, with a crowned head and long golden locks entwined with pearls. The housings of her palfry were of crimson velvet embroidered with gold, and swept the earth; but she rode all disconsolate, with eyes ever fixed upon the ground.

Then succeeded a train of courtiers magnificently arrayed in robes and turbans of divers colors, and amidst them, on a cream-colored charger, rode king Boabdil el Chico, in a royal mantle covered with jewels, and a crown sparkling with diamonds. The little Sanchica knew him by his yellow beard, and his resemblance to his portrait, which she had often seen in the picture gallery of the Generalife. She gazed in wonder and admiration at this royal pageant, as it passed glistening among the trees; but though she knew these monarchs and courtiers and warriors, so pale and silent, were out of the common course of nature, and things of magic and enchantment, yet she looked on with a bold heart, such courage did she derive from the mystic talisman of the hand, which was suspended about her neck.

The cavalcade having passed by, she rose and followed. It continued on to the great Gate of Justice, which stood wide open; the old invalid sentinels on duty lay on the stone benches of the barbican, buried in profound and apparently charmed sleep, and the phantom pageant swept noiselessly by them with flaunting banner and triumphant state. Sanchica would have followed; but to her surprise she beheld an opening in the earth, within the barbican, leading down beneath the foundations of the tower. She entered for a little distance, and was encouraged to proceed by finding steps rudely hewn in the rock, and a vaulted passage here and there lit up by a silver lamp, which, while it gave light, diffused likewise a grateful fragrance. Venturing on, she came at last to a great hall, wrought out of the heart of the mountain, magnificently furnished in the Moorish style, and lighted up by silver and crystal lamps. Here, on an ottoman, sat an old man in Moorish dress, with a long white beard, nodding and dozing, with a staff in his hand, which seemed ever to be slipping from his grasp; while at a little distance sat a beautiful lady, in ancient Spanish dress, with a coronet all sparkling with diamonds, and her hair entwined with pearls, who was softly playing on a silver lyre. The little Sanchica now recollected a story she had heard among the old people of the Alhambra, concerning a Gothic princess confined in the centre of the mountain by an old Arabian magician, whom she kept bound up in magic sleep by the power of music.

The lady paused with surprise at seeing a mortal in that enchanted hall. "Is it the eve of the blessed St. John?" said she.

"It is," replied Sanchica.

"Then for one night the magic charm is suspended. Come hither, child, and fear not. I am a Christian like thyself, though bound here by enchantment. Touch my fetters with the talisman that hangs about thy neck, and for this night I shall be free."

So saying, she opened her robes and displayed a broad golden band round her waist, and a golden chain that fastened her to the ground. The child hesitated not to apply the little hand of jet to the golden band, and immediately the chain fell to the earth. At the sound the old man woke and began to rub his eyes; but the lady ran her fingers over the chords of the lyre, and again he fell into a slumber and began to nod, and his staff to falter in his hand. "Now," said the lady, "touch his staff with the talismanic hand of jet." The child did so, and it fell from his grasp, and he sank in a deep sleep on the ottoman. The lady gently laid the silver lyre on the ottoman, leaning it against the head of the sleeping magician; then touching the chords until they vibrated in his ear—"O potent spirit of harmony," said she, "continue thus to hold his senses in thraldom till the return of day. Now follow me, my child," continued she, "and thou shalt behold the Alhambra as it was in the days of its glory, for thou hast a magic talisman that reveals all enchantments." Sanchica followed the lady in silence. They passed up through the entrance of the cavern into the barbican of the Gate of Justice, and thence to the Plaza de los Algibes, or esplanade within the fortress.

This was all filled with Moorish soldiery, horse and foot, marshalled in squadrons, with banners displayed. There were royal guards also at the portal, and rows of African blacks with drawn cimeters. No one spoke a word, and Sanchica passed on fearlessly after her conductor. Her astonishment increased on entering the royal palace, in which she had been reared. The broad moonshine lit up all the halls and courts and gardens almost as brightly as if it were day, but revealed a far different scene from that to which she was accustomed. The walls of the apartments were no longer stained and rent by time. Instead of cobwebs, they were now hung with rich silks of Damascus, and the gildings and arabesque paintings were restored to their original brilliancy and freshness. The halls, no longer naked and unfurnished, were set out with divans and ottomans of the rarest stuffs, embroidered with pearls and studded with precious gems, and all the fountains in the courts and gardens were playing.

The kitchens were again in full operation; cooks were busy preparing shadowy dishes, and roasting and boiling the phantoms of pullets and partridges: servants were hurrying to and fro with silver dishes heaped up with dainties, and arranging a delicious banquet. The Court of Lions was thronged with guards, and courtiers, and alfaquis, as in the old times of the Moors; and at the upper end, in the saloon of judgment, sat Boabdil on his throne, surrounded by his court, and swaying a shadowy sceptre for the night. Notwithstanding all this throng and seeming bustle, not a voice nor a footstep was to be heard; nothing interrupted the midnight silence but the splashing of the fountains. The little Sanchica followed her conductress in mute amazement about the palace, until they came to a portal opening to the vaulted passages beneath the great tower of Comares. On each side of the portal sat the figure of a nymph, wrought out of alabaster. Their heads were turned aside, and their regards fixed upon the same spot within the vault. The enchanted lady paused, and beckoned the child to her. "Here," said she, "is a great secret, which I will reveal to thee in reward for thy faith and courage. These discreet statues watch over a treasure hidden in old times by a Moorish king. Tell thy father to search the spot on which their eyes are fixed, and he will find what will make him richer than any man in Granada. Thy innocent hands alone, however, gifted as thou art also with the talisman, can remove the treasure. Bid thy father use it discreetly, and devote a part of it to the performance of daily masses for my deliverance from this unholy enchantment."

When the lady had spoken these words, she led the child onward to the little garden of Lindaraxa, which is hard by the vault of the statues. The moon trembled upon the waters of the solitary fountain in the centre of the garden, and shed a tender light upon the orange and citron trees. The beautiful lady plucked a branch of myrtle and wreathed it round the head of the child. "Let this be a memento," said she, "of what I have revealed to thee, and a testimonial of its truth. My hour is come; I must return to the enchanted hall; follow me not, lest evil befall thee—farewell. Remember what I have said, and have masses performed for my deliverance." So saying, the lady entered a dark passage leading beneath the tower of Comares, and was no longer seen.

The faint crowing of a cock was now heard from the cottages below the Alhambra, in the valley of the Darro, and a pale streak of light began to appear above the eastern mountains. A slight wind arose, there was a sound like the rustling of dry leaves through the courts and corridors, and door after door shut to with a jarring sound.

Sanchica returned to the scenes she had so lately beheld thronged with the shadowy multitude, but Boabdil and his phantom court were gone. The moon shone into empty halls and galleries stripped of their transient splendor, stained and dilapidated by time, and hung with cobwebs. The bat flitted about in the uncertain light, and the frog croaked from the fish-pond.

Sanchica now made the best of her way to a remote staircase that led up to the humble apartment occupied by her family. The door as usual was open, for Lope Sanchez was too poor to need bolt or bar; she crept quietly to her pallet, and, putting the myrtle wreath beneath her pillow, soon fell asleep.

In the morning she related all that had befallen her to her father. Lope Sanchez, however, treated the whole as a mere dream, and laughed at the child for her credulity. He went forth to his customary labors in the garden, but had not been there long when his little daughter came running to him almost breathless. "Father! father!" cried she, "behold the myrtle wreath which the Moorish lady bound round my head!"

Lope Sanchez gazed with astonishment, for the stalk of the myrtle was of pure gold, and every leaf was a sparkling emerald! Being not much accustomed to precious stones, he was ignorant of the real value of the wreath, but he saw enough to convince him that it was something more substantial than the stuff of which dreams are generally made, and that at any rate the child had dreamt to some purpose. His first care was to enjoin the most absolute secrecy upon his daughter; in this respect, however, he was secure, for she had discretion far beyond her years or sex. He then repaired to the vault, where stood the statues of the two alabaster nymphs. He remarked that their heads were turned from the portal, and that the regards of each were fixed upon the same point in the interior of the building. Lope Sanchez could not but admire this most discreet contrivance for guarding a secret. He drew a line from the eyes of the statues to the point of regard, made a private mark on the wall, and then retired.

All day, however, the mind of Lope Sanchez was distracted

with a thousand cares. He could not help hovering within distant view of the two statues, and became nervous from the dread that the golden secret might be discovered. Every footstep that approached the place made him tremble. He would have given any thing could he but have turned the heads of the statues, forgetting that they had looked precisely in the same direction for some hundreds of years, without any person being the wiser.

"A plague upon them," he would say to himself, "they'll betray all; did ever mortal hear of such a mode of guarding a secret?" Then on hearing any one advance, he would steal off, as though his very lurking near the place would awaken suspicion. Then he would return cautiously, and peep from a distance to see if every thing was secure, but the sight of the statues would again call forth his indignation. "Ay, there they stand," would he say, "always looking, and looking, and looking, just where they should not. Confound them! they are just like all their sex; if they have not tongues to tattle with, they'll be sure to do it with their eyes."

At length, to his relief, the long anxious day drew to a close. The sound of footsteps was no longer heard in the echoing halls of the Alhambra; the last stranger passed the threshold, the great portal was barred and bolted, and the bat and the frog and the hooting owl gradually resumed their nightly vocations in the deserted palace.

Lope Sanchez waited, however, until the night was far advanced before he ventured with his little daughter to the hall of the two nymphs. He found them looking as knowingly and mysteriously as ever at the secret place of deposit. "By your leaves, gentle ladies," thought Lope Sanchez, as he passed between them, "I will relieve you from this charge that must have set so heavy in your minds for the last two or three centuries." He accordingly went to work at the part of the wall which he had marked, and in a little while laid open a concealed recess, in which stood two great jars of porcelain. He attempted to draw them forth, but they were immovable, until touched by the innocent hand of his little daughter. With her aid he dislodged them from their niche, and found, to his great joy, that they were filled with pieces of Moorish gold, mingled with jewels and precious stones. Before daylight he managed to convey them to his chamber, and left the two guardian statues with their eyes still fixed on the vacant wall.

Lope Sanchez had thus on a sudden become a rich man; but riches, as usual, brought a world of cares to which he had hitherto been a stranger. How was he to convey away his wealth with safety? How was he even to enter upon the enjoyment of it without awakening suspicion? Now, too, for the first time in his life the dread of robbers entered into his mind. He looked with terror at the insecurity of his habitation, and went to work to barricade the doors and windows; yet after all his precautions he could not sleep soundly. His usual gayety was at an end; he had no longer a joke or a song for his neighbors, and, in short, became the most miserable animal in the Alhambra. His old comrades remarked this alteration, pitied him heartily, and began to desert him; thinking he must be falling into want, and in danger of looking to them for assistance. Little did they suspect that his only calamity was riches.

The wife of Lope Sanchez shared his anxiety, but then she had ghostly comfort. We ought before this to have mentioned that Lope, being rather a light inconsiderate little man, his wife was accustomed, in all grave matters, to seek the counsel and ministry of her confessor Fray Simon, a sturdy, broad-shouldered, blue-bearded, bullet-headed friar of the neighboring convent of San Francisco, who was in fact the spiritual comforter of half the good wives of the neighborhood. He was moreover in great esteem among divers sisterhoods of nuns; who requited him for his ghostly services by frequent presents of those little dainties and knick-knacks manufactured in convents, such as delicate confections, sweet biscuits, and bottles of spiced cordials, found to be marvellous restoratives after fasts and vigils.

Fray Simon thrived in the exercise of his functions. His oily skin glistened in the sunshine as he toiled up the hill of the Alhambra on a sultry day. Yet notwithstanding his sleek condition, the knotted rope round his waist showed the austerity

of his self-discipline; the multitude doffed their caps to him as
a mirror of piety, and even the dogs scented the odor of sanctity
that exhaled from his garments, and howled from their kennels
as he passed.

Such was Fray Simon, the spiritual counsellor of the comely
wife of Lope Sanchez; and as the father confessor is the domestic
confidant of women in humble life in Spain, he was soon acquainted, in great secrecy, with the story of the hidden treasure.

The friar opened his eyes and mouth and crossed himself a
dozen times at the news. After a moment's pause, "Daughter
of my soul!" said he, "know that thy husband has committed a
double sin—a sin against both state and church! The treasure
he hath thus seized upon for himself, being found in the royal
domains, belongs of course to the crown; but being infidel
wealth, rescued as it were from the very fangs of Satan, should
be devoted to the church. Still, however, the matter may be
accommodated. Bring hither thy myrtle wreath."

When the good father beheld it, his eyes twinkled more than
ever with admiration of the size and beauty of the emeralds.
"This," said he, "being the first-fruits of this discovery, should
be dedicated to pious purposes. I will hang it up as a votive
offering before the image of San Francisco in our chapel, and
will earnestly pray to him, this very night, that your husband
be permitted to remain in quiet possession of your wealth."

The good dame was delighted to make her peace with heaven
at so cheap a rate, and the friar putting the wreath under his
mantle, departed with saintly steps toward his convent.

When Lope Sanchez came home, his wife told him what had
passed. He was excessively provoked, for he lacked his wife's
devotion, and had for some time groaned in secret at the domestic visitations of the friar. "Woman," said he, "what hast thou
done? thou hast put every thing at hazard by thy tattling."

"What!" cried the good woman, "would you forbid my dis-
burdening my conscience to my confessor?"

"No, wife! confess as many of your own sins as you please;
but as to this money-digging, it is a sin of my own, and my conscience is very easy under the weight of it."

There was no use, however, in complaining; the secret was told, and, like water spilled on the sand, was not again to be gathered. Their only chance was, that the friar would be discreet.

The next day, while Lope Sanchez was abroad there was a humble knocking at the door, and Fray Simon entered with meek and demure countenance.

"Daughter," said he, "I have earnestly prayed to San Francisco, and he has heard my prayer. In the dead of the night the saint appeared to me in a dream, but with a frowning aspect. 'Why,' said he, 'dost thou pray to me to dispense with this treasure of the Gentiles, when thou seest the poverty of my chapel? Go to the house of Lope Sanchez, crave in my name a portion of the Moorish gold, to furnish two candlesticks for the main altar, and let him possess the residue in peace.'"

When the good woman heard of this vision, she crossed herself with awe, and going to the secret place where Lope had hid the treasure, she filled a great leathern purse with pieces of Moorish gold, and gave it to the friar. The pious monk bestowed upon her, in return, benedictions enough, if paid by Heaven, to enrich her race to the latest posterity; then slipping the purse into the sleeve of his habit, he folded his hands upon his breast, and departed with an air of humble thankfulness.

When Lope Sanchez heard of this second donation to the church, he had well nigh lost his senses. "Unfortunate man," cried he, "what will become of me? I shall be robbed by piecemeal; I shall be ruined and brought to beggary!"

It was with the utmost difficulty that his wife could pacify him, by reminding him of the countless wealth that yet remained, and how considerate it was for San Francisco to rest contented with so small a portion.

Unluckily, Fray Simon had a number of poor relations to be provided for, not to mention some half-dozen sturdy bullet-headed orphan children, and destitute foundlings that he had taken under his care. He repeated his visits, therefore, from day to day, with solicitations on behalf of Saint Dominick, Saint Andrew, Saint James, until poor Lope was driven to despair, and found that unless he got out of the reach of this holy friar, he should have to make peace-offerings to every saint in the calendar. He determined, therefore, to pack up his remaining wealth, beat a secret retreat in the night, and make off to another part of the kingdom.

Full of his project, he bought a stout mule for the purpose, and tethered it in a gloomy vault underneath the tower of the seven floors; the very place whence the Belludo, or goblin horse, is said to issue forth at midnight, and scour the streets of Granada, pursued by a pack of hell-hounds. Lope Sanchez had little faith in the story, but availed himself of the dread occasioned by it, knowing that no one would be likely to pry into the subterranean stable of the phantom steed. He sent off his family in the course of the day with orders to wait for him at a distant village of the Vega. As the night advanced, he conveyed his treasure to the vault under the tower, and having loaded his mule, he led it forth, and cautiously descended the dusky avenue.

Honest Lope had taken his measures with the utmost secrecy, imparting them to no one but the faithful wife of his bosom. By some miraculous revelation, however, they became known to Fray Simon. The zealous friar beheld these infidel treasures on the point of slipping for ever out of his grasp, and determined to have one more dash at them for the benefit of the church and San Francisco. Accordingly, when the bells had rung for animas, and all the Alhambra was quiet, he stole out of his convent, and descending through the Gate of Justice, concealed himself among the thickets of roses and laurels that border the great avenue. Here he remained, counting the quarters of hours as they were sounded on the bell of the watch-tower, and listening to the dreary hootings of owls, and the distant barking of dogs from the gipsy caverns.

At length he heard the tramp of hoofs, and, through the gloom of the overshadowing trees, imperfectly beheld a steed descending the avenue. The sturdy friar chuckled at the idea of the knowing turn he was about to serve honest Lope.

Tucking up the skirts of his habit, and wriggling like a cat watching a mouse, he waited until his prey was directly before him, when darting forth from his leafy covert, and putting one hand on the shoulder and the other on the crupper, he made a vault that would not have disgraced the most experienced master of equitation, and alighted well-forked astride the steed. "Ah ha!" said the sturdy friar, "we shall now see who best understands the game." He had scarce uttered the words when the mule began to kick, and rear, and plunge, and then set off full speed down the hill. The friar attempted to check him, but in vain. He bounded from rock to rock, and bush to bush; the friar's habit was torn to ribbons and fluttered in the wind, his shaven poll received many a hard knock from the branches of the trees, and many a scratch from the brambles. To add to his terror and distress, he found a pack of seven hounds in full cry at his heels, and perceived, too late, that he was actually mounted upon the terrible Belludo!

Away then they went, according to the ancient phrase, "pull devil, pull friar," down the great avenue, across the Plaza Nueva, along the Zacatin, around the Vivarrambla—never did huntsman and hound make a more furious run, or more infernal uproar. In vain did the friar invoke every saint in the calendar, and the holy Virgin into the bargain; every time he mentioned a name of the kind it was like a fresh application of the spur, and made the Belludo bound as high as a house. Through the remainder of the night was the unlucky Fray Simon carried hither and thither and whither he would not, until every bone in his body ached, and he suffered a loss of leather too grievous to be mentioned. At length the crowing of a cock gave the signal of returning day. At the sound the goblin steed wheeled about, and galloped back for his tower. Again he scoured the Vivarrambla, the Zacatin, the Plaza Nueva, and the avenue of fountains, the seven dogs yelling and barking, and leaping up, and snapping at the heels of the terrified friar. The first streak of day had just appeared as they reached the tower; here the goblin steed kicked up his heels, sent the friar a somerset through the air, plunged into the dark vault followed by the infernal pack, and a profound silence succeeded to the late deafening clamor.

Was ever so diabolical a trick played off upon a holy friar?
A peasant going to his labors at early dawn found the unfortunate Fray Simon lying under a fig-tree at the foot of the tower,
but so bruised and bedevilled that he could neither speak nor
move. He was conveyed with all care and tenderness to his cell,
and the story went that he had been waylaid and maltreated by
robbers. A day or two elapsed before he recovered the use of
his limbs; he consoled himself, in the meantime, with the
thoughts that though the mule with the treasure had escaped
him, he had previously had some rare pickings at the infidel
spoils. His first care on being able to use his limbs, was to
search beneath his pallet, where he had secreted the myrtle
wreath and the leathern pouches of gold extracted from the
piety of dame Sanchez. What was his dismay at finding the
wreath, in effect, but a withered branch of myrtle, and the
leathern pouches filled with sand and gravel!

Fray Simon, with all his chagrin, had the discretion to hold
his tongue, for to betray the secret might draw on him the
ridicule of the public, and the punishment of his superior; it
was not until many years afterwards, on his death-bed, that he
revealed to his confessor his nocturnal ride on the Belludo.

Nothing was heard of Lope Sanchez for a long time after his
disappearance from the Alhambra. His memory was always
cherished as that of a merry companion, though it was feared,
from the care and melancholy observed in his conduct shortly
before his mysterious departure, that poverty and distress had
driven him to some extremity. Some years afterwards one of
his old companions, an invalid soldier, being at Malaga, was
knocked down and nearly run over by a coach and six. The
carriage stopped; an old gentleman magnificently dressed, with
a bag-wig and sword, stepped out to assist the poor invalid.
What was the astonishment of the latter to behold in this grand
cavalier his old friend Lope Sanchez, who was actually cele-
brating the marriage of his daughter Sanchica with one of the
first grandees in the land.

The carriage contained the bridal party. There was dame
Sanchez, now grown as round as a barrel, and dressed out with

feathers and jewels, and necklaces of pearls, and necklaces of diamonds, and rings on every finger, altogether a finery of apparel that had not been seen since the days of Queen Sheba. The little Sanchica had now grown to be a woman, and for grace and beauty might have been mistaken for a duchess, if not a princess outright. The bridegroom sat beside her—rather a withered spindle-shanked little man, but this only proved him to be of the true-blue blood; a legitimate Spanish grandee being rarely above three cubits in stature. The match had been of the mother's making.

Riches had not spoiled the heart of honest Lope. He kept his old comrade with him for several days; feasted him like a king, took him to plays and bull-fights, and at length sent him away rejoicing, with a big bag of money for himself, and another to be distributed among his ancient messmates of the Alhambra.

Lope always gave out that a rich brother had died in America and left him heir to a copper mine; but the shrewd gossips of the Alhambra insist that his wealth was all derived from his having discovered the secret guarded by the two marble nymphs of the Alhambra. It is remarked that these very discreet statues continue, even unto the present day, with their eyes fixed most significantly on the same part of the wall; which leads many to suppose there is still some hidden treasure remaining there well worthy the attention of the enterprising traveller. Though others, and particularly all female visitors, regard them with great complacency as lasting monuments of the fact that women can keep a secret.

CHAPTER XX.   THE CAMP OF THE WILD HORSE

HUNTERS' STORIES—HABITS OF THE WILD HORSE—THE HALF-BREED AND HIS PRIZE—A HORSE CHASE—A WILD SPIRIT TAMED

We had encamped in a good neighborhood for game, as the reports of rifles in various directions speedily gave notice. One of our hunters soon returned with the meat of a doe, tied up in the skin, and slung across his shoulders. Another brought a fat buck across his horse. Two other deer were brought in, and a number of turkeys. All the game was thrown down in front of the Captain's fire, to be portioned out among the various messes. The spits and camp kettles were soon in full employ, and throughout the evening there was a scene of hunters' feasting and profusion.

We had been disappointed this day in our hopes of meeting with buffalo, but the sight of the wild horse had been a great novelty, and gave a turn to the conversation of the camp for the evening. There were several anecdotes told of a famous gray horse, which has ranged the prairies of this neighborhood for six or seven years, setting at naught every attempt of the hunters to capture him. They say he can pace and rack (or amble) faster than the fleetest horses can run. Equally marvellous accounts were given of a black horse on the Brassos,[77] who grazed the prairies on that river's banks in the Texas. For years he outstripped all pursuit. His fame spread far and wide; offers were made for him to the amount of a thousand dollars; the boldest and most hard-riding hunters tried incessantly to make prize of him, but in vain. At length he fell a victim to his gallantry, being decoyed under a tree by a tame mare, and a noose dropped over his head by a boy perched among the branches.

The capture of the wild horse is one of the most favorite achievements of the prairie tribes; and, indeed, it is from this source that the Indian hunters chiefly supply themselves. The wild horses which range those vast grassy plains, extending from the Arkansas to the Spanish settlements, are of various forms and colors, betraying their various descents. Some resemble the common English stock, and are probably descended from horses which have escaped from our border settlements. Others are of a low but strong make, and are supposed to be of the Andalusian breed, brought out by the Spanish discoverers.

Some fanciful speculatists have seen in them descendants of the Arab stock, brought into Spain from Africa, and thence transferred to this country; and have pleased themselves with the idea, that their sires may have been of the pure coursers of the desert, that once bore Mahomet and his warlike disciples across the sandy plains of Arabia.

The habits of the Arab seem to have come with the steed. The introduction of the horse on the boundless prairies of the Far West, changed the whole mode of living of their inhabitants. It gave them that facility of rapid motion, and of sudden and distant change of place, so dear to the roving propensities of man. Instead of lurking in the depths of gloomy forests, and patiently threading the mazes of a tangled wilderness on foot, like his brethren of the north, the Indian of the West is a rover of the plain; he leads a brighter and more sunshiny life; almost always on horseback, on vast flowery prairies and under cloudless skies.

I was lying by the Captain's fire, late in the evening, listening to stories about those coursers of the prairies, and weaving speculations of my own, when there was a clamor of voices and a loud cheering at the other end of the camp; and word was passed that Beatte, the half-breed, had brought in a wild horse.

In an instant every fire was deserted; the whole camp crowded to see the Indian and his prize. It was a colt about two years old, well grown, finely limbed, with bright prominent eyes, and a spirited yet gentle demeanor. He gazed about him with an air of mingled stupefaction and surprise, at the men, the horses, and the camp-fires; while the Indian stood before him with folded arms, having hold of the other end of the cord which noosed his captive, and gazing on him with a most imperturbable aspect. Beatte, as I have before observed, has a greenish olive complexion, with a strongly marked countenance, not unlike the bronze casts of Napoleon; and as he stood before his captive horse, with folded arms and fixed aspect, he looked more like a statue than a man.

If the horse, however, manifested the least restiveness, Beatte would immediately worry him with the lariat, jerking him first on one side, then on the other, so as almost to throw him on the ground; when he had thus rendered him passive, he would resume his statue-like attitude and gaze at him in silence.

The whole scene was singularly wild; the tall grove, partially illumined by the flashing fires of the camp, the horses tethered here and there among the trees, the carcasses of deer hanging around, and in the midst of all, the wild huntsman and his wild horse, with an admiring throng of rangers, almost as wild.

In the eagerness of their excitement, several of the young rangers sought to get the horse by purchase or barter, and even offered extravagant terms; but Beatte declined all their offers. "You give great price now;" said he, "to-morrow you be sorry, and take back, and say d—d Indian!"

The young men importuned him with questions about the mode in which he took the horse, but his answers were dry and laconic; he evidently retained some pique at having been undervalued and sneered at by them; and at the same time looked down upon them with contempt as greenhorns, little versed in the noble science of woodcraft.

Afterwards, however, when he was seated by our fire, I readily drew from him an account of his exploit; for, though taciturn among strangers, and little prone to boast of his actions, yet his taciturnity, like that of all Indians, had its times of relaxation.

He informed me, that on leaving the camp, he had returned to the place where we had lost sight of the wild horse. Soon getting upon its track, he followed it to the banks of the river.

Here, the prints being more distinct in the sand, he perceived that one of the hoofs was broken and defective, so he gave up the pursuit.

As he was returning to the camp, he came upon a gang of six horses, which immediately made for the river. He pursued them across the stream, left his rifle on the river bank, and putting his horse to full speed, soon came up with the fugitives. He attempted to noose one of them, but the lariat hitched on one of his ears, and he shook it off. The horses dashed up a hill, he followed hard at their heels, when, of a sudden, he saw their tails whisking in the air, and they plunging down a precipice. It was too late to stop. He shut his eyes, held in his breath, and went over with them—neck or nothing. The descent was between twenty and thirty feet, but they all came down safe upon a sandy bottom.

He now succeeded in throwing his noose round a fine young horse. As he galloped alongside of him, the two horses passed each side of a sapling, and the end of the lariat was jerked out of his hand. He regained it, but an intervening tree obliged him again to let it go. Having once more caught it, and coming to a more open country, he was enabled to play the young horse with the line until he gradually checked and subdued him, so as to lead him to the place where he had left his rifle.

He had another formidable difficulty in getting him across the river, where both horses stuck for a time in the mire, and Beatte was nearly unseated from his saddle by the force of the current and the struggles of his captive. After much toil and trouble, however, he got across the stream, and brought his prize safe into camp.

For the remainder of the evening, the camp remained in a high state of excitement; nothing was talked of but the capture of wild horses; every youngster of the troop was for this harum-scarum kind of chase; every one promised himself to return from the campaign in triumph, bestriding one of these wild coursers of the prairies. Beatte had suddenly risen to great importance; he was the prime hunter, the hero of the day. Offers were made him by the best mounted rangers, to let him ride their horses in the chase, provided he would give them a share of the spoil. Beatte bore his honors in silence, and closed with none of the offers. Our stammering, chattering, gasconading little Frenchman, however, made up for his taciturnity, by vaunting as much upon the subject as if it were he that had caught the horse. Indeed he held forth so learnedly in the matter, and boasted so much of the many horses he had taken, that he began to be considered an oracle; and some of the youngsters were inclined to doubt whether he were not superior even to the taciturn Beatte.

The excitement kept the camp awake later than usual. The hum of voices, interrupted by occasional peals of laughter, was heard from the groups around the various fires, and the night was considerably advanced before all had sunk to sleep.

With the morning dawn the excitement revived, and Beatte and his wild horse were again the gaze and talk of the camp. The captive had been tied all night to a tree among the other horses. He was again led forth by Beatte, by a long halter or lariat, and, on his manifesting the least restiveness, was, as before, jerked and worried into passive submission. He appeared to be gentle and docile by nature, and had a beautifully mild expression of the eye. In his strange and forlorn situation, the poor animal seemed to seek protection and companionship in the very horse which had aided to capture him.

Seeing him thus gentle and tractable, Beatte, just as we were about to march, strapped a light pack upon his back, by way of giving him the first lesson in servitude. The native pride and independence of the animal took fire at this indignity. He reared, and plunged, and kicked, and tried in every way to get rid of the degrading burden. The Indian was too potent for him. At every paroxysm he renewed the discipline of the halter, until the poor animal, driven to despair, threw himself prostrate on the ground, and lay motionless, as if acknowledging himself vanquished. A stage hero, representing the despair of a captive prince, could not have played his part more dramatically. There was absolutely a moral grandeur in it.

The imperturbable Beatte folded his arms, and stood for a

time, looking down in silence upon his captive; until seeing him perfectly subdued, he nodded his head slowly, screwed his mouth into a sardonic smile of triumph, and, with a jerk of the halter, ordered him to rise. He obeyed, and from that time forward offered no resistance. During that day he bore his pack patiently, and was led by the halter; but in two days he followed voluntarily at large among the supernumerary horses of the troop.

I could not but look with compassion upon this fine young animal, whose whole course of existence had been so suddenly reversed. From being a denizen of these vast pastures, ranging at will from plain to plain and mead to mead, cropping of every herb and flower, and drinking of every stream, he was suddenly reduced to perpetual and painful servitude, to pass his life under the harness and the curb, amid, perhaps, the din and dust and drudgery of cities. The transition in his lot was such as sometimes takes place in human affairs, and in the fortunes of towering individuals:—one day, a prince of the prairies—the next day, a pack-horse!

From ABBOTSFORD [78]

I sit down to perform my promise of giving you an account of a visit made many years since to Abbotsford. I hope, however, that you do not expect much from me, for the travelling notes taken at the time are so scanty and vague, and my memory so extremely fallacious, that I fear I shall disappoint you with the meagreness and crudeness of my details.

Late in the evening of the 29th of August, 1817, I arrived at the ancient little border town of Selkirk, where I put up for the night. I had come down from Edinburgh, partly to visit Melrose Abbey and its vicinity, but chiefly to get a sight of the "mighty minstrel of the north." I had a letter of introduction to him from Thomas Campbell the poet, and had reason to think, from the interest he had taken in some of my earlier scribblings, that a visit from me would not be deemed an intrusion.

On the following morning, after an early breakfast, I set off in a postchaise for the Abbey. On the way thither I stopped at the gate of Abbotsford, and sent the postillion to the house with the letter of introduction and my card, on which I had written that I was on my way to the ruins of Melrose Abbey, and wished to know whether it would be agreeable to Mr. Scott (he had not yet been made a Baronet) to receive a visit from me in the course of the morning.

While the postillion was on his errand, I had time to survey the mansion. It stood some short distance below the road, on the side of a hill sweeping down to the Tweed; and was as yet but a snug gentleman's cottage, with something rural and picturesque in its appearance. The whole front was overrun with evergreens, and immediately above the portal was a great pair of elk horns, branching out from beneath the foliage, and giving the cottage the look of a hunting lodge. The huge baronial pile, to which this modest mansion in a manner gave birth, was just emerging into existence: part of the walls, surrounded by scaffolding, already had risen to the height of the cottage, and the court-yard in front was encumbered by masses of hewn stone.

The noise of the chaise had disturbed the quiet of the establishment. Out sallied the warder of the castle, a black greyhound, and, leaping on one of the blocks of stone, began a furious barking. His alarum brought out the whole garrison of dogs:

> "Both mongrel, puppy, whelp, and hound,
>   And curs of low degree;"

all open-mouthed and vociferous.——I should correct my quotation;—not a cur was to be seen on the premises: Scott was too true a sportsman, and had too high a veneration for pure blood, to tolerate a mongrel.

In a little while the "lord of the castle" himself made his appearance. I knew him at once by the descriptions I had read and heard, and the likenesses that had been published of him. He was tall, and of a large and powerful frame. His dress was simple, and almost rustic. An old green shooting-coat, with a dog-whistle at the button hole, brown linen pantaloons, stout shoes that tied at the ankles, and a white hat that had evidently seen service. He came limping up the gravel walk, aiding himself by a stout walking-staff, but moving rapidly and with vigor. By his side jogged along a large iron-gray stag hound of most grave demeanor, who took no part in the clamor of the canine rabble, but seemed to consider himself bound, for the dignity of the house, to give me a courteous reception.

Before Scott had reached the gate he called out in a hearty tone, welcoming me to Abbotsford, and asking news of Campbell. Arrived at the door of the chaise, he grasped me warmly by the hand: "Come, drive down, drive down to the house," said he, "ye're just in time for breakfast, and afterwards ye shall see all the wonders of the Abbey."

I would have excused myself, on the plea of having already made my breakfast. "Hout, man," cried he, "a ride in the morning in the keen air of the Scotch hills is warrant enough for a second breakfast."

I was accordingly whirled to the portal of the cottage, and in a few moments found myself seated at the breakfast table. There was no one present but the family, which consisted of Mrs. Scott, her eldest daughter Sophia, then a fine girl about seventeen, Miss Ann Scott, two or three years younger, Walter, a well-grown stripling, and Charles, a lively boy, eleven or twelve years of age. I soon felt myself quite at home, and my heart in a glow with the cordial welcome I experienced. I had thought to make a mere morning visit, but found I was not to be let off so lightly. "You must not think our neighborhood is to be read in a morning, like a newspaper," said Scott. "It takes several days of study for an observant traveller that has a relish for auld world trumpery. After breakfast you shall make your visit to Melrose Abbey; I shall not be able to accompany you, as I have some household affairs to attend to, but I will put you in charge of my son Charles, who is very learned in all things touching the old ruin and the neighborhood it stands in, and he and my friend Johnny Bower will tell you the whole truth about it, with a good deal more that you are not called upon to believe—unless you be a true and nothing-doubting antiquary. When you come back, I'll take you out on a ramble about the neighborhood. To-morrow we will take a look at the Yarrow, and the next day we will drive over to Dryburgh Abbey, which is a fine old ruin well worth your seeing"—in a word, before Scott had got through with his plan, I found myself committed for a visit of several days, and it seemed as if a little realm of romance was suddenly opened before me.

* * *

After my return from Melrose Abbey, Scott proposed a ramble to show me something of the surrounding country. As we sallied forth, every dog in the establishment turned out to attend us. There was the old stag-hound Maida, that I have already mentioned, a noble animal, and a great favorite of Scott's, and Hamlet, the black greyhound, a wild thoughtless youngster, not yet arrived to the years of discretion; and Finette, a beautiful setter, with soft silken hair, long pendent ears, and a mild eye, the parlor favorite. When in front of the house, we were joined by a superannuated greyhound, who came from the kitchen wagging his tail, and was cheered by Scott as an old friend and comrade.

In our walks, Scott would frequently pause in conversation to notice his dogs and speak to them, as if rational companions; and indeed there appears to be a vast deal of rationality in these faithful attendants on man, derived from their close intimacy with him. Maida deported himself with a gravity becoming his age and size, and seemed to consider himself called upon to preserve a great degree of dignity and decorum in our society. As he jogged along a little distance ahead of us, the young dogs would gambol about him, leap on his neck, worry at his ears, and endeavor to tease him into a frolic. The old dog would keep on for a long time with imperturbable solemnity, now and then seeming to rebuke the wantonness of his young companions. At length he would make a sudden turn, seize one of them, and tumble him in the dust; then giving a glance at us, as much as to say, "You see, gentlemen, I can't help giving way to this nonsense," would resume his gravity and jog on as before.

Scott amused himself with these peculiarities. "I make no doubt," said he, "when Maida is alone with these young dogs, he throws gravity aside, and plays the boy as much as any of them; but he is ashamed to do so in our company, and seems to say, 'Ha' done with your nonsense, youngsters; what will the laird and that other gentleman think of me if I give way to such foolery?' "

Maida reminded him, he said, of a scene on board an armed yacht in which he made an excursion with his friend Adam Ferguson. They had taken much notice of the boatswain, who was a fine sturdy seaman, and evidently felt flattered by their attention. On one occasion the crew were "piped to fun," and the sailors were dancing and cutting all kinds of capers to the music of the ship's band. The boatswain looked on with a wistful eye, as if he would like to join in; but a glance at Scott and Ferguson showed that there was a struggle with his dignity, fearing to lessen himself in their eyes. At length one of his messmates came up, and seizing him by the arm, challenged him to a jig. The boatswain, continued Scott, after a little hesitation complied, made an awkward gambol or two, like our friend Maida, but soon gave it up. "It's of no use," said he, jerking up his waistband and giving a side glance at us, "one can't dance always nouther."

Scott amused himself with the peculiarities of another of his dogs, a little shamefaced terrier, with large glassy eyes, one of the most sensitive little bodies to insult and indignity in the world. If ever he whipped him, he said, the little fellow would sneak off and hide himself from the light of day, in a lumber garret, whence there was no drawing him forth but by the sound of the chopping-knife, as if chopping up his victuals, when he would steal forth with humbled and downcast look, but would skulk away again if any one regarded him.

While we were discussing the humors and peculiarities of our canine companions, some object provoked their spleen, and produced a sharp and petulant barking from the smaller fry, but it was some time before Maida was sufficiently aroused to ramp forward two or three bounds and join in the chorus, with a deep-mouthed bow-wow!

It was but a transient outbreak, and he returned instantly, wagging his tail, and looking up dubiously in his master's face; uncertain whether he would censure or applaud.

"Aye, aye, old boy!" cried Scott, "you have done wonders. You have shaken the Eildon hills with your roaring; you may now lay by your artillery for the rest of the day. Maida is like the great gun at Constantinople," continued he; "it takes so long to get it ready, that the small guns can fire off a dozen times first, but when it does go off it plays the very d—l."

These simple anecdotes may serve to show the delightful play of Scott's humors and feelings in private life. His domestic animals were his friends; every thing about him seemed to rejoice in the light of his countenance: the face of the humblest dependent brightened at his approach, as if he anticipated a cordial and cheering word. I had occasion to observe this particularly in a visit which we paid to a quarry, whence several men were cutting stone for the new edifice; who all paused from their labor to have a pleasant "crack wi' the laird." One of them was a burgess of Selkirk, with whom Scott had some joke about the old song:

> "Up with the Souters o' Selkirk,
> And down with the Earl of Home."

Another was precentor at the Kirk, and, beside leading the psalmody on Sunday, taught the lads and lasses of the neighborhood dancing on week days, in the winter time, when out-of-door labor was scarce.

Among the rest was a tall, straight old fellow, with a healthful complexion and silver hair, and a small round-crowned white hat. He had been about to shoulder a hod, but paused, and stood looking at Scott, with a slight sparkling of his blue eye, as if waiting his turn; for the old fellow knew himself to be a favorite.

Scott accosted him in an affable tone, and asked for a pinch of snuff. The old man drew forth a horn snuff-box. "Hoot, man," said Scott, "not that old mull: where's the bonnie French one that I brought you from Paris?" "Troth, your honor," replied the old fellow, "sic a mull as that is nae for week days."

On leaving the quarry, Scott informed me that when absent at Paris, he had purchased several trifling articles as presents for his dependents, and among others the gay snuff-box in question, which was so carefully reserved for Sundays, by the veteran. "It was not so much the value of the gifts," said he, "that pleased them, as the idea that the laird should think of them when so far away."

The old man in question, I found, was a great favorite with Scott. If I recollect right, he had been a soldier in early life, and his straight, erect person, his ruddy yet rugged countenance, his gray hair, and an arch gleam in his blue eye, reminded me of the description of Edie Ochiltree. I find that the old fellow has since been introduced by Wilkie, in his picture of the Scott family.

* * *

Scott went on to expatiate on the popular songs of Scotland. "They are a part of our national inheritance," said he, "and something that we may truly call our own. They have no foreign taint; they have the pure breath of the heather and the mountain breeze. All the genuine legitimate races that have descended from the ancient Britons; such as the Scotch, the Welsh, and the Irish, have national airs. The English have none, because they are not natives of the soil, or, at least, are mongrels. Their music is all made up of foreign scraps, like a harlequin jacket, or a piece of mosaic. Even in Scotland, we have comparatively few national songs in the eastern part, where we have had most influx of strangers. A real old Scottish song is a cairn gorm—a gem of our own mountains: or rather, it is a precious relic of old times, that bears the national character stamped upon it;—like a cameo, that shows what the national visage was in former days, before the breed was crossed."

While Scott was thus discoursing, we were passing up a narrow glen, with the dogs beating about, to right and left, when suddenly a black cock burst upon the wing.

"Aha!" cried Scott, "there will be a good shot for master Walter; we must send him this way with his gun, when we go home. Walter's the family sportsman now, and keeps us in game. I have pretty nigh resigned my gun to him; for I find I cannot trudge about as briskly as formerly."

Our ramble took us on the hills commanding an extensive prospect. "Now," said Scott, "I have brought you, like the pilgrim in the Pilgrim's Progress, to the top of the Delectable Mountains, that I may show you all the goodly regions hereabouts. Yonder is Lammermuir, and Smalholme; and there you have Gallashiels, and Torwoodlie, and Gallawater; and in that direction you see Teviotdale, and the Braes of Yarrow; and Ettrick stream, winding along, like a silver thread, to throw itself into the Tweed."

He went on thus to call over names celebrated in Scottish song, and most of which had recently received a romantic interest from his own pen. In fact, I saw a great part of the border country spread out before me, and could trace the scenes of those poems and romances which had, in a manner, bewitched the world. I gazed about me for a time with mute surprise, I may almost say with disappointment. I beheld a mere succession of gray waving hills, line beyond line, as far as my eye could reach; monotonous in their aspect, and so destitute of trees, that one could almost see a stout fly walking along their profile; and the far-famed Tweed appeared a naked stream, flowing between bare hills, without a tree or thicket on its banks; and yet, such had been the magic web of poetry and romance thrown over the whole, that it had a greater charm for me than the richest scenery I beheld in England.

I could not help giving utterance to my thoughts. Scott hummed for a moment to himself, and looked grave; he had no idea of having his muse complimented at the expense of his native hills. "It may be partiality," said he, at length; "but to my eye, these gray hills and all this wild border country have beauties peculiar to themselves. I like the very nakedness of the land; it has something bold, and stern, and solitary about it. When I have been for some time in the rich scenery about Edinburgh, which is like ornamented garden land, I begin to wish myself back again among my own honest gray hills; and if I did not see the heather at least once a year, *I think I should die!*"

The last words were said with an honest warmth, accompanied with a thump on the ground with his staff, by way of emphasis, that showed his heart was in his speech. He vindicated the Tweed, too, as a beautiful stream in itself, and observed that he did not dislike it for being bare of trees, probably from having been much of an angler in his time, and an angler does not like to have a stream overhung by trees, which embarrass him in the exercise of his rod and line.

I took occasion to plead, in like manner, the associations of early life, for my disappointment, in respect to the surrounding scenery. I had been so accustomed to hills crowned with forests, and streams breaking their way through a wilderness of trees, that all my ideas of romantic landscape were apt to be well wooded.

"Aye, and that's the great charm of your country," cried Scott. "You love the forest as I do the heather—but I would not have you think I do not feel the glory of a great woodland prospect. There is nothing I should like more than to be in the midst of one of your grand, wild, original forests: with the idea of hundreds of miles of untrodden forest around me. I once saw, at Leith, an immense stick of timber, just landed from America. It must have been an enormous tree when it stood on its native soil, at its full height, and with all its branches. I gazed at it with admiration; it seemed like one of the gigantic obelisks which are now and then brought from Egypt, to shame the pigmy monuments of Europe; and, in fact, these vast aboriginal trees, that have sheltered the Indians before the intrusion of the white men, are the monuments and antiquities of your country."

The conversation here turned upon Campbell's poem of Gertrude of Wyoming, as illustrative of the poetic materials furnished by American scenery. Scott spoke of it in that liberal style in which I always found him to speak of the writings of his contemporaries. He cited several passages of it with great delight. "What a pity it is," said he, "that Campbell does not write more and oftener, and give full sweep to his genius. He has wings that would bear him to the skies; and he does now and then spread them grandly, but folds them up again and resumes his perch, as if he was afraid to launch away. He don't know or won't trust his own strength. Even when he has done a thing well, he has often misgivings about it. He left out several fine passages of his Lochiel, but I got him to restore some of them." Here Scott repeated several passages in a magnificent style. "What a grand idea is that," said he, "about prophetic boding, or, in common parlance, second sight—

'Coming events cast their shadows before.'

It is a noble thought, and nobly expressed. And there's that, glorious little poem, too, of Hohenlinden; after he had written it, he did not seem to think much of it, but considered some of it 'd—d drum and trumpet lines.' I got him to recite it to me, and I believe that the delight I felt and expressed had an effect in inducing him to print it. The fact is," added he, "Campbell is, in a manner, a bugbear to himself. The brightness of his early success is a detriment to all his further efforts. *He is afraid of the shadow that his own fame casts before him.*"

While we were thus chatting, we heard the report of a gun among the hills. "That's Walter, I think," said Scott, "he has finished his morning's studies, and is out with his gun. I should not be surprised if he had met with the black cock; if so, we shall have an addition to our larder, for Walter is a pretty sure shot."

I inquired into the nature of Walter's studies. "Faith," said Scott, "I can't say much on that head. I am not over bent upon making prodigies of any of my children. As to Walter, I taught him, while a boy, to ride, and shoot, and speak the truth; as to the other parts of his education, I leave them to a very worthy young man, the son of one of our clergymen, who instructs all my children."

* * *

After dinner we adjourned to the drawing-room, which served also for study and library. Against the wall on one side was a long writing-table, with drawers; surmounted by a small cabinet of polished wood, with folding doors richly studded with brass ornaments, within which Scott kept his most valuable papers. Above the cabinet, in a kind of niche, was a complete corslet of glittering steel, with a closed helmet, and flanked by gauntlets and battle-axes. Around were hung trophies and relics of various kinds: a cimeter of Tippoo Saib; a Highland broadsword from Floddenfield; a pair of Rippon spurs from Bannockburn; and above all, a gun which had belonged to Rob Roy, and bore his initials, R. M. G., an object of peculiar interest to me at the time, as it was understood Scott was actually engaged in printing a novel founded on the story of that famous outlaw.

On each side of the cabinet were book-cases, well stored with works of romantic fiction in various languages, many of them rare and antiquated. This, however, was merely his cottage library, the principal part of his books being at Edinburgh.

From this little cabinet of curiosities Scott drew forth a manuscript picked up on the field of Waterloo, containing copies of several songs popular at the time in France. The paper was dabbled with blood—"the very life-blood, very possibly," said Scott, "of some gay young officer, who had cherished these songs as a keepsake from some lady love in Paris."

He adverted in a mellow and delightful manner to the little half gay, half melancholy campaigning song, said to have been composed by General Wolfe, and sung by him at the mess table, on the eve of the storming of Quebec, in which he fell so gloriously.

> "Why, soldiers, why,
> Should we be melancholy, boys?
> Why, soldiers, why,
> Whose business 'tis to die!
> For should next campaign
> Send us to him who made us, boys,
> We're free from pain:
> But should we remain,
> A bottle and kind landlady
> Makes all well again."

"So," added he, "the poor lad who fell at Waterloo, in all probability, had been singing these songs in his tent the night before the battle, and thinking of the fair dame who had taught him them, and promising himself, should he outlive the campaign, to return to her all glorious from the wars."

I find since that Scott published translations of these songs among some of his smaller poems.

The evening passed away delightfully in this quaint-looking apartment, half study, half drawing-room. Scott read several passages from the old romance of Arthur, with a fine deep sonorous voice, and a gravity of tone that seemed to suit the antiquated, black-letter volume. It was a rich treat to hear such a work, read by such a person, and in such a place; and his appearance as he sat reading, in a large armed chair, with his favorite hound Maida at his feet, and surrounded by books and relics, and border trophies, would have formed an admirable and most characteristic picture.

While Scott was reading, the sage grimalkin already mentioned had taken his seat in a chair beside the fire, and remained with fixed eye and grave demeanor, as if listening to the reader. I observed to Scott that his cat seemed to have a black-letter taste in literature.

"Ah," said he, "these cats are a very mysterious kind of folk. There is always more passing in their minds than we are aware of. It comes no doubt from their being so familiar with witches and warlocks." He went on to tell a little story about a gude man who was returning to his cottage one night, when, in a lonely out of the way place, he met with a funeral procession of cats all in mourning, bearing one of their race to the grave in a coffin covered with a black velvet pall. The worthy man, astonished and half frightened at so strange a pageant, hastened home and told what he had seen to his wife and children. Scarce had he finished, when a great black cat that sat beside the fire raised himself up, exclaimed "Then I am king of the cats!" and vanished up the chimney. The funeral seen by the gude man, was one of the cat dynasty.

"Our grimalkin here," added Scott, "sometimes reminds me of the story, by the airs of sovereignty which he assumes; and I am apt to treat him with respect from the idea that he may be a great prince incog., and may some time or other come to the throne."

In this way Scott would make the habits and peculiarities of even the dumb animals about him, subjects for humorous remark or whimsical story.

Our evening was enlivened also by an occasional song from Sophia Scott, at the request of her father. She never wanted to be asked twice, but complied frankly and cheerfully. Her songs were all Scotch, sung without any accompaniment, in a simple manner, but with great spirit and expression, and in their native

dialects, which gave them an additional charm. It was delightful
to hear her carol off in sprightly style, and with an animated air,
some of those generous-spirited old Jacobite songs, once current among the adherents of the Pretender in Scotland, in
which he is designated by the appellation of "The Young
Chevalier."

These songs were much relished by Scott, notwithstanding
his loyalty; for the unfortunate "Chevalier" has always been a
hero of romance with him, as he has with many other stanch
adherents to the House of Hanover, now that the Stuart line
has lost all its terrors. In speaking on the subject, Scott mentioned as a curious fact, that, among the papers of the "Chevalier," which had been submitted by government to his inspec-
tion, he had found a memorial to Charles from some adherents
in America, dated 1778, proposing to set up his standard in the
back settlements. I regret that, at the time, I did not make more
particular inquiries of Scott on the subject; the document in
question, however, in all probability, still exists among the
Pretender's papers, which are in the possession of the British
Government.

In the course of the evening, Scott related the story of a
whimsical picture hanging in the room, which had been drawn
for him by a lady of his acquaintance. It represented the doleful
perplexity of a wealthy and handsome young English knight of
the olden time, who, in the course of a border foray, had been
captured and carried off to the castle of a hard-headed and high-
handed old baron. The unfortunate youth was thrown into a
dungeon, and a tall gallows erected before the castle gate for
his execution. When all was ready, he was brought into the
castle hall where the grim baron was seated in state, with his
warriors armed to the teeth around him, and was given his
choice, either to swing on the gibbet or to marry the baron's
daughter. The last may be thought an easy alternative, but
unfortunately, the baron's young lady was hideously ugly, with
a mouth from ear to ear, so that not a suitor was to be had for
her, either for love or money, and she was known throughout
the border country by the name of Muckle-mouthed Mag!

The picture in question represented the unhappy dilemma of the handsome youth. Before him sat the grim baron, with a face worthy of the father of such a daughter, and looking daggers and rat's-bane. On one side of him was Muckle-mouthed Mag, with an amorous smile across the whole breadth of her countenance, and a leer enough to turn a man to stone; on the other side was the father confessor, a sleek friar, jogging the youth's elbow, and pointing to the gallows, seen in perspective through the open portal.

The story goes, that after long laboring in mind between the altar and the halter, the love of life prevailed, and the youth resigned himself to the charms of Muckle-mouthed Mag. Contrary to all the probabilities of romance, the match proved a happy one. The baron's daughter, if not beautiful, was a most exemplary wife; her husband was never troubled with any of those doubts and jealousies which sometimes mar the happiness of connubial life, and was made the father of a fair and undoubtedly legitimate line, which still flourishes on the border.

I give but a faint outline of the story from vague recollection; it may, perchance, be more richly related elsewhere, by some one who may retain something of the delightful humor with which Scott recounted it.

When I retired for the night, I found it almost impossible to sleep; the idea of being under the roof of Scott; of being on the borders of the Tweed, in the very centre of that region which had for some time past been the favorite scene of romantic fiction; and above all, the recollections of the ramble I had taken, the company in which I had taken it, and the conversation which had passed, all fermented in my mind, and nearly drove sleep from my pillow.

On the following morning, the sun darted his beams from over the hills through the low lattice window. I rose at an early hour, and looked out between the branches of eglantine which overhung the casement. To my surprise Scott was already up and forth, seated on a fragment of stone, and chatting with the workmen employed on the new building. I had supposed, after the time he had wasted upon me yesterday, he would be closely occupied this morning: but he appeared like a man of leisure, who had nothing to do but bask in the sunshine and amuse himself.

I soon dressed myself and joined him. He talked about his proposed plans of Abbotsford: happy would it have been for him could he have contented himself with his delightful little vine-covered cottage, and the simple, yet hearty and hospitable style, in which he lived at the time of my visit. The great pile of Abbotsford, with the huge expense it entailed upon him, of servants, retainers, guests, and baronial style, was a drain upon his purse, a tax upon his exertions, and a weight upon his mind, that finally crushed him.

As yet, however, all was in embryo and perspective, and Scott pleased himself with picturing out his future residence, as he would one of the fanciful creations of his own romances. "It was one of his air castles," he said, "which he was reducing to solid stone and mortar." About the place were strewed various morsels from the ruins of Melrose Abbey, which were to be incorporated in his mansion. He had already constructed out of similar materials a kind of Gothic shrine over a spring, and had surmounted it by a small stone cross.

* * *

A summons to breakfast broke off our conversation, when I begged to recommend to Scott's attention my friend the little red lion, who had led to such an interesting topic, and hoped he might receive some niche or station in the future castle, worthy of his evident antiquity and apparent dignity. Scott assured me, with comic gravity, that the valiant little lion should be most honorably entertained; I hope, therefore, that he still flourishes at Abbotsford.

Before dismissing the theme of the relics from the Abbey, I will mention another, illustrative of Scott's varied humors. This was a human skull, which had probably belonged of yore to one of those jovial friars, so honorably mentioned in the old border ballad:

> "O the monks of Melrose made gude kale
>   On Fridays, when they fasted;
> They wanted neither beef nor ale,
>   As long as their neighbors lasted."

This skull Scott had caused to be cleaned and varnished, and placed it on a chest of drawers in his chamber, immediately opposite his bed; where I have seen it, grinning most dismally. It was an object of great awe and horror to the superstitious housemaids; and Scott used to amuse himself with their apprehensions. Sometimes, in changing his dress, he would leave his neckcloth coiled round it like a turban, and none of the "lasses" dared to remove it. It was a matter of great wonder and speculation among them that the laird should have such an "awsome fancy for an auld girning skull."

*   *   *

His daughter Sophia and his son Charles were those of his family who seemed most to feel and understand his humors, and to take delight in his conversation. Mrs. Scott did not always pay the same attention, and would now and then make a casual remark which would operate a little like a damper. Thus, one morning at breakfast, when Dominie Thompson the tutor was present, Scott was going on with great glee to relate an anecdote of the laird of Macnab, "who, poor fellow!" premised he, "is dead and gone—" "Why, Mr. Scott," exclaimed the good lady, "Macnab's not dead, is he?" "Faith, my dear," replied Scott, with humorous gravity, "if he's not dead they've done him great injustice,—for they've buried him."

The joke passed harmless and unnoticed by Mrs. Scott, but hit the poor Dominie just as he had raised a cup of tea to his lips, causing a burst of laughter which sent half of the contents about the table.

After breakfast, Scott was occupied for some time correcting proof sheets, which he had received by the mail. The novel of Rob Roy, as I have already observed, was at that time in the press, and I supposed them to be the proof sheets of that work. The authorship of the Waverley novels was still a matter of conjecture and uncertainty; though few doubted their being principally written by Scott. One proof to me of his being the author, was that he never adverted to them. A man so fond of any thing Scottish, and any thing relating to national history or local legend, could not have been mute respecting such productions, had they been written by another. He was fond of quoting the works of his contemporaries; he was continually reciting scraps of border songs, or relating anecdotes of border story. With respect to his own poems, and their merits, however, he was mute, and while with him I observed a scrupulous silence on the subject.

I may here mention a singular fact, of which I was not aware at the time, that Scott was very reserved with his children respecting his own writings, and was even disinclined to their reading his romantic poems. I learnt this, some time after, from a passage in one of his letters to me, adverting to a set of the American miniature edition of his poems, which, on my return to England, I forwarded to one of the young ladies. "In my hurry," writes he, "I have not thanked you, in Sophia's name, for the kind attention which furnished her with the American volumes. I am not quite sure I can add my own, since you have made her acquainted with much more of papa's folly, than she would otherwise have learned; for I have taken special care they should never see any of these things during their earlier years."

To return to the thread of my narrative. When Scott had got through his brief literary occupation, we set out on a ramble. The young ladies started to accompany us, but had not gone far, when they met a poor old laborer and his distressed family, and turned back to take them to the house, and relieve them.

On passing the bounds of Abbotsford, we came upon a bleak-looking farm, with a forlorn crazy old manse, or farmhouse, standing in naked desolation. This, however, Scott told me was an ancient hereditary property called Lauckend, about as valuable as the patrimonial estate of Don Quixote, and which,

in like manner, conferred an hereditary dignity upon its pro-
prietor, who was a laird, and, though poor as a rat, prided
himself upon his ancient blood, and the standing of his house.
He was accordingly called Lauckend, according to the Scottish
custom of naming a man after his family estate, but he was more
generally known through the country round by the name of
Lauckie Long Legs, from the length of his limbs. While Scott
was giving this account of him, we saw him at a distance
striding along one of his fields, with his plaid fluttering about
him, and he seemed well to deserve his appellation, for he looked
all legs and tartan.

Lauckie knew nothing of the world beyond his neighborhood. Scott told me that on returning to Abbotsford from his
visit to France, immediately after the war, he was called on by
his neighbors generally, to inquire after foreign parts. Among
the number, came Lauckie Long Legs and an old brother as
ignorant as himself. They had many inquiries to make about
the French, whom they seemed to consider some remote and
semi-barbarous horde—"And what like are thae barbarians in
their own country?" said Lauckie, "can they write?—can they
cipher?" He was quite astonished to learn that they were
nearly as much advanced in civilization as the gude folks of
Abbotsford.

After living for a long time in single blessedness, Lauckie all
at once, and not long before my visit to the neighborhood, took
it into his head to get married. The neighbors were all surprised; but the family connection, who were as proud as they
were poor, were grievously scandalized, for they thought the
young woman on whom he had set his mind quite beneath him.
It was in vain, however, that they remonstrated on the misalli-
ance he was about to make: he was not to be swayed from his
determination. Arraying himself in his best, and saddling a
gaunt steed that might have rivalled Rosinante, and placing a
pillion behind his saddle, he departed to wed and bring home
the humble lassie who was to be made mistress of the venerable
hovel of Lauckend, and who lived in a village on the opposite
side of the Tweed.

A small event of the kind makes a great stir in a little quiet country neighborhood. The word soon circulated through the village of Melrose, and the cottages in its vicinity, that Lauckie Long Legs had gone over the Tweed to fetch home his bride. All the good folks assembled at the bridge to await his return. Lauckie, however, disappointed them; for he crossed the river at a distant ford, and conveyed his bride safe to his mansion, without being perceived.

Let me step forward in the course of events and relate the fate of poor Lauckie, as it was communicated to me a year or two afterwards in letter by Scott. From the time of his marriage he had no longer any peace, owing to the constant intermeddlings of his relations, who would not permit him to be happy in his own way, but endeavored to set him at variance with his wife. Lauckie refused to credit any of their stories to her disadvantage; but the incessant warfare he had to wage, in defence of her good name, wore out both flesh and spirit. His last conflict was with his own brothers, in front of his paternal mansion. A furious scolding match took place between them; Lauckie made a vehement profession of faith in favor of her immaculate honesty, and then fell dead at the threshold of his own door. His person, his character, his name, his story, and his fate, entitled him to be immortalized in one of Scott's novels, and I looked to recognize him in some of the succeeding works from his pen; but I looked in vain.

* * *

I think it was in the course of this ramble that my friend Hamlet, the black greyhound, got into a sad scrape. The dogs were beating about the glens and fields as usual, and had been for some time out of sight, when we heard a barking at some distance to the left. Shortly after we saw some sheep scampering on the hills, with the dogs after them. Scott applied to his lips the ivory whistle, always hanging at his button-hole, and soon called in the culprits, excepting Hamlet. Hastening up a bank which commanded a view along a fold or hollow of the hills, we beheld the sable prince of Denmark standing by the bleeding body of a sheep. The carcass was still warm, the throat bore marks of the fatal grip, and Hamlet's muzzle was stained with blood. Never was culprit more completely caught in *flagrante delictu*. I supposed the doom of poor Hamlet to be sealed; for no higher offence can be committed by a dog in a country abounding with sheep walks. Scott, however, had a greater value for his dogs than for his sheep. They were his companions and friends. Hamlet, too, though an irregular, impertinent kind of youngster, was evidently a favorite. He would not for some time believe it could be he who had killed the sheep. It must have been some cur of the neighborhood, that had made off on our approach, and left poor Hamlet in the lurch. Proofs, however, were too strong, and Hamlet was generally condemned. "Well, well," said Scott, "it's partly my own fault. I have given up coursing for some time past, and the poor dog has had no chance after game to take the fire edge off of him. If he was put after a hare occasionally he never would meddle with sheep."

I understood, afterwards, that Scott actually got a pony, and went out now and then coursing with Hamlet, who, in consequence, showed no further inclination for mutton.

* * *

Whenever Scott touched, in this way, upon local antiquities, and in all his familiar conversations about local traditions and superstitions, there was always a sly and quiet humor running at the bottom of his discourse, and playing about his countenance, as if he sported with the subject. It seemed to me as if he distrusted his own enthusiasm, and was disposed to droll upon his own humors and peculiarities, yet, at the same time, a poetic gleam in his eye would show that he really took a strong relish and interest in them. "It was a pity," he said, "that antiquarians were generally so dry, for the subjects they handled were rich in historical and poetic recollections, in picturesque details, in quaint and heroic characteristics, and in all kinds of curious and obsolete ceremonials. They are always groping among the rarest materials for poetry, but they have no idea of turning them to poetic use. Now every fragment from old times has, in some degree, its story with it, or gives an inkling of something characteristic of the circumstances and manners of its day, and so sets the imagination at work."

For my own part I never met with antiquarian so delightful, either in his writings or his conversation; and the quiet subacid humor that was prone to mingle in his disquisitions, gave them, to me, a peculiar and an exquisite flavor. But he seemed, in fact, to undervalue every thing that concerned himself.

* * *

The only sad moment that I experienced at Abbotsford, was that of my departure; but it was cheered with the prospect of soon returning; for I had promised, after making a tour in the Highlands, to come and pass a few more days on the banks of the Tweed, when Scott intended to invite Hogg the poet to meet me.... He accompanied me on foot ... to a small ... gate, when he halted, and took my hand. "I will not say fare-well," said he, "for it is always a painful word, but I will say, come again. When you have made your tour to the Highlands, come here and give me a few more days—but come when you please, you will always find Abbotsford open to you, and a hearty welcome."

* * *

When I consider how much he has thus contributed to the better hours of my past existence, and how independent his works still make me, at times, of all the world for my enjoy-ment, I bless my stars that cast my lot in his days, to be thus cheered and gladdened by the outpourings of his genius. I con-sider it one of the greatest advantages that I have derived from my literary career, that it has elevated me into genial communion with such a spirit; and as a tribute of gratitude for his friend-ship, and veneration for his memory, I cast this humble stone upon his cairn, which will soon, I trust, be piled aloft with the contributions of abler hands.

From OLIVER GOLDSMITH: A BIOGRAPHY[79]

PREFACE

In the course of a revised edition of my works I have come to
a biographical sketch of Goldsmith, published several years
since. It was written hastily, as introductory to a selection from
his writings; and, though the facts contained in it were collected from various sources, I was chiefly indebted for them to
the voluminous work of Mr. James Prior, who had collected
and collated the most minute particulars of the poet's history
with unwearied research and scrupulous fidelity; but had rendered them, as I thought, in a form too cumbrous and overlaid
with details and disquisitions, and matters uninteresting to the
general reader.

When I was about of late to revise my biographical sketch,
preparatory to republication, a volume was put into my hands,
recently given to the public by Mr. John Forster, of the Inner
Temple, who, likewise availing himself of the labors of the
indefatigable Prior, and of a few new lights since evolved, has
produced a biography of the poet, executed with a spirit, a feeling, a grace and an eloquence, that leave nothing to be desired.
Indeed it would have been presumption in me to undertake the
subject after it had been thus felicitously treated, did I not stand
committed by my previous sketch. That sketch now appeared
too meager and insufficient to satisfy public demand; yet it had
to take its place in the revised series of my works unless something more satisfactory could be substituted. Under these circumstances I have again taken up the subject, and gone into it
with more fulness than formerly, omitting none of the facts
which I considered illustrative of the life and character of the
poet, and giving them in as graphic a style as I could command.
Still the hurried manner in which I have had to do this amidst
the pressure of other claims on my attention, and with the press
dogging at my heels, has prevented me from giving some parts

of the subject the thorough handling I could have wished. Those who would like to see it treated still more at large, with the addition of critical disquisitions and the advantage of collateral facts, would do well to refer themselves to Mr. Prior's circumstantial volumes, or to the elegant and discursive pages of Mr. Forster.

For my own part, I can only regret my short comings in what to me is a labor of love; for it is a tribute of gratitude to the memory of an author whose writings were the delight of my childhood, and have been a source of enjoyment to me throughout life; and to whom, of all others, I may address the beautiful apostrophe of Dante to Virgil:

> Tu se' lo mio maestro, e 'l mio autore:
> Tu se' solo colui, da cu' io tolsi
> Lo bello stile, che m' ha fatto onore.

W. I.

Sunnyside, Aug. 1, 1849.

From CHAPTER II

. . . The time had now arrived for him to be sent to the University; and, accordingly, on the 11th June, 1745, when seventeen years of age, he entered Trinity College, Dublin; but his father was no longer able to place him there as a pensioner, as he had done his eldest son Henry; he was obliged, therefore, to enter him as a sizer, or "poor scholar." He was lodged in one of the top rooms adjoining the library of the building, numbered 35, where it is said his name may still be seen, scratched by himself upon a window frame.

A student of this class is taught and boarded gratuitously, and has to pay but a very small sum for his room. It is expected, in return for these advantages, that he will be a diligent student, and render himself useful in a variety of ways. In Trinity College, at the time of Goldsmith's admission, several derogatory, and, indeed, menial offices were exacted from the sizer, as if the college sought to indemnify itself for conferring benefits by inflicting indignities. He was obliged to sweep part of the courts in the morning; to carry up the dishes from the kitchen to the fellows' table, and to wait in the hall until that body had dined. His very dress marked the inferiority of the "poor student" to his happier classmates. It was a black gown of coarse stuff without sleeves, and a plain black cloth cap without a tassel. We can conceive nothing more odious and ill-judged than these distinctions, which attached the idea of degradation to poverty, and placed the indigent youth of merit below the worthless minion of fortune. They were calculated to wound and irritate the noble mind, and to render the base mind baser.

Indeed, the galling effect of these servile tasks upon youths of proud spirits and quick sensibilities became at length too notorious to be disregarded. About fifty years since, on a Trinity Sunday, a number of persons were assembled to witness the college ceremonies; and as a sizer was carrying up a dish of meat to the fellows' table, a burly citizen in the crowd made some sneering observation on the servility of his office. Stung to the quick, the high-spirited youth instantly flung the dish and its contents at the head of the sneerer. The sizer was sharply reprimanded for this outbreak of wounded pride, but the degrading task was from that day forward very properly consigned to menial hands.

It was with the utmost repugnance that Goldsmith entered college in this capacity. His shy and sensitive nature was affected by the inferior station he was doomed to hold among his gay and opulent fellow-students, and he became, at times, moody and despondent. A recollection of these early mortifications induced him, in after years, most strongly to dissuade his brother Henry, the clergyman, from sending a son to college on a like footing. "If he has ambition, strong passions, and an exquisite sensibility of contempt, do not send him there, unless you have no other trade for him except your own."

To add to his annoyances, the fellow of the college who had the peculiar control of his studies, the Rev. Theaker Wilder, was a man of violent and capricious temper, and of diametrically opposite tastes. The tutor was devoted to the exact sciences;

Goldsmith was for the classics. Wilder endeavored to force his favorite studies upon the student by harsh means, suggested by his own coarse and savage nature. He abused him in presence of the class as ignorant and stupid; ridiculed him as awkward and ugly, and at times in the transports of his temper indulged in personal violence. The effect was to aggravate a passive distaste into a positive aversion. Goldsmith was loud in expressing his contempt for mathematics and his dislike of ethics and logic; and the prejudices thus imbibed continued through life. Mathematics he always pronounced a science to which the meanest intellects were competent. . . .

He had two college associates from whom he would occasionally borrow small sums; one was an early schoolmate, by the name of Beatty; the other a cousin, and the chosen companion of his frolicks, Robert (or rather Bob) Bryanton, of Ballymulvey House, near Ballymahon. When these casual supplies failed him he was more than once obliged to raise funds for his immediate wants by pawning his books. At times he sank into despondency, but he had what he termed "a knack at hoping," which soon buoyed him up again. He began now to resort to his poetical vein as a source of profit, scribbling street-ballads, which he privately sold for five shillings each at a shop which dealt in such small wares of literature. He felt an author's affection for these unowned bantlings, and we are told would stroll privately through the streets at night to hear them sung, listening to the comments and criticisms of by-standers, and observing the degree of applause which each received.

Edmund Burke was a fellow-student with Goldsmith at the college. Neither the statesman nor the poet gave promise of their future celebrity, though Burke certainly surpassed his contemporary in industry and application, and evinced more disposition for self-improvement, associating himself with a number of his fellow-students in a debating club, in which they discussed literary topics, and exercised themselves in composition.

Goldsmith may likewise have belonged to this association, but his propensity was rather to mingle with the gay and thoughtless. On one occasion we find him implicated in an affair that came nigh producing his expulsion. A report was brought to college that a scholar was in the hands of the bailiffs. This was an insult in which every gownsman felt himself involved. A number of the scholars flew to arms, and sallied forth to battle, headed by a hair-brained fellow nicknamed Gallows Walsh, noted for his aptness at mischief and fondness for riot. The stronghold of the bailiff was carried by storm, the scholar set at liberty, and the delinquent catchpole borne off captive to the college, where, having no pump to put him under, they satisfied the demands of collegiate law by ducking him in an old cistern.

Flushed with this signal victory, Gallows Walsh now harangued his followers, and proposed to break open Newgate, or the Black Dog, as the prison was called, and effect a general jail delivery. He was answered by shouts of concurrence, and away went the throng of madcap youngsters, fully bent upon putting an end to the tyranny of law. They were joined by the mob of the city, and made an attack upon the prison with true Irish precipitation and thoughtlessness, never having provided themselves with cannon to batter its stone walls. A few shots from the prison brought them to their senses, and they beat a hasty retreat, two of the townsmen being killed, and several wounded.

A severe scrutiny of this affair took place at the University. Four students, who had been ringleaders, were expelled; four others, who had been prominent in the affray, were publicly admonished; among the latter was the unlucky Goldsmith.

To make up for this disgrace, he gained, within a month afterward, one of the minor prizes of the college. It is true it was one of the very smallest, amounting in pecuniary value to but thirty shillings, but it was the first distinction he had gained in his whole collegiate career. This turn of success and sudden influx of wealth proved too much for the head of our poor student. He forthwith gave a supper and dance at his chamber to a number of young persons of both sexes from the city, in direct violation of college rules. The unwonted sound of the fiddle reached the ears of the implacable Wilder. He rushed to the scene of unhallowed festivity, inflicted corporal punishment on the "father of the feast," and turned his astonished guests neck and heels out of doors.

This filled the measure of poor Goldsmith's humiliations; he felt degraded both within college and without. He dreaded the ridicule of his fellow-students for the ludicrous termination of his orgie, and he was ashamed to meet his city acquaintances after the degrading chastisement received in their presence, and after their own ignominious expulsion. Above all, he felt it impossible to submit any longer to the insulting tyranny of Wilder: he determined, therefore, to leave, not merely the college, but also his native land, and to bury what he conceived to be his irretrievable disgrace in some distant country. He accordingly sold his books and clothes, and sallied forth from the college walls the very next day, intending to embark at Cork for —he scarce knew where—America, or any other part beyond sea. With his usual heedless imprudence, however, he loitered about Dublin until his finances were reduced to a shilling; with this amount of specie he set out on his journey.

For three whole days he subsisted on his shilling; when that was spent, he parted with some of the clothes from his back, until, reduced almost to nakedness, he was four-and-twenty hours without food, insomuch that he declared a handful of gray pease, given to him by a girl at a wake, was one of the most delicious repasts he had ever tasted. Hunger, fatigue, and destitution brought down his spirit and calmed his anger. Fain would he have retraced his steps, could he have done so with any salvo for the lingerings of his pride. In his extremity he conveyed to his brother Henry information of his distress, and of the rash project on which he had set out. His affectionate brother hastened to his relief; furnished him with money and clothes; soothed his feelings with gentle counsel; prevailed upon him to return to college, and effected an indifferent reconciliation between him and Wilder.

After this irregular sally upon life he remained nearly two years longer at the University, giving proofs of talent in occa-

sional translations from the classics, for one of which he received
a premium, awarded only to those who are the first in literary
merit. Still he never made much figure at college, his natural
disinclination to study being increased by the harsh treatment
he continued to experience from his tutor.

Among the anecdotes told of him while at college is one indicative of that prompt, but thoughtless and often whimsical
benevolence which throughout life formed one of the most
eccentric, yet endearing points of his character. He was engaged to breakfast one day with a college intimate, but failed
to make his appearance. His friend repaired to his room,
knocked at the door, and was bidden to enter. To his surprise,
he found Goldsmith in his bed, immersed to his chin in feathers.
A serio-comic story explained the circumstance. In the course
of the preceding evening's stroll he had met with a woman with
five children, who implored his charity. Her husband was in
the hospital; she was just from the country, a stranger, and destitute, without food or shelter for her helpless offspring. This
was too much for the kind heart of Goldsmith. He was almost
as poor as herself, it is true, and had no money in his pocket;
but he brought her to the college gate, gave her the blankets
from his bed to cover her little brood, and part of his clothes for
her to sell and purchase food; and, finding himself cold during
the night, had cut open his bed and buried himself among the
feathers.

At length, on the 27th of February, 1749, O. S., he was
admitted to the degree of Bachelor of Arts, and took his final
leave of the University. He was freed from college rule, that
emancipation so ardently coveted by the thoughtless student,
and which too generally launches him amid the cares, the hardships, and vicissitudes of life. . . .

None of his relatives were in circumstances to aid him with
any thing more than a temporary home, and the aspect of every
one seemed somewhat changed. In fact, his career at college
had disappointed his friends, and they began to doubt his being
the great genius they had fancied him. . . .

The only one of his relatives who did not appear to lose faith

in him was his uncle Contarine. This kind and considerate
man, it is said, saw in him a warmth of heart requiring some skill
to direct, and a latent genius that wanted time to mature, and
these impressions none of his subsequent follies and irregularities wholly obliterated. His purse and affection, therefore,
as well as his house, were now open to him, and he became his
chief counsellor and director after his father's death. He urged
him to prepare for holy orders; and others of his relatives concurred in the advice. Goldsmith had a settled repugnance to a
clerical life. This has been ascribed by some to conscientious
scruples, not considering himself of a temper and frame of mind
for such a sacred office: others attributed it to his roving propensities and his desire to visit foreign countries; he himself gives a
whimsical objection in his biography of the "Man in Black:"—
"To be obliged to wear a long wig when I liked a short one, or
a black coat when I generally dressed in brown, I thought such
a restraint upon my liberty that I absolutely rejected the
proposal."

In effect, however, his scruples were overruled, and he agreed
to qualify himself for the office. . . .

From CHAPTER III

The time had now arrived for Goldsmith to apply for orders,
and he presented himself accordingly before the Bishop of
Elphin for ordination. We have stated his great objection to
clerical life, the obligation to wear a black coat; and, whimsical
as it may appear, dress seems in fact to have formed an obstacle
to his entrance into the church. He had ever a passion for cloth-
ing his sturdy, but awkward little person in gay colors; and on
this solemn occasion, when it was to be supposed his garb
would be of suitable gravity, he appeared luminously arrayed
in scarlet breeches! He was rejected by the bishop: some say
for want of sufficient studious preparation; his rambles and
frolics with Bob Bryanton, and his revels with the club at
Ballymahon, having been much in the way of his theological
studies; others attribute his rejection to reports of his college
irregularities, which the Bishop had received from his old

tyrant Wilder; but those who look into the matter with more
knowing eyes, pronounce the scarlet breeches to have been the
fundamental objection. "My friends," says Goldsmith, speaking through his humorous representative, the "Man in Black"
—"my friends were now perfectly satisfied I was undone; and
yet they thought it a pity for one that had not the least harm in
him, and was so very good-natured." His uncle Contarine,
however, still remained unwavering in his kindness, though
much less sanguine in his expectations. He now looked round
for a humbler sphere of action, and through his influence and
exertions Oliver was received as tutor in the family of a Mr.
Flinn, a gentleman of the neighborhood. The situation was
apparently respectable; he had his seat at the table; and joined
the family in their domestic recreations and their evening game
at cards. There was a servility, however, in his position, which
was not to his taste: nor did his deference for the family increase
upon familiar intercourse. He charged a member of it with un-
fair play at cards. A violent altercation ensued, which ended in
his throwing up his situation as tutor. On being paid off he
found himself in possession of an unheard of amount of money.
His wandering propensity and his desire to see the world, were
instantly in the ascendency. Without communicating his plans
or intentions to his friends, he procured a good horse, and with
thirty pounds in his pocket, made his second sally forth into
the world.

The worthy niece and housekeeper of the hero of La Mancha
could not have been more surprised and dismayed at one of the
Don's clandestine expeditions, than were the mother and friends
of Goldsmith when they heard of his mysterious departure.
Weeks elapsed, and nothing was seen or heard of him. It was
feared that he had left the country on one of his wandering
freaks, and his poor mother was reduced almost to despair, when
one day he arrived at her door almost as forlorn in plight as the
prodigal son. Of his thirty pounds not a shilling was left; and,
instead of the goodly steed on which he had issued forth on his
errantry, he was mounted on a sorry little pony, which he had
nicknamed Fiddle-back. . . .

From CHAPTER XVIII

The social position of Goldsmith had undergone a material change since the publication of The Traveller. Before that event he was but partially known as the author of some clever anonymous writings, and had been a tolerated member of the club and the Johnson circle, without much being expected from him. Now he had suddenly risen to literary fame, and become one of the *lions* of the day. The highest regions of intellectual society were now open to him; but he was not prepared to move in them with confidence and success. Ballymahon had not been a good school of manners at the outset of life; nor had his experience as a 'poor student' at colleges and medical schools contributed to give him the polish of society. He had brought from Ireland, as he said, nothing but his "brogue and his blunders," and they had never left him. He had travelled, it is true; but the Continental tour which in those days gave the finishing grace to the education of a patrician youth, had, with poor Goldsmith, been little better than a course of literary vagabondizing. It had enriched his mind, deepened and widened the benevolence of his heart, and filled his memory with enchanting pictures, but it had contributed little to disciplining him for the polite intercourse of the world. His life in London had hitherto been a struggle with sordid cares and sad humiliations. "You scarcely can conceive," wrote he some time previously to his brother, "how much eight years of disappointment, anguish, and study, have worn me down." Several more years had since been added to the term during which he had trod the lowly walks of life. He had been a tutor, an apothecary's drudge, a petty physician of the suburbs, a bookseller's hack, drudging for daily bread. Each separate walk had been beset by its peculiar thorns and humiliations. It is wonderful how his heart retained its gentleness and kindness through all these trials; how his mind rose above the "meannesses of poverty," to which, as he says, he was compelled to submit; but it would be still more wonderful, had his manners acquired a tone corresponding to the innate grace and refinement of his intellect. He was near forty years of age when he published The Traveller, and was lifted by it into celebrity. As is beautifully said of him by one of his biographers, "he has fought his way to consideration and esteem; but he bears upon him the scars of his twelve years' conflict; of the mean sorrows through which he has passed; and of the cheap indulgences he has sought relief and help from. There is nothing plastic in his nature now. His manners and habits are completely formed; and in them any further success can make little favorable change, whatever it may effect for his mind or genius."[80]

We are not to be surprised, therefore, at finding him make an awkward figure in the elegant drawing-rooms which were now open to him, and disappointing those who had formed an idea of him from the fascinating ease and gracefulness of his poetry. . . .

From CHAPTER XXV

Boswell, in his memoirs, has rendered one of his suits for ever famous. That worthy, on the 16th of October in this same year, gave a dinner to Johnson, Goldsmith, Reynolds, Garrick, Murphy, Bickerstaff, and Davies. Goldsmith was generally apt to bustle in at the last moment, when the guests were taking their seats at table, but on this occasion he was unusually early. While waiting for some lingerers to arrive, "he strutted about," says Boswell, "bragging of his dress, and I believe, was seriously vain of it, for his mind was undoubtedly prone to such impressions. 'Come, come,' said Garrick, 'talk no more of that. You are perhaps the worst—eh, eh?' Goldsmith was eagerly attempting to interrupt him, when Garrick went on, laughing ironically. 'Nay, you will always *look* like a gentleman; but I am talking of your being well or *ill dressed*.' 'Well, let me tell you,' said Goldsmith, 'when the tailor brought home my bloom-colored coat, he said, "Sir, I have a favor to beg of you; when any body asks you who made your clothes, be pleased to mention John Filby, at the Harrow, in Water Lane." 'Why, sir,' cried Johnson, 'that was because he knew the strange color would attract crowds to gaze at it, and thus they might hear of him, and see how well he could make a coat of so absurd a color.'"

But though Goldsmith might permit this raillery on the part of his friends, he was quick to resent any personalities of the kind from strangers. As he was one day walking the Strand in grand array with bag-wig and sword, he excited the merriment of two coxcombs, one of whom called to the other to "look at that fly with a long pin stuck through it." Stung to the quick, Goldsmith's first retort was to caution the passers-by to be on their guard against "that brace of disguised pickpockets"—his next was to step into the middle of the street, where there was room for action, half-draw his sword, and beckon the joker, who was armed in like manner, to follow him. This was literally a war of wit which the other had not anticipated. He had no inclination to push the joke to such an extreme, but abandoning the ground, sneaked off with his brother wag amid the hootings of the spectators.

This proneness to finery in dress, however, which Boswell and others of Goldsmith's contemporaries, who did not understand the secret plies of his character, attributed to vanity, arose, we are convinced, from a widely different motive. It was from a painful idea of his own personal defects, which had been cruelly stamped upon his mind in his boyhood, by the sneers and jeers of his playmates, and had been ground deeper into it by rude speeches made to him in every step of his struggling career, until it had become a constant cause of awkwardness and embarrassment. This he had experienced the more sensibly since his reputation had elevated him into polite society; and he was constantly endeavoring by the aid of dress to acquire that personal *acceptability*, if we may use the phrase, which nature had denied him. If ever he betrayed a little self-complacency on first turning out in a new suit, it may, perhaps, have been because he felt as if he had achieved a triumph over his ugliness. . . .

From CHAPTER XLIV

He was not aware of his critical situation, and intended to be at the club on the 25th of March, on which occasion Charles Fox, Sir Charles Bunbury (one of the Horneck connection),

and two other new members were to be present. In the afternoon, however, he felt so unwell as to take to his bed, and his
symptoms soon acquired sufficient force to keep him there.
His malady fluctuated for several days, and hopes were entertained of his recovery, but they proved fallacious. He had
skilful medical aid and faithful nursing, but he would not follow
the advice of his physicians, and persisted in the use of James's
powders, which he had once found beneficial, but which were
now injurious to him. His appetite was gone, his strength failed
him, but his mind remained clear, and was perhaps too active
for his frame. Anxieties and disappointments which had previously sapped his constitution, doubtless aggravated his present complaint and rendered him sleepless. In reply to an inquiry
of his physician, he acknowledged that his mind was ill at ease.
This was his last reply: he was too weak to talk, and in general
took no notice of what was said to him. He sank at last into a
deep sleep, and it was hoped a favorable crisis had arrived. He
awoke, however, in strong convulsions, which continued without intermission until he expired, on the fourth of April, at five
o'clock in the morning; being in the forty-sixth year of his age.

His death was a shock to the literary world, and a deep
affliction to a wide circle of intimates and friends; for, with all
his foibles and peculiarities, he was fully as much beloved as he
was admired. Burke, on hearing the news, burst into tears.
Sir Joshua Reynolds threw by his pencil for the day, and
grieved more than he had done in times of great family distress. "I was abroad at the time of his death," writes Dr.
M'Donnell, the youth whom when in distress he had employed
as an amanuensis, "and I wept bitterly when the intelligence
first reached me. A blank came over my heart as if I had lost
one of my nearest relatives, and was followed for some days by
a feeling of despondency." Johnson felt the blow deeply and
gloomily. In writing some time afterwards to Boswell, he observed, "Of poor Dr. Goldsmith there is little to be told more
than the papers have made public. He died of a fever, made, I
am afraid, more violent by uneasiness of mind. His debts
began to be heavy, and all his resources were exhausted. Sir

Joshua is of opinion that he owed no less than two thousand pounds. Was ever poet so trusted before?"

Among his debts were seventy-nine pounds due to his tailor, Mr. William Filby, from whom he had received a new suit but a few days before his death. "My father," said the younger Filby, "though a loser to that amount, attributed no blame to Goldsmith; he had been a good customer, and had he lived, would have paid every farthing." Others of his tradespeople evinced the same confidence in his integrity, notwithstanding his heedlessness. Two sister milliners in Temple Lane, who had been accustomed to deal with him, were concerned when told, some time before his death, of his pecuniary embarrassments. "Oh, sir," said they to Mr. Cradock, "sooner persuade him to let us work for him gratis than apply to any other; we are sure he will pay us when he can."

On the stairs of his apartment there was the lamentation of the old and infirm, and the sobbing of women; poor objects of his charity, to whom he had never turned a deaf ear, even when struggling himself with poverty.

But there was one mourner, whose enthusiasm for his memory, could it have been foreseen, might have soothed the bitterness of death. After the coffin had been screwed down, a lock of his hair was requested for a lady, a particular friend, who wished to preserve it as a remembrance. It was the beautiful Mary Horneck—the Jessamy Bride. The coffin was opened again, and a lock of hair cut off; which she treasured to her dying day. Poor Goldsmith! could he have foreseen that such a memorial of him was to be thus cherished! . . .

From CHAPTER XLV

Never was the trite, because sage apothegm, that "The child is father to the man," more fully verified than in the case of Goldsmith. He is shy, awkward, and blundering in childhood, yet fully of sensibility; he is a butt for the jeers and jokes of his companions, but apt to surprise and confound them by sudden and witty repartees; he is dull and stupid at his tasks, yet an

eager and intelligent devourer of the travelling tales and campaigning stories of his half military pedagogue; he may be a
dunce, but he is already a rhymer; and his early scintillations of
poetry awaken the expectations of his friends. He seems from
infancy to have been compounded of two natures, one bright,
the other blundering; or to have had fairy gifts laid in his
cradle by the "good people" who haunted his birth-place, the
old goblin mansion on the banks of the Inny.

He carried with him the wayward elfin spirit, if we may so
term it, throughout his career. His fairy gifts are of no avail at
school, academy, or college: they unfit him for close study and
practical science, and render him heedless of every thing that
does not address itself to his poetical imagination and genial and
festive feelings; they dispose him to break away from restraint,
to stroll about hedges, green lanes, and haunted streams, to revel
with jovial companions, or to rove the country like a gipsy in
quest of odd adventures.

As if confiding in these delusive gifts, he takes no heed of the
present nor care for the future, lays no regular and solid foundation of knowledge, follows out no plan, adopts and discards
those recommended by his friends, at one time prepares for the
ministry, next turns to the law, and then fixes upon medicine.
He repairs to Edinburgh, the great emporium of medical science, but the fairy gifts accompany him; he idles and frolics
away his time there, imbibing only such knowledge as is agreeable to him; makes an excursion to the poetical regions of the
Highlands; and having walked the hospitals for the customary
time, sets off to ramble over the Continent, in quest of novelty
rather than knowledge. His whole tour is a poetical one. He
fancies he is playing the philosopher while he is really playing
the poet; and though professedly he attends lectures and visits
foreign universities, so deficient is he on his return, in the studies
for which he set out, that he fails in an examination as a sur-
geon's mate; and while figuring as a doctor of medicine, is out-
vied on a point of practice by his apothecary. Baffled in every
regular pursuit, after trying in vain some of the humbler callings of commonplace life, he is driven almost by chance to the

exercise of his pen, and here the fairy gifts come to his assistance. For a long time, however, he seems unaware of the magic
properties of that pen: he uses it only as a make-shift until he
can find a *legitimate* means of support. He is not a learned man,
and can write but meagerly and at second-hand on learned subjects; but he has a quick convertible talent that seizes lightly on
the points of knowledge necessary to the illustration of a theme:
his writings for a time are desultory, the fruits of what he has
seen and felt, or what he has recently and hastily read; but his
gifted pen transmutes every thing into gold, and his own genial
nature reflects its sunshine through his pages.

Still unaware of his powers he throws off his writings anony-
mously, to go with the writings of less favored men; and it is a
long time, and after a bitter struggle with poverty and humiliation, before he acquires confidence in his literary talent as a
means of support, and begins to dream of reputation.

From this time his pen is a wand of power in his hand, and
he has only to use it discreetly, to make it competent to all his
wants. But discretion is not a part of Goldsmith's nature; and
it seems the property of these fairy gifts to be accompanied by
moods and temperaments to render their effect precarious. The
heedlessness of his early days; his disposition for social enjoyment; his habit of throwing the present on the neck of the
future, still continue. His expenses forerun his means; he in-
curs debts on the faith of what his magic pen is to produce, and
then, under the pressure of his debts, sacrifices its productions
for prices far below their value. It is a redeeming circumstance
in his prodigality, that it is lavished oftener upon others than
upon himself; he gives without thought or stint, and is the continual dupe of his benevolence and his trustfulness in human
nature. We may say of him as he says of one of his heroes,
"He could not stifle the natural impulse which he had to do
good, but frequently borrowed money to relieve the distressed;
and when he knew not conveniently where to borrow, he has
been observed to shed tears as he passed through the wretched
suppliants who attended his gate."   *   *   *   *   *

"His simplicity in trusting persons whom he had no previous

reasons to place confidence in, seems to be one of those lights of his character which, while they impeach his understanding, do honor to his benevolence. The low and the timid are ever suspicious; but a heart impressed with honorable sentiments, expects from others sympathetic sincerity." [81]

His heedlessness in pecuniary matters, which had rendered his life a struggle with poverty even in the days of his obscurity, rendered the struggle still more intense when his fairy gifts had elevated him into the society of the wealthy and luxurious, and imposed on his simple and generous spirit fancied obligations to a more ample and bounteous display.

"How comes it," says a recent and ingenious critic, "that in all the miry paths of life which he had trod, no speck ever sullied the robe of his modest and graceful muse? How amidst all that love of inferior company, which never to the last forsook him, did he keep his genius so free from every touch of vulgarity?"

We answer that it was owing to the innate purity and goodness of his nature; there was nothing in it that assimilated to vice and vulgarity. Though his circumstances often compelled him to associate with the poor, they never could betray him into companionship with the depraved. His relish for humor and for the study of character, as we have before observed, brought him often into convivial company of a vulgar kind; but he discriminated between their vulgarity and their amusing qualities, or rather wrought from the whole those familiar pictures of life which form the staple of his most popular writings.

Much, too, of this intact purity of heart may be ascribed to the lessons of his infancy under the paternal roof; to the gentle, benevolent, elevated, unworldly maxims of his father, who "passing rich with forty pounds a year," infused a spirit into his child which riches could not deprave nor poverty degrade. Much of his boyhood, too, had been passed in the household of his uncle, the amiable and generous Contarine; where he talked of literature with the good pastor, and practised music with his daughter, and delighted them both by his juvenile attempts at poetry. These early associations breathed a grace and refine-

ment into his mind and tuned it up, after the rough sports on
the green, or the frolics at the tavern. These led him to turn
from the roaring glees of the club, to listen to the harp of his
cousin Jane; and from the rustic triumph of "throwing sledge,"
to a stroll with his flute along the pastoral banks of the Inny.

The gentle spirit of his father walked with him through life,
a pure and virtuous monitor; and in all the vicissitudes of his
career, we find him ever more chastened in mind by the sweet
and holy recollections of the home of his infancy.

It has been questioned whether he really had any religious
feeling. Those who raise the question have never considered
well his writings; his Vicar of Wakefield, and his pictures of
the Village Pastor, present religion under its most endearing
forms, and with a feeling that could only flow from the deep
convictions of the heart. When his fair travelling companions
at Paris urged him to read the Church Service on a Sunday, he
replied that "he was not worthy to do it." He had seen in early
life the sacred offices performed by his father and his brother,
with a solemnity which had sanctified them in his memory; how
could he presume to undertake such functions? His religion
has been called in question by Johnson and by Boswell: he certainly had not the gloomy hypochondriacal piety of the one,
nor the babbling mouth-piety of the other; but the spirit of
Christian charity, breathed forth in his writings and illustrated
in his conduct, give us reason to believe he had the indwelling
religion of the soul.

We have made sufficient comments in the preceding chapters
on his conduct in elevated circles of literature and fashion.
The fairy gifts which took him there, were not accompanied by
the gifts and graces necessary to sustain him in that artificial
sphere. He can neither play the learned sage with Johnson,
nor the fine gentleman with Beauclerc: though he has a mind
replete with wisdom and natural shrewdness, and a spirit free
from vulgarity. The blunders of a fertile but hurried intellect,
and the awkward display of the student assuming the man of
fashion, fix on him a character for absurdity and vanity which,
like the charge of lunacy, it is hard to disprove, however weak

the grounds of the charge and strong the facts in opposition to it.

In truth, he is never truly in his place in these learned and fashionable circles, which talk and live for display. It is not the kind of society he craves. His heart yearns for domestic life; it craves familiar, confiding intercourse, family firesides, the guileless and happy company of children; these bring out the heartiest and sweetest sympathies of his nature.

"Had it been his fate," says the critic we have already quoted, "to meet a woman who could have loved him, despite his faults, and respected him despite his foibles, we cannot but think that his life and his genius would have been much more harmonious; his desultory affections would have been concentred, his craving self-love appeased, his pursuits more settled, his character more solid. A nature like Goldsmith's, so affectionate, so confiding—so susceptible to simple, innocent enjoyments—so dependent on others for the sunshine of existence, does not flower if deprived of the atmosphere of home."

The cravings of his heart in this respect are evident, we think, throughout his career; and if we have dwelt with more significancy than others, upon his intercourse with the beautiful Horneck family, it is because we fancied we could detect, amid his playful attentions to one of its members, a lurking sentiment of tenderness, kept down by conscious poverty and a humiliating idea of personal defects. A hopeless feeling of this kind— the last a man would communicate to his friends—might account for much of that fitfulness of conduct, and that gathering melancholy, remarked, but not comprehended by his associates, during the last year or two of his life; and may have been one of the troubles of the mind which aggravated his last illness, and only terminated with his death.

We shall conclude these desultory remarks, with a few which have been used by us on a former occasion. From the general tone of Goldsmith's biography, it is evident that his faults, at the worst, were but negative, while his merits were great and decided. He was no one's enemy but his own; his errors, in the main, inflicted evil on none but himself, and were so blended with humorous, and even affecting circumstances, as to disarm anger and conciliate kindness. Where eminent talent is united to spotless virtue, we are awed and dazzled into admiration, but our admiration is apt to be cold and reverential; while there is something in the harmless infirmities of a good and great, but erring individual, that pleads touchingly to our nature; and we turn more kindly towards the object of our idolatry, when we find that, like ourselves, he is mortal and is frail. The epithet so often heard, and in such kindly tones, of "poor Goldsmith," speaks volumes. Few, who consider the real compound of admirable and whimsical qualities which form his character, would wish to prune away its eccentricities, trim its grotesque luxuriance, and clip it down to the decent formalities of rigid virtue. "Let not his frailties be remembered," said Johnson; "he was a very great man." But, for our part, we rather say "Let them be remembered," since their tendency is to endear; and we question whether he himself would not feel gratified in hearing his reader, after dwelling with admiration on the proofs of his greatness, close the volume with the kind-hearted phrase, so fondly and familiarly ejaculated, of "POOR GOLDSMITH."

GUESTS FROM GIBBET-ISLAND[82]

A Legend of Communipaw

FOUND AMONG THE KNICKERBOCKER PAPERS
AT WOLFERT'S ROOST

Whoever has visited the ancient and renowned village of Communipaw, may have noticed an old stone building, of most ruinous and sinister appearance. The doors and window-shutters are ready to drop from their hinges; old clothes are stuffed in the broken panes of glass, while legions of half-starved dogs prowl about the premises, and rush out and bark at every passer by; for your beggarly house in a village is most apt to swarm with profligate and ill-conditioned dogs. What adds to the sinister appearance of this mansion, is a tall frame in front, not a little resembling a gallows, and which looks as if waiting to accommodate some of the inhabitants with a well-merited airing. It is not a gallows, however, but an ancient sign-post; for this dwelling in the golden days of Communipaw, was one of the most orderly and peaceful of village taverns, where public affairs were talked and smoked over. In fact, it was in this very building that Oloffe the Dreamer, and his companions, concerted that great voyage of discovery and colonization, in which they explored Buttermilk Channel, were nearly shipwrecked in the strait of Hell-gate, and finally landed on the island of Manhattan, and founded the great city of New-Amsterdam.

Even after the province had been cruelly wrested from the sway of their High Mightinesses, by the combined forces of the British and the Yankees, this tavern continued its ancient loyalty. It is true the head of the Prince of Orange disappeared from the sign, a strange bird being painted over it, with the explanatory legend of "DIE WILDE GANS," or, The Wild Goose; but this all the world knew to be a sly riddle of the landlord, the worthy

349

Teunis Van Gieson, a knowing man, in a small way, who laid his finger beside his nose and winked, when any one studied the signification of his sign, and observed that his goose was hatching, but would join the flock whenever they flew over the water; an enigma which was the perpetual recreation and delight of the loyal but fat-headed burghers of Communipaw.

Under the sway of this patriotic, though discreet and quiet publican, the tavern continued to flourish in primeval tranquillity, and was the resort of true-hearted Nederlanders, from all parts of Pavonia; who met here quietly and secretly, to smoke and drink the downfall of Briton and Yankee, and success to Admiral Van Tromp.

The only drawback on the comfort of the establishment, was a nephew of mine host, a sister's son, Yan Yost Vanderscamp by name, and a real scamp by nature. This unlucky whipster showed an early propensity to mischief, which he gratified in a small way, by playing tricks upon the frequenters of the Wild Goose; putting gunpowder in their pipes, or squibs in their pockets, and astonishing them with an explosion, while they sat nodding round the fireplace in the bar-room; and if perchance a worthy burgher from some distant part of Pavonia lingered until dark over his potation, it was odds but young Vanderscamp would slip a brier under his horse's tail, as he mounted, and send him clattering along the road, in neck-or-nothing style, to the infinite astonishment and discomfiture of the rider.

It may be wondered at, that mine host of the Wild Goose did not turn such a graceless varlet out of doors; but Teunis Van Gieson was an easy-tempered man, and having no child of his own, looked upon his nephew with almost parental indulgence. His patience and good nature were doomed to be tried by another inmate of his mansion. This was a cross-grained curmudgeon of a negro, named Pluto, who was a kind of enigma in Communipaw. Where he came from, nobody knew. He was found one morning, after a storm, cast like a sea-monster on the strand, in front of the Wild Goose, and lay there, more dead than alive. The neighbors gathered round, and speculated on this production of the deep; whether it were fish or flesh, or a compound of both, commonly yclept a merman. The kind-hearted Teunis Van Gieson, seeing that he wore the human form, took him into his house, and warmed him into life. By degrees, he showed signs of intelligence, and even uttered sounds very much like language, but which no one in Communi-paw could understand. Some thought him a negro just from Guinea, who had either fallen overboard, or escaped from a slave-ship. Nothing, however, could ever draw from him any account of his origin. When questioned on the subject, he merely pointed to Gibbet-Island, a small rocky islet, which lies in the open bay, just opposite Communipaw, as if that were his native place, though every body knew it had never been in-habited.

In the process of time, he acquired something of the Dutch language, that is to say, he learnt all its vocabulary of oaths and maledictions, with just words sufficient to string them together. "Donder en blicksem!" (thunder and lightning), was the gen-tlest of his ejaculations. For years he kept about the Wild Goose, more like one of those familiar spirits, or household gob-lins, we read of, than like a human being. He acknowledged allegiance to no one, but performed various domestic offices, when it suited his humor; waiting occasionally on the guests; grooming the horses, cutting wood, drawing water; and all this without being ordered. Lay any command on him, and the stubborn sea urchin was sure to rebel. He was never so much at home, however, as when on the water, plying about in skiff or canoe, entirely alone, fishing, crabbing, or grabbing for oysters, and would bring home quantities for the larder of the Wild Goose, which he would throw down at the kitchen door, with a growl. No wind nor weather deterred him from launch-ing forth on his favorite element: indeed, the wilder the weather, the more he seemed to enjoy it. If a storm was brewing, he was sure to put off from shore; and would be seen far out in the bay, his light skiff dancing like a feather on the waves, when sea and sky were in a turmoil, and the stoutest ships were fain to lower their sails. Sometimes on such occasions he would be absent for days together. How he weathered the tempest, and how and where he subsisted, no one could divine, nor did any one venture to ask, for all had an almost superstitious awe of him. Some of the Communipaw oystermen declared they had more than once seen him suddenly disappear, canoe and all, as if plunged beneath the waves, and after a while come up again, in quite a different part of the bay; whence they concluded that he could live under water like that notable species of wild duck, commonly called the hell-diver. All began to consider him in the light of a foul-weather bird, like the Mother Carey's Chicken, or stormy petrel; and whenever they saw him putting far out in his skiff, in cloudy weather, made up their minds for a storm.

The only being for whom he seemed to have any liking, was Yan Yost Vanderscamp, and him he liked for his very wickedness. He in a manner took the boy under his tutelage, prompted him to all kinds of mischief, aided him in every wild harum-scarum freak, until the lad became the complete scape-grace of the village; a pest to his uncle, and to every one else. Nor were his pranks confined to the land; he soon learned to accompany old Pluto on the water. Together these worthies would cruise about the broad bay, and all the neighboring straits and rivers; poking around in skiffs and canoes; robbing the set nets of the fishermen; landing on remote coasts, and laying waste orchards and water-melon patches; in short, carrying on a complete system of piracy, on a small scale. Piloted by Pluto, the youthful Vanderscamp soon became acquainted with all the bays, rivers, creeks, and inlets of the watery world around him; could navigate from the Hook to Spiting-devil on the darkest night, and learned to set even the terrors of Hell-gate at defiance.

At length, negro and boy suddenly disappeared, and days and weeks elapsed, but without tidings of them. Some said they must have run away and gone to sea; others jocosely hinted that old Pluto, being no other than his namesake in disguise, had spirited away the boy to the nether regions. All however, agreed in one thing, that the village was well rid of them.

In the process of time, the good Teunis Van Gieson slept with his fathers, and the tavern remained shut up, waiting for a claimant, for the next heir was Yan Yost Vanderscamp, and he had not been heard of for years. At length, one day, a boat was seen pulling for shore, from a long, black, rakish-looking schooner, that lay at anchor in the bay. The boat's crew seemed worthy of the craft from which they debarked. Never had such a set of noisy, roistering, swaggering varlets landed in peaceful Communipaw. They were outlandish in garb and demeanor, and were headed by a rough, burly, bully ruffian, with fiery whiskers, a copper nose, a scar across his face, and a great Flaunderish beaver slouched on one side of his head, in whom, to their dismay, the quiet inhabitants were made to recognise their early pest, Yan Yost Vanderscamp. The rear of this hopeful gang was brought up by old Pluto, who had lost an eye, grown grizzly-headed, and looked more like a devil than ever. Vanderscamp renewed his acquaintance with the old burghers, much against their will, and in a manner not at all to their taste. He slapped them familiarly on the back, gave them an iron grip of the hand, and was hail fellow well met. According to his own account, he had been all the world over; had made money by bags full; had ships in every sea, and now meant to turn the Wild Goose into a country-seat, where he and his comrades, all rich merchants from foreign parts, might enjoy themselves in the interval of their voyages.

Sure enough, in a little while there was a complete metamorphose of the Wild Goose. From being a quiet, peaceful Dutch public house, it became a most riotous, uproarious private dwelling, a complete rendezvous for boisterous men of the seas, who came here to have what they called a "blow out" on dry land, and might be seen at all hours, lounging about the door, or lolling out of the windows; swearing among themselves, and cracking rough jokes on every passer by. The house was fitted up, too, in so strange a manner: hammocks slung to the walls, instead of bedsteads; odd kinds of furniture, of foreign fashion; bamboo couches, Spanish chairs; pistols, cutlasses, and blunderbusses, suspended on every peg; silver crucifixes on the mantelpieces, silver candlesticks and porringers on the tables, contrasting oddly with the pewter and Delf ware of the original establishment. And then the strange amusements of these sea-monsters! Pitching Spanish dollars, instead of quoits; firing blunderbusses out of the window; shooting at a mark, or at any unhappy dog, or cat, or pig, or barn-door fowl, that might happen to come within reach.

The only being who seemed to relish their rough waggery, was old Pluto; and yet he led but a dog's life of it; for they prac-tised all kinds of manual jokes upon him; kicked him about like a football; shook him by his grizzly mop of wool, and never spoke to him without coupling a curse by way of adjective to his name, and consigning him to the infernal regions. The old fellow, however, seemed to like them the better, the more they cursed him, though his utmost expression of pleasure never amounted to more than the growl of a petted bear, when his ears are rubbed.

Old Pluto was the ministering spirit at the orgies of the Wild Goose; and such orgies as took place there! Such drinking, sing-ing, whooping, swearing; with an occasional interlude of quar-relling and fighting. The noisier grew the revel, the more old Pluto plied the potations, until the guests would become frantic in their merriment, smashing every thing to pieces, and throw-ing the house out of the windows. Sometimes, after a drinking bout, they sallied forth and scoured the village, to the dismay of the worthy burghers, who gathered their women within doors, and would have shut up the house. Vanderscamp, how-ever, was not to be rebuffed. He insisted on renewing acquaint-ance with his old neighbors, and on introducing his friends, the merchants, to their families; swore he was on the look-out for a wife, and meant, before he stopped, to find husbands for all their daughters. So, will-ye, nill-ye, sociable he was; swaggered about their best parlors, with his hat on one side of his head; sat on the good wife's nicely-waxed mahogany table, kicking his heels against the carved and polished legs; kissed and tousled the young vrouws; and, if they frowned and pouted, gave them a gold rosary, or a sparkling cross, to put them in good humor again.

Sometimes nothing would satisfy him, but he must have some

of his old neighbors to dinner at the Wild Goose. There was no refusing him, for he had the complete upper hand of the community, and the peaceful burghers all stood in awe of him. But what a time would the quiet, worthy men have, among these rake-hells, who would delight to astound them with the most extravagant gunpowder tales, embroidered with all kinds of foreign oaths; clink the can with them; pledge them in deep potations; bawl drinking songs in their ears; and occasionally fire pistols over their heads, or under the table, and then laugh in their faces, and ask them how they liked the smell of gunpowder.

Thus was the little village of Communipaw for a time like the unfortunate wight possessed with devils; until Vanderscamp and his brother merchants would sail on another trading voyage, when the Wild Goose would be shut up, and every thing relapse into quiet, only to be disturbed by his next visitation.

The mystery of all these proceedings gradually dawned upon the tardy intellects of Communipaw. These were the times of the notorious Captain Kidd, when the American harbors were the resorts of piratical adventurers of all kinds, who, under pretext of mercantile voyages, scoured the West Indies, made plundering descents upon the Spanish Main, visited even the remote Indian Seas, and then came to dispose of their booty, have their revels, and fit out new expeditions, in the English colonies.

Vanderscamp had served in this hopeful school, and having risen to importance among the buccaneers, had pitched upon his native village and early home, as a quiet, out-of-the-way, unsuspected place, where he and his comrades, while anchored at New York, might have their feasts, and concert their plans, without molestation.

At length the attention of the British government was called to these piratical enterprises, that were becoming so frequent and outrageous. Vigorous measures were taken to check and punish them. Several of the most noted freebooters were caught and executed, and three of Vanderscamp's chosen comrades, the most riotous swashbucklers of the Wild Goose, were hanged in chains on Gibbet-Island, in full sight of their favorite resort. As to Vanderscamp himself, he and his man Pluto again disappeared, and it was hoped by the people of Communipaw that he had fallen in some foreign brawl, or been swung on some foreign gallows.

For a time, therefore, the tranquillity of the village was restored; the worthy Dutchmen once more smoked their pipes in peace, eyeing, with peculiar complacency, their old pests and terrors, the pirates, dangling and drying in the sun, on Gibbet-Island.

This perfect calm was doomed at length to be ruffled. The fiery persecution of the pirates gradually subsided. Justice was satisfied with the examples that had been made, and there was no more talk of Kidd, and the other heroes of like kidney. On a calm summer evening, a boat, somewhat heavily laden, was seen pulling into Communipaw. What was the surprise and disquiet of the inhabitants, to see Yan Yost Vanderscamp seated at the helm, and his man Pluto tugging at the oar! Vanderscamp, however, was apparently an altered man. He brought home with him a wife, who seemed to be a shrew, and to have the upper hand of him. He no longer was the swaggering, bully ruffian, but affected the regular merchant, and talked of retiring from business, and settling down quietly, to pass the rest of his days in his native place.

The Wild Goose mansion was again opened, but with diminished splendor, and no riot. It is true, Vanderscamp had frequent nautical visitors, and the sound of revelry was occasionally overheard in his house; but every thing seemed to be done under the rose; and old Pluto was the only servant that officiated at these orgies. The visitors, indeed, were by no means of the turbulent stamp of their predecessors; but quiet, mysterious traders, full of nods, and winks, and hieroglyphic signs, with whom, to use their cant phrase, "every thing was smug." Their ships came to anchor at night, in the lower bay; and, on a private signal, Vanderscamp would launch his boat, and accompanied solely by his man Pluto, would make them mysterious visits. Sometimes boats pulled in at night, in front of the Wild Goose, and various articles of merchandise were landed in the dark, and spirited away, nobody knew whither. One of the more curious of the inhabitants kept watch, and caught a glimpse of the features of some of these night visitors, by the casual glance of a lantern, and declared that he recognized more than one of the freebooting frequenters of the Wild Goose, in former times; whence he concluded that Vanderscamp was at his old game, and that this mysterious merchandise was nothing more nor less than piratical plunder. The more charitable opinion, however, was, that Vanderscamp and his comrades, having been driven from their old line of business, by the "oppressions of government," had resorted to smuggling to make both ends meet.

Be that as it may: I come now to the extraordinary fact, which is the butt-end of this story. It happened late one night, that Yan Yost Vanderscamp was returning across the broad bay, in his light skiff, rowed by his man Pluto. He had been carousing on board of a vessel, newly arrived, and was somewhat obfuscated in intellect, by the liquor he had imbibed. It was a still, sultry night; a heavy mass of lurid clouds was rising in the west, with the low muttering of distant thunder. Vanderscamp called on Pluto to pull lustily, that they might get home before the gathering storm. The old negro made no reply, but shaped his course so as to skirt the rocky shores of Gibbet-Island. A faint creaking overhead caused Vanderscamp to cast up his eyes, when, to his horror, he beheld the bodies of his three pot companions and brothers in iniquity dangling in the moonlight, their rags fluttering, and their chains creaking, as they were slowly swung backward and forward by the rising breeze.

"What do you mean, you blockhead!" cried Vanderscamp, "by pulling so close to the island?"

"I thought you'd be glad to see your old friends once more," growled the negro: "you were never afraid of a living man, what do you fear from the dead?"

"Who's afraid?" hiccupped Vanderscamp, partly heated by liquor, partly nettled by the jeer of the negro; "who's afraid! Hang me, but I would be glad to see them once more, alive or dead, at the Wild Goose. Come, my lads in the wind!" continued he, taking a draught, and flourishing the bottle above his head, "here's fair weather to you in the other world; and if you should be walking the rounds to-night, odds fish! but I'll be happy if you will drop in to supper."

A dismal creaking was the only reply. The wind blew loud and shrill, and as it whistled round the gallows, and among the bones, sounded as if they were laughing and gibbering in the air. Old Pluto chuckled to himself, and now pulled for home. The storm burst over the voyagers, while they were yet far from shore. The rain fell in torrents, the thunder crashed and pealed, and the lightning kept up an incessant blaze. It was stark midnight before they landed at Communipaw.

Dripping and shivering, Vanderscamp crawled homeward. He was completely sobered by the storm; the water soaked from without, having diluted and cooled the liquor within. Arrived at the Wild Goose, he knocked timidly and dubiously at the door, for he dreaded the reception he was to experience from his wife. He had reason to do so. She met him at the threshold, in a precious ill-humor.

"Is this a time," said she, "to keep people out of their beds, and to bring home company, to turn the house upside down?"

"Company?" said Vanderscamp, meekly; "I have brought no company with me, wife."

"No indeed! they have got here before you, but by your invitation; and blessed-looking company they are, truly!"

Vanderscamp's knees smote together. "For the love of heaven, where are they, wife?"

"Where?—why in the blue room up stairs, making themselves as much at home as if the house were their own."

Vanderscamp made a desperate effort, scrambled up to the room, and threw open the door. Sure enough, there at a table on which burned a light as blue as brimstone, sat the three guests from Gibbet-Island, with halters round their necks, and bobbing their cups together, as if they were hob-or-nobbing, and trolling the old Dutch freebooter's glee, since translated into English:

> "For three merry lads be we,
> And three merry lads be we;

> I on the land, and thou on the sand,
> And Jack on the gallows-tree."

Vanderscamp saw and heard no more. Starting back with horror, he missed his footing on the landing place, and fell from the top of the stairs to the bottom. He was taken up speechless, and, either from the fall or the fright, was buried in the yard of the little Dutch church at Bergen, on the following Sunday.

From that day forward, the fate of the Wild Goose was sealed. It was pronounced a *haunted house*, and avoided accordingly. No one inhabited it but Vanderscamp's shrew of a widow, and old Pluto, and they were considered but little better than its hob-goblin visitors. Pluto grew more and more haggard and morose, and looked more like an imp of darkness than a human being. He spoke to no one, but went about muttering to himself; or, as some hinted, talking with the devil, who, though unseen, was ever at his elbow. Now and then he was seen pulling about the bay alone, in his skiff, in dark weather, or at the approach of nightfall; nobody could tell why, unless on an errand to invite more guests from the gallows. Indeed it was affirmed that the Wild Goose still continued to be a house of entertainment for such guests, and that on stormy nights, the blue chamber was occasionally illuminated, and sounds of diabolical merriment were overheard, mingling with the howling of the tempest. Some treated these as idle stories, until on one such night, it was about the time of the equinox, there was a horrible uproar in the Wild Goose, that could not be mistaken. It was not so much the sound of revelry, however, as strife, with two or three piercing shrieks, that pervaded every part of the village. Nevertheless, no one thought of hastening to the spot. On the contrary, the honest burghers of Communipaw drew their nightcaps over their ears, and buried their heads under the bed-clothes, at the thoughts of Vanderscamp and his gallows companions.

The next morning, some of the bolder and more curious undertook to reconnoitre. All was quiet and lifeless at the Wild Goose. The door yawned wide open, and had evidently been open all night, for the storm had beaten into the house.

Gathering more courage from the silence and apparent deser-
tion, they gradually ventured over the threshold. The house
had indeed the air of having been possessed by devils. Every
thing was topsy-turvy; trunks had been broken open, and chests
of drawers and corner cupboards turned inside out, as in a time
of general sack and pillage; but the most woeful sight was the
widow of Yan Yost Vanderscamp, extended a corpse on the
floor of the blue chamber, with the marks of a deadly gripe on
the windpipe.

All now was conjecture and dismay at Communipaw; and
the disappearance of old Pluto, who was nowhere to be found,
gave rise to all kinds of wild surmises. Some suggested that
the negro had betrayed the house to some of Vanderscamp's
buccaneering associates, and that they had decamped together
with the booty; others surmised that the negro was nothing
more nor less than a devil incarnate, who had now accomplished
his ends, and made off with his dues.

Events, however, vindicated the negro from this last imputa-
tion. His skiff was picked up, drifting about the bay, bottom
upward, as if wrecked in a tempest; and his body was found,
shortly afterward, by some Communipaw fishermen, stranded
among the rocks of Gibbet-Island, near the foot of the pirates'
gallows. The fishermen shook their heads, and observed that
old Pluto had ventured once too often to invite Guests from
Gibbet-Island.

HOWE HEARS OF THE AFFAIR AT TRENTON—CORNWALLIS SENT
BACK TO THE JERSEYS—RECONNOITERING EXPEDITION OF
REED—HIS EXPLOITS—WASHINGTON IN PERIL AT TRENTON
—REINFORCED BY TROOPS UNDER CADWALADER AND
MIFFLIN—POSITION OF HIS MEN—CORNWALLIS AT TREN-
TON—REPULSED AT THE ASSUNPINK—THE AMERICAN
CAMP MENACED—NIGHT MARCH OF WASHINGTON—AFFAIR
AT PRINCETON—DEATH OF MERCER—ROUT OF BRITISH
TROOPS—PURSUED BY WASHINGTON—CORNWALLIS AT
PRINCETON—BAFFLED AND PERPLEXED—WASHINGTON AT
MORRISTOWN—HIS SYSTEM OF ANNOYANCE—THE TABLES
TURNED UPON THE ENEMY

General Howe was taking his ease in winter quarters at New
York, waiting for the freezing of the Delaware to pursue his
triumphant march to Philadelphia, when tidings were brought
him of the surprise and capture of the Hessians at Trenton.
"That three old established regiments of a people who made
war their profession, should lay down their arms to a ragged
and undisciplined militia, and that with scarcely any loss on
either side," was a matter of amazement. He instantly stopped
Lord Cornwallis, who was on the point of embarking for England, and sent him back in all haste to resume the command in
the Jerseys.

The ice in the Delaware impeded the crossing of the American troops, and gave the British time to draw in their scattered
cantonments and assemble their whole force at Princeton.
While his troops were yet crossing, Washington sent out Colonel Reed to reconnoitre the position and movements of the
enemy and obtain information. Six of the Philadelphia light-
horse, spirited young fellows, but who had never seen service,
volunteered to accompany Reed. They patrolled the country

to the very vicinity of Princeton, but could collect no information from the inhabitants; who were harassed, terrified, and bewildered by the ravaging marches to and fro of friend and enemy.

Emerging from a wood almost within view of Princeton, they caught sight, from a rising ground, of two or three red coats passing from time to time from a barn to a dwelling house. Here must be an outpost. Keeping the barn in a line with the house so as to cover their approach, they dashed up to the latter without being discovered, and surrounded it. Twelve British dragoons were within, who, though well armed, were so panic-stricken that they surrendered without making defence. A commissary, also, was taken; the sergeant of the dragoons alone escaped. Colonel Reed and his six cavaliers returned in triumph to head-quarters. Important information was obtained from their prisoners. Lord Cornwallis had joined General Grant the day before at Princeton, with a reinforcement of chosen troops. They had now seven or eight thousand men, and were pressing waggons for a march upon Trenton.[84]

Cadwalader, stationed at Crosswicks, about seven miles distant, between Bordentown and Trenton, sent intelligence to the same purport, received by him from a young gentleman who had escaped from Princeton.

Word, too, was brought from other quarters, that General Howe was on the march with a thousand light troops, with which he had landed at Amboy.

The situation of Washington was growing critical. The enemy were beginning to advance their large pickets towards Trenton. Every thing indicated an approaching attack. The force with him was small; to retreat across the river, would destroy the dawn of hope awakened in the bosoms of the Jersey militia by the late exploit; but to make a stand without reinforcements was impossible. In this emergency, he called to his aid General Cadwalader from Crosswicks, and General Mifflin from Bordentown, with their collective forces, amounting to about three thousand six hundred men. He did it with reluctance, for it seemed like involving them in the common danger, but the exigency of the case admitted of no alternative. They promptly answered to his call, and marching in the night, joined him on the 1st of January.

Washington chose a position for his main body on the east side of the Assunpink. There was a narrow stone bridge across it, where the water was very deep; the same bridge over which part of Rahl's brigade had escaped in the recent affair. He planted his artillery so as to command the bridge and the fords. His advance guard was stationed about three miles off in a wood, having in front a stream called Shabbakong Creek.

Early on the morning of the 2d, came certain word that Cornwallis was approaching with all his force. Strong parties were sent out under General Greene, who skirmished with the enemy and harassed them in their advance. By twelve o'clock they reached the Shabbakong, and halted for a time on its northern bank. Then crossing it, and moving forward with rapidity, they drove the advance guard out of the woods, and pushed on until they reached a high ground near the town. Here Hand's corps of several battalions was drawn up, and held them for a time in check. All the parties in advance ultimately retreated to the main body, on the east side of the Assunpink, and found some difficulty in crowding across the narrow bridge.

From all these checks and delays, it was nearly sunset before Cornwallis with the head of his army entered Trenton. His rear-guard under General Leslie rested at Maiden Head, about six miles distant, and nearly half way between Trenton and Princeton. Forming his troops into columns, he now made repeated attempts to cross the Assunpink at the bridge and the fords, but was as often repulsed by the artillery. For a part of the time Washington, mounted on a white horse, stationed himself at the south end of the bridge, issuing his orders. Each time the enemy was repulsed there was a shout along the American lines. At length they drew off, came to a halt, and lighted their camp fires. The Americans did the same, using the neighboring fences for the purpose. Sir William Erskine, who was with Cornwallis, urged him, it is said, to attack Washington that evening in his camp; but his lordship declined; he felt sure of the game which had so often escaped him; he had at length, he thought, got Washington into a situation from which he could not escape, but where he might make a desperate stand, and he was willing to give his wearied troops a night's repose to prepare them for the closing struggle. He would be sure, he said, to "bag the fox in the morning."

A cannonade was kept up on both sides until dark; but with little damage to the Americans. When night closed in, the two camps lay in sight of each other's fires, ruminating the bloody action of the following day. It was the most gloomy and anxious night that had yet closed in on the American army, throughout its series of perils and disasters; for there was no concealing the impending danger. But what must have been the feelings of the commander-in-chief, as he anxiously patrolled his camp, and considered his desperate position? A small stream, fordable in several places, was all that separated his raw, inexperienced army, from an enemy vastly superior in numbers and discipline, and stung to action by the mortification of a late defeat. A general action with them must be ruinous; but how was he to retreat? Behind him was the Delaware, impassable from floating ice. Granting even (a thing not to be hoped) that a retreat across it could be effected, the consequences would be equally fatal. The Jerseys would be left in possession of the enemy, endangering the immediate capture of Philadelphia, and sinking the public mind into despondency.

In this darkest of moments a gleam of hope flashed upon his mind: a bold expedient suggested itself. Almost the whole of the enemy's force must by this time be drawn out of Princeton, and advancing by detachments toward Trenton, while their baggage and principal stores must remain weakly guarded at Brunswick. Was it not possible by a rapid night-march along the Quaker road, a different road from that on which General Leslie with the rear-guard was resting, to get past that force undiscovered, come by surprise upon those left at Princeton, capture or destroy what stores were left there, and then push on to Brunswick? This would save the army from being cut off; would avoid the appearance of a defeat; and might draw the enemy away from Trenton, while some fortunate stroke might give additional reputation to the American arms. Even should the enemy march on to Philadelphia, it could not in any case be prevented; while a counterblow in the Jerseys would be of great consolation.

Such was the plan which Washington revolved in his mind on the gloomy banks of the Assunpink, and which he laid before his officers in a council of war, held after nightfall, at the quarters of General Mercer. It met with instant concurrence, being of that hardy, adventurous kind, which seems congenial with the American character. One formidable difficulty presented itself. The weather was unusually mild; there was a thaw, by which the roads might be rendered deep and miry, and almost impassable. Fortunately, or rather providentially, as Washington was prone to consider it, the wind veered to the north in the course of the evening; the weather became intensely cold, and in two hours the roads were once more hard and frostbound. In the mean time, the baggage of the army was silently removed to Burlington, and every other preparation was made for a rapid march. To deceive the enemy, men were employed to dig trenches near the bridge within hearing of the British sentries, with orders to continue noisily at work until daybreak; others were to go the rounds; relieve guards at the bridge and fords; keep up the camp fires, and maintain all the appearance of a regular encampment. At daybreak they were to hasten after the army.

In the dead of the night, the army drew quietly out of the encampment and began its march. General Mercer, mounted on a favorite gray horse, was in the advance with the remnant of his flying camp, now but about three hundred and fifty men, principally relics of the brave Delaware and Maryland regiments, with some of the Pennsylvania militia. Among the latter were youths belonging to the best families in Philadelphia. The main body followed, under Washington's immediate command.

The Quaker road was a complete roundabout, joining the main road about two miles from Princeton, where Washington expected to arrive before daybreak. The road, however, was new and rugged; cut through woods, where the stumps of trees broke the wheels of some of the baggage trains, and retarded the march of the troops; so that it was near sunrise of a bright, frosty morning, when Washington reached the bridge over Stony Brook, about three miles from Princeton. After crossing the bridge, he led his troops along the bank of the brook to the edge of a wood, where a by-road led off on the right through low grounds, and was said by the guides to be a short cut to Princeton, and less exposed to view. By this road Washington defiled with the main body, ordering Mercer to continue along the brook with his brigade, until he should arrive at the main road, where he was to secure, and, if possible, destroy a bridge over which it passes; so as to intercept any fugitives from Princeton, and check any retrograde movements of the British troops which might have advanced towards Trenton.

Hitherto the movements of the Americans had been undiscovered by the enemy. Three regiments of the latter, the 17th, 40th, and 55th, with three troops of dragoons, had been quartered all night in Princeton, under marching orders to join Lord Cornwallis in the morning. The 17th regiment, under Colonel Mawhood, was already on the march; the 55th regiment was preparing to follow. Mawhood had crossed the bridge by which the old or main road to Trenton passes over Stony Brook, and was proceeding through a wood beyond, when, as he attained the summit of a hill about sunrise, the glittering of arms betrayed to him the movement of Mercer's troops to the left, who were filing along the Quaker road to secure the bridge, as they had been ordered.

The woods prevented him from seeing their number. He supposed them to be some broken portion of the American army flying before Lord Cornwallis. With this idea, he faced about and made a retrograde movement, to intercept them or hold them in check; while messengers spurred off at all speed, to hasten forward the regiments still lingering at Princeton, so as completely to surround them.

The woods concealed him until he had recrossed the bridge

of Stony Brook, when he came in full sight of the van of Mercer's brigade. Both parties pushed to get possession of a rising ground on the right near the house of a Mr. Clark, of the peaceful Society of Friends. The Americans being nearest, reached it first, and formed behind a hedge fence which extended along a slope in front of the house; whence, being chiefly armed with rifles, they opened a destructive fire. It was returned with great spirit by the enemy. At the first discharge Mercer was dismounted, "his gallant gray" being crippled by a musket ball in the leg. One of his colonels, also, was mortally wounded and carried to the rear. Availing themselves of the confusion thus occasioned, the British charged with the bayonet; the American riflemen having no weapon of the kind, were thrown into disorder and retreated. Mercer, who was on foot, endeavored to rally them, when a blow from the butt end of a musket felled him to the ground. He rose and defended himself with his sword, but was surrounded, bayoneted repeatedly, and left for dead.

Mawhood pursued the broken and retreating troops to the brow of the rising ground, on which Clark's house was situated, when he beheld a large force emerging from a wood and advancing to the rescue. It was a body of Pennsylvania militia, which Washington, on hearing the firing, had detached to the support of Mercer. Mawhood instantly ceased pursuit, drew up his artillery, and by a heavy discharge brought the militia to a stand.

At this moment Washington himself arrived at the scene of action, having galloped from the by-road in advance of his troops. From a rising ground he beheld Mercer's troops retreating in confusion, and the detachment of militia checked by Mawhood's artillery. Every thing was at peril. Putting spurs to his horse he dashed past the hesitating militia, waving his hat and cheering them on. His commanding figure and white horse, made him a conspicuous object for the enemy's marksmen; but he heeded it not. Galloping forward under the fire of Mawhood's battery, he called upon Mercer's broken brigade. The Pennsylvanians rallied at the sound of his voice, and caught fire from his example. At the same time the 7th Virginia regiment emerged from the wood, and moved forward with loud cheers, while a fire of grapeshot was opened by Captain Moulder of the American artillery, from the brow of a ridge to the south.

Colonel Mawhood, who a moment before had thought his triumph secure, found himself assailed on every side, and separated from the other British regiments. He fought, however, with great bravery, and for a short time the action was desperate. Washington was in the midst of it; equally endangered by the random fire of his own men, and the artillery and musketry of the enemy. His aide-de-camp, Colonel Fitzgerald, a young and ardent Irishman, losing sight of him in the heat of the fight when enveloped in dust and smoke, dropped the bridle on the neck of his horse and drew his hat over his eyes; giving him up for lost. When he saw him, however, emerge from the cloud, waving his hat, and beheld the enemy giving way, he spurred up to his side. "Thank God," cried he, "your excellency is safe!" "Away, my dear colonel, and bring up the troops," was the reply; "the day is our own!" It was one of those occasions in which the latent fire of Washington's character blazed forth.

Mawhood, by this time, had forced his way, at the point of the bayonet, through gathering foes, though with heavy loss, back to the main road, and was in full retreat towards Trenton to join Cornwallis. Washington detached Major Kelly with a party of Pennsylvania troops, to destroy the bridge at Stony Brook, over which Mawhood had retreated, so as to impede the advance of General Leslie from Maiden Head.

In the mean time the 55th regiment, which had been on the left and nearer Princeton, had been encountered by the American advance-guard under General St. Clair, and after some sharp fighting in a ravine had given way, and was retreating across fields and along a by-road to Brunswick. The remaining regiment, the 40th, had not been able to come up in time for the action; a part of it fled toward Brunswick; the residue took refuge in the college at Princeton, recently occupied by them as barracks. Artillery was now brought to bear on the college, and a few shot compelled those within to surrender.

In this brief but brilliant action, about one hundred of the British were left dead on the field, and nearly three hundred taken prisoners, fourteen of whom were officers. Among the slain was Captain Leslie, son of the Earl of Leven. His death was greatly lamented by his captured companions.

The loss of the Americans was about twenty-five or thirty men and several officers. Among the latter was Colonel Haslet, who had distinguished himself throughout the campaign, by being among the foremost in services of danger. He was indeed a gallant officer, and gallantly seconded by his Delaware troops.

A greater loss was that of General Mercer. He was said to be either dead or dying, in the house of Mr. Clark, whither he had been conveyed by his aide-de-camp, Major Armstrong, who found him, after the retreat of Mawhood's troops, lying on the field gashed with several wounds, and insensible from cold and loss of blood. Washington would have ridden back from Princeton to visit him, and have him conveyed to a place of greater security; but was assured, that, if alive, he was too desperately wounded to bear removal; in the mean time he was in good hands, being faithfully attended to by his aide-de-camp, Major Armstrong, and treated with the utmost care and kindness by Mr. Clark's family.[85]

Under these circumstances Washington felt compelled to leave his old companion in arms to his fate. Indeed, he was called away by the exigencies of his command, having to pursue the routed regiments which were making a headlong retreat to Brunswick. In this pursuit he took the lead at the head of a detachment of cavalry. At Kingston, however, three miles to the northeast of Princeton, he pulled up, restrained his ardor, and held a council of war on horseback. Should he keep on to Brunswick or not? The capture of the British stores and baggage would make his triumph complete; but, on the other hand, his troops were excessively fatigued by their rapid march all night and hard fight in the morning. All of them had been one night without sleep, and some of them two, and many were half-starved. They were without blankets, thinly clad, some of them barefooted, and this in freezing weather. Cornwallis would be upon them before they could reach Brunswick. His rear-guard, under General Leslie, had been quartered but six miles from Princeton, and the retreating troops must have roused them. Under these considerations, it was determined to discontinue the pursuit and push for Morristown. There they would be in a mountainous country, heavily wooded, in an abundant neighborhood, and on the flank of the enemy, with various defiles by which they might change their position according to his movements.

Filing off to the left, therefore, from Kingston, and breaking down the bridges behind him, Washington took the narrow road by Rocky Hill to Pluckamin. His troops were so exhausted, that many in the course of the march would lie down in the woods on the frozen ground and fall asleep, and were with difficulty roused and cheered forward. At Pluckamin he halted for a time, to allow them a little repose and refreshment. While they are taking breath we will cast our eyes back to the camp of Cornwallis, to see what was the effect upon him of this masterly movement of Washington.

His lordship had retired to rest at Trenton with the sportsman's vaunt that he would "bag the fox in the morning." Nothing could surpass his surprise and chagrin, when at daybreak the expiring watchfires and deserted camp of the Americans told him that the prize had once more evaded his grasp; that the general whose military skill he had decried had outgeneralled him.

For a time he could not learn whither the army, which had stolen away so silently, had directed its stealthy march. By sunrise, however, there was the booming of cannon, like the rumbling of distant thunder, in the direction of Princeton. The idea flashed upon him that Washington had not merely escaped, but was about to make a dash at the British magazines at Brunswick. Alarmed for the safety of his military stores, his lordship forthwith broke up his camp, and made a rapid march towards

Princeton. As he arrived in sight of the bridge over Stony Brook, he beheld Major Kelly and his party busy in its destruction. A distant discharge of round shot from his field-pieces drove them away, but the bridge was already broken. It would take time to repair it for the passage of the artillery; so Cornwallis in his impatience urged his troops breast-high through the turbulent and icy stream, and again pushed forward. He was brought to a stand by the discharge of a thirty-two pounder from a distant breastwork. Supposing the Americans to be there in force, and prepared to make resistance, he sent out some horsemen to reconnoitre, and advanced to storm the battery. There was no one there. The thirty-two pounder had been left behind by the Americans, as too unwieldy, and a match had been applied to it by some lingerer of Washington's rearguard.

Without further delay Cornwallis hurried forward, eager to save his magazines. Crossing the bridge at Kingston, he kept on along the Brunswick road, supposing Washington still before him. The latter had got far in the advance, during the delays caused by the broken bridge at Stony Brook, and the discharge of the thirty-two pounder; and the alteration of his course at Kingston had carried him completely out of the way of Cornwallis. His lordship reached Brunswick towards evening, and endeavored to console himself, by the safety of the military stores, for being so completely foiled and outmanœuvred.

Washington, in the mean time, was all on the alert; the lion part of his nature was aroused; and while his weary troops were in a manner panting upon the ground around him, he was despatching missives and calling out aid to enable him to follow up his successes. In a letter to Putnam, written from Pluckamin during the halt, he says: "The enemy appear to be panic-struck. I am in hopes of driving them out of the Jerseys. March the troops under your command to Crosswicks, and keep a strict watch upon the enemy in this quarter. Keep as many spies out as you think proper. A number of horsemen in the dress of the country must be kept constantly going backwards and for-

wards for this purpose. If you discover any motion of the
enemy of consequence, let me be informed thereof as soon as
possible, by express."

To General Heath, also, who was stationed in the Highlands
of the Hudson, he wrote at the same hurried moment. "The
enemy are in great consternation; and as the panic affords us a
favorable opportunity to drive them out of the Jerseys, it has
been determined in council that you should move down towards
New York with a considerable force, as if you had a design upon
the city. That being an object of great importance, the enemy
will be reduced to the necessity of withdrawing a considerable
part of their force from the Jerseys, if not the whole, to secure
the city."

These letters despatched, he continued forward to Morristown, where at length he came to a halt from his incessant and
harassing marchings. There he learnt that General Mercer was
still alive. He immediately sent his own nephew, Major George
Lewis, under the protection of a flag, to attend upon him.
Mercer had indeed been kindly nursed by a daughter of Mr.
Clark and a negro woman, who had not been frightened from
their home by the storm of battle which raged around it. At the
time that the troops of Cornwallis approached, Major Armstrong was binding up Mercer's wounds. The latter insisted on
his leaving him in the kind hands of Mr. Clark's household,
and rejoining the army. Lewis found him languishing in great
pain; he had been treated with respect by the enemy, and great
tenderness by the benevolent family who had sheltered him.
He expired in the arms of Major Lewis on the 12th of January,
in the fifty-sixth year of his age. Dr. Benjamin Rush, afterwards celebrated as a physician, was with him when he died.

He was upright, intelligent and brave; esteemed as a soldier
and beloved as a man, and by none more so than by Washington.
His career as a general had been brief; but long enough to secure
him a lasting renown. His name remains one of the consecrated
names of the Revolution.

From Morristown, Washington again wrote to General
Heath, repeating his former orders. To Major-general Lincoln,

also, who was just arrived at Peekskill, and had command of the Massachusetts militia, he writes on the 7th, "General Heath will communicate mine of this date to you, by which you will find that the greater part of your troops are to move down towards New York, to draw the attention of the enemy to that quarter; and if they do not throw a considerable body back again, you may, in all probability, carry the city, or at least blockade them in it. * * * * Be as expeditious as possible in moving forward, for the sooner a panic-struck enemy is followed the better. If we can oblige them to evacuate the Jerseys, we must drive them to the utmost distress; for they have depended upon the supplies from that State for their winter's support."

Colonel Reed was ordered to send out rangers and bodies of militia to scour the country, waylay foraging parties, cut off supplies, and keep the cantonments of the enemy in a state of siege. "I would not suffer a man to stir beyond their lines," writes Washington, "nor suffer them to have the least communication with the country."

The expedition under General Heath toward New York, from which much had been anticipated by Washington, proved a failure. It moved in three divisions, by different routes, but all arriving nearly at the same time at the enemy's outposts at King's Bridge. There was some skirmishing, but the great feature of the expedition was a pompous and peremptory summons of Fort Independence to surrender. "Twenty minutes only can be allowed," said Heath, "for the garrison to give their answer, and, should it be in the negative, they must abide the consequences." The garrison made no answer but an occasional cannonade. Heath failed to follow up his summons by corresponding deeds. He hovered and skirmished for some days about the outposts and Spyt den Duivel Creek, and then retired before a threatened snow-storm, and the report of an enemy's fleet from Rhode Island, with troops under Lord Percy, who might land in Westchester, and take the besieging force in rear.

Washington, while he spoke of Heath's failure with indulgence in his despatches to government, could not but give him a rebuke in a private letter. "Your summons," writes he, "as you did not attempt to fulfil your threats, was not only idle, but farcical; and will not fail of turning the laugh exceedingly upon us. These things I mention to you as a friend, for you will perceive they have composed no part of my public letter."

But though disappointed in this part of his plan, Washington, having received reinforcements of militia, continued, with his scanty army, to carry on his system of annoyance. The situation of Cornwallis, who, but a short time before, traversed the Jerseys so triumphantly, became daily more and more irksome. Spies were in his camp, to give notice of every movement, and foes without to take advantage of it; so that not a foraging party could sally forth without being waylaid. By degrees he drew in his troops which were posted about the country, and collected them at New Brunswick and Amboy, so as to have a communication by water with New York, whence he was now compelled to draw nearly all his supplies; "presenting," to use the words of Hamilton, "the extraordinary spectacle of a powerful army, straitened within narrow limits by the phantom of a military force, and never permitted to transgress those limits with impunity."

In fact, the recent operations in the Jerseys had suddenly changed the whole aspect of the war, and given a triumphant close to what had been a disastrous campaign.

The troops, which for months had been driven from post to post, apparently an undisciplined rabble, had all at once turned upon their pursuers, and astounded them by brilliant stratagems and daring exploits. The commander, whose cautious policy had been sneered at by enemies, and regarded with impatience by misjudging friends, had all at once shown that he possessed enterprise, as well as circumspection, energy as well as endurance, and that beneath his wary coldness lurked a fire to break forth at the proper moment. This year's campaign, the most critical one of the war, and especially the part of it which occurred in the Jerseys, was the ordeal that made his great qualities fully appreciated by his countrymen, and gained for him from the statesmen and generals of Europe the appellation of the AMERICAN FABIUS.

NOTES

LETTERS OF JONATHAN OLDSTYLE

1. This, the third of the nine contributions to the *Morning Chronicle*, a daily paper edited by Irving's brother Peter, appeared originally in the issue of Dec. 1, 1802. Concerning the effect of such portions of the Oldstyle papers as treat of the drama, William Dunlap, in his *History of the American Theatre* (New York, 1832), remarked: "Though always playful, the irritation caused was excessive," meaning, of course, among the actors, for to the town they afforded much amusement.

2. The Park Theatre, which stood opposite the Park, midway between Ann and Beekman Streets, offered the chief theatrical entertainment in New York at the time of these letters.

3. Mrs. Whitlock, a sister of Mrs. Siddons. [Pierre M. Irving.]

4. Hodgkinson, a versatile actor who filled all parts, from Falstaff to a Harlequin. [Pierre M. Irving.]

5. Mrs. Johnson, a great favorite with the author and the public. [Pierre M. Irving.]

SALMAGUNDI

6. The title-page read: SALMAGUNDI;/or the/Whim-Whams and Opinions/of/Launcelot Langstaff, & Others./In hoc est hoax, cum quiz et jokesez,/Et smokem, toastem, roastem folksez,/Fe, faw, fum. *Psalm-anaʒar.*/With baked, and broiled, and stew'd and toasted,/And fried, and boil'd, and smok'd and roasted,/We treat the town./New-York:/Published by David Longworth,/At the Shakespeare-Gallery./1807.

The text of these selections remains (except for minor verbal changes made by Irving himself in the Paris edition of 1834) that of the work as it was first published by David Longworth, an eccentric theatrical publisher of the day, who, himself a gentleman much given to whim-whams, had a flair for elegant titles and fine books, and who called his shop, in the neighborhood of the old Park Theatre, "The Sentimental Epicure's Ordinary."

7. A mixed dish, as of chopped meat and pickled herring, with oil, vinegar, pepper, and onions; a miscellany; an olio. *Salmagundi*, the joint production of William Irving, James K. Paulding, and Washington Irving, is so truly a mixed dish that the individual authorship of many of the selections is not easily determined. External evidence is scarce, and internal evidence not always conclusive. In many of the essays all three had a hand. The two herewith reprinted are mainly by Washington Irving, though Paulding had a hand in both.

8. Subsequently, however, somewhat lengthy but whimsical sketches of the editors are given: Anthony Evergreen, Esq., in charge of the department of fashionable society; William Wizard, Esq., the territory of theatrical and general literary criticism; Pindar Cockloft, the poetical effusions; and Launcelot Langstaff, Esq., a sort of "Spectator," who roamed as whim or will dictated from one subject to another.

9. The parallelism of purpose between the editors of *Salmagundi* and Steele and Addison in the *Tatler* and *Spectator* is obvious.

10. The title of a newspaper published in New York, the columns of which, among other miscellaneous topics, occasionally contained strictures on the performances at the theatres. [Irving's note in the Paris edition of his works of 1834.]

11. Paulding, during Irving's absence from New York (in attendance upon the trial of Burr in Richmond), had concluded the first volume at No. X, dated May 16, 1807, thus affording the editors a splendid opportunity to review their work.

12. Dr. Francis, in his remarks on the life and character of Washington Irving, before the Historical Society, alludes to this conflict of spelling-books at the school in which they were both instructed. "There was a curious conflict existing in the school between the principal and his assistant instructor; the former a legitimate burgher of the city, the latter a New England pedagogue. So far as I can remember, something depended on the choice of the boy's parents in the selection of his studies; but if not expressed otherwise, the principal stuck earnestly to Dilworth, while the assistant, for his section of instruction, held to Noah Webster." [Pierre M. Irving.] See also Dr. John Francis, "Characteristics of Washington Irving," *Irvingiana*, p. xxxiii.

13. Dancing, particularly the waltz, is often burlesqued, as in No. VII. No. XX, containing an account of the City Assembly from the pen of Mustapha, is a take-off on a fashionable New York ball.

14. Scandal and gossip are as often and as cleverly satirized as they are in the *Tatler* and the *Spectator*.

15. A reference to Anthony Evergreen's strictures on "nudity being all the rage," in his essay on "Fashions," in No. III.

16. A reference to Tom Straddle, a "gemmen" just arrived from Birmingham, England, in an importation of hardware—half beau, half button-maker—whose shoddy social pretensions and foppish Anglomania are objects of satire in No. XII.

17. A reference to William Wizard's satire in No. VIII on the family of old Timothy Giblet, typical social climbers of the day.

18. Punning is frequently the object of attack, particularly in No. X.

19. The twenty numbers of *Salmagundi* contain nine letters supposedly written by a Tripolitan prisoner detained in New York, Mustapha Rub-a-Dub Keli Khan, who, addressing himself principally to Asem Hacchem, Principal Slave-Driver to His Highness the Bashaw of Tripoli, recounts

his observations and experiences in America. His first letter, in No. III, relates his reception in this "most enlightened nation under the sun," where women have souls,—some of them "soul enough to swear,"—and whose government is in the hands of "a grand and most puissant bashaw, whom they dignify with the title of president."

"He is chosen by persons, who are chosen by an assembly, elected by the people—hence the mob is called the sovereign people—and the country, free; the body politic doubtless resembling a vessel, which is best governed by its tail. The present bashaw is a very plain old gentleman—something they say of a humorist, as he amuses himself with impaling butterflies and pickling tadpoles; he is rather declining in popularity, having given great offense by wearing red breeches and tying his horse to a post."

These, of course, are allusions to President Jefferson's philosophical and scientific activities and to his several eccentricities, such as his fondness for wearing red breeches and his democratic manner of riding unattended, himself hitching his horse to the handiest post—all of which the young Federalist editors thus slyly poked fun at.

Next, Mustapha descants upon the nature of the American government:

"To let thee at once into a secret, which is unknown to these people themselves, their government is a pure unadulterated *logocracy*, or government of words. The whole nation does everything *vivâ voce*, or by word of mouth; and in this manner is one of the most military nations in existence. Every man who has what is here called the gift of the gab, that is, a plentiful stock of verbosity, becomes a soldier outright; and is forever in a militant state. The country is entirely defended *vi et linguâ;* that is to say, by force of tongues. . . .

"There has been a civil war carrying on with great violence for some time past, in consequence of a conspiracy, among the higher classes, to dethrone his highness, the present bashaw, and place another in his stead. I was mistaken when I formerly asserted to thee that this dissatisfaction arose from his wearing red breeches. It is true, the nation have long held that color in great detestation, in consequence of a dispute they had some twenty years since with the barbarians of the British Islands. The color, however, is again rising into favor, as the ladies have transferred it to their heads from the bashaw's —— body. The true reason, I am told, is, that the bashaw absolutely refuses to believe in the deluge, and in the story of Balaam's ass; maintaining that this animal was never yet permitted to talk except in a genuine logocracy; where, it is true, his voice may often be heard, and is listened to with reverence, as 'the voice of the sovereign people.' Nay, so far did he carry his obstinacy, that he absolutely invited a professed antediluvian from the Gallic empire, who illuminated the whole country with his principles—and his nose. [This is doubtless a reference to Tom Paine.] This was enough to set the nation in a blaze—every slang-whanger resorted to his tongue or his pen; and for seven years they have carried on a most inhuman war, in which volumes of words have been expended, oceans of ink have been shed; nor has any mercy been shown to age, sex, or condition. Every day have these slang-whangers made furious attacks on each other and upon their respective adherents; discharging their heavy artillery, consisting of large sheets, loaded with scoundrel! villain! liar! rascal! numskull! nincompoop! dunderhead! wiseacre! blockhead! jackass! and I do swear by my beard, though I know thou wilt scarcely credit me, that in some of these skirmishes the grand bashaw himself has been wofully pelted! yea, most ignominiously pelted! and yet have these talking desperadoes escaped without the bastinado! . . .

"But in nothing is the verbose nature of this government more evident than in its grand national divan, or Congress, where the laws are framed: this is a blustering, windy assembly, where everything is carried by noise, tumult, and debate; for thou must know, that the members of this assembly do not meet together to find wisdom in the multitude of counselors, but to wrangle, call each other hard names, and hear themselves talk. . . ." (*Salmagundi*, No. VII.)

In this logocratic country, where even wars with foreign countries are waged by the grand bashaw's issuing a document or uttering a speech (referring to Jefferson's numerous official proclamations), Mustapha finds himself much discomfited in consequence of his needing a new pair of breeches. Since he is a prisoner of the United States, this need can be supplied only by direct action of Congress, where, after running the gauntlet of the national slang-whangers in the great divan, his request finally founders on the all-important Jeffersonian watch-word "Economy," so that a benefit at the theatre is resorted to to supply his pressing want. In other letters Mustapha comments upon the American manner of conducting elections, military reviews, and balls.

20. John Carr, Esq., of the Honorable Society of the Middle Temple, wrote several slipshod travel books, one of which, *The Stranger in Ireland, a Tour in 1805*, seems to have been popular in America, where it reached a third edition in 1807.

21. Aunt Charity Cockloft, we are told in No. IX, "died of a Frenchman," *i.e.*, in consequence of her inability to satisfy her curiosity regarding "a little, meagre, weazel-faced Frenchman" who moved into a house across the street from the Cockloft mansion. Her failure "to get at the bottom" of "what he could possibly do with so much baggage, and particularly with his parrots and monkeys, or how so small a carcass could have occasion for so many trunks of clothes" so frustrated her scandal-mongering curiosity that she left her window, drooped daily, and in "one little month" died, being "the seventh Cockloft that has died of a whim-wham."

22. The wooden gentlemen, because of their social gaucherie, were Miss Sophie Sparkle's (Mary Fairlie's) particular aversions.

A HISTORY OF NEW YORK

23. Printed in Philadelphia and published simultaneously on Dec. 6, 1809, in New York, Philadelphia, Boston, Baltimore, and Charleston. The full title read: "A History of New York, from the Beginning of the World to the End of the Dutch Dynasty. Containing among many Surprising and Curious Matters, the Unutterable Ponderings of Walter the Doubter, the Disastrous Projects of William the Testy, and the Chivalric Achievments [*sic*] of Peter the Headstrong, the three Dutch Governors of New Amsterdam; being the only Authentic History of the Times that ever hath been, or ever will be Published. By Diedrich Knickerbocker."

Irving made numerous changes in subsequent editions, notably in those of 1812 and 1848. All the selections here given follow the text of the "author's revised edition." For a verbatim reprint of the 1809 text, see the edition prepared by Stanley T. Williams and Tremaine McDowell (New York, 1927).

24. Van Twiller really arrived in 1633, and was in reality the fifth governor, not the first, as Irving intimates.

25. William Kieft in this book is in many respects a satirical delineation of Thomas Jefferson. The political satire in the other books is negligible by comparison. In Books I and II, Irving's targets are pedantic historians. Book III possibly contains half-concealed allusions to President Adams; while Book V, on Stuyvesant, possibly makes some allusions to Madison's departure from Jeffersonian pedantry and from Jeffersonian democracy. Book IV, however, is a palpable and clever burlesque on the archenemy of the Federalists and Federalism.

"Irving had obviously no ready-made parallel in two individuals so dissimilar as this governor of the New Netherlands and the fourth president of the new republic, but Kieft's 'cocked hat and corduroy small clothes' and his 'raw-boned charger' would easily suggest to a reader in 1809 Jefferson's notorious saddle-horse which he rode between Washington and Monticello, and his democratic taste in breeches, so annoying to American aristocrats. The reader would, then, at the very first think of Kieft in terms of Jefferson, and though the satire ranges from definite analogies to mere faint intimations, he could not escape the fact that Irving was laughing at Jefferson. Thus, the absurd characteristics of heavy scholarship, eccentric inventive genius, and philosophical accomplishments are less in the known facts about Kieft than in the reputation of Jefferson. An opponent of Jefferson would readily apprehend, in Kieft's smattering of languages, the linguistic pretensions of the President; in Kieft's metaphysical 'fog of contradictions and perplexities,' his studies in eighteenth century philosophy; in the Dutchman's '*universal acquire-*

ments,' which 'were very much in his way,' his alleged encyclopædic learning.

"Certainly Kieft's odd propensity for inventions squares with popular stories of Jefferson. Kieft goes to his country estate and makes 'patent smoke-jacks—carts that went before the horses, and . . . wind-mills,' to which Irving later adds 'Dutch ovens for roasting meat without fire and weather-cocks that turned against the wind.' Yet these burlesque fictions hardly outdo Jefferson's weather-vane, with its indicator on the ceiling of his porch, his machine for breaking hemp, his leather tops for carriages, his plough, and his other experiments. Is 'Dog's Misery,' Kieft's estate where in his experiments he paralyzed animals, an ironical allusion to Jefferson's interest in vivisection? Is the 'sweet, sequestered swamp,' where Kieft conducts his researches, merely Monticello, where Jefferson spent more than a fourth of his time as president? Kieft is in the *History* a 'wrangler,' a 'scolder,' and as savage as an ugly dog. Here Irving is closer perhaps to the actual Kieft than to the real Jefferson, but the Federalists spoke in these same terms of Jefferson's supposed bursts of violent anger.

"In his account of Kieft as governor, Irving follows Jefferson through his two administrations, from his inauguration in 1801 to his retirement in 1809. The governor's régime begins with an address which Irving introduces with a significant comment (quite as significantly omitted in the revision of 1848): '. . . Everybody knows what a glorious opportunity a governor, a president, or even an emperor has, of drubbing his enemies in his speeches, messages and bulletins.' After expressions of mock humility and pedantic references to ancient history, Kieft attacks the Yankees. We look in vain in the Dutch chronicles for such a speech, but Jefferson's second inaugural supplies it. Here, as so often in this 'concealed satire,' Irving satirizes less particular phrases than the general tone of Jefferson's animadversions on the New Englanders.

"Throughout his term of office, Kieft is 'fond of trying . . . political experiments' whereby he 'entangled the government . . . in more knots during his administration than half a dozen successors could have untied.' Irving had already attacked, in the same fashion, the progressive policies of Jefferson in *Salmagundi*, notably the President's program of Economy. Now in four pages he celebrates Kieft's devotion to 'that cabalistic word, economy': 'By its magic influence seventy-fours shrink into frigates— frigates into sloops, and sloops into gunboats.' . . . Jefferson advocated gunboats and deplored the folly of a navy. For this policy and for his scheme for a dry dock he was severely censored. Irving's references, therefore, do not appear uninspired, to Dutch boats 'laid up (or dry docked) in a cove . . . where they quietly rotted in the mud.'

"Nor could his enemies forgive Jefferson's high-flown notion of substituting negotiations and economic pressure for warfare. Actual history was in this point Irving's ally, for Kieft, too, had a weakness for manifestoes, even against Yankees. Yet the exaggeration of the Dutch governor's habit is evidently part of the satire. First, he promulgates a decree ordering all Yankees out of the province. He then resolves to 'double the dose,' and issues 'a kind of non-intercourse bill, forbidding and prohibiting all commerce and connexion' with the Yankees, and ordering the Dutch to buy none of their 'pacing horses, meazly pork, apple brandy, Yankee rum, cyder water, apple sweetmeats, Weathersfield onions or wooden bowls.' Since a number of these items had not yet been produced in quantity by the New England settlers in the 1640's, this passage appears to burlesque Jefferson's Non-Importation Act of 1806. This 'new and cheap method of fighting' the Yankees ignored. Thereupon Kieft 'flew in a passion, . . . and swore that, though it was slow in operating, yet once it began to work, it would purge the land.' In a similar fashion Jefferson, when his Embargo Act of 1807 was evaded, insisted that it was 'a measure which, if persevered in a little longer . . . would have effected its object completely.' Kieft's policies on these and allied questions are strikingly like Jefferson's: both are pacifists; both oppose adequate national defense; both encourage farcical military preparations. It is difficult to believe that Irving has not here in mind the limited appropriation for the national defense. Kieft is an obstinate muddler who would 'govern by the wind,' and his collection of windmills and his official trumpeter would seem to enemies fair allusions to the man who said, 'Peace is our passion.' Contemporaries did not fail to discover that these passages referred to Jefferson and his associates, for a Federalist journal, *The Monthly Anthology* for February, 1810, remarks: 'If anything can be hoped from ridicule, the rash imbecility of these ignoble plagiarists who have been for some years past carrying on war by proclamations and resolutions, might by this work be shamed into a retreat and concealment.' " (Williams and McDowell, *op. cit.*, intro., pp. lxi-lxvi.) For further interesting parallels see *ibid.*, pp. lxvii–lxxiii, and E. A. Greenlaw's paper on political satire in *Knickerbocker* in *The Texas Review* for April, 1916.

26. Although this date is disputed, 1638 is probably the correct one.

27. The following cases in point appear in Hazard's Collection of State Papers.

"In the meantime, they of Hartford have not onely usurped and taken in the lands of Connecticott, although unrighteously and against the lawes of nations but have hindered our nation in sowing theire own purchased broken up lands, but have also sowed them with corne in the night, which the Nederlanders had broken up and intended to sowe: and have beaten the servants of the high and mighty the honored companie, which were laboring upon theire master's lands, from theire lands, with sticks and plow staves in hostile manner laming, and among the rest, struck Ever Duckings [Evert Duyckink] a hole in his head, with a stick, so that the bloode ran downe very strongly downe upon his body."

"Those of Hartford sold a hogg, that belonged to the honored com-

panie, under pretence that it had eaten of theire grounde grass, when they
had not any foot of inheritance. They proffered the hogg for 5s. if the
commissioners would have given 5s. for damage; which the commissioners
denied, because noe man's own hogg (as men used to say) can trespass
upon his owne master's grounde." [Irving's note.]

28. The bridge here mentioned by Mr. Knickerbocker still exists; but it
is said that the toll is seldom collected nowadays, excepting on sleighing-
parties, by the descendants of the patriarchs, who still preserve the traditions of the city. [Irving's note.]

29. Irving's Federalism is clearly discernible in this satirization of the
expedients of self-government, political societies, and beclouded democratic opinions which, in the Federalist's mind, were associated with
Jeffersonian democracy.

30. Out of the "Pipe Plot" (possibly an expansion of the consequences
of Kieft's tax on tobacco) grew the three political parties: the Long Pipes
(Federalists), the Short Pipes (Anti-Federalists), and the Quids ("political
mongrels, which sometimes spring up between two great parties, as a mule
is produced between a horse and an ass")—in short, the mob who follow
blindly first one, then the other.

31. The old Welsh bards believed that King Arthur was not dead, but
carried awaie by the fairies into some pleasant place, where he sholde
remaine for a time, and then returne againe and reigne in as great authority
as ever.—Hollinshed.

The Britons suppose that he shall come yet and conquere all Britaigne,
for certes, this is the prophicye of Merlyn—He say'd that his deth shall
be doubteous; and said soth, for men thereof yet have doubte and shullen
for ever more—for men wyt not whether that he lyveth or is dede.—Dr.
Leew, Chron. [Irving's note.]

32. Diedrich Knickerbocker, in his scrupulous search after truth, is
sometimes too fastidious in regard to facts which border a little on the
marvellous. The story of the golden ore rests on something better than
mere tradition. The venerable Adrian Van der Donck, Doctor of Laws,
in his description of the New Netherlands, asserts it from his own observation as an eye-witness. He was present, he says, in 1645, at a treaty between Governor Kieft and the Mohawk Indians, in which one of the latter,
in painting himself for the ceremony, used a pigment, the weight and
shining appearance of which excited the curiosity of the governor and
Mynheer Van der Donck. They obtained a lump and gave it to be proved
by a skilful doctor of medicine, Johannes de la Montagne, one of the
councillors of the New Netherlands. It was put into a crucible, and yielded
two pieces of gold, worth about three guilders. All this, continues Adrian
Van der Donck, was kept secret. As soon as peace was made with the
Mohawks, an officer and a few men were sent to the mountain (in the
region of the Kaatskill) under the guidance of an Indian, to search for the
precious mineral. They brought back a bucket full of ore; which, being

submitted to the crucible, proved as productive as the first. William Kieft now thought the discovery certain. He sent a confidential person, Arent Corsen, with a bag full of the mineral, to New Haven, to take passage in an English ship for England, thence to proceed to Holland. The vessel sailed at Christmas, but never reached her port. All on board perished.

In the year 1647, Wilhelmus Kieft himself embarked on board the Princess, taking with him specimens of the supposed mineral. The ship was never heard of more!

Some have supposed that the mineral in question was not gold, but pyrites; but we have the assertion of Adrian Van der Donck, an eye-witness, and the experiment of Johannes de la Montagne, a learned doctor of medicine, on the golden side of the question. Cornelius Van Tienhoo-ven, also, at that time secretary of the New Netherlands, declared in Holland that he had tested several specimens of the mineral, which proved satisfactory. (See Van der Donck's "Description of the New Nether-lands." Collect. New York Hist. Society, Vol. I, p. 161.)

It would appear, however, that these golden treasures of the Kaatskill always brought ill luck; as is evidenced in the fate of Arent Corsen and Wilhelmus Kieft, and the wreck of the ships in which they attempted to convey the treasure across the ocean. The golden mines have never since been explored, but remain among the mysteries of the Kaatskill mountains, and under the protection of the goblins which haunt them. [Irving's note.]

33. See the histories of Masters' Josselyn and Blome. [Irving's note.] The reference here is to John Josselyn's *Chronological Observations of America* (London, 1674) and Richard Blome's *Present State of His Majesty's Isles and Territories* (London, 1687).

34. Modern historians assert that when the New Netherlands were thus overrun by the British, as Spain in ancient days by the Saracens, a resolute band refused to bend the neck to the invader. Led by one Garret Van Horne, a valorous and gigantic Dutchman, they crossed the bay and buried themselves among the marshes and cabbage-gardens of Communipaw; as did Pelayo and his followers among the mountains of Asturias. Here their descendants have remained ever since, keeping themselves apart, like seed-corn, to re-people the city with the genuine breed whenever it shall be effectually recovered from its intruders. It is said the genuine descendants of the Nederlanders who inhabit New York, still look with longing eyes to the green marshes of ancient Pavonia, as did the conquered Spaniards of yore to the stern mountains of Asturias, considering these the regions whence deliverance is to come. [Irving's note.]

THE SKETCH BOOK

35. Published originally in seven installments, or numbers, at irregular intervals from May 15, 1819, to Sept. 13, 1820, by C. S. Van Winkle of New York. The first four numbers were re-issued, in England, in Febru-

ary, 1820, by John Miller. When Miller failed shortly after, John Murray
was induced by Scott to undertake all future publications of the work.

36. This, after a short "Prospectus," formed the first part of No. I.

37. This is the last part of No. I.

38. Note. The foregoing tale, one would suspect, had been suggested
to Mr. Knickerbocker by a little German superstition about the Emperor
Frederick *der Rothbart*, and the Kypphaüser [*sic*] mountain: the subjoined
note, however, which he had appended to the tale, shows that it is an
absolute fact, narrated with his usual fidelity:

"The story of Rip Van Winkle may seem incredible to many, but
nevertheless I give it my full belief, for I know the vicinity of our old
Dutch settlements to have been very subject to marvellous events and
appearances. Indeed, I have heard many stranger stories than this, in the
villages along the Hudson; all of which were too well authenticated to
admit of a doubt. I have even talked with Rip Van Winkle myself, who,
when last I saw him, was a very venerable old man, and so perfectly
rational and consistent on every other point, that I think no conscientious
person could refuse to take this into the bargain; nay, I have seen a cer-
tificate on the subject taken before a country justice and signed with a
cross, in the justice's own handwriting. The story, therefore, is beyond
the possibility of doubt. D.K." [Irving's note.]

39. Part of No. IV.

40. The erudite reader, well versed in good-for-nothing lore, will perceive that the above tale must have been suggested to the old Swiss by a
little French anecdote, a circumstance said to have taken place at Paris.
[Irving's note.]

41. *i.e.*, Cat's Elbow. The name of a family of those parts very powerful in former times. The appellation, we are told, was given in compliment
to a peerless dame of the family, celebrated for her fine arm. [Irving's
note.]

42. This essay and "Philip of Pokanoket" (both of which had previously appeared in the *Analectic Magazine*) were included by Irving in
No. VII of the English edition of *The Sketch Book;* both were subsequently incorporated in the American volumes.

43. The American government has been indefatigable in its exertions
to ameliorate the situation of the Indians, and to introduce among them
the arts of civilization, and civil and religious knowledge. To protect
them from the frauds of the white traders, no purchase of land from them
by individuals is permitted; nor is any person allowed to receive lands
from them as a present, without the express sanction of government.
These precautions are strictly enforced. [Irving's note.]

44. Originally intended for No. IV, but later reserved for No. VI.

45. Part of No. VI. This tale is a good example of Irving's more sentimental productions.

46. Part of No. VI.

47. The whip-poor-will is a bird which is heard only at night. It receives its name from its note, which is thought to resemble those words. [Irving's note.]

48. *Postscript, Found in the Handwriting of Mr. Knickerbocker.*

The preceding Tale is given, almost in the precise words in which I heard it related at a Corporation meeting of the ancient city of Manhattoes, at which were present many of its sagest and most illustrious burghers. The narrator was a pleasant, shabby, gentlemanly old fellow, in pepper-and-salt clothes, with a sadly humorous face; and one whom I strongly suspected of being poor,—he made such efforts to be entertaining. When his story was concluded, there was much laughter and approbation, particularly from two or three deputy aldermen, who had been asleep the greater part of the time. There was, however, one tall, dry-looking old gentleman, with beetling eyebrows, who maintained a grave and rather severe face throughout: now and then folding his arms, inclining his head, and looking down upon the floor, as if turning a doubt over in his mind. He was one of your wary men, who never laugh, but upon good grounds—when they have reason and the law on their side. When the mirth of the rest of the company had subsided, and silence was restored, he leaned one arm on the elbow of his chair, and, sticking the other akimbo, demanded with a slight but exceedingly sage motion of the head, and contraction of the brow, what was the moral of the story, and what it went to prove?

The story-teller, who was just putting a glass of wine to his lips, as a refreshment after his toils, paused for a moment, looked at his inquirer with an air of infinite deference, and, lowering the glass slowly to the table, observed, that the story was intended most logically to prove:—

"That there is no situation in life but has its advantages and pleasures—provided we will but take a joke as we find it:

"That, therefore, he that runs races with goblin troopers is likely to have rough riding of it.

"Ergo, for a country schoolmaster to be refused the hand of a Dutch heiress, is a certain step to high preferment in the state."

The cautious old gentleman knit his brows tenfold closer after this explanation, being sorely puzzled by the ratiocination of the syllogism; while, methought, the one in pepper-and-salt eyed him with something of a triumphant leer. At length, he observed, that all this was very well, but still he thought the story a little on the extravagant—there were one or two points on which he had his doubts.

"Faith, sir," replied the story-teller, "as to that matter, I don't believe one-half of it myself." D. K. [Irving's note.]

BRACEBRIDGE HALL

49. Published in America originally in two volumes in 1822, and almost simultaneously by Murray in London. However, the English edi-

tion, the printing of which Irving himself supervised, contained many alterations and additions.

50. Mirror for Magistrates. [Irving's note.]

TALES OF A TRAVELLER

51. Published in London by Murray in two parts, Aug. 25, 1824. In New York, it was published in four installments between Aug. 24 and Oct. 9, 1824, the first part consisting of "Strange Stories by a Nervous Gentleman"; the second, of "Buckthorne and His Friends"; the third, of "The Italian Banditti"; and the fourth, of "The Money Diggers."

52. Many years later Irving had a good laugh out of a flattering review of his works, in which it was asserted: "His most comical pieces have always a serious end in view." "You laugh," said Irving to his nephew, with that air of whimsical significance so natural to him, "but it is true. I have kept that to myself hitherto, but that man has found me out He has detected the moral of the 'Stout Gentleman.'" (*Life*, I, 399.)

53. This caper at the end of Irving's tales is typical.

THE LIFE AND VOYAGES OF CHRISTOPHER COLUMBUS

54. Published originally in three volumes in 1828.

55. Hist. del Almirante, cap. 19. Herrera, Hist. Ind., decad i. lib. i. cap. 10. [Irving's note.] The notes on this chapter of Columbus are all Irving's, and are illustrative of his method of documenting his historical and biographical works.

56. Journal of Columb., Primer Viage, Navarrete, tom. i. [Irving's note.]

57. Navarrete, tom. i. p. 16. [Irving's note.]

58. Journ. of Columbus, Navarrete, tom. i. p. 17. [Irving's note.]

59. Hist. del Almirante, cap. 20. Journ. of Columbus, Navarrete, tom. i. [Irving's note.]

60. Hist. del Almirante, cap. 20. Las Casas, lib. i. Journal of Columb., Navarrete, Colec. tom. i, p. 19.

It has been asserted by various historians, that Columbus, a day or two previous to coming in sight of the New World, capitulated with his mutinous crew, promising, if he did not discover land within three days, to abandon the voyage. There is no authority for such an assertion, either in the history of his son Fernando or that of the Bishop Las Casas, each of whom had the admiral's papers before him. There is no mention of such a circumstance in the extracts made from the journal by Las Casas, which have recently been brought to light, nor is it asserted by either Peter Martyr or the Curate of Los Palacios, both contemporaries and acquaintances of Columbus, and who could scarcely have failed to mention so striking a fact, if true. It rests merely upon the authority of Oviedo, who is of inferior credit to either of the authors above cited, and was grossly misled as to many of the particulars of this voyage by a pilot of the name of Hernan Perez Matheo, who was hostile to Columbus. In the manuscript process of the memorable lawsuit between Don Diego, son of the admiral, and the fiscal of the crown, is the evidence of one Pedro de Bilbao, who testifies that he heard many times that some of the pilots and mariners wished to turn back, but that the admiral promised them presents, and entreated them to wait two or three days, before which time he should discover land. ("Pedro de Bilbao oyo muchas veces que algunos pilotos y marineros querian volverse sino fuera por el Almirante que les prometio donos, les rogó esperasen dos o tres dias i que antes del termino descubriera tierra.") This, if true, implies no capitulation to relinquish the enterprise.

On the other hand, it was asserted by some of the witnesses in the above-mentioned suit, that Columbus, after having proceeded some few hundred leagues without finding land, lost confidence and wished to turn back; but was persuaded and even piqued to continue by the Pinzons. This assertion carries falsehood on its very face. It is in total contradiction to that persevering constancy and undaunted resolution displayed by Columbus, not merely in the present voyage, but from first to last of his difficult and dangerous career. This testimony was given by some of the mutinous men, anxious to exaggerate the merits of the Pinzons, and to depreciate that of Columbus. Fortunately, the extracts from the journal of the latter, written from day to day with guileless simplicity, and all the air of truth, disprove these fables, and show that on the very day previous to his discovery, he expressed a peremptory determination to persevere, in defiance of all dangers and difficulties. [Irving's note.]

61. Hist. del Almirante, cap. 21. [Irving's note.]

A CHRONICLE OF THE CONQUEST OF GRANADA

62. First published in 1829 under the pseudonym of Fray Antonio Agapida, and completely revised in 1850. This selection follows the revised edition.

63. Alcantara, t. 4, c. 18. [Irving's note.]

64. Conde, part 4. [Irving's note.]

65. Mariana. [Irving's note.]

66. Salazar de Mendoza. Chron. del Gran. Cardinal, lib. 1, c. 69, p. 1. Mondaja: His. MS. as cited by Alcantara, t. 4, c. 18. [Irving's note.]

67. Abarca, Anales de Aragon, Rey 30, c. 3. [Irving's note.]

68. This ring remained in the possession of the count until the death of the marques Don Inigo, the last male heir, who died in Malaga without children, in 1656. The ring was then lost through inadvertence and ignorance of its value, Dona Maria, the sister of the marques, being absent in Madrid. Alcantara, l. 4. c. 18. [Irving's note.]

69. Zurita, Anales de Aragon, lib. 20, cap. 92. [Irving's note.]

70. Abarca, lib. sup. Zurita, &c. [Irving's note.]

71. Cid Hiaya was made cavalier of the order of Santiago. He and his

son intermarried with the Spanish nobility, and the marqueses of Compotejar are among their descendants. Their portraits, and the portraits of their grandsons, are to be seen in one of the rooms of the Generalife at Granada. [Irving's note.]

72. The words of Fray Antonio Agapida are little more than an echo of those of the worthy Jesuit father Mariana (l. 25, c. 18). [Irving's note.]

73. Garibay, Compend. Hist. lib. 40, c. 42. The existence of this gateway, and the story connected with it, are perhaps known to few; but were identified, in the researches made to verify this history. The gateway is at the bottom of the tower, at some distance from the main body of the Alhambra. The tower has been rent and ruined by gunpowder, at the time when the fortress was evacuated by the French. Great masses lie around half-covered by vines and fig-trees. A poor man, by the name of Matteo Ximenes, who lives in one of the halls among the ruins of the Alhambra, where his family has resided for many generations, pointed out to the author the gateway, still closed up with stones. He remembered to have heard his father and grandfather say, that it had always been stopped up, and that out of it King Boabdil had gone when he surrendered Granada. The route of the unfortunate king may be traced thence across the garden of the convent of Los Martyros, and down a ravine beyond, through a street of Gipsy caves and hovels, by the gate of Los Molinos, and so on to the Hermitage of St. Sebastian. None but an antiquarian, however, will be able to trace it, unless aided bv the humble historian of the place, Matteo Ximenes. [Irving's note.]

THE ALHAMBRA

74. Published originally in 1832. In 1851 Irving rearranged and revised the whole as it now stands in the "author's revised edition," which this selection follows.

75. *Note to The Arabian Astrologer.* Al Makkari, in his history of the Mahommedan Dynasties in Spain, cites from another Arabian writer an account of a talismanic effigy somewhat similar to the one in the foregoing legend.

In Cadiz, says he, there formerly stood a square tower upwards of one hundred cubits high, built of huge blocks of stone, fastened together with clamps of brass. On the top was the figure of a man, holding a staff in his right hand, his face turned to the Atlantic, and pointing with the forefinger of his left hand to the Straits of Gibraltar. It was said to have been set up in ancient times by the Gothic kings of Andalus, as a beacon or guide to navigators. The Moslems of Barbary and Andalus, considered it a talisman which exercised a spell over the seas. Under its guidance, swarms of piratical people of a nation called Majus, appeared on the coast in large vessels with a square sail in the bow, and another in the stern. They came every six or seven years; captured everything they met with on the sea;

guided by the statue, they passed through the Straits into the Mediterranean, landed on the coasts of Andalus, laid every thing waste with fire and sword; and sometimes carried their depredations on the opposite coasts even as far as Syria.

At length, it came to pass in the time of the civil wars, a Moslem Admiral who had taken possession of Cadiz, hearing that the statue on top of the tower was of pure gold, had it lowered to the ground and broken to pieces; when it proved to be of gilded brass. With the destruction of the idol, the spell over the seas was at an end. From that time forward, nothing more was seen of the piratical people of the ocean, excepting that two of their barks were wrecked on the coast, one at Marsu-l-Majus (the port of the Majus), the other close to the promontory of Al-Aghan.

The maritime invaders above mentioned by Al Makkari must have been the Northmen. [Irving's note.]

A TOUR ON THE PRAIRIES

76. *A Tour on the Prairies* formed vol. I of *The Crayon Miscellany* (3 vols., Philadelphia, 1835).

77. Usually spelled *Brazos*.

ABBOTSFORD

78. "Abbotsford," together with "Newstead Abbey," formed vol. II of *The Crayon Miscellany*.

OLIVER GOLDSMITH

79. These selections are from the 1849 edition, not to be confused with the briefer sketch of 1840. The preface is generally indicative of Irving's attitude and manner as a biographer.

80. Forster's Goldsmith. [Irving's note.]

81. Goldsmith's Life of Nash. [Irving's note.]

WOLFERT'S ROOST

82. This is a selection from *Wolfert's Roost and Other Papers Now First Collected* (1855), a miscellany of sketches and stories which had appeared many years before in various periodicals, chiefly in *Knickerbocker's Magazine*.

LIFE OF GEORGE WASHINGTON

83. Published in 5 vols., 1855–1859.

84. Life of Reed, i. 282. [Irving's note.]

85. See Washington to Col. Reed, Jan. 15. [Irving's note.]